George L. Browne

Narratives of State Trials in the Nineteenth Century

First period: from the union with Ireland to the death of George the Fourth,

1801-1830. Vol. 1

George L. Browne

Narratives of State Trials in the Nineteenth Century
First period: from the union with Ireland to the death of George the Fourth, 1801-1830. Vol. 1

ISBN/EAN: 9783337323295

Printed in Europe, USA, Canada, Australia, Japan

Cover: Foto ©ninafisch / pixelio.de

More available books at **www.hansebooks.com**

NTH CENTURY

FIRST PERIOD.

WITH IRELAND TO THE DEATH OF
GEORGE THE FOURTH,
1801—1830.

BY
LATHOM BROWNE,
MIDDLE TEMPLE, BARRISTER-AT-LAW.

IN TWO VOLUMES.

VOL. I.
UNION TO THE REGENCY, 1801—1811.

SECOND EDITION.

London:
MARSTON, SEARLE, & RIVINGTON,
BUILDINGS, 188, FLEET STREET.
1882.
[*All rights reserved.*]

TO THE

RIGHT HONOURABLE JOHN DUKE, BARON COLERIDGE,

OF OTTERY ST. MARY, DEVON,

LORD CHIEF JUSTICE OF ENGLAND,

THESE VOLUMES

ARE,

BY HIS KIND PERMISSION,

RESPECTFULLY DEDICATED

BY

THE AUTHOR.

PREFACE.

IT is proposed, in these volumes, to present in a popular form the incidents of such of the State Trials during the first thirty years of the present century as appear most clearly to exhibit the political and social phases of that period, and as "rich storehouses of curious and authentic facts illustrative of human character and conduct." Hence the cases now given are not confined to mere judicial inquiries in our criminal courts, but embrace investigations by other competent jurisdictions — such as the humiliating inquiry instituted by the House of Commons, in 1809, into the gross traffic in commissions and promotion in the army, and in civil appointments, through immoral female influence, and the claim to the Berkeley Peerage in 1811, characterized by Lord Lyndhurst as "a dreadful measure of perjury and guilt."

On the dry records of the evidence given in these cases, much light has been thrown by the publication of the Diaries and Correspondence of cotemporaries, which would be materially increased were the official papers in the hands of Government open to investigation. In the case of Colonel Despard's wild attempt at rebellion in London, in 1802, I have been allowed to consult the official papers now in the Public Record Office, including the original brief of the Attorney-General (Spencer Perceval) by whom the prosecution was conducted. I had hoped that a similar permission would have been granted in the case of Emmet's attempt in Dublin, in the following year, and thus a more satisfactory solution obtained of the apparent connexion between these two events, as well as of the conduct of the Irish Government. There are, however, I am told, "strong reasons in the interest of the country why this request should be refused."[1] What these reasons may be, beyond the chronic sensitiveness of every Government on Irish questions, I have no means of judging. The case against the Government of that day, in connexion with this mad but most dangerous attempt, has been so materially strengthened by the publication in the Correspondence of Lord Castlereagh and the Diary of Mr. Speaker Abbot, of the secret despatches between those persons and the Irish Government, that if it could be rebutted by the official records it is surely in the interest of the country that the use of them, under proper supervision, should be permitted. The refusal of this information necessarily increases the

---

[1] Letter from Mr. Under-Secretary Liddell, July 8, 1879, "I am directed by Mr. Secretary Cross to inform you, that after communicating with the Irish Government and other departments he finds that there are strong reasons why, in the interest of the country, the request should not be complied with."

impression given by other authorities, that the case of the Government of Lord Hardwicke cannot be improved.

In the case of General Picton I have had the advantage of consulting and taking extracts from a volume of official and other cotemporary documents lodged with the Privy Council during the progress of this lingering investigation, and lately collected together by the learned Registrar, Mr. Henry Reeve, to whom, and to Mr. Kingston, of the Public Record Office, I desire to offer my thanks. The Committee of the Stock Exchange have also permitted me to make use of the papers in their possession relating to the De Berenger frauds; whose Secretary, Mr. Levien, I have also to thank for the assistance he has rendered to me in their examination.

The trials and investigations given in the first of these volumes treat of subjects as varied as they are socially and politically important. The *trial of Governor Wall* for flogging a soldier to death and the *Libels of Leigh Hunt and Cobbett* on the military punishments of the time, painfully illustrate the atrocious severity of the military discipline of the period. Those of *Colonel Despard*, and the ill-fated enthusiast, *Emmet*, mark the baneful effects of the secret intrigues so persistently persevered in by the French Government, to turn to its advantage the widespread discontent with the Act of Union felt by the lower classes in Ireland. They also prove the existence, though in secret, of the Rebels of "98" (cowed but not crushed by their bitter punishment), and the encouragement afforded to them by the fatal feeling of distrust of their Roman Catholic neighbours entertained by the Protestant landowners. From the curious cases of the *Libels of the Trojan Horse*, so clearly traced to a Judge on the Irish Bench, we learn not only how bitter was the feeling against the Government of Lord Hardwicke in connexion with Emmet's rebellion, but to what an extent that animosity pervaded other than the lower and uneducated classes. The cruel and cowardly acts of *The Threshers*, in 1809, and of the *Caravats and Shanavests*, in 1811, in Ireland, have a special interest, when the selfsame acts are being committed in that unfortunate island, with the same objects. The trial of *Peltier* for suggesting the assassination of the First Consul, derives additional interest from that of Herr Most so lately convicted of a similar offence against the Czar. The trials of *General Picton* for allowing torture to be administered to a prisoner under the old Spanish law at Trinidad, bring out prominently the liability under which the Governors of our Colonies labour in the discharge of their arduous duties, and present a vivid picture of the rules and practices of the Spanish law in the Indies, and of the harshness of its rules towards non-Catholic residents.

The *Impeachment of Lord Melville*, despite the strong party bias that characterized the proceeding—the disgusting case of the *Duke of York and Mrs. Mary Ann Clarke*, and the astounding and impudent frauds of *Alexander Davison and Valentine Jones*, each in its way exposes the negligence that prevailed among the higher officers of our Administrative Government, permitting, if not creating, a system of corruption among subordinates, perilous alike to good government and the great services of the country. The *Berkeley Peerage* cases reveal a state of Society in high and low life as humiliating as it was immoral, and are in their details as astonishing for the effrontery as for the wickedness of the attempts.

The second volume carries down these narratives to the death of George the Fourth—the close of the system of persistent interference on the part of the Sovereign with the formation and measures of his Cabinets. In this volume are included the cases of *Bellingham*, for the murder of Spencer Perceval; the *Luddite Rioters* of 1812; the trial of *Lord Cochrane*, for the Berenger frauds; the *Spa Fields Riot* in 1816; the trials of *Sir Charles Wolseley and Harrison* for sedition; the *Peterloo Riot* and trials of *Hunt and others* for conspiracy, and *Sir F. Burdett* for libel; the *Cato Street Conspiracy* of *Thistlewood;* the *Trial of Queen Caroline;* and the assault on Lord Wellesley, in Dublin, in 1823, known as *The Bottle Conspiracy*. These are all sources of legitimate interest, fraught with instruction. In order to show more clearly how these trials bear on the political and social events of the period, I have prefixed to each volume a brief historical summary of the period covering the cases included in it.

For the details of these trials the shorthand writers' notes necessarily furnish the only reliable source. Much information may, however, be gathered from the biographies and diaries of cotemporaries who were behind the scenes, and thus enabled to reveal the machinery by which many of these performances were conducted in public. Of cotemporary reports, and pamphlets, and the leading serials of the time, use has also been made.

In adopting the form of narratives (in the hope that the information and instruction to be drawn from these trials will thus be more widely diffused) instead of reporting the evidence, with notes and explanations, I have necessarily been compelled to state points of law with succinctness. Still, I trust they are given in sufficient detail to render these volumes not useless to my professional brethren.

I am indebted to my son, Mr. H. W. Lathom, for the preparation of the Indexes.

G. L. B.

King's Bench Walk,
   Temple,
     January, 1882.

PREFACE TO SECOND EDITION.

A SECOND Edition having been so soon required, I have been able only to correct some clerical errors in the text and notes, and to add, in Appendices C, D, and E, in Volume II., a brief account of the trial of Lord Cochrane at Guildford, for his escape from the King's Bench Prison, from a copy of a report lately obtained; some interesting incidents of the last days and death of Queen Caroline; and an example of the libels on her, taken from a volume kindly lent to me by a friend.

One word to some of my critics. I am not going to question my own demerits, and am sincerely obliged for their calling my attention to them. I must, however, repudiate the assertion of one critic, that I have taken the law of the cases mainly from the biography of persons interested in them. In truth, in only three cases—those of Picton, Cochrane, and Perceval—are any biographies available, and in all of these the writers have either eschewed or misreported legal questions. The shorthand writers' reports of the trials, and the authorized law reports, have been my sole authorities—the only reliable ones—on all points of law. The same reviewer has taken exception to the "looseness" with which I have used the title "State Trials," and consequently included the cases of Governor Wall, Lord Cochrane, and the Berkeley Peerage. The first trial is included by Mr. Howell in his invaluable volumes; the second in those of the late Mr. Townsend, the Recorder of Macclesfield. Indeed, both these great authorities have been far more "loose" in their use of the title— Mr. Howell including the case of "the wilful destruction of a trading brig by its captain and crew," and Mr. Townsend "the abduction of Miss Turner by the brothers Wakefield," and the "Libel on the Directors of the African Company." My excuse for giving the case of the "Berkeley Peerage" is, as stated in my work, its exposure of the state of society in those dark days.

Whilst I regret my lack of "narrative power," I shall feel that my three years' of work have been amply rewarded if others of my critics are right in saying that "the work when completed will be invaluable to all modern historians"—"that I have seldom omitted to give my readers the necessary material for forming an independent judgment," and that "it presents the past before our eyes in its true form and colour, thus affording accurate grounds for comparison between the old and the present time." I am glad to find that the "Historical Summaries" are generally acceptable.

G. L. B.

TEMPLE, *May*, 1882.

CONTENTS.

CHAPTER I.
PAGE

Historical Summary from the Union with Ireland to the Regency, 1801 to 1811 I

Population and revenue at the commencement of the century—Mr. Pitt and the Catholic Question—Resignation of Pitt and accession of Addington's Cabinet—Copenhagen—Egypt—Peace of Amiens—Distress and disaffection in England—*Conspiracy of Colonel Despard*—Chronic agitation in Ireland—*Emmet's Rebellion, and the libels on the Irish Government*—The First Consul's complaints of the English Press—*Peltier's trial*—Renewal of the war with France—Pitt's return to office—New Continental Coalition—Ulm, Austerlitz, Trafalgar—Death of Pitt—The Cabinet of "All the Talents"—*Impeachment of Lord Melville*—Death of Fox, and break-up of the ministry—Cabinet of the Duke of Portland and Mr. Perceval—*Duke of York and Mrs. Clarke*—Military punishment—*Governor Wall, Cobbett, and Leigh Hunt*—*Persecution of Picton*—Rising in Spain—Moore and Wellesley in Portugal and Spain—Madness of the King—The Regency—Social morality of the period—*The Berkeley Peerage case*.

CHAPTER II.

Trial of Governor Wall, of Goree, for the murder of a soldier by flogging: tried January 20, 1802 28

CHAPTER III.

The conspiracy of Colonel Despard in 1802, in London, to murder the King and revolutionize the Government: tried February 7, 1803 43

CHAPTER IV.

The trial of Jean Gabriel Peltier for a series of libels, in 1802, on Bonaparte, as First Consul: tried February 21, 1803 78

CHAPTER V.

The rebellion of Robert Emmet and others in Dublin in July, 1803: trials of the rebels from August 31 to September 19, 1803 97

CHAPTER VI.

The libels of "The Trojan Horse" on the Government of Ireland at the period of the Emmet Rebellion, in Cobbett's *Political Register* and on Dr. Troy in the *Anti-Jacobin*, February, 1804, to November, 1805 . 142

CHAPTER VII.

Impeachment of Viscount Melville, as Treasurer of the Navy: House of Lords, April 29 to May 17, 1806   170

CHAPTER VIII.

Trials of Alexander Davison and Valentine Jones for frauds on the Commissariat, December 7, 1808, and May 26, 1809 223

CHAPTER IX.

The Duke of York and Mary Ann Clarke: investigation by Committee of the whole House of Commons, February 1

PAGE

to March 20, 1809.—Inquiries into patronage of the Directors of the East India Company—Lord Castlereagh, and others 243

CHAPTER X.

Trials of General Picton, as Governor of Trinidad, for the torture of Louisa Calderon, and investigation before the Privy Council into charges brought against him by Colonel Fullarton.—Trial of Lieutenant-Colonel Draper for libels on the Right Honourable John Sullivan and Colonel Fullarton, February, 1806, to June, 1810. . 295

CHAPTER XI.

Press prosecutions: James Perry, libel on the King; Cobbett, Leigh Hunt, and Drakard, on military punishments: October, 1809, to November, 1811 . . . 330

CHAPTER XII.

The Berkeley Peerage : House of Lords, May, 1799 ; Court of Chancery, April, 1801 ; House of Lords, March 7 to June, 21, 1811 346

BERKELEY PEERAGE :
Facsimiles of Registers of Banns and Marriage of Earl of Berkeley and Mary Ann Cole. . . . 366

CHAPTER XIII.

Agrarian conspiracies in Ireland: The Threshers, 1806 ; Caravats and Shanavests, 1810 390

APPENDIX.

A. Extract from Plowden's "History of Ireland" relative to the quotations from that work made by Garrow in Dr. Troy's case 409
B. Trial of Herr Most, the editor of the *Freiheit*, for inciting to the murder of the Czar 410

INDEX TO VOL. I. 427

NARRATIVES OF STATE TRIALS.

CHAPTER I.

HISTORICAL SUMMARY FROM THE UNION WITH IRELAND TO THE REGENCY.

1801 TO 1811.

Population and revenue at the commencement of the century—Mr. Pitt and the Catholic Question—Resignation of Pitt and accession of Addington's Cabinet — Copenhagen — Egypt —Peace of Amiens—Distress and disaffection in England—*Conspiracy of Colonel Despard*—Chronic agitation in Ireland —*Emmet's rebellion, and the libels on the Irish Government* —The First Consul's complaints of the English Press—*Peltier's trial*—Renewal of the war with France—Pitt's return to office — New Continental Coalition — Ulm, Austerlitz, Trafalgar—Death of Pitt—The Cabinet of "All the Talents" —*Impeachment of Lord Melville*—Death of Fox, and break-up of the ministry—Cabinet of the Duke of Portland and Mr. Perceval—*Duke of York and Mrs. Clarke*—Military punishment—*Governor Wall, Cobbett, and Leigh Hunt— Persecution of Picton*—Rising in Spain—Moore and Wellesley in Portugal and Spain—Madness of the king—The Regency —Social morality of the period—*The Berkeley Peerage case.*

AT the commencement of the present century England was the only country in Europe that had effectually resisted the military despotism of France,

VOL. I. B

and could boast of free institutions and a free press. The pride we so justly feel, whatever may be our political views, at the success with which we resisted that ever-growing power, and at the perseverance with which, after a few months of a precarious peace, we fought on until we had shown the world the way to shatter it, would be heightened were we to consider with what a comparatively small population and limited resources we renewed the struggle. In 1801 the entire population of the United Kingdom did not amount to fifteen millions. The whole population of the counties did not exceed that which is now crowded into some of their cities and towns, and that of Middlesex was hardly one-fourth of what is now included in modern London. The assessed taxes, though then a very drag-net of taxable articles, produced less than three-and-a-half millions, and a five per cent. property[1] tax brought in less than six millions to the national revenue. Though the crowning victory of Trafalgar had yet to be fought, we had practically won the mastery of the seas. As yet, however, our soldiers had not met those of the great conqueror. If we reigned on the ocean, he reigned on the land.

The war of the French Revolution was lingering to a close when the century opened, and the first parlia-

[1] In his last budget, in the spring of 1801, Pitt had to provide for an expenditure of 43,538,000*l.*, of which 30,000,000*l.* were nearly equally divided between the army and navy. To meet this the Ways and Means produced only 16,744,000*l.*, and the deficiency had to be made up by a loan of 25,000,000*l.*, to meet the interest on which new taxes, estimated to produce 1,794,000*l.*, were imposed. To raise this loan 125*l.* 15*s.* consols and 50*l.* 15*s.* reduced were given for every 100*l.*

ment of the United Kingdom assembled. Apparently the cabinet of Mr. Pitt was still in power as well as place; in reality it was on the eve of dissolution. Pitt's statesmanlike policy of following up the union with Ireland by ameliorating the position of its Roman Catholic inhabitants was no secret, and was equally distasteful to some of his colleagues as to his royal master. In the previous winter the king had learnt from the Chancellor[2] and another minister the intentions of the majority of the Cabinet in favour of a modified measure of Catholic Emancipation, and had openly expressed his opinions, that "he should reckon any man his personal enemy who should propose such a measure." On the 1st of February Mr. Pitt had written to the king that whilst regretting his Majesty's sentiments on that subject, he and the majority of his colleagues felt that it would be expedient to repeal the laws excluding Catholics from

---

[2] Chancellor Lord Loughborough and Lord Auckland communicated this to the king by the Archbishop of Canterbury. January 29 the king wrote to Mr. Addington, wishing "that he would from himself open Pitt's eyes on the danger of agitating this improper question, which may prevent his ever speaking to me on a subject on which I can hardly keep my temper." Addington saw Pitt, and persuaded himself that he had succeeded, and wrote to the king encouragingly. On 31st January the king replied to Addington, expressing his pleasure at the communication, and inviting him to see him on that or the next evening. In the interval Pitt had decided to proceed or resign, and Addington, on his arrival, was desired to form a cabinet. On his begging to be excused, the king said, "Lay your hand on your heart, and ask yourself where I am to turn for support, if you don't stand by me."—Pellew's "Life of Lord Sidmouth," i. 385, and Abbot's Diary of the date.

Parliament and place, as well as those excluding Dissenters from offices. He promised, indeed, to do his best to postpone the introduction of the measure, if the king on his part would avoid expressing his opinion so as to influence others in their conduct. George the Third was the last man to entertain such a suggestion. Rightly or wrongly, he regarded concession to the Catholics as a violation of his coronation oath, and as he truly replied, "he was not in the habit of concealing his sentiments on important occasions." Though he still hoped that "Mr. Pitt would not leave him while he lived," he had already consulted with the section of politicians in and out of the Cabinet known as "The King's Friends," and had summoned Mr. Addington to undertake the responsibility of forming a Cabinet, from the deliberations of which the question of Catholic Emancipation should be rigorously excluded. It is needless, even if the limited nature of this summary allowed of it, to enter here into the various details of the political intrigues which preceded the accession of the Addington ministry. The precarious condition of the king's health increased the difficulties of the ministerial crisis. He had again become temporarily insane, and for a month was incapable of attending to business. On his recovery the change of ministry was effected.[3] The change of men was thorough—Henry Addington in the place of Pitt; Lord Hawkesbury at the Foreign Office in that of Lord Grenville, and Windham replaced at the War Office by Mr. Yorke—respectable, well-intentioned mediocrities for men who had made a

[3] March 7, 1801.

European reputation. The only strong man was Lord Eldon, who stepped into the Chancellorship which Lord Loughborough had schemed in vain to secure by being foremost in betraying his late colleagues. Had not Pitt given a cold promise of support and urged his friends to assist, the ministry of Mr. Addington must have died almost in its birth.[4]

From its predecessors the new Cabinet inherited two expeditions, that to the Baltic, in which Nelson achieved the victory of Copenhagen; that to Egypt, in which, under Abercromby, English soldiers first met the hitherto unconquered troops of the First Consul, and commenced that long series of victories over their rivals which ended only on the plains of Waterloo. Paul, the mad Emperor of Russia, so lately become an idolater of Bonaparte, readily fell into the views of his new idol, and with Denmark and Sweden created the armed neutrality of the northern powers, by which Bonaparte vainly hoped to counteract our naval supremacy and thus to obtain in neutral ships the supplies which we so constantly inter-

---

[4] According to Lord Sidmouth's biographer, Addington consulted Pitt on receiving the king's commands, and he replied, " I see nothing but ruin, Addington, if you hesitate." Canning, in a letter to a Mr. Newbolt, February 17, communicating the resignation of Pitt and formation of a new Cabinet, says, "in which Mr. Pitt earnestly presses all those of his own friends who are now in office to take part, and to which he intends personally to give *the most decided and active support.*" Subsequent events soon proved that Canning had written too strongly. Perceval was more correct when he wrote Vansittart that he was authorized to tell Pitt's friends " that he wishes as many as agree with the king on the Catholic Question to accept office under Addington."

cepted. The fleet of Denmark was not only powerful in ships, but more so in the courageous and hardy crews by which they were manned. Had we not prevented its union with that of France, the consequences to our credit and our commerce would have been most serious. It is needless to tell over again in detail the grand old story, how Nelson, in despite of the signal for his recall, conquered that gallant navy, and gave the first blow to the Northern Confederacy. When the battle was fought and won, it was not known that the mad emperor, on whose life and power the Confederacy depended, had been assassinated and the key of the edifice broken.

Whilst the fleet under Parker and Nelson was struggling through the narrow seas of the North, another under Sidney Smith was landing an army on the shore of the Bay of Aboukir under the command of Abercromby. The landing in Egypt, though in the face of a determined resistance by the French, was "like a movement on the opera stage—in five or six minutes 5500 men stood in battle array."[5] A fortnight after the landing the important battle of Alexandria broke the French power in Egypt, a victory dearly earned by the death of the veteran leader of the victorious troops. Within a few months Egypt was cleared of the French, and the Sultan resumed the dominion of his valuable province.

Contemporaneously with the victories of Copenhagen and Alexandria, negotiations for peace were being secretly carried on in London, in continuation of

[5] General Bertrand, quoted by Alison, from La Casas.

those which had been broken off a year before, and
conducted on the part of Bonaparte by the same
negotiator, M. Otto.[6]

Though France now reached to the Rhine, ruled
Italy as a dependency, and Holland and Spain
were little better than her servants, the First
Consul had good reason for obtaining a truce under
the more specious title of peace. He had failed
in the Baltic, and a doubtful neutral occupied the
throne of his idolater the Emperor Paul. Every semblance of his power was swept away from Syria and
Egypt, and the boasted "forty centuries" looked
down only on French reverses. On the seas his way
was barred by our fleets. Hardly a foreign dependency remained under his power, and though he
threatened invasion and made a vigorous display of
his boats, his transports, and his troops on the
opposite coast of our Channel (which even Nelson had
failed to destroy), without the command of the sea
he knew full well that invasion was a bravado, and

[6] M. Otto, nominally Superintendent of Exchange of Prisoners,
was a Protestant of Strasburg, and originally in the French
Foreign Office. In 1793 he drew up the peace proposals brought
to England by M. Maret, and refused by Lord Grenville. After
a short imprisonment in France, on suspicion of secret correspondence with England, he came to England in 1799, just after
Bonaparte's letter to the king. Recalled on the plea of English
aggression on French fisheries, he delayed his departure, and
through Sir J. Macpherson, a friend of Prince Augustus, got
introduced to Mr. Addington and Lord Hawkesbury unofficially,
and eventually opened the negotiations and concluded the
preliminaries of peace on 1st October, 1801. See Pellew's
"Sidmouth," which contains much more curious information on
this subject.

that without a breathing-time any attempts at the re-creation of his marine was an impossibility.

In England the times were opportune for his apparently peaceful designs. The state of Ireland was so unsatisfactory that in May, on the report of a secret committee of both Houses of Parliament, the Habeas Corpus Act had been suspended, and martial law established.[7] The dogged perseverance of Pitt had been replaced by the placable pliancy of Addington. Pecuniary difficulties had no power over the one, but were all-powerful with the other minister. Hence the overtures of M. Otto were met half way by Lord Hawkesbury, and on the 1st of October the preliminaries of the precarious Peace of Amiens were signed. From then until the spring of 1802 the battle of the diplomatists continued with varied fortunes, all turning on the eventual cause of quarrel, the possession of Malta. At length, on the 27th of March, 1802, the definite treaty was signed. All our conquests except Ceylon and Trinidad were surrendered; Naples and the Papal States were evacuated by the French; Egypt was formally restored to the Sultan; the republic of the Ionian Isles recognized; the integrity of Portugal guaranteed, and Malta agreed to be given up by us to the Knights of Malta, by whom it had been surrendered to the French, and who had neither men nor money to provide for its effective defence.

The king was right when he described the Peace of Amiens as "an experimental peace;" and very

[7] See Cases of the Threshers, Caravats and Shanavests.

short-lived was the experiment; it was at the best "a precarious armistice." Within two months of its signature the First Consul had begun his complaints of our press and his remonstrances against the countenance and protection we gave to the Bourbon princes and their adherents. On the continent his restless ambition and devouring activity seemed boundless. He had already become First Consul for life, with power to select his successor; had made himself Dictator of the Cisalpine Republic; invaded Switzerland, annexed Piedmont, and refused to withdraw his troops from Holland. When a new Parliament met on the 23rd of November, 1802, the dissatisfaction of the Cabinet at these encroachments on the liberties of other states was dispassionately, yet clearly expressed, and additional forces by land and sea were readily voted in accordance with the recommendations in the Royal speech. As a set-off to these acts of Bonaparte, we kept our hold on Malta, and refused to violate the rights of hospitality on which our liberties were founded, so long as the emigrants did not break the law. In one point, however, we yielded to Bonaparte's demands, in prosecuting the public writers under whose withering sarcasms and libels the great man writhed like a whipped child.

Jean Gabriel Peltier was indicted for his fierce attack on the First Consul, and his ill-disguised incitement of his assassination. The story is told elsewhere in detail.[8] Though it resulted in a conviction, no punishment followed. Almost before the verdict was

* Trial of Peltier for Libel.

given, our relations with France were so strained that peace or war hung on a thread. On the 8th of March, 1803, in consequence of the armaments preparing in the ports of France and Holland, the militia were called out. Five days after occurred the scene of vulgar violence at the Tuileries, when Bonaparte openly insulted our ambassador, Lord Whitworth, and though for two months more the semblance of diplomatic intercourse was maintained, it is certain that the First Consul had already taken the "Fatal oath to destroy England or perish," and that we only anticipated him in declaring war. On the 18th of May the "experimental peace" had come to an untimely end. Two days after, the first blow—the capture of two small French vessels—had been given in that fearful contest into which, one by one, every nation of Europe was dragged, and which continued without intermission until the fall of Paris in 1815. By his detention of the thousands of Englishmen who were visiting or residing in France, Bonaparte gave strength to the Ministry, weak as it was, and "made the war universally popular in England."

The sudden cessation of the extravagance of a war expenditure on the signature of the peace of Amiens, without a corresponding fall in the prices of the necessaries of life seriously affected the working classes and made them disaffected to the Government, whilst the disbanding of soldiers added to the ranks of the idle and therefore dangerous classes. One result of these events was the mad conspiracy of Colonel Despard, in the winter of 1802, for the murder of the king and the revolutionizing of the Government of the country.[9] In the details of his trial, given in this volume, the spy system of the Government of the day and the steps by which a gallant soldier, the comrade of Nelson, smarting under neglect, was led from remonstrance to rebellion are painfully exposed. This mad plot, however, was not due to any French emissaries or supported by foreign funds. Not so that of Robert Emmet, in the summer of 1803, when for many hours the capital of Ireland was in the power of a small band of ill-armed conspirators, whilst, thanks to the culpable apathy of the authorities, a large garrison was lying idle in its barracks, and no attempt was made to quell the outbreak, until after a couple of companies of soldiers and a few yeomen, on their own responsibility and without an order from headquarters, had driven the mob from the streets and crushed a dangerous rebellion.[1]

Never before had there been such unanimity in England. No one cared for parliamentary reform, for relief from taxation, or for the harsh measures which the Government had of late adopted in dealing with the lower classes. As for the political intrigues for the return of Pitt to office in conjunction with Addington, no one but the individuals concerned and their immediate adherents wasted a moment's thought on them. The cry throughout the length and breadth of the land was "for our hearths and homes." In less than a year in addition to a reserve force of 50,000 soldiers, nearly 380,000 volunteers had

[9] Trial of Colonel Despard for High Treason.
[1] See Emmet's trial, and the trial of the libel of the " Trojan Horse."

been accepted and enrolled for the defence of the country against the threatened invasion. The Government looked but coldly on these citizen soldiers, but Pitt, himself active in training his own regiments as Warden of the Cinque Ports, stood up boldly in their support and forced the Government from its apathy. Men we had in thousands and tens of thousands, but arms were with difficulty obtained even for portions of the musters. It seems hardly credible in this age of Mechanism to learn that in 1803 "London could not supply more than 500 muskets a week, and that Birmingham sent none." [2]

Our navy too was neglected. The old ships were wearing out, and no new ones had been built. Gradually the necessity for Pitt's return to power became more and more evident, and Pitt himself, tired of giving a half-hearted support to the Ministry, "could not forbear any longer a direct opposition to the measures of the administration." [3]

A recurrence of the king's mental malady in February, 1804, postponed the ministerial change for several months, during which only the formal acts of his sovereignty, such as attaching the Sign Manual, were performed by him, on the responsibility of ministers, though severely questioned and condemned by the opposition. On the 22nd of April Pitt had announced to the king his intention of going openly into opposition. From then to the 2nd of May verbal communications through the Chancellor passed between the king and the ex-minister. Some attempt no doubt

[2] Abbot's Diary, December 30, 1803.
[3] Pitt to the king, April 22, 1804.

was made at a union with the Grenville party, which failed ; and Pitt having at length submitted to the Royal condition of not agitating for Catholic Emancipation during the king's lifetime, the Addington Cabinet resigned, and Pitt, on the 18th of May, returned to office. Strange coincidence, on the same day Napoleon Bonaparte, by the decree of his obsequious senate, became Emperor of the French.

Though Mr. Pitt on his return to office could command what would now be regarded as a good working majority of about fifty in the House of Commons, he realized the necessity for securing further support before the opening of Parliament in 1805. This he obtained by the adhesion of the Addington section, "The King's Friends," some fifty in number, whose leader was raised to the Peerage as Lord Sidmouth, and made President of the Council. At home the measures of the new Government provided for the strengthening of our offensive and defensive forces, imperatively demanded by the parade of invasion in which the new emperor indulged, and which, though postponed from month to month, he professed to be on the point of converting into action.[4] Abroad the

---

[4] The difference between the policy of Addington and Pitt is said by the biographer of the former to be that Addington would have confined our exertions to home defence and blockades, and attacks on distant possessions of France, until the Continental powers had sufficiently recovered for a new coalition, whilst Pitt proposed to increase the regular army, subsidize foreign powers without delay, and stir up the Continent at once. The result was that a good excuse was created for the abandonment of the threatened invasion, and that Austria, Prussia, and Russia fell one after the other before the armies of the invader.

minister laboured to revive the Continental coalition, on the one hand, whilst on the other he tore the mask of neutrality from Spain, in reality a vassal of France, capturing her treasure-ships containing the subsidy which Napoleon had longed for so eagerly, and forcing her openly to declare war, which it was now admitted she had contemplated from the moment Bonaparte had renewed the contest with England.

Though eminently successful in his home policy, so far as the raising of finances, and the improvement of our forces, Pitt met with one rebuff which inflicted on him the deepest mortification. It was painful enough to one so strictly honest in dealing with public money, to learn, through the reports of the commissioners appointed to inquire into our naval and military expenditure during the late war, how prevalent had been the frauds of contractors and officials; how nearly the success of important expeditions had been thwarted by their artifices, and the necessarily large expenditure of war budgets increased by their systematic deception.[5] When, however, his own most trusted friend and colleague, Lord Melville, was accused of being implicated in similar transactions, the blow fell with additional severity on so proud, so sensitive, and so confiding a spirit. Personal corruption in its worst sense was not indeed imputed to Lord Melville, but his careless and negligent mode of administration, bordering so closely on connivance at the misdeeds of his Paymaster, Trotter, could not be gainsaid. Pitt had to sacrifice his old friend, to see his

[5] See trials of Alexander Davison and Valentine Jones for commissariat frauds.

name erased from the list of Privy Councillors, and at the same moment to have his political following seriously weakened by the defection of Lord Sidmouth and his followers. At any time such a defection would have been serious. It was doubly so now when his health was daily getting more and more impaired, and the position of affairs on the Continent demanded his undivided attention.[6]

By subsidies the Continental coalition had been revived, and treaties arranged with Russia and Austria for the union of their armies against the emperor. Russia had never hesitated, but Austria, with her usual dilatoriness, kept on negotiations with Napoleon until the autumn, and then came into the field with ill-prepared armies. The rapidity of Napoleon's movements was extraordinary, even for him. On the 23rd of September he announced the passage of the river Inn by the Austrian forces. At once the huge army broke up from the camp at Boulogne, and headed by Napoleon, crossed the Rhine on the 1st of October. Two severe defeats of the Austrians followed in quick succession, and on the 20th the capitulation of Ulm, with 30,000 men and sixty pieces of cannon, completed the destruction of their army in Bavaria. Following up his successes, Vienna was entered by Napoleon on the 13th of November. On the 2nd of December the united armies of Russia and Austria were utterly routed on the field of Austerlitz. Before the end of the year peace with Austria was signed at Presburg, and the Continental coalition practically at an end. Against these overwhelming

[6] Impeachment of Lord Melville.

disasters there was but one event to be set—the crowning victory of Trafalgar. On the day after the capitulation of Ulm, Nelson and Collingwood led the British fleet against the united navies of France and Spain. It is almost needless to say how complete the defeat was. Before the hero expired twenty of the enemy's ships had struck, and four more were afterwards captured. Napoleon could no longer hope to keep the narrow seas against us for the passage of his flotilla—the invasion was at an end. Though Pitt revived for a few days at the news of Trafalgar from the depression caused by the capitulation of Ulm, the calamity of Austerlitz struck so deeply on his enfeebled frame that he never recovered it. With some intermittent days of temporary revival, the great minister—great, whatever might be his faults from a party view—gradually sank, and died on the 23rd of January, 1806, the twenty-fifth anniversary of his entry into Parliament. It has been well said of him, "He was indeed 'The top of Eloquence'—the most ardent amongst the lovers of his country; had he lived to behold the war triumph, he might have vindicated his claim to be a great peace minister and a sincere social reformer."[7]

On the death of Pitt the accession of the Opposition to office was inevitable. Amongst his colleagues there was no one courageous enough to attempt to be his successor, and certainly no one capable of supplying his place. After a little coquetting on the part of the king, Lord Grenville put together the cabinet of "All the Talents," in which Lord Sidmouth and Lord Ellenborough, the Chief Justice of England,

[7] C. Knight's "Popular History," vol. vii. p. 452.

represented the king's friends, and Lord Grenville and Mr. Fox the two sections into which the Opposition had separated. Erskine became Chancellor, and Lord Henry Petty, so well known in later days as the veteran Lord Lansdowne, Chancellor of the Exchequer. The mischievous consequences of reducing the head of the Criminal Law to the level of a political partisan were vigorously exposed in both Houses of Parliament, and it is somewhat humiliating to find men like Fox and Romilly defending such an appointment on the narrowest grounds of worn-out precedents, merely in the temporary-interests of party politics. Apart from the sessional work incidental to the prosecution of the war, three incidents occupied the public mind—the impeachment of Lord Melville, in which Romilly made his first mark as a political speaker; the protracted debates on the charges against Lord Wellesley for his annexation policy in India; and the so-called delicate inquiry into the conduct of the Princess of Wales. It would be inconsistent with the scope of this summary to enter into the details of the Wellesley scandals. The other incidents are fully considered in the reports of the impeachment of Lord Melville and the trial of Queen Caroline.

The Coalition Cabinet came to an untimely end, hastened undoubtedly by the early death of Fox, ere he had been in office a year, removing not only a master-mind from the ministry, but a controlling influence tempered by time and official responsibilities which might, had it remained, have averted the mistakes by which his colleagues wrecked their own vessel. He had hoped, but hoped in vain, that before he died he should have secured a solid and honourable peace with France, and struck an effectual blow at the hateful trade in slaves. In the one case, despite all his energy and honesty, or perhaps rather because of the latter, he utterly failed. Napoleon, through the wily Talleyrand, made a plausible show of peace-making and no more; he felt that the Cabinet could not last, and he had no faith in treating with a decaying authority. Towards the accomplishment of the other wish of his life, the abolition of the Slave-Trade, Fox made an all-important step when, on the 10th of June, he carried by an overwhelming majority his resolution pledging the Commons to proceed with all practical expedition to take effectual measures for its abolition. Within six months after his death the great measure on which he had set his heart was carried, and the trade in slaves scotched but not killed. The two great leaders of the people were gone, sleeping side by side in the hallowed dust of the Abbey. The statesmen that were left, with hardly an exception, were of a far inferior caste, and yet despite mistakes in policy and acts, seriously endangering the power of the country abroad and its peace at home, by patient perseverance they carried England through years of trouble and danger, and at last, though at a cost on which it frightens us to look back, broke down the would-be universal monarchy of Napoleon, and freed Europe from the tyranny of a despot.

On the day on which the royal assent was given to the Slave-Trade Abolition Bill, the Coalition Ministry resigned. Each side had its own story to tell. The ostensible cause was again the king's feelings on the

Catholic question. Presumably as a Cabinet measure Lord Howick, the Lord Grey of the Reform period, on the 5th of March, 1807, introduced a Bill to Extend Service in the Army and Navy to the Catholics. Lord Sidmouth and his friends at once seceded, and the Commander-in-Chief, the Chancellor, and the Duke of Portland pressed the king to put his pressure on the Grenville party to abandon the proposed measure, notwithstanding the state of Ireland and the danger at such a moment of excluding so large and influential a portion of the nation from its defence. The measure was abandoned, in a Cabinet minute to the king which reiterated the expression of its advisability on the part of its proposers. The king was still not satisfied, and required " a written and positive engagement never, under any circumstances, to propose any measure of concession to the Catholics or even connected with the question." This unconstitutional pledge was unhesitatingly refused, and a new Cabinet formed without delay, with the Duke of Portland as its nominal chief, but Perceval, as Chancellor of the Exchequer, its real leader. Lord Eldon returned to the woolsack; Lord Hawkesbury became Home Secretary; Mr. Canning went to the Foreign Office; Lord Castlereagh assumed the direction of the war; and Sir Arthur Wellesley entered political office for the first time as Secretary for Ireland. Backed by the strong cry of "No Popery," ministers dissolved Parliament without delay, and at once obtained a powerful majority. Thus recommenced the reign of the Tory party, which lasted almost without interruption, until the Reform Cabinet of Earl Grey, in 1830.

Whilst our party politicians were intriguing and disputing at home, or frittering away our strength in distant and unsuccessful expeditions in South America, Egypt, and the Dardanelles, Napoleon, keeping his huge armies together as one gigantic machine, was rapidly achieving the conquest of the Continent. Prussia, who, with fatal inopportuneness, waited to break her stubborn neutrality until Austria had been crushed at Austerlitz, herself fell before the conqueror on the field of Jena. Within seven weeks of the commencement of the war, Berlin was entered by Napoleon, and only 15,000 men left to follow the defeated king to the banks of the Vistula. Further resistance was hopeless, and the unfortunate king had to submit to the hardest terms of peace to save the remnant of his kingdom. Napoleon marked this success by issuing from Berlin the decrees which formally put the whole coasts of the Continent under a blockade against the admission of English cargoes. A hopeless scheme, which in reality pressed far more heavily on his own subjects and those of his vassals than on those of the power which he flattered himself he should paralyze by his paper blockade. The humiliation of Russia followed quickly on that of Prussia and Austria. Though driven to a standstill for a time by the fearful but indecisive battle of Eylau, from a new conscription Napoleon soon recruited his forces, and utterly defeated the Russians. Peace followed without delay, and at Tilsit, in July, 1807, Alexander and Napoleon practically agreed to divide the world between them, and Napoleon obtained formal recognition of the kinglets whom he had placed on the thrones of Naples, Holland and Westphalia. England was left without an ally. Anxious to re-create a fleet, Napoleon had tried in vain to persuade the Regent of Portugal to join him, but was more successful with the Danish king. Stoutly as it was denied at the time, it is now certain that, but for the much-abused expedition against Copenhagen, the Danish fleet would have joined that of France, and given material aid to the new crusade against England, which Napoleon had initiated. On the 12th of August the English expedition—powerful alike by land and sea—was in the Sound to back the demand for the surrender of the Danish fleet into our custody until the war was ended. The demand was rejected, and without the loss of a day the expedition moved on, the troops were landed, Copenhagen severely bombarded, and on the 8th of September the much-coveted fleet and enormous naval stores surrendered to Sir Arthur Wellesley, who had thrown up his political appointment at the first intimation of the intended expedition, to become the second in command. It was one of those cases, regret it and dispute about it as we may, which State expediency, and that alone, could justify.

At the opening of the year 1808 the position of Great Britain was one of painful and dangerous isolation. Thanks to the action of Napoleon, the ambassadors of Austria, Prussia, and Russia had been withdrawn, Denmark kept from open hostility only by force, Spain practically a vassal of France, Portugal temporarily independent, only by sufferance, and Sweden alone friendly. Nominally our commerce, our right hand of power, was excluded from the whole range of the Continent, and the sea alone remained our hardly disputed territory. It was at this moment of the apparent completion of his autocracy that Napoleon made his first false move by the overthrow of the Bourbon dynasty in Spain and his attempt to seize the crown of the Peninsula for another of his brothers. For the first time in these long years of war the cry of resistance came from the people, and not from their king. Demanding the enforcement of his Continental system by Portugal, he, towards the close of 1807, required the Prince Regent to confiscate all British property within his kingdom and join his fleet to those of the Continental States. Unable to offer effectual resistance, the Regent issued the decree demanded, so far as to formally declare war with us, but hesitated to carry out the order for the confiscation of British property. Napoleon seized the occasion. Junot was hurried through Spain with an army. An article in the official *Moniteur* intimated, though not in so many words, that "The house of Braganza had ceased to reign," and at the close of November the fleet of Portugal, instead of joining that of Napoleon, sailed from the Tagus, loaded with the court, the archives, and many thousands of loyal Portuguese, for their great dependency in South America. Junot found neither resistance nor obedience. The people were biding their time.

The intrigues for the seizure of Spain followed the attack on Portugal. Taking advantage of a family quarrel, Napoleon forced the imbecile king to surrender his crown to his son Ferdinand, entrapped both father and son into his power at Bayonne, crushed an insurrection in Madrid, excited by this kidnapping of the king, and then disclosed the real object of the whole intrigue, by placing his weak brother Joseph on the throne. The Spanish people were thoroughly roused. Provincial juntas were rapidly established, help was invoked from England for a nation that was animated with one spirit of resistance. The appeal was received with enthusiasm by the English, and the required assistance at once given by the Government. On the 12th of July, 1808, the forces assembled at Cork, under Sir Arthur Wellesley, for the projected recovery of our credit in South America, so miserably shattered by the imbecility of General Whitelock, were directed to Portugal, and the Peninsular War begun. It is as needless to rewrite as it would be impossible to equal the record of the war immortalized by Napier. Every one knows how the first efforts of the future conqueror of Napoleon were arrested by the mismanagement at the Horse Guards by which he was subordinated in the moment of victory to a succession of inferior generals, and how the remnants of the French army were saved by the miserable Convention of Cintra. One good the Convention did. It temporarily freed the Portuguese from the French army, and gave a little breathing-time to the nation, in which to prepare for the great coming struggle. Wellesley returned home, whilst Sir John Moore, misled by the ignorance of the Government of the interior of Spain, pushed forward without adequate information, only to find himself in danger of being surrounded by the rapidly gathering divisions of the enemy. Then com-

menced the famous retreat to Corunna, and its more
famous battle, when the British "leopards" instead of
being driven into the sea, defeated their assailants, and
the nation mourned the death, in the moment of
victory, of the kindest and bravest of her generals.
On the 16th of January, 1809, the British troops re-
embarked, and the Peninsula was left at the mercy of
Napoleon. Within two months after Wellesley was
back in Portugal with the first detachments of that
army which fighting on, year after year, with almost
uniform success, never left the soil of the Peninsula
until, four years after, it crossed the Bidassoa, and stood
victorious on French territory. How, by firmness,
patience, and perseverance, that army was created out
of the most disheartening materials, is told in the
Wellington despatches. Why those materials were
so disheartening may be traced in the disclosures in
the case of the Duke of York, the Commander-in-
Chief, and his leman, Mrs. Clarke, and in the exposure of the barbarities of the military discipline of the
time in the indictments of Cobbett and Leigh Hunt.[8]
When the general system of corruption not only in
military patronage, but in all the departments of State,
of which Mrs. Clarke was the leading operator, became
fully known, it is not to be wondered that reasonable
statesmen doubted of the success of any future military
enterprise. Had the noble army which was wasted
by disease in the fœtid island of Walcheren been
directed to Portugal, the liberation of the Peninsula

[8] Trial of Governor Wall, investigation in House of Commons of the charges against the Duke of York, and indictments of Cobbett, Leigh Hunt, and Drakard for libel.

might have been secured within a third of the time consumed in its accomplishment.

At home there was but little to disturb the monotony of the ministerial policy. A half-hearted support was given to the campaign in the Peninsula. Ministers quarrelled amongst themselves, and intrigued against each other: Canning and Castlereagh fought a duel to decide who should conduct the war, and in the end together deserted the Cabinet; the Duke of Portland, broken in health, and almost on the point of death, resigned the Premiership, and at the close of 1809, after many negotiations and intrigues, Mr. Perceval became Premier, Lord Wellesley assumed the seal of the Foreign Office, and to Lord Palmerston, as Secretary at War, fell the direction of the war, in the conduct of which Wellington's astute policy was misunderstood even by his friends, and of course misrepresented by his enemies.[9] Hitherto, though sorely afflicted, the blind old king had been able to perform the duties of his state. In the autumn of 1810 the serious illness of his favourite daughter, the Princess Amelia, had so affected his mind that he was unable to sign the commission for the further prorogation of Parliament, and from the moment of her death his intellect gave way and a regency became a necessity. Following the precedent of 1788, Parliament passed resolutions affirming the king's incapacity—the right and duty of the two Houses to provide

---

[9] It was for remarks based on these negotiations between Lords Grenville and Grey on the one side and Mr. Perceval and Lord Liverpool on the other, that Perry of the *Morning Chronicle* was indicted for libel. See Press Prosecutions.

for the emergency, and the determination of the powers of the future Regent. The temporary limitations of the Regent's power, which ministers carried, though by small majorities, and only after acrimonious debates, were offensive to the Prince of Wales and his political friends, especially that which left the king in the care of his consort. It was, however, useless to resist. The prince consoled himself with the fact of these lasting only for a year, and his political friends with their faith in his oft-repeated assurances that when he had the power he would place them in office. Before the Regency Bill passed on the 5th of February, 1811, the prince's friends were aware that he had deserted them, and that he had told Mr. Perceval that he did not intend to remove any of his father's official servants, "lest any act of his might, in the smallest degree, have the effect of interfering with the progress of his sovereign's recovery." On the 6th of February the prince took the oaths as Regent, and the reign of George the Third practically closed.[1]

This brief sketch of the leading incidents of the

---

[1] The principal instrument in effecting the change was one of the king's physicians, who had been accustomed to furnish reports of the king's real state of health to the prince and had latterly represented the strong probability of his recovery. He reported that "the king asked most anxiously after the prince (this was fabulous), and that a change of ministers would, in all probability, produce such an exacerbation as might put an end to his life."—Romilly's "Diary," ii. 366. Wilberforce confirms this, and adds, "I am assured that before the prince determined on keeping his ministers, he sent to Mrs. Fitzherbert and Lady Hertford, and they both advised it."—"Life of Wilberforce," iii. 494.

period, of which the trials here selected form apt illustrations, would be incomplete without an allusion to the social habits of the decade. Though since the close of the previous century manners had lost somewhat of their external grossness, there was but little real improvement in our social morals. The good example set by the king and his consort was counteracted by the open immorality of so many of the royal princes, whose evil courses were naturally imitated by their friends and dependents.[2] Such examples in high places naturally had their effect on the middle and lower classes. Duelling was rife, actions for seduction and adultery more than usually frequent, the footpad still lingered outside London, and the streets, practically unwatched, were not to be used after dark without imminent danger of violence and robbery. Gambling and drunkenness were not the prerogative of the habitués at White's or the Cocoa Tree, but pervaded every class. A Christian spirit was indeed struggling to leaven the mass, but as yet its good work was hardly felt amid the immorality of the period.

[2] See the Berkeley Peerage case.

CHAPTER II.

TRIAL OF GOVERNOR WALL OF GOREE.

MURDER OF A SOLDIER BY FLOGGING.

JANUARY 20TH, 1802.

ABOUT a mile to the south of Cape Verd, on the north-west coast of Africa, lies the island of Goree, a mere rock, half a mile in length and less than a quarter in breadth, and valuable only as sheltering a good anchorage from which it originally derived its name.[1] Occupied originally by the Dutch in 1617, it was repeatedly captured and recaptured by the fleets of England, France, and Holland, but eventually ceded to the French Crown at the peace of Nimeguen. So well did the French utilize their new possession, that in less than a century they had engrossed the whole

---

[1] Goree, from the Dutch word Gorree, "a good road for shipping," occupied by the Dutch, 1617; captured by Admiral Holmes, 1653; and soon after recaptured by De Ruyter. Taken in 1677 by the French fleet under Count d'Estrées, and ceded to France, 1678. Captured by Commodore Keppel in 1759; restored to France, 1763. Captured by British, 1779; restored to France at the peace of Paris, 1782. Retaken in 1809, and finally ceded with Senegal in 1816. At the time of its capture in 1779 it was inhabited by some 5000 free blacks, and 120 Europeans of various races.

trade along 500 miles of coast, from Cape Blanco to the River Gambia, and strengthened their position by forts in the Senegal river and on the island of Goree. The effect of this practical monopoly of the most valuable portion of the African trade was so severely felt by the African merchants of our country, that when the seven years' war commenced, the capture of the French African possessions was strongly urged on the Government, and Goree again retaken by us in 1759, only to be again surrendered at the peace of Paris in 1763; and again recaptured in 1779, when the French king openly joined the Americans in their struggle for independence. Its sole value to us was in its commanding the approach to the French settlements on the Gambia river, and the opportunity it offered to our merchants of pushing their goods into markets previously closed to their trade.

So unhealthy was the place that in three years three governors had been appointed in succession, and the garrison reduced to about 150 men of the African Corps, and a small detachment of artillery. Dangerous as were the classes of men which in those days were too often found in the ranks of the army, those in the African corps were of the worst description—mainly military convicts exchanging a portion of their punishment for this deadly service, and the refuse of the people whom the recruiting-sergeants could tempt into the ranks. Dependent for their supplies entirely on the uncertain arrivals of store-ships, the garrison of Goree was frequently reduced to short rations, and a custom had sprung up of crediting the men with the value of the arrears of food in the books of the commissary of the garrison, and liquidating this either in money or in additional stores, when opportunity offered.

Of this wretched spot, in 1782, Colonel Joseph Wall was the Governor. As Lieutenant-Governor he had succeeded Governor Adams some two years before, and at the time when this sad history begins, was about to leave the island, with the Commissary and the Commandant of the Artillery, in order to escape the approaching unhealthy season. Governor Wall came of a good Irish family, and by his marriage with a sister of Lord Seaforth was well connected. His gallantry when a subaltern at the capture of the Havannah in 1762, under General Forbes, had won him early promotion, and though his temper was hasty, perhaps violent, he was known as a good officer and a gallant soldier. During his government of Goree he had done his best to keep the garrison supplied, but periods of short rations could not be avoided, and no settlement of these arrears had apparently been made in his time. When, therefore, in July of 1782 it was known in the garrison that he and the other officers were about to leave, the men became anxious for their arrears, and having got one of their number to make out an account of them, agreed to send some of their comrades to press the Commissary for a settlement before he embarked. Armstrong, the victim of this tragedy, a sergeant of some standing in the African Corps, headed the party. On their way to the Commissary's they had to pass the Governor's house, and were met at the gate by Wall himself. On what passed then and at a subsequent meeting a few hours afterwards, the whole case turned. Wall declared it was mutiny ; what ensued was, that a sort of drumhead court-martial was called on parade a little before sunset, Armstrong sentenced to 800 lashes, which were at once inflicted by negroes with a short knotted rope, led away to hospital, and a dead man in less than a week.

Wall, with the Commissary, left the island on the day after the punishment, and apparently knew nothing of its sad result until some time after his arrival in England. He at once reported himself to the authorities, and in his despatch was strangely silent about the mutiny.[2] Other charges against him as Governor, however, were made to the Privy Council by an officer of the African Corps, but proved to be so groundless that his accuser was severely reprimanded.[3] On this Wall retired to Bath. His conduct in Goree, however, soon became a topic in the newspapers, and if they were to be believed, he was a veritable monster, who had not only murdered men under the lash, but subjected them to most ingenious tortures, and even fired more than one victim from the guns of the fortress. Captain Lacy, who had succeeded him in the Governorship, arrived soon after in England, and from him the Government obtained a detailed account of the supposed mutiny and of Armstrong's

[2] Letter of August 26, 1782, to the Right Hon. Thomas Townsend, Secretary of State, with a return of the state of the garrison of Goree on July 11th of same year.
[3] There is no mention of these charges in the records of the Privy Council.

fate. Hence in October, 1784, warrants for his arrest for murder were issued by the Secretary of State, and he was arrested at Bath by the Council's messengers.[4] On the way to London, whilst at Reading, whether by the connivance or not of these officers, he escaped, got abroad, and for eighteen years the matter slept.

According to his own story he knew nothing of the charges for which he was arrested, he did not even know that the messengers held warrants for his arrest, but believed that they were sent only to require him to come to London to see the Secretary of State. The popular outcry against him, he said, was such that he deemed it best to leave the country, professedly to obtain evidence to rebut the calumnies so popularly circulated against him.[5] Yet at that time Captain Lacy, who must have known the truth, and, probably, several of the other officers who were pre-

[4] Proclamation for his arrest, 8th March, 1784.
[5] Letters from Wall to the Right Hon. Lord Pelham, Secretary of State, Oct. 5 and 6, 1801. According to a paragraph in the London *Evening Post*, Dec. 3 to 6, 1808, Wall, after escaping from the officers, remained for many years in the south of France, but at length, from poverty and distress, determined to surrender. He came to Calais. When waiting in the inn-room with other intending passengers, and it was reported that the weather was too bad for the packet to sail, Mr. Brooks, a government messenger, came in and said he would go. On this Wall told him who he was, and called on him, as an officer of justice, to take him over as a prisoner. Brooks declined, but asked Wall to write his name on a piece of paper, which he would take over to be compared with his official signature. When the necessary materials were brought, Wall rushed out. Brooks, thinking him a madman, embarked without him, and was drowned within a short distance of the shore by the upsetting of the boat.

sent at the punishment were alive and in England, and could have been called to explain the tragic incidents of that day. Eighteen years after—October, 1801—he suddenly returned to England, and offered himself for trial. By that time every officer who had been a witness of the tragedy, save one, was dead, and Wall apparently felt himself safe.

He was at once arraigned and tried by Chief Baron Macdonald, at the Old Bailey, on the 20th of January. For the Crown the Attorney-General, Sir E. Law, with the Solicitor-General, Spencer Perceval, and some five other counsel, appeared to prosecute,[6] and the defence was entrusted to Knowles, Allen, and Gurney. Five questions arose on the trial. Was there a mutiny: was Armstrong its leader: was there a legal court-martial: was the punishment excessive, and was it the immediate cause of Armstrong's death?

The witnesses for the prosecution, mostly soldiers in the African Corps, told a plain and a consistent story, confirming in all important particulars the account given by the orderly sergeant, Evan Lewis, who was on duty that day at the gate of the

[6] Edward Law, son of the Bishop of Carlisle, born 1748, on Erskine's refusal of the brief, acted as counsel for Warren Hastings. Attorney-General, 1801, and next year, on the death of Lord Kenyon, Lord Chief Justice of England, and created a peer. An acute and profound lawyer, but notably harsh as a judge, and a bitter partisan. The acquittal of Hone by the jury, in despite of his charge, weighed on his then sinking health, he died 1818. Spencer Perceval, born in 1762, practised at the Chancery Bar. Attorney-General, 1801. Entered cabinet 1807, as Chancellor of the Exchequer. Prime Minister, 1809. Shot by Bellingham, May 11, 1812.

Governor's house. According to Lewis, early in the morning of the fatal 10th of July he saw some fifteen or twenty men of his corps, headed by Armstrong, pass by Government House on their way to that of Commissary Deering. Being told by Armstrong that they were on their way to the Commissary's to request a settlement of the arrears of the allowance for short rations before he embarked for England, Lewis reported it to the Governor, and was ordered by him to tell them to return at once to barracks, or he would flog them. On this he said the men left and returned towards their barracks. In about an hour and a half afterwards they came again, probably in rather larger numbers, headed by two other sergeants as well as Armstrong. Wall went out, met them, and asked Armstrong what they wanted. Hat in hand, Armstrong, as spokesman, repeated what he had told Lewis. Wall again threatened them, and they left. They had no arms, and were only in their undress jackets. On that day some of the officers dined with the Governor and left early. As soon as they had gone, Wall went to the ramparts and main guard of the fort, where he appears to have roughly treated a half-drunken sentinel at the guard-room, ordered the drum to beat for parade, and sent Lewis to the barracks to order the men to fall in without arms. At the parade, which was called rather earlier than usual, the men fell in in a circle with the officers in the midst. A gun-carriage was rolled in by the negro assistants of the interpreter. Wall spoke a few words to the officers, then Armstrong was called out from the ranks, ordered to strip, tied to the carriage, and flogged by the blacks with a half-inch rope knotted at the end. Whilst the punishment was being inflicted, Wall stood by, urging the blacks to their work. "Lay it on," he said, "or I will lay it on you. Cut him to the heart." How many lashes were given Lewis did not know (it was admitted, however, that they were 800); but he remembered that the blacks were repeatedly changed during the punishment. Armstrong was then led away to hospital, and Lewis never saw him again alive. He saw no signs of a court-martial nor of a mutiny.

Moore, another private in the corps, spoke also to the punishment. Previously to it he saw the officers talking together, and heard the Governor call Armstrong out of the ranks and say he was the ringleader, and afterwards instructing the negro linguist and his men how to flog. He remembered the men discussing the question of the arrears in the barracks, and Armstrong telling them that he had been to the Governor, and that the Governor would see them righted before he left. The absence of mutiny was spoken to also by other soldiers, and confirmed by the official report of the state of the garrison on that day, in which no mention appeared of such a fact.

The testimony of the garrison surgeon was decided on the one point, that the punishment was the cause of death, but by no means satisfactory on other points, from his want of experience, both of military floggings and of the effect of such a climate on so severe a punishment. He had heard, of course, of the brutal extent to which the cat was used in those days, when six hundred, eight hundred, and even a thousand lashes were not unfrequently awarded, and that men endured these tortures and yet lived through them. He admitted that the instrument used was more likely from the bruises it would inflict to cause mortification than the sharply-cutting whipcords of the cat; but he saw no reason to interfere during the infliction of the torture, or to remonstrate against its continuance. He forbade the sufferer to take spirits or wine, but otherwise treated it as an ordinary case, and was somewhat surprised when it had a sudden and fatal termination. But though he warned the sufferer against ardent drink, he did not deem it necessary to warn his assistant, who had care of the hospital, against its use, with the inevitable result that the daily allowance of brandy or wine was sent in, and in all probability drunk by the patient. The letters of 26th of August, 1782, reporting the state of the garrison on that day, of October, 1784, to the Secretary of State, excusing his flight abroad, and to Lord Pelham of October, 1801, announcing his return for trial, having been put in, the case for the prosecution closed.

The story for the defence, set out in Wall's own statement, was boldly confirmed by Mrs. Lacy, the widow of the officer who succeeded Wall in the government of the garrison. According to her tale, she had been in Government House at the time when the men came there, making preparations for its being occupied by herself and her husband. If she told the truth, the existence of a serious mutiny was established. Looking from the open window of one of the rooms across the very small courtyard in front of Government House, she saw seventy or eighty of the soldiers come to the gate in a noisy and riotous manner, and heard them threaten Wall that if they did not get the arrears due in his predecessor's time, they would break open the stores and help themselves. The Governor, she declared, remonstrated with them, and then desired them to return to their barracks, and give him time to consider their demand. In about an hour's time they returned, headed by Armstrong and two other sergeants, in a most mutinous and riotous manner. Wall again went out to them, when they threatened that he should not leave the island until their claims were satisfied, and then went off, headed by Armstrong, all holloaing and shouting together. On this, Wall sent one of the officers, O'Shanley, to summon those off duty to Government House, who shortly after returned with Captain Lacy and Lieutenant Fall. Wall related to them what had happened, when it was decided not to attempt to confine the men to barracks for fear of resistance, but to pick out the ringleaders and try them by a drum-head court-martial. On O'Shanley reporting that the cat had been destroyed that morning by some of the mutineers, it was suggested by Lacy that the negro linguist and his assistants should inflict the punishment, as the drummers were believed to be entirely unreliable. Wall then left Government House to prepare for the court-martial, and the linguist came there to receive his instructions from the officers.

Here Mrs. Lacy's part of the story ended. Throughout her cross-examination she showed temper in a way that threw discredit on her testimony, fenced with the questions put to her about her husband's state of mind when in England in 1784, and in command of his corps at Chichester, stoutly denied that Lewis was the orderly of the day, and professed not to know him when confronted with her in court. Her story, however, was confirmed by Mary Faulkener, the wife of a gunner, who happened to be passing Government House when the men came there for the second time, and who stood near the gate and heard what passed. If she could be trusted, her evidence carried the mutiny much further, as she also swore that through the door of the room in the barracks she heard the three sergeants, when asking one Besson to make out their claims for allowances, threaten to take the Governor's life if he attempted to leave without a settlement of their arrears.

Fawcett, another gunner, besides explaining the incident of Wall's beating the sentry on the main guard, entirely in the Governor's favour, declared that after the circle was formed on parade, he heard Armstrong charged with threatening to stop the embarkation of the Governor and to detain his stores, and asked what he had to say in reply. Williams, also a gunner, here took up the tale. Though in the outer ring of the circle, he saw Wall go in, heard him order the officers to form a court-martial, and then charge Armstrong as the ringleader. On this the officers consulted together, and then spoke to Wall and told Armstrong that he was sentenced to 800 lashes. He saw the punishment inflicted, and agreed with Fawcett that Armstrong walked away apparently little the worse for its infliction. Turner, a private in the African Corps, saw one of the drummers taking the cat to pieces in the afternoon of the day, and in the evening witnessed a drinking-bout between Armstrong and two or three other soldiers in the hospital.

The testimony to character called by Wall was far from favourable. Those witnesses who spoke of his distinguished kindness, and of his being "brim-full of the best feelings of humanity," had known him only during his retirement abroad. Of the two who had served with him, General Forbes had not seen him since they were together in the Havannah, forty years before; and Major Phipps, who commanded the artillery at Goree during Wall's career there, was obliged to admit that his reputation for humanity was very doubtful.

To rebut the prisoner's witnesses, Lieutenant Poplett, who was at the time temporarily under arrest, spoke confidently of Captain Lacy's good health on his return to England. Besson, who, as a witness for the prosecution, had spoken to making out the claims for arrears, distinctly denied the threat which Mrs. Faulkener had sworn she overheard, and declared that the men were not riotous, and that he only told them it was unsoldierlike for four or five of them together to trouble the officers. That Lewis was the Governor's orderly on the day was confirmed by another non-commissioned officer, and Williams, who had given so clear an account of the drum-head courtmartial, was proved by Captain Williams, under whose command he had been subsequently at Gibraltar, to bear the character of "a lying, shuffling fellow."

To the prisoner's evidence the Attorney-General did not consider it necessary to reply. Had Mrs. Lacy's tale been true, how much better would it have come from her husband in 1784 than from her when he had been removed from the scene? How strongly would it have told if it had been confirmed by Fall and O'Shanley, both of whom were alive at that period? If there was such a serious mutiny on the 10th of July, how came it that not a word was written about it in the Governor's report, or a note made of it in the daily state of the garrison, and that the Governor and two officers could risk leaving the island with the knowledge that it was left in the power of a garrison only a few hours before in open mutiny? "Allowance," said the Chief Baron in his charge to the jury, "should be made for a man in such a position as Governor Wall, far away from England, and with but few British subjects to rely on, if his conduct did not show malevolence but only human infirmity. But he was bound by the rules of good sense and common humanity not to administer excessive punishment, and to use the ordinary instrument in its infliction. Hence, he said, arose the question whether the use of one more likely to injure was not evidence of malice. Spirits," he continued, "no doubt were dangerous in such a climate, but no man was entitled to place another by violence in such a situation, that mortification was not unlikely to come on by the careless mistreatment of himself."

There could not be a doubt about the verdict. After a brief delay of half an hour the jury returned a verdict of Guilty, and Wall was left for execution.

On his sentence the unhappy man made no remark, beyond begging a short delay to enable him to prepare for death. To this extent his request was granted—the usual brief interval of twenty-four hours between sentence and execution was extended to eight days. From his rank, his age, and the circumstances not only of his crime but of his voluntary surrender, a hitherto unequalled curiosity was excited in the public mind, and his appearance on the scaffold was hailed by crowds with three rounds of cheers, which appeared to completely unnerve him. By some sad mismanagement his sufferings were protracted, to the evident satisfaction of the wretches who surrounded the scaffold.[7]

Though the justice of the verdict was accepted by all but a few of his friends, the conduct of the Government in leaving him for execution was freely canvassed. Had he been convicted in 1784, it was admitted that if ever the extreme penalty was deserved, it would have been in his case. The lapse of time between the act and the trial, however, led many to doubt of the justice of the execution, even in those days when criminals died by scores on the scaffold for what are now regarded as trifling offences. They did

[7] Wall was a man of commanding stature and presence, and in his sixty-fifth year when executed. During his protracted trial, which lasted nearly fourteen hours, he behaved with great steadiness and composure. He was connected with many good families, and left several young children. His brother, a member of the Irish Bar in good practice, was the first to publish reports of the speeches in Parliament with the real names of the speakers, and the author of several literary works.—*Gentleman's Magazine*, 1802, part 2, p. 81.

not, however, consider that the delay of justice was not due to any neglect on the part of the authorities, but solely to the ingenuity of the prisoner. Apart from the difficulties thrown in the way of capturing him abroad by the prevalence of a state of war, extradition treaties were not dreamed of in those times, nor for many a long year afterwards. What, however apparently swayed the decision of the Government was the almost contemporaneous execution of the mutinous sailors at Portsmouth for resistance to their officers. In the temper of the public they could not dare to spare the officer for brutality to soldiers, when they had so lately executed the sailor for resistance to his officers.[8]

[8] According to an anecdote of Lord Sidmouth, given by Dean Pellew in his life of that statesman, Lord Eldon as usual "doubted." " He would not say he ought to be hanged, and he would not say he ought not."—Vol. i. 478.

CHAPTER III.

THE DESPARD CONSPIRACY OF 1802.

FEBRUARY 7TH, 1803.

AT the opening of the present century, the satisfaction of the nation in the almost uniform success that had attended its arms, and the hopes entertained that the lately accomplished union with Ireland had quelled that restless country, were sadly diminished by the condition of the working classes, especially in the great towns where the war prices of provisions pressed heavily on their limited means. To such a height had the price of wheat risen, that the manufacture of pure wheaten bread was prohibited by statute and the law against corn engrossers rigidly enforced. Projects for reforms of the constitution based on the new French models were popularly discussed, but generally wisely allowed by the Government to be talked to death without the interference of the law. The Government of the day, however, was far too weak for the situation. Its intentions were no doubt good, but its remedial performances weak, and its policy savoured too much of forcible repression. By Mr. Pitt's retirement, the reins had fallen into the hands of Speaker Addington—hands far too weak at such a period to drive the state car, even if strenuously supported by those of the ex-premier.

The prospect of peace too, though welcome, in the existing condition of the country, and at first hailed with acclamation, gradually became less and less acceptable as the terms were known, and it was found to be purchased at the cost of the concession of some of our most important conquests. Yet even these would have been parted with readily, could it have been believed that, on the part of the 'First Consul, peace was honestly entered into, and not merely contrived to afford him time to prepare for a more bitter contest. To the great bulk of Englishmen, Bonaparte, despite the civil things now said of him by Ministers who had so lately abused him, was still little better than an incarnate fiend. In the navy there was much discontent, and the prospect of peace brought no comfort to sailors only too eager to continue the contest in that arena where victory seemed to be the monopoly of our flag. Early in 1802, when it was reported in the fleet in Bantry Bay that they were ordered to the West Indies, a mutiny of a very serious character broke out, for which several of the mutineers eventually suffered death. Again at the close of the same year a similar outbreak occurred on board the fleet at Gibraltar, during which one of the men-of-war was for a time completely in the hands of its crew, and only recovered by her officers on the crews of the other ships of the fleet not responding to the cheers of the mutineers. In the army, the disbanding of many regiments, and the discharge of men from others, so as to reduce them to a peace footing, increased the numbers of the unemployed, and thus added to the ranks of the dangerous classes in the manufacturing towns and the metropolis. In such well-prepared soil it was not difficult to sow the seeds of conspiracy, and it only required a clever and desperate leader to raise and bring to maturity the dangerous crop of disaffection. Such a man was apparently ready to hand in a brave and meritorious officer, Colonel Despard, smarting under a bitter grievance, whose rank and gallant deeds gave him a great and most dangerous influence among the soldiers, whilst the sudden blight that had fallen on his military career might well have rendered him careless alike of life and character.

Marcus Edward Despard was born in Queen's County, Ireland, in 1750 or '51, of an old and respectable family, the youngest of six brothers, all of whom except the eldest served in our army or navy.[1] At the age of sixteen, Marcus was gazetted as an ensign in the 50th Regiment, in which he obtained his lieutenancy, and in 1782 was promoted to his company in the 79th or Liverpool Volunteers. On the disbanding of this regiment in the following year, he was placed on half pay, and employed on detached service in important offices in the West Indies and the Spanish Main, with the local rank of lieutenant-colonel and field engineer. It was during this time that he was the comrade of Nelson. "We slept many

[1] Memoirs of Colonel Marcus Edward Despard, by James Bannatyne, his Secretary when Superintendent of H.M. Affairs in Honduras, 1798.—Cited in *Gentleman's Magazine*, vol. lxxiii. part 1, p. 377.

nights together in our clothes on the ground," said the hero, when testifying to his late comrade's character on his trial. "We have measured the height of the enemies' wall together. In all that time no man could have shown more zealous attachment to his sovereign and his country. I formed the highest opinion of him at that time as a man and an officer, seeing him so willing in the service of his country. Having lost sight of him for the last twenty years, if I had been asked my opinion of him, I should certainly have said, If he is alive, he is certainly one of the highest ornaments of the British army." [2] For his services in Jamaica he twice received the thanks of the Governor and Council, and his well-merited promotion to his colonelcy soon followed. In 1784 he assisted as first commissioner in settling and receiving the territory in the Spanish Main ceded by the treaty with Spain, and was appointed superintendent of English affairs at Honduras. This position proved the bane of his life. He appears to have got into disputes with the English there, and such serious complaints of his conduct were sent home, that he was suspended, and returned to England to demand the fullest inquiry

[2] In April, 1789, Nelson, just made a post-captain, was sent to capture Fort San Juan on the Nicaragua river, running from that lake to the Atlantic, with only a few British troops and some Mosquito Indians. After heavy loss and suffering, they reached an outlying fort, which Nelson determined to board. At the head of a few sailors he leaped on the beach, followed by Despard, and together they stormed the battery. Two days after they came in sight of the Castle of San Juan, and speedily reduced it on the 24th. Out of 1800 men engaged, only 380 returned unhurt.

into his conduct. For two years he pressed ministers for their decision, without success. At last he was told that there was no charge against him worth investigating, that, had not his previous post been abolished, he would have been sent back, and promised that in due time he should be rewarded. In 1795 he was made major of the 107th regiment, but in the next year his name disappears from the army list.

Irritated at his treatment by the ministry of the day, he appears to have taken a violent part in politics, and from his family connexion with Ireland to have fallen under suspicion during the rebellion of "98," and to have been arrested (under the powers given by the suspension of the Habeas Corpus Act to the Secretary of State), on the general charge of "treasonable practices."[3] Under this warrant he was committed to Cold Bath Fields Bridewell, where his harsh treatment became the subject of animated discussions in both Houses of Parliament, and the validity of the warrant itself was ineffectually tested in the Queen's Bench on the ground of the general nature of the charge.[4] From his first prison he was transferred to the house of correction at Shrewsbury, and thence back to the Bridewell in Tothill Fields, without even being able to learn the particulars of the

[3] Hansard's Debates, House of Commons, Dec.21, 26, 1798, House of Lords, January 4, 1799.

[4] June 25, 1788. 7 Term Reports, p. 736. Under 38 George III. c. 36, the right to a writ of Habeas Corpus was suspended until 1st February, 1799, and no person allowed to try or bail persons committed by warrant of Secretary of State without a licence from the Privy Council.

charges against him, much less to obtain the verdict of a jury on their truth or falsehood. In prison he passed three weary years, and only obtained his release on the expiry of the Suspension Act, when apparently the Irish rebellion had been stamped out, and the impending peace with France led many to hope against hope, that a period of tranquillity at home and abroad had at last arrived.

In 1802, London on the south side of the Thames was but sparsely built over, and the majority of the houses dated from the time when Newington and Lambeth were suburban villages, and young city sportsmen flushed small birds in the hedges and fields of Kennington and South Lambeth. From the Southwark side the communication was still by old London Bridge, which, though cleared of its houses, was narrow even for the traffic of that day, as it crept slowly thence down the picturesque street until at the point where the old town hall faced the older Tabard Inn, it opened on a broader thoroughfare as far as St. George's Church. To this point the lines of houses were continuous, broken only on the north side by the gloomy gates of the gloomier Marshalsea, and on the southern by Union Street, a new road leading towards Blackfriars; then by a lane between tenements, each floor of which projected above the lower one, leading to the ill-cared-for church of St. Saviour's with its ancient school-house, and lower down by the narrow entrance to the still vilely built, and more vilely inhabited, alleys of the Mint. Thence to the "Stones End" the scattered houses were of newer character, and at this point whence the Newington Causeway ran towards the country, the then lately erected county jail for Surrey stood in open fields, and the dark high walls of the King's Bench towered over the lately opened road towards the obelisk at Blackfriars. Lock's Fields on the one side contained only a few scattered hovels; on the other, St. George's Fields were without a decent habitation until the shops and sheds of the Borough Market were reached. Kennington was a rural village separated from Westminster by the open land on which Bethlehem now stands, and the Westminster Bridge Road practically ended at the turnpike within a quarter of a mile of the then new bridge over the Thames.

Since the construction of the bridge at Blackfriars buildings had sprung up in the road leading from it towards the obelisk, due mainly to the fact of its lower portion being included in the rules of the bench, within which, under the easy administration of the Bankruptcy Act of the day, debtors lived in comparative luxury, whilst their creditors pined for dividends. Pedlars' acre with its halfpenny hatch bridge cut off Westminster from what is now known as the Waterloo Road, which extended nearly to the New Cut, then, as now badly inhabited, whilst lower down ran Oakley Street, still as narrow as it was in those days, completing the line of road from Rowland Hill's Octagon Chapel in the Blackfriars Road, erected some twenty-five years before, *viâ* Charlotte Street, to the spot where in after-years the present Orphan Asylum was erected. In this street, worse built, and less creditably inhabited than at present, stood a low public-house, called the Oakley Arms, with a club-room of fair size on its first floor; a popular hostelry among the working classes of the South of London, the scene of the last act of the Despard Conspiracy.

Though by no means unaccustomed to the visits of the guardians of the peace, the inhabitants of this locality were somewhat startled at the numbers of the patrol gathered in front of the Oakley Arms on the evening of the 16th of November, 1802, and the subsequent procession of lumbering hackney coaches filled with persons strongly guarded driving off as fast as their poor cattle could go towards the lock-up-houses of Westminster, and the Borough. The news soon spread that a large body of rebels under the command of a veteran soldier had been captured and that the vigilance of the government alone had saved the capital from a renewal of riots of a far more dangerous character than those of which the remembrance was still keen, and thus prevented the assassination of the king and the overthrow of the constitution. Rumour of course exaggerated the danger, whilst the newspapers of the day by their vague reports increased the public anxiety, and it was not until the reputed leader, and his chief agents stood on their trial in the February of the following year, that it was known how mad had been the project, and how contemptible the machinery by which this threatened revolution was to have been accomplished.[5]

---

[5] *Gentleman's Magazine*, 1802, p. 1216. "Annual Register," 1802, November 19. The prisoners were first examined by Sir R. Ford, and afterwards by the Privy Council. Seven were committed to the new prison at Clerkenwell, twenty-three to Tothill Fields Bridewell. Colonel Despard, after being examined

The time for the execution of the project was well selected. The new Parliament had lately met, and the swearing-in of members had proceeded so rapidly that it was expected that on the very day on which the conspirators were arrested the king would have attended its formal opening. In those days the royal procession assembled in the park at the back of St. James's Palace and crossed the Mall on its way to St. Stephen's. Hence one of the mad projects of these men was to get one of the soldier conspirators to be selected as sentry over the long Indian gun on the Mall, and to load and fire it through the crowd at the moment when the state coach came within range. Parliament, happily, was not ready, and the Royal visit was in consequence postponed to the 23rd. In the meantime the conspirators were arrested, and the miserable project was stifled in its cradle.

In this conspiracy Colonel Despard was the only man above the working classes who apparently had a share, the others were soldiers, either disbanded, or allowed in that day to pursue their trades, and to be only nominally attached to their regiment, and workmen. Among them, from the very inception of the plot, there was a traitor, Thomas Windsor, a soldier in the Guards, allowed, though still borne on the strength of his regiment, to pursue his trade as a bricklayer, and undoubtedly in regular communication with some Government official. To the soldiers rank and increased pay were held out as a bait. To the workmen

at Lord Pelham's office (Home Secretary) in the presence of several Cabinet ministers, was sent to Newgate.

the prospect of sharing in the expected plunder and being raised from their dependent position through the anticipated revolution were the inducements offered. With their leader, whilst a vague idea of improving the condition of the working classes, by a radical change in the Constitution, no doubt animated his efforts, revenge for the neglect of his grievances by the Cabinet, and especially for his long and unexplained imprisonment was the chief motive. As an Irishman he imbibed Irish ideas of liberty, and if the remark made by Emmet, in his proclamation in the year following this mad attempt, may be trusted, looked with no ill-will on the designs that for some time had been in agitation by the remnants of the United Irishmen.[6]

From the moment of his release from prison, Despard appears to have sought out kindred spirits, and, as far as he dared, to have openly agitated against the Government in the manufacturing districts, where the working classes were suffering severely from the depression of trade and the high price of provisions. How far he succeeded in making treasonable arrangements for a rising in these parts of England is not clearly known. He, however, is said to have persuaded himself that, in Birmingham, Leeds, Manchester, and Sheffield, the workmen were ripe for rebellion, and that it only required an outbreak in the metropolis to ensure a general insurrection in those towns, for which the stoppage of the mail

[6] It will be seen subsequently that the majority of the conspirators were Irishmen and affiliated members of the London branch of the Corresponding Society.

coaches was to be the agreed signal. With this object he seems to have sought out some of those disaffected spirits which are always to be found in a great city and especially soldiers, among whom his rank and acknowledged gallantry necessarily gave him great influence. With the exception of these latter, some of whom turned King's evidence against him, and some of whom died with him on the scaffold, his followers were of the lowest and almost poorest class of workmen, utterly ignorant of military tactics, and uniformly strangers to arms. These confederates, it was sworn, he met from time to time, with dangerous and inconceivable openness, in small and low public houses in the lower parts of London, in the purlieus of the Haymarket and St. Giles's, in Hatton Garden, and near the Tower, in the Mint, in the Borough, at Newington, and finally in Oakley Street, where they were arrested. At several of these meetings it was proved that the following oath was administered, either by Despard or by those of his companions to whom he had given military titles as generals. The oath was headed—

CONSTITUTION.

The Independence of Great Britain and Ireland.
An Equalization of Civil, Political, and Religious Rights.
An ample Provision for the Families of the Heroes who shall fall in the contest.
A liberal Reward for Distinguished Merit.
These are the objects for which we contend, and to obtain these objects we swear to be united.

In the awful presence of Almighty God, I, A. B., do voluntarily declare that I will endeavour to the utmost of my power to obtain the objects of this union, namely, to recover those rights which the Supreme Being in His infinite bounty has given to all men; that neither hopes nor fears, rewards nor punishments, shall ever induce me to give any information, directly or indirectly, concerning the business, or of any member of this or any similar society.

So help me God.

It was not, apparently, until the spring of 1802 that the Colonel commenced his operations in London, taking advantage of the return to the metropolis of a portion of the foot guards from Chatham, many of whom from the idleness due to the declaration of peace with France, he found ready for any mischief. Among those who were early sworn in, according to his own account, was Windsor, the Government spy, to whom the oath was, as he said, administered by another of the foot guards, John Francis, who had already joined and taken an active part in the conspiracy. Whether instructed or not by the Government to put himself in the way of joining the confederates, no sooner did Windsor take the oath and obtain from Francis other copies that he might make more converts, than he took some of them to an army agent of the name of Bownas, who told him "to keep an eye on those people, and to put himself as forward as possible."[7] From that moment Wind-

[7] "Bownas was applied to by Windsor in May to get his dis-

sor pretended to be zealous in the cause, tried to draw others into it, and doubtless kept the Government fully apprised of the proceedings of the conspirators. The secret of this man's treachery was well kept. When the rest of the party were being arrested at the Oakley Arms, Windsor, who had been invited and agreed to go to the meeting, walked with well-assumed unconcern into the tap-room, in the dress and with the marks of his calling on him, and sat down, as apparently a chance customer, to his beer and pipe. In this position he was seen by Mr. Stafford, the chief clerk of the Union Street police office, as he came down from the club-room, where he had arrested the others. According to that gentleman's naive evidence on this point, it was quite by accident that he spoke to this man and drew from him his knowledge of the plot. And so well satisfied was he of his innocence, that he was content to leave him free and merely to take his word that he would meet him the next morning at Union

charge, on the reduction of his regiment. About July he came again to him, and mentioned that there was a meeting of men who called themselves United Irishmen, and were of the lowest description by their appearance, and told him where they met. Bownas told him he had better wait a little while, and try and find out whether there were any better sort of persons with them, and come and tell him. At this interview he gave him some of the cards with the Constitution printed on them. Saw him again about two months ago (September 18 ?), when he said that he had not found out any names of consequence." Bownas' evidence as given in the proofs attached to the Attorney General's brief. Public Record Office, Treasury papers Re Despard. It will be seen, hereafter, that Windsor took a most active part in suggesting measures and inciting the others to proceed.

Hall to be examined. On his examination Mr. Stafford declared that he did not know the man then. We suppose that he must be believed. He may not have seen him before, but that he knew that a Government spy would be there to fall in his way can hardly be doubted. The sad farce was well played by both the actors, and probably some sign of recognition had been given him by authority. Otherwise it would be a reflection on Stafford's capability as a lawyer, had he allowed a confessed conspirator to go away with no further security than his promise to attend as a witness on the morrow.

Another and most important approver was William Francis, whose testimony helped to send his own brother to the scaffold. This man was also a guardsman, and if this man's story was true, Colonel Despard was a fool as well as a traitor. According to his evidence, though he refused to take the oath, when repeatedly pressed by the Colonel, and openly told him that he did not hold with his brother's views, and could not join in the conspiracy, every detail of the plot was disclosed to him by its leader. Strange, too, that having refused to take the treasonable oath and to join the plot, he should, at one of the meetings of the conspirators, have crossed his bayonet with those of the rest of the party of soldiers, and sworn with them that "they would have a time fixed for the attack on the Tower before they left the room, or would do it themselves." Emblin, too, another witness, though he steadily refused the oath, was made fully acquainted with all the details by Colonel Despard himself. The last approver was also a guardsman, Thomas Blades. He, indeed, had taken the oath. 'I ask you," said Sergeant Best to the jury in his powerful speech for the defence, "whether a man who has so abused the solemnity of an oath is afterwards to be believed, recollecting at the same time that he has already falsified one oath by another, for, as a soldier, he has sworn to be true to his Sovereign, and by this oath he has pledged himself to betray him."

The plot which these witnesses professed to reveal was of the wildest and most reckless character. The new constitution which the society were to establish was to consist of an executive government, of course self-elected, at any rate at the commencement, and a parliament, based on the parochial system, composed of one delegate from each parish, for the meeting of whose thousands Salisbury Plain or Kirkstall Moor would have been appropriate places. Any general organization in London was regarded as too dangerous, as it would be under the immediate eye of the Government. What was proposed to be done there was, rather to strike a paralyzing blow by the assassination of the king than to seriously attempt (unless suddenly aided by kindred spirits who were not as yet in the society, but who were likely to be attracted by the prospect of plunder and licence) to seize the Tower, and obtain military possession of the metropolis. If they could only get sufficient temporary command in London to enable them to stop the evening mails, the lower classes, in the great manufacturing towns, taking their non-arrival as the agreed sign of success, it was said, would at once rise and so divide the attention of the Government as to paralyze its action, and ensure the ultimate success of the conspiracy.

With this object clubs were to be formed in various low districts of the city to collect subscriptions to be devoted to the organization of other clubs in the country, and for the secret purchase of arms. The basis of these funds was the shilling paid by each man who took the oath, a miserable source of revenue, as the whole exchequer appears not to have exceeded sixteen shillings, beyond what no doubt was furnished from the purse of Colonel Despard. These clubs were companies of ten men each, over whom an eleventh man was put as captain—this rank being the reward of any one who could recruit the other ten. Over five of these companies a colonel was to be appointed by the executive government, and though, generally, soldiers were selected for these posts, a breeches-maker and a watchmaker were not considered unfit for these important positions. Each of these officers had a district assigned to him, Colonel Despard himself taking the dangerous duty of attacking the royal procession, aided by the soldier Wood, who undertook to get himself placed as sentry over the Indian gun, to load it with two balls or chain shot and fire it at the royal carriage, should the Colonel's desperate attempt on the king previously miscarry. Much stress was laid on the reported disaffection of the Tower guard, several hundreds of whom were said to have secretly joined "The Constitution Society." In this there was no truth, and in reality, though at each of the numerous meetings held in the various public-houses, from a dozen to a score of persons attended, the real force of the conspirators never exceeded forty, as the same parties appeared over and over again at the different meetings, walking off and returning to the scene like a stage procession.

The day for the attempt was several times postponed, but eventually the 17th of November decided on, and a preliminary meeting called for the previous evening at the Oakley Arms. At that place some thirty persons assembled in the club-room, many of whom came solely out of curiosity, and were not as yet sworn to the plot, others were accomplices ready to betray their comrades, and some fifteen only really in the conspiracy. Here they were met by Colonel Despard. According to the witness Emblin, the proposal of Wood to fire the Indian gun was boasted of by the conspirator Broughton in the immediate hearing of the colonel, who discussed with Emblin the feasibility of attacking the Tower and the Bank, and taking the guns at the artillery-ground. He relied apparently on the disaffected among the garrison to secure the Tower, but questioned the wisdom of attacking the artillery-ground, as it was a "sort of garrison to annoy the association." At this moment the police officers came into the room, headed by Mr. Stafford, who at Colonel Despard's request showed his warrant, and after an attempt to leave the room, at the call of Despard, "for all to follow him," the parties were searched, the black sheep divided off, and the remainder of the flock allowed to stray away without further notice. Of those that were arrested, three, William Francis, Emblin, and Blades were admitted as king's evidence. Of the rest, after a further weeding of the list, thirteen, including Colonel Despard, were reserved for trial.[8]

On the 21st of January, 1803, a special commission for the trial of treasons committed within the County of Surrey was opened at the new sessions house Newington, by Lord Ellenborough and other judges, and the cases of Colonel Despard and his companions sent before the grand jury.[9] On the same day a true bill was found, the prisoners at once put to the bar, copies of the indictment with lists of the witnesses who might be called, and the jury panel handed to them, and at his request Mr. Serjeant Best and Mr. Gurney assigned as counsel for the colonel. On the 5th of February, to which day the court then adjourned, counsel was assigned to the other prisoners, and on the 7th the trial of Colonel Despard commenced. During this interval no pains were spared by the government in finding out the political opinions of the jurors and the nature of the defence likely to be attempted by the prisoners. Lists of jurors were sent

[8] *John Wood*, Thomas Broughton, *John Francis*, Thomas Phillips, Thomas Newman, Daniel Tyndall, John Doyle, James Sedgwick Wratten, William Lander, Arthur Graham, Samuel Smith, and John Macnamara. Wood and Francis were guardsmen, the others working men.

[9] The judges were Lord Ellenborough, Baron Thomson, and Justices Le Blanc and Chambre. The counsel for the Crown, Attorney-General (Spencer Perceval), Solicitor-General (Sir Thomas Manners Sutton, afterwards Lord Chancellor Manners, of Ireland), Mr. Plumer (afterwards Master of the Rolls), the Common Sergeant, Mr. Garrow and Mr. Wood (afterwards Barons of the Exchequer), Mr. Fielding, and Mr. Abbott (afterwards Lord Chief Justice of the King's Bench).

to the Lord Mayor, the magistrates of the Southwark Bench and others, and from the information thus obtained marked lists prepared.[1] The proceedings of the prisoners friends in the provinces, where they were collecting funds, and witnesses for their defence were carefully watched by a government agent. The most unscrupulous means were used by him to worm himself into their confidence and with such marked success that the prosecution was fully apprised of the nature of the evidence, and the names of the witnesses likely to be called on behalf of the accused.[2]

The accused on the contrary, beyond knowing the names, and addresses of the proposed witnesses, knew but little of the evidence they were prepared to give against them. Could they have had copies of the original depositions, the cross-examination of the approvers, and the spy might have been made far more effective. We now know what their original statements were, and how materially they fell short of the carefully dovetailed story to which they swore in court.[3]

On the 5th of February the court again met, and as the prisoners elected to sever in their challenges, Spencer Perceval, the Attorney-General, claimed to

---

[1] Letters from Birchwood to J. King, and from Raye, 25th January, 1803; ditto from J. Bowles, February 4, 1803, enclosing list of jurors marked bad or doubtful. Treasury papers, Re Despard.

[2] Unsigned letter, dated February 2, 1803, apparently to Treasury Solicitor, detailing the steps taken by the Government agent. Treasury papers, Re Despard.

[3] Brief of the Attorney-General, and proofs attached to it. Treasury papers, Re Despard.

try Colonel Despard separately, acting no doubt, on the suggestion of one of the parties who had been engaged in branding the jurors, that otherwise, by the repeated challenges of the accused, " All good, and true men would be struck off."[4] Though a full jury of eighty-four answered to their names, so many were excused for age or bodily infirmities, or disqualified as not being freeholders in the county, that the jury was not completed until the last name had been called.[5]

On the 7th at nine o'clock, the trial of the colonel commenced. Not to occupy space with any full analysis of the verbose indictment, it will be sufficient to note that it was grounded partly on the old statute of King Edward the Third, and partly on one passed seven years before the trial, by which it was enacted that treason must be made out by " printing, writing, or any other overt act or deed." The treason charged against the prisoner was twofold, compassing and intending the king's death, and conspiring to imprison and restrain his person. The overt acts under both statutes were the same, seduction of soldiers, administering illegal oaths, and holding meetings for agreeing on the means for carrying out these treasonable objects. Serjeant Best for the prisoner urged on the court that mere words could not be regarded as overt acts, however treasonable such would have been if joined to acts. But Lord Ellenborough at once put aside the objection affirming that it always had been

---

[4] Letter from J. Bowles, previously referred to.
[5] Excused for age or illness, twenty-four and one Quaker. Disqualified as not freeholders, twenty. Challenged by the prisoner, twenty-seven; by the Crown, nine.

laid down as good law, that, if such words were used at meetings held for the purpose of forwarding treasonable designs, and addressed to others to incite them to such acts, such words were overt acts. If the witnesses were to be believed, such overt acts were clearly provable against the prisoner.

Now Windsor the spy swore that soon after the return of his regiment from Chatham in the spring of 1802, John Francis one of the accused gave him some of the cards containing the oath (which he afterwards gave to Mr. Bownas), and swore him in a conspirator. From that time, acting of course under Bownas's advice, he frequented numerous meetings at various public-houses in the lower parts of London, at which the design was repeatedly declared to be the overthrow of the government, and the destruction of the royal family. That with this object London was divided into districts, in each of which meetings were held, and men, disbanded or idle soldiers, and workmen of the lowest class sworn in. For many months he neither saw nor heard of the colonel on the matter, but on the 12th of November, 1802, he was invited by Broughton, a brother-conspirator to meet "good company" at a public house in Newington, called the "Flying Horse." On going there in the evening, he met and was introduced by Wood, another conspirator, to the colonel, who according to his story at once invited him "to meet him next day on Tower Hill, and bring with him four or five intelligent men to consult on the best mode of taking the Tower, and securing the arms."

At this his first interview he swore that the death

of the king was discussed, and that Despard used the words pressed against him by the Crown: "*I have weighed the matter well, and my heart is callous.*" At this meeting on Tower Hill, where others also were present, nothing was apparently said about the professed object for which it was held, but some of the party with the colonel adjourned to another rendezvous, the "Two Bells" in Whitechapel, and afterwards to a third, the "Coach and Horses" in the same locality, where some soldiers were offered refreshment which they declined, and in their presence, Heron Winterbottom and himself after a frugal meal of bread and cheese and beer, discussed the project. Then it was that without any apparent connexion with the previous conversation Despard said privately to Windsor, "*His Majesty must be put to death, and the people will be at liberty.*" *He would make the attack himself on the day his Majesty went to the house, if he could get no assistance from this side of the water.*" Again the Colonel invited him to meet him; this time at the "Oakley Arms," for the same object as on the previous occasion, the capture of the Tower. On this, Windsor invited Despard "to show himself at different meetings, and then the people would be satisfied that there was such a person as that to lead them." He no doubt remembered the anxiety of Mr. Bownas to discover whether any better class of person was in the plot, and did not miss the opportunity of thoroughly implicating Despard in it. It is impossible not to believe that he communicated this to his friend Mr. Bownas, and that on his information the arrest of the conspirators was so safely planned.

To this meeting at the Oakley Arms he took good care to come just too late to be found in the room with his fellows. He played the part of a casual visitor to perfection; and when he had seen that the rest were in custody, and on their way to safe keeping, "he introduced himself" to Mr. Stafford, made him acquainted with the previous steps in the matter, admitted of course how deeply implicated he was in it, and volunteered to attend as a witness next day at the police court. His word was taken, and next day he appeared in the double character of an accomplice and a spy. Can one come to any more charitable conclusion than that the whole scene had been arranged, if not with, at any rate, for Mr. Stafford?

In addition to these statements, made directly to him by Colonel Despard, Windsor stated that at the first interview—that at the Flying Horse—he heard Emblin, another accomplice and Crown witness, urge on Despard the necessity for a regular organization in London, and the Colonel in reply refused to attempt it as too dangerous because under the eyes of the government. Despard then said "*A regular organization in the country is necessary, and I believe is already general; the people are everywhere ripe and anxious for the moment of the attack. I believe this to be the moment: the people, particularly in Birmingham, in Leeds, in Sheffield, and in every town in England, are ripe; I have walked twenty miles to-day, and the people were everywhere ripe where I have been. The attack is to be made on the day his Majesty goes to the House, and his Majesty must be put to death. The mail coaches are to be stopped, as a signal to the people in the country that they have revolted in town."*

In confirmation of any of these statements only one independent witness was produced; otherwise they depended upon the oaths of accomplices. This independent witness was a Mrs. Plowman, the landlady of the Flying Horse. She stated that whilst in the bar, which was separated by a wainscot petition from the room in which the parties sat, at a distance admitted by the witness to be as far as she was from the Judge in court, though the person was not speaking very loud she heard some one say, "*he had weighed everything well within him, and God may know, his heart was callous.*" Now it is a very awkward fact, that on the proofs attached to the brief of the Attorney-General, not one word of this statement by Colonel Despard appears, either in the evidence of Windsor or of Emblin, who was also present, and who was called to confirm his comrade. It is difficult to understand, why Mrs. Plowman should have heard only these words out of the many stated to have been then spoken by Despard; and it is almost impossible not to believe that the words were suggested to Windsor and Emblin, after they had heard or been told the the statement of the landlady.

Emblin, on whose confirmation of the statements said to have been made by Despard at the Flying Horse so much was made by the prosecution, to judge merely by his evidence given in court was brought into the conspiracy only a month before his arrest at the Oakley Arms. He was a watchmaker at Vauxhall, and apparently in no way previously connected with such associations. Though he gives a somewhat different account of Despard's conversations with himself, and inserts others of which Windsor made no mention, substantially they are the same, at any rate in intention. In addition, however, he swore that Broughton suggested shooting two of the horses of the royal carriage, and then directly seizing the King; and that when he replied that any one attempting this would be cut to pieces by the horse guards, Despard said "*he would do it with his own hand.*" Still he was silent about the Colonel weighing the circumstances and being callous, until it was almost put into his mouth by Mr. Garrow, who was examining him. Then he remembered the words to a letter, though, as we have previously said, he never mentioned them when giving his proof for use of the Crown counsel. One extraordinary statement indeed, he did volunteer in his proof. At this meeting at the Flying Horse, "he pressed Despard to ask Lord Holland, the Duke of Norfolk, and Lord Thanet for money to help," that the Colonel said "it would be an absurdity, and that he did not know where to go to for a shilling," when he made the following reply: "That he (Emblin) was a delegate sent from the Corresponding Society to the late Duke of Buckingham begging for assistance, and that Sir Thomas Erskine had come out and told him that the duke could not, consistent with his honour and estate, come forth in any such way, but if the people were of sufficient body, and conducted themselves properly, money should not be wanted." No wonder that against this portion of Emblin's evidence Spencer Perceval has written, "This will not be believed," How damaging could have been the cross-examination of this man and Windsor, had the prisoner's counsel known that the words said to have been heard by Mrs. Plowman, were not to be found in the original deposition of these witnesses, and that the professedly loyal and seduced watchmaker had been, according to his own statement, an active member of the London "Corresponding Society."[6]

William Francis, a brother of one of the prisoners, though he refused to take the oath was to all intents as much an accomplice as his less favoured brother. According to his tale, after having refused the oath when asked by his brother and Wood, he was pressed by Colonel Despard himself to join. This meeting with Despard he fixed as somewhere about Bartholomew Fair time,[7] and at either the King or Queen's Head on Tower Hill. Who was also present, or how the conversation commenced, does not appear in the notes of either the evidence-in-chief or the cross-examination. The Colonel, he said, asked him "*what were his principles, and his desire towards the cause that was going forth of taking the Tower.*" To which he replied that "he did not approve." Yet he asked Despard what was to be done that day; and was told by him "Nothing, as he expected some money and news to come from France." A few days after, though he

[6] For hanging this man in effigy on the paling of Vauxhall Gardens, on the 19th of February, a person of the name of Smith was indicted by the Crown, Mr. Attorney and Solicitor-General giving a solemn opinion that it was a proper case for prosecution. See case and opinion, Treasury papers, Re Despard.

[7] 24th August.

still "did not approve," this witness went to the meeting at the Bleeding Heart in Hatton Garden, and there met Despard, his own brother, Wood, Macnamara, and seven others. This was a few days after the fair. He was asked by Mr. Plumer "whether he heard anything pass with Colonel Despard." "A paper," he said, "was read over concerning the plan of taking the Tower, the Bank, and the Horse Guards." " Did the Colonel," he was next asked, " say anything to you that day about yourself?" " He read over the *same* paper to me in the corner at the top of the table: then my brother John and he desired me to kiss it. Colonel Despard said, 'he hoped my principles were mended from the last time he saw me.'" Q. " Did you comply with his desire?" A. "I did not. He said, 'It is very odd that my principles were not the same as my brother's, or something of that sort." Again he met Despard, about a week after, accidentally, and after drinking with him and his own brother he swore "Despard offered me a small card, which my brother gave him. He looked it over, and then handed it down to me, meaning for me to kiss it, if I would. He said 'he was sorry I was not of the same principles as my brother.'" Q. " Did you kiss the card?" A. "I did not." Q. "Did you tell him why?" A. "I told him, that I had been sworn once to my king and country, and would never be again." Yet he had before admitted that between the second and last interview with Despard he had met the other leading spirits at another rendezvous, and that during the discussion of their plans *he* and other soldiers present " *drawed our bayonets and protested we should have a time fixed to make the grand attack upon the Tower before we left the company."*

Well might the prisoners' counsel comment on the inconsistency of such a story. Well might he have again and again urged this point, had he known that this man, who had refused the oath, was so eager in the cause that, when no date was fixed for the attack, he and his brother, with Wood and Newman, drew their bayonets, and swore that they would have the lives of the others if they did not go with them at once to another rendezvous ; that to secure their company they took them arm-in-arm to a public-house at the end of Oxford Street, and there, in a room upstairs, repeated their threat, with drawn bayonets, to make the attack themselves if the day was not fixed ; and that for some time he had been quite as active as his brother in the plot, and had gone down with him to Windsor, to assist in practising on the soldiers there.[8] It will be borne in mind that this witness in his statement in court had nothing to relate about the interview with Despard on Tower Hill, beyond his urging him to join. In his proof, in Perceval's brief, he says, that at that interview the full details of the scheme had been told him, "how the Tower was to be taken, the army stopped at Blackfriars Bridge, the cellars of

[8] Proofs of evidence of Patrick Connell, attached to Attorney-General's brief; Treasury papers, Re Despard. The name of this witness having been given as "John Connell" in the list of witnesses delivered to the prisoner, he was objected to for improper description, and withdrawn by the Attorney-General. Lord Ellenborough said this was "extremely fair and candid in the Attorney-General." Considering what he might have said, was it not rather "judicious"?

the Bank drowned, the guns taken from the parade in the park and planted so as to command Parliament Street, the magazine in Hyde Park seized; how all these details were on a paper which his brother and Doyle read over to Despard, who then signed it; and how he had quarrelled with his brother on this matter.[9]

One more accomplice was called—Thomas Blades, also a guardsman—the bulk of whose evidence went to the cases of the other prisoners, especially J. Francis and Macnamara, with whom he had frequent meetings. By the former of these he was sworn; by the latter afterwards appointed a colonel. Of Despard he neither saw nor heard anything until, invited by Broughton, he went to a meeting at the Oakley Arms on the 9th of November, at which he was told the heads of the people would be, to settle the attack for the following 17th. There he found Despard and others. Soon after he entered, Despard invited "those who had come to settle the business to go to one end of the room, and those who came only to show their goodwill to remain in the other. What passed in conclave Blades did not hear; and though Wood, he declared, explained to him when and where the King could be most safely attacked, it is clear from the original proof of this witness that it was not said in the hearing of Despard. He, too, bore a bad character in his regiment, was a deserter—he called it absenting himself—and had made away with—he repudiated the idea of

[9] Proof of W. Francis, attached to Attorney-General's brief; Treasury papers.

theft—some of the property of his master for whom he had worked.

The evidence given by these men, of direct threats against the King's life used by Despard in the company of others of the conspirators from their general agreement, was urged by Lord Ellenborough as satisfactory confirmation of their story, when taken with the statement of Mrs. Plowman as to overhearing one sentence. These witnesses also gave accounts of the parts played by the others, and especially John Francis, Macnamara, and Wood, in trying to seduce the soldiers and in making arrangements for the attack. That Colonel Despard was present at the rendezvous where some of these meetings were held was undoubtedly proved by independent witnesses, and admitted by his counsel; and it was argued for the prosecution that a soldier of his position would not be consorting with such persons, except for the same ends. Special stress was laid on his being a friend of Wood, who had offered to fire the gun in the park.

In defence it was urged that the accomplices were not sufficiently confirmed, and that if so, there was no sufficient evidence that Despard's attendance at any of these meetings was for a treasonable purpose. The characters and statements of the accomplices were criticized with just severity, and the improbability of so brave and distinguished a soldier having for a moment thought of, much less suggested, such mad schemes with such an absurdly inadequate force, without arms and without money, pressed on the jury. The villanies and the absurdities of the plot, it was said, were kept from him, and the men who really began it and devised its mad suggestions, only enticed him into it towards its end, when they found out that nothing "could be done, and could only want Colonel Despard to deliver him up as a victim, as the means of purchasing their own indemnity." No witnesses were called for the defence, except to character. That given by Lord Nelson has been cited before. It had, as the Attorney-General elicited, on cross-examination, the defect of being based on a knowledge twenty years old. He had heard nothing of him since 1780. That of Sir Alfred Clarke, under whose orders as Governor of Jamaica he had been for six years, brought that knowledge down to 1790; and though Sir Evan Nepean carried it down a few years more, his evidence was too general to be very valuable.

Despicable as was the character of the witness Windsor, and unreliable by itself as was the evidence of each of the accomplices, had there been even less satisfactory evidence than was given in confirmation of the Colonel's attendance at some of the meetings, and of the discussion at them, whether to his knowledge or not, of the mad projects, a conviction must have been secured by the trenchant charge of the most convicting of judges. In it every discrepancy was plausibly explained, the fullest effect given to the statements of the few independent witnesses, and every expression—even that at the time of his arrest, "All follow me!"—urged on the jury as proofs that Despard was the contriver and leader in the plot, and not the all too-ready tool of his inferior comrades. In a few minutes a verdict of Guilty was returned, but coupled with a strong recommendation to mercy on the score of his eminent services. For fifteen hours, with but slight intervals, the Court had sat, and every one engaged, except the iron Judge, was worn out. Though the trial was not over till three in the morning, Lord Ellenborough was in his seat at nine the next day, when the other conspirators were put on their trial,[1] and after an ordeal of twenty-three hours all found Guilty, and at once, together with Colonel Despard, condemned to all the cruel horrors of a traitor's death.

In his sentence the Chief Justice did not even allude to the recommendation of the jury in Despard's case, much less promise to forward it to the authorities. He had persuaded himself that the conspiracy was "of enormous extent and most alarming magnitude"—of which no evidence was certainly given in Court, whatever might have been the secret information of the Government. Treachery among conspirators he seemed to regard as a Providential intervention for the safety of the public; and alluding apparently to the real part played by Windsor in the plot, warned the prisoners that "such leagues and unions are at all times false and hollow. They begin in treachery to their king and country, and they end, *if they do not immediately begin*, in schemes of treachery towards each other." The lives of Newman, Tyndall, and Lander were spared; the remainder died with their leader on the scaffold.

[1] See previous list.

The execution of the sentence was deferred until Monday the 21st; and in deference to the improved spirit of the age, the disgusting details legally attendant on an execution for high treason were omitted by Royal command, and that of dragging the prisoners on hurdles round the prison yard on the road to execution, and the subsequent decapitation of the lifeless bodies, alone retained.

The scene of execution was the then newly-erected gaol of the county, known in late days as Horsemonger Lane, in front of which the scaffold stood surrounded by a strong detachment of the foot guards, whilst bodies of cavalry patrolled all the road leading to it. On the scaffold, Broughton, Graham, Wood, and Wratten behaved with decorum, and expressed their sincere regret for the part they had taken, Broughton addressing a few words of warning to young men "to avoid low public-houses and mixing with certain company, or perhaps they would see more executions of a similar character." Macnamara, who had been attended by his priest, evinced commendable though late piety; and Colonel Despard alone refused either to attend the prison chapel or to receive the ministrations of the chaplain, protesting his entire innocence, and declaring that Ministers knew that he was guiltless.

At his trial Despard had confined his own statement, after sentence had been passed, to denying that evidence had been given to show that he had seduced the others, following the line taken by Serjeant Best, who admitted the existence of a conspiracy, that he had been drawn into it by Francis and the other active agents, and that though he had attended some of their meetings, he was no party to, if not entirely ignorant of, the reckless design of attempting the King's life, or making the wild and absurd attempts to which the spy and accomplices had testified. Colonel Despard's dying denial was not believed by the crowd, who looked upon the other sufferers as his victims. On his severed head being exhibited by the executioner, the crowd hooted, but when the others were held up in turn preserved a marked silence. Six days afterwards the bodies of the minor actors in this deadly drama were interred in one vault under the Roman Catholic chapel in the London Road, on the site of which the South London Music Hall now stands.[2] On the 1st of March that of Colonel Despard was removed from his late residence in Mount Street, Westminster, and interred in the burial-ground of old St. Faith's, on the north side of the enclosure of St. Paul's.[3]

[2] *Gentleman's Magazine,* February 27, 1803. When this chapel and its ground was given up on the erection of St. George's Cathedral in the Westminster Road, the only bodies removed to the new place of sepulture were those of the priests who were there buried, and a Mr. James Kievnau. Letter from the Venerable Provost Doyle, March 13, 1879, to the author, who regrets to have now to record the death, in his ninetieth year, of the good priest.

[3] *Gentleman's Magazine,* March 1, 1803. It is said erroneously "on the south side of St. Paul's." That is St. Gregory's churchyard, St. Faith's being on the north side. Letter from Parish Clerk of St. Faith's, March 4, 1879.

Thus fell a gallant officer, who had he met with that speedy justice against unfounded charges which his conduct in his difficult position on the Spanish Main demanded, but which a negligent Government withheld until disappointment worked its baneful effects on a naturally sensitive mind, would in all probability have proved himself worthy of the character given him by the Hero of the Nile.

CHAPTER IV.

JEAN GABRIEL PELTIER FOR A LIBEL ON THE FIRST CONSUL.

FEBRUARY 21ST, 1803.

AMONG the numerous refugees from France who sought safety in London after the dreadful massacres of August and September, 1792, was Jean Gabriel Peltier, a journalist and pamphleteer, who had already proved the power and bitterness of his wit in the Parisian capital. In a serial, entitled *Les Actes de Apôtres*, in conjunction with other Royalists he had for two years unceasingly defended the old regime and attacked the ways and works of the Constituent Assembly. In England he continued these attacks in the *Courrier de Londres*, and other similar publications, with the same vigour; and supported the cause of loyalty, social order, and religion, with the same hearty devotion as in Paris. On the signature of the Peace of Amiens his attacks ceased for a time. When, however, he heard of the mission of the Consul's spies in England—sent here under the guise of commercial agents—as well as of Bonaparte's conduct towards his weaker continental neighbours, and read the libellous letters on England of the Jacobin

Frevée in the *Mercure de France*, he seems to have thought that the time was ripe for a revival of his diatribes. With this object, in August, 1802, he commenced a serial in his native tongue, entitled *L'Ambigu, ou Variétés Atroces et Amusantes, Journal dans le Genre Egyptien*, on the front of which appeared the Sphynx, with the features of the First Consul, surrounded by emblems reflecting severely on his political and military actions.

To a free Press Bonaparte entertained the most bitter antipathy. On the continent he had crushed every attempt to criticize himself or his actions hostilely, and reduced the Press to a mere machine for circulating his decrees and eulogizing his policy. In England alone the Press was still free, and in too many instances had perverted its freedom into licence. Calculating on the anxiety of the weak Government of Mr. Addington for the continuance of peace, and judging of their timidity by the feeble remonstrances they had made against Bonaparte's treatment of English ships since the treaty was signed, he attempted through them to extinguish the last remnant of freedom of speech and writing in Europe, and to deprive England of its well-earned title of the refuge of the political exile.

Within three months of the signature of the peace, the First Consul called on the English Government to adopt the most effectual measures for stopping "the seditious and unbecoming attacks made on his Government in the English journals, to send out of the country certain parties whom he named as obnoxious to himself, to compel the Bourbon princes to join the head of their family at Warsaw, and to drive out all emigrees who still dared to wear the decorations and orders of the old Government. This dictatorial and contemptuous demand met with but a mild response. No surprise was expressed at its demands or its tone; the question of wearing the old French orders was put aside as not needing interference; and it was simply replied that so long as the emigrees conducted themselves peaceably they could not be removed. Thus encouraged the First Consul pushed his demands one step further, and marked out the individual journals whom he required the Government to prosecute. By his orders M. Otto now distinctly charged M. Peltier with the attacks on Bonaparte and his Government in the *Ambigu*, and implicated in a similar charge the editor of the *Courrier de Londres*, and Cobbett, adding the significant threat that, "in the event of such writings not being stopped, similar writers would be found in France willing to avenge their countrymen by filling their pages with odious reflections on the most respectable persons and the dearest interests of Great Britain." This letter produced the desired effect. Lord Hawkesbury expressed the displeasure of the Government at the articles denounced by M. Otto and their anxious desire to have the writer punished. He lamented the existing licence of the Press, and the legal difficulties in the way of proving the guilt of an individual so as to obtain a verdict of guilty, but promised to refer the articles to the law officers of the Crown, to see if they were proper objects for a prosecution.[1] In furtherance of this promise, M. Peltier was indicted for a series of libels on the First Consul and his Government, Spencer Percival, now Attorney-General, leading for the Crown, and Mackintosh, known as yet only by his fluent "Vindication of the French Revolution," for the defence.[2]

The libels were threefold—an Ode, ascribed to Chenier; another piece of verse entitled "The Wish of a Good Patriot on the 14th July, 1802; an Address to the French Nation, modelled on the attack of Lepidus against Sylla in the Roman Senate. The supposed Ode of Chenier opened with a description of a storm, which the author pretends to believe the gods have raised to protect the liberties of the French people and to avenge their wrongs on the author of the 19th Brumaire. On second thoughts he finds that heaven is blind or cruel, that vessels laden with things good

---

[1] Lord Glenbervie to Mr. Addington, May 24, 1802. M. Otto to Lord Hawkesbury, July 25, with specific demands for the punishment of Cobbett, the editor of the *Courrier Français de Londres*, and others. Reply of Lord Hawkesbury that the case of Peltier should be submitted to the law officers, August 17. M. Otto to Lord Hawkesbury, with the six demands. As an instance of the anxiety of the Government at the bitter paper war then raging between France and England, J. Heriot, the editor of a Government paper, appears to have been threatened with the withdrawal of the Government support on account of some paragraphs which had through inadvertence appeared in his journal.—J. Heriot to Mr. Addington, August 10, 1802. Rev. R. Hill to same. Pellew's "Sidmouth," vol. 2.

[2] In addition, the Solicitor-General, Sir Thomas Manvers, afterwards Lord Chancellor of Ireland; Abbott, eventually Lord Chief Justice of England; and Garrow, afterwards a Baron of the Exchequer, were for the Crown.

for man are shattered and lost; whilst the guilty ship of the rebel Corsican sails tranquilly on the waves and announces the fortunes and designs of Cæsar. "O eternal disgrace of France," continues the poet. "Cæsar on the banks of the Rubicon has against him in the quarrel the Senate, Pompey, and Cato; and if fortune is unequal on the plains of Pharsalia, if you must yield to the destinies of Rome in this sad reverse, *at least there remains to avenge you a poniard among the last of the Romans.*"[3] Again he said, "Is it to give you a master—is it to crown a traitor, that France has punished her kings? No! no! Guilty ambition shall know that there is nothing inviolable, but the rights of the people and their laws." The hints of the dagger of Brutus and the fate of the Bourbon monarch, could hardly be misunderstood.

The second poem, "The Wish of a Good Patriot on the 14th of July, 1802," was shorter, but even more clear in its suggestions. "What fortune has the son of Lætitia? A Corsican, he becomes a Frenchman. His new country adopts him, nourishes him in the rank of its children, and already promises him the greatest destinies." Five tyrants shared his power. He forces

> [3] "De la France à honte éternelle!
> Cæsar au bord du Rubicon
> A contre lui dans sa querelle
> Le Sénat, Pompée, et Caton;
> Et dans les plaines de Pharsale
> Si large fortune est inégale,
> S'il te faut céder aux destins,
> Rome, dans ce revers funeste,
> Pour te venger au moins il reste
> Une poignard aux derniers Romains."

from their hands the sceptre and the censer. Behold him seated where the throne is raised. What is wanting to his wishes? a sceptre, a crown? Consul, he governs all; he makes and unmakes kings. Little careful to be beloved, terror establishes his right over a people degraded even to the rank of slaves. He reigns: he is a despot: they kiss his chains: he is proclaimed Chief and Consul for life." Severe in its truth as this was, and hardly to be borne by one of Bonaparte's temperament, there was worse to come in the concluding lines. "As for me," said the supposed patriot, "far from envying his lot, let him name—I consent to it—his successor. Carried on the shield, let him be proclaimed Emperor. *Finally, and Romulus recalls the story to my mind, I wish that on the morrow he may have his apotheosis. Amen.*"[4] Explain such words as you may, remembering the legend of the assassination of Romulus, the Roman practice of deifying their kings and emperors after death, and the wished for deification on the morrow of his elevation to the empire, they could only mean his death by the hand of the assassin only a few hours after his acceptance of the imperial crown.

The parody of the diatribe of Lepidus was a long and laboured bit of prose, cleverly adapted to the hankering after classical models so popular and so

[4] " Pour moi, loin qu'à sort je porte quelqu' envie,
Qu'il nomme, j'y consens, son digne *successeur*.
Sur le pavois porté, qu'on l'élise *empereur*.
Enfin, et Romulus nous rappelle la chose,
Je fais vœu . . . des demains qu'il ait l'apothéose!
Amen."

intelligible among Frenchmen from the first day of the Revolution. Bonaparte was "the tiger who dares to call himself the regenerator of France, who enjoys the fruits of your labours as of spoil taken from the enemy" . . "who is not content with the destruction of the king, nor of so many brave men, nor of so many princes whom the war has mown down, but becomes more covetous and more cruel in circumstances under which prosperity changes fury into pity among the greater part of mankind.". . . "You must act, citizens ; you must march ; you must oppose what is passing, if you would not wish that he should seize upon all you have." His mamelukes were characterized "as a foreign banditti". . ."his mutes, his cut-throats, and his hangmen." "You see at every moment arbitrary arrests, judges punished for having acquitted citizens, individuals put to death after having been acquitted by a lawful sentence, and sentences of death extorted from judges by threats. Remains there for men who would deserve that name, anything else to do but to avenge their wrongs or to perish with glory?" In this diatribe, though there was no suggestion of assassination, there was the clearest incitement to rebellion against the Government which France had accepted, and with which we were nominally at peace. Legally, therefore, the jury had before them only three questions—were these productions written or published by Peltier? what was their intention and tendency? and what, in law, their character of guilt or innocence?

In opening the case to the jury Spencer Perceval anticipated two points of the probable defence—that they were historical narratives written with honest zeal, though with a freedom approaching licentiousness; or mere pieces of flippant insolence or impudence, to be treated only with contempt. With much force he pressed on the jury that they were libels in law and in fact; that the defamation of the First Consul and his Government was their general object; and that their ulterior intention was to incite his subjects to rebellion against their chief magistrate and to excite them to his assassination. Aware of the public feeling that had arisen against this prosecution, he sought to justify it by the previous cases in which that religious madman, Lord George Gordon, had been prosecuted and punished, in 1787, for his reckless libel on Marie Antoinette, and the printer and publishers of the *Courier* for a libel on the Emperor of Russia—the madman Paul.⁵ Not content with the verses, and the

⁵ John Vint, printer, G. Ross, publisher, and J. Parry, proprietor, for paragraph in the *Courier*, November, 1798 : " The Emperor of Russia is rendering himself obnoxious to his subjects by various acts of tyranny, and ridiculous in the eyes of Europe by his inconsistency. He has lately passed an edict to prohibit the exportation of deals and other naval stores. In consequence of this ill-judged law, 100 sail of vessels are likely to return to this country without freight." In reality Paul had made an exception in favour of England. Erskine defended. They were all found guilty, and Parry was fined 100*l*., with six months' imprisonment, and the others only imprisoned for two months, without a fine.

Lord George Gordon, tried June 6, 1787, for two libels; one a petition from the prisoners convicted for the No-Popery riots, to preserve their lives and liberties, and to prevent their banishment to Botany Bay; the other for an account published in the *Public Advertiser*, accusing the Queen and the French Ambassador in London of a plot to get the adventurer Cagliostri who was then living in Gordon's house, back to France, and speech of Lepidus, he discovered libel and defamation in the features of the sphynx and the emblems on the cover. He prayed in aid of his interpretation, the words with which the prospectus to the paper concluded "the editor will so manage all the materials which he may employ to build the edifice he is about to erect to the glory of Bonaparte, that he will take care that they shall be worthy of the Temple."

The evidence in the case was confined to proof of the purchase of the numbers of the *Ambigu* at M. de Boffe's, its publisher; the admission by him—he having allowed judgment to go by default—that they were published by him for and by the orders of Peltier; and the reading of an authorized translation of the poems and speech as well as the French originals. Thus it was that, after a very brief interval, Mackintosh had to make what defence he could to a prosecution, so plain in law, so ill-judged in fact. The Court was crowded to

stating that the affair of the diamond necklace was a plot to ruin Prince de Rohan. Woodfall, before allowing Lord Gordon to send him paragraphs of news, had obtained an indemnity for costs, and on proceedings being threatened at once gave up the author. The French Ambassador would himself have prosecuted, but the Government interfered, as the attack on the Queen was of such a brutal nature. Lord Gordon, who was found guilty on both charges, escaped for a time to Holland, but was sent away from there by the Government, and concealed until 1787 at Birmingham. When brought up, January 28, 1788, for sentence, he claimed to be a Jew, having been circumcised, and calling himself Israel Abraham George Gordon, and claiming as such to remain covered in court. He was sentenced to five years' imprisonment—two on the first charge and three on the second —and to find sureties for good behaviour. These not being satisfactory, he was sent back (January 18, 1793), to Newgate, and died there on the 1st of the November following.

excess. Throughout the week preceding the trial "it was the general opinion that Peltier's acquittal would be considered in France as tantamount to a declaration of war against the First Consul; wagers had been laid that a verdict of *Not Guilty* would lower the funds five per cent., and runners were waiting in court to hasten to the Stock Exchange with the verdict, should it be given before the house closed for the day." Whether or not an acquittal would have precipitated the war which so soon broke out, the Government were keenly alive to the necessity for a conviction. Half the special jurors summoned were challenged, and it was only by adding from common jurymen that the jury had been formed. The anxiety on the part of Bonaparte to seal the odium of such a prosecution of the Press with the verdict of the jury was little less. The Secretary and Aide-de-Camp of his Ambassador occupied a position beneath the jury box, and if they were linguists enough to follow the fluent eloquence of the defendants' counsel, must have reaped but little satisfaction from the pictures of the revolutionary leaders, and the history of the steady manacling of the Press of Europe by their autocratic master, with which his speech abounded.

Mackintosh's speech was undoubtedly "one of the most splendid displays of eloquence," in a period when eloquence was the characteristic of forensic speaking; and as affording a series of historical sketches of the rise and progress of the freedom of the Press in England, and exposing the atrocities and plots, not only of the worst men of the earlier days of the Revolution, but of some who had become useful instruments of the new Government, is still well worthy of careful study. But it was little more. As Percival said, "there were in it some things to observe on, some things to apply in his own favour, and some things to be interpreted differently than had been attempted by his learned friend. There were undoubtedly many topics on which he had expatiated which, without derogation to him, were irrelevant to the discussion." It made the fortune of the speaker, but it had no effect on the verdict of the jury.

Commencing, as was almost the universal custom of the Bar in his day, by eulogizing the intrepidity of his profession in the cause of justice and in the defence of innocence and professing his unbounded respect for the laws of his country and the judges who administered them, he gave a brief sketch of the adventurous life of his client. Driven from his country by the violence of its rulers, he had refused to accept the only terms on which he could return to it—that of allegiance to the present Government. During his stay in England he had devoted his time and talents to political discussion so long as we were not at peace with France; had desisted as soon as the peace was signed; and now, driven to it by the acts of the emissaries of Bonaparte, had indeed recommenced his criticisms, but confined them to this obscure journal, written entirely in the language of his own people, little likely, therefore, to have any large circulation in England, and less likely to penetrate into France, whence it and similar journals were vigorously excluded by the decrees of a master whose word was law, and whose law few dared to evade, much more to violate. In a rapid but clear sketch of the history of the law of libel in England, he showed that no precise rule had been laid down marking the boundary between that and historical discussions, and urged that in our insular position it had been and still was our true policy to consider with great indulgence even the boldest animadversions of political writers on the ambitious projects of foreign states. The jury, he said, must be convinced that the intention of the productions was to libel, and not to state facts which the writer believed to be true, however injudicious or violent might be language in which he related them. Professing to regard the Odes and the Address to the French Nation as original documents, only republished by Peltier, he claimed the right of *republishing historically* those documents (whatever their original malignity might be) which display the character and unfold the intentions of Governments, or factions, or individuals. The intention of the original writer might be to vilify, but that of the compiler only to gratify curiosity. He admitted, however, that he had no evidence to prove that the Ode was really by Chenier and sent over here for republication, and sought to evade this difficulty by contending, that as it appeared on the face of it to be so, it was for the Crown to prove the negative. If it was a mere republication, in what respect was M. Peltier more guilty than the editors of those journals in which General Sebastiani's report accusing General Stuart of inciting persons to assassinate the First Consul had been published, or the atrocious libel on the king inserted in the *Moniteur*, and thus circulated throughout the kingdom? Why, he asked, were not these journalists prosecuted? The answer was plain, because, as Percival said "when they published the libels, they exposed their falsehood—they gave the antidote with the poison." As a last explanation of the Ode, Mackintosh suggested that it was a satire on Chenier and the Jacobin party, after the manner of Swift's arguments against Christianity. The ideas, he argued, were not those of a loyalist. If addressed to such, it was the production of a lunatic. As the production of a loyalist assuming the mask of a Jacobin, it had ridicule of that party and defamation of the Consul and his Government, for its objects. This line of defence was far too fine-drawn to be of any practical value.

Passing to the second libel, "The Wish of a True Patriot," Mackintosh suggested that it might be the composition of a Dutch patriot, and only republished by Peltier, and that the imputed suggestion of assassination meant no more than that the writer would not be sorry to hear of Bonaparte's death. As for the wish for his apotheosis on the morrow of his elevation to the imperial crown, it by no means followed that he also wished his death. Augustus, Tiberius, Nero, and other Roman Emperors, had been deified during their lifetime. If it was not really a Dutchman's work, might it not be a satire on a Dutch Jacobin? By such a one assassination was not looked on as a crime. "Besides," he added, "such a wish for a man's death is very often little more than a strong, though he would admit a not very decent way, of expressing detestation for his character." Certainly the mildest interpretation of such a detestable crime. He did not care, perhaps, to remember, that the reference of the writer was not to Augustus, Tiberius, or Nero, but to Romulus, whose deification, according to the legend, did not precede, but followed his assassination.

The third libel—the parody on the speech attributed to Lepidus in the fragments of Sallust, remained to be excused. Assuming the truth of the story told of it in the journal, that it had been written and clandestinely placed among the papers of M. Camille Jourdan by Fouché, for the purpose of involving him in a charge of conspiracy, Mackintosh treated it as a satire on Fouché's manufacture of plots for political purposes; and illustrated his character by reading some of the letters of Collot d'Herboise, and Fouché justifying and glorying in the horrible executions at Lyons in 1793, laying especial stress on the postscript to one of them, in which he wrote: "We have but one way of celebrating victory; we send this evening two hundred and fifty rebels to be shot." If, he said, such Fouché was, he could not understand why M. Peltier should have stigmatized his work, and deprived it of all authority and power of persuasion, by prefixing to it his infamous name—if it were not in reality a parody on Fouché himself and his mode of acting, and not at all the libel of a loyalist on Bonaparte. The assumption was ingenious, but in the absence of any evidence to justify the supposed history of the production, it was not of much, or indeed, any value as a legal defence to the charge of libel.

The defence, such as it was, was now really ended. Mackintosh however had much more to say, and said it well. Looking upon the prosecution as in reality that of Bonaparte, and as "the first battle between reason and power," and as making the jury "the trustees of the only remains of free discussion in Europe," he sought to "strengthen their spirits by the contemplation of great examples of constancy," and "to seek for these in the annals of our forefathers." In language hardly to be equalled by any historian, he recalled the manner in which Elizabeth spoke of her Spanish foes, and excited the enthusiam of her people by her grand and powerful utterances. He pictured her, by some prophetic instinct foreseeing the effect of the Press for rousing and guiding the minds of men; and spoke of her publication of the first Gazettes in the time of the Armada "as one of the greatest discoveries of political genius—one of the most striking anticipations of future experience, that we find in history."

Passing on to the times of the Grand Monarque, he claimed the reception of the refugees on the revocation of the Edict of Nantes, as establishing the right of refuge for the political exile, when, "though a Jefferies disgraced the bench, no refugee was deterred by prosecution for libel from giving vent to his feelings, from arraigning the oppressor in the face of Europe." The invasion of Holland by Louis was due, he said, to the freedom with which the Dutch Press discussed that monarch's conduct; and its defeat was the triumph of "the free and public exercise of reason. Raised from obscurity by that struggle, William of Orange defended and fostered the same liberty of thought and speech as King of England, reviving among us the feelings and principles of our ancestors and resuming our former station and former duties as the protectors of the independence of Europe." The interval between the conclusion of the struggle by the Peace of Ryswick and the commencement of the War of Succession, was in reality only a truce. "It was desirable, however, not to provoke the enemy by unreasonable hostility; but it was still more desirable to keep up the national jealousy and indignation against him who was to be so soon our enemy." The application to the present crisis was evident. "I can venture to say that at no period were the system and projects of Louis XIV. animadverted on with more freedom and boldness than during that interval. Our ancestors, and the heroic Prince who governed them, did not deem it wise policy to disarm the national mind for the sake of prolonging a truce. They were both too proud and too wise to pay so great a price for so small a benefit."

The outburst of popular feeling in England on the obnoxious partitions of Poland was pressed into his service by the eager advocate. "Rapine was not then called policy—nor was the oppression of an innocent people termed a mediation in their domestic differences. No prosecutions, no criminal informations, followed the liberty and the boldness of the language then employed. No complaints even appear to have been made from abroad—much less any insolent menaces against the English Press. The people of England were too long known throughout Europe, for the proudest potentate to expect to silence our Press by such means."

As instances of "the terrible consequences" of enforcing the law of libel against political writers,

Mackintosh pictured the position of a Government intent on such a policy. "Had we been at peace when Robespierre ruled in France, when Marat called for two hundred and seventy thousand heads, when Cartier ordered five hundred children to be shot, and when the poor victims, too small of stature to be hit by the bullets, ran for protection to the soldiers, and were bayonetted as they clung to their knees,—even if we had been at peace with these men, would it have been endured that Government should have come into Court to ask a verdict against the libellers of Barrére and Collot d'Herboise," or have instructed the Attorney-General to file a criminal information against M. Peltier for "wickedly and maliciously intending to vilify and degrade Maximilian Robespierre, President of the Committee of Safety of the French Republic?" "Then, indeed, we should have seen the last humiliation fall on England—the spotless and venerable tribunals of this free country reduced to be the ministers of the vengeance of Robespierre. What would have rescued us from this last disgrace? The honesty and the courage of a jury." With a reminder that in that very Court, Cromwell, at the height of his power, was twice defeated in his attempts to obtain a verdict against Lilburne⁶ as a libeller, and expressing

⁶ John Lilburne, a violent and enthusiastic republican, born 1618, died 1657. Sentenced by the Star Chamber, during his absence in Holland, to 500 lashes and the pillory, for libels on the Government of Charles, for which the Long Parliament voted him reparation, he fought throughout the war, and rose to be colonel of dragoons. After Marston Moor he was committed by the House of Lords for a libel on the Earl of Manchester; and whilst in prison wrote numerous pamphlets, accusing

his firm belief that the same spirit that existed then in the hearts of English jurors was not extinct, the accomplished orator concluded his brilliant battle-cry against the tyranny of Bonaparte.

Brief as was the reply of Percival, the only important points of which have been noticed in this summary of Mackintosh's speech, the summing up of Lord Ellenborough was still more brief. Without even a word of recognition of the speech for the defence, the hard-headed and cold-hearted Judge briefly explained the law, which neither side had questioned, read again the passages in the Ode and in "The Wish of the Patriot," on which the two first counts of the indictment rested, and told the jury it was for them to say whether they did not import a direct incitement to assassination. He gave it as his judicial opinion that their direct tendency, if so interpreted, was to interrupt and destroy the peace and amity then existing between the two kingdoms, and that therefore they were libels within the terms of the indictment. Of the parody on the speech of Lepidus he took no notice, satisfied that the strength of the case lay in the poetical libels, and that any further criticism would only weaken the effect of his brief but trenchant charge. Without retiring from the box, the jury almost at once returned their verdict of Guilty, and with that the solemn farce ended.

Though the oration of Mackintosh was useless as a

Cromwell and Ireton of high treason. When tried for these, he defended himself so successfully that he was twice acquitted by juries.

legal defence of his client, it was so entirely in accordance with public opinion that it protected him as fully as any acquittal could have done. The delicate position of the negotiations with the First Consul were daily becoming more delicate, and his determination to trap us into a war more evident. No one therefore was surprised when, on the 8th of March, a Royal Message called upon the Commons to provide for a large increase of both the army and the navy, in the face of those warlike preparations in the ports of Holland and France, which were lamely enacted under the pretence of the necessities of the colonial dominions of the Republic. Before the end of April that war commenced, which did not end in reality until 1815. Under this state of our international relations the Attorney-General never called up Peltier for judgment; and when once war was declared, *L'Ambigu* reappeared, and flourished for nearly twenty years.[7]

It is sad to think, that though M. Peltier escaped any punishment in England, the vengeance of Bonaparte fell on his aged father and his sister, whose property was confiscated, and whose death was in all probability hastened by the danger in which they believed that their son stood of being transported to France at the demand of the First Consul—a demand happily resisted even by the feeble Government of Addington.

[7] No prosecution of a similar class of libel has been attempted until that of Herr Most for the article in the Nihilist journal *Freiheit* advocating the assassination of the Czar, tried May, 1881, of which an abstract is given in the Appendix.

CHAPTER V.

EMMET'S REBELLION.

JULY 23RD, 1803.

TRIALS OF REBELS, AUGUST 31ST TO SEPTEMBER 19TH, 1803.

BITTER and recriminatory as had been the public utterances during the passage of the Union Act, and openly violent the opposition to its enactment, when it had once become law it was succeeded by a political calm and popular tranquillity, justifying apparently the anticipations of its promoters.[1] This sudden cessation of the open discussion of Catholic claims and parliamentary reform was painfully deceptive. The old ill feeling between the rival religionists was all the more bitter, because concealed; and the late peace with France, by allowing the Irish refugees of "'98" to return home, increased the

[1] On Addington resigning the Speakership (February, 1801), Sir J. Mitford was elected, and Lord Hardwicke and Mr. Abbot sent to Ireland as Lord Lieutenant and Irish Secretary. On September 19, Abbot writes to Addington, " Dublin is still quiet, but we are watchful." On Lord Clare's death, Sir J. Mitford was made Chancellor of Ireland, with title of Lord Redesdale, and Abbot elected Speaker, Mr. Wickham being made Irish Secretary in his place.

influence of the Republican party on the middle and lower classes of the people.[2] The open assistance previously rendered by the French Government to the Irish Republicans had, of course, been checked, only to be replaced by a more dangerous, because secret influence, exercised by so-called "Commercial Agents" of the French Government. These emissaries, settled in Dublin and other large towns, especially at the commercial ports, besides formally discharging the duties of ordinary trade agents, were instructed to "furnish plans of the ports of their districts, with the soundings for mooring vessels; and if no plans could be obtained, to point out the winds favourable for entering and leaving each port, and the greatest depth of water with which heavily-laden ships could enter." Money was freely at their command, and their relations with the returned refugees were of the most confidential nature. The painful

[2] Lord Redesdale to Mr. Abbot, early in 1803, urging the necessity for Mr. Wickham being sent to Limerick, "where the lower orders were rife for any disturbance—formidable as banditti, as rebels nothing; the gentry are so divided into parties, and those parties are so hostile to each other, that authority was necessary to bring them even to act together cordially for the public safety, and this it is hoped Mr. Wickham's visit would effect;" a resident Protestant clergy wanted, and a general commutation of tithes recommended. Pellew's "Lord Sidmouth," vol. ii. In a previous letter to Mr. Addington, towards the close of 1802, Lord Redesdale had pressed on the Premier the want of a resident Protestant clergy, and that the bishops and clergy should "exert themselves to make that which was established also superior in weight and influence; to introduce law and order into the country, to render it safe for a Protestant to reside wherever he pleased, and to afford him the means of freely exercising his religion." Ib.

recollections of the events of " '98" were still fresh in the memories of the lower classes of the Catholics, and the subject of constant conversation in the workshop and the cabin. Among the middle and higher classes of the same faith the impolitic conduct of the Protestant gentry in forming a "league of exclusion, suspicion, and security," as it was called, had created a feeling of indifference towards the existing Government, and raised a wall of separation between those who would otherwise have united in its defence. Had the Protestant landowners and clergy, at the first rumours of the suspicious visits of the Irish refugees among the peasantry, and of the designs of French agents, invited their Catholic neighbours to join them in the good work, instead of restraining them from any participation in it, the new rising would have been crushed in its birth, and the capital of Ireland would have been spared that most painful exhibition of reckless conspiracy and Government apathy—the Emmet Rebellion.

Robert Emmet, the youthful instigator of this foolish and wicked outbreak, was the third son of Dr. Emmet, a physician of eminence in Dublin, attached to the Viceregal Court, and, at the time of his death, head of the Royal Hospital of Kilmainham. "His eldest brother," said Lord Norbury, "whom an early death had snatched away, was one of the greatest ornaments of the Irish Bar. The laws of his country were the study of his youth, and the study of his maturer life was to cultivate and support them." Another brother, also a member of the Bar, had been so deeply involved in the rebellion of "'98" that with difficulty he escaped to France, and subsequently to America, where he rose to a good position in his profession. By this brother Robert was early innoculated with Republican principles. As a mere boy of sixteen he had been Secretary of the Secret Committee of United Irishmen,[3] and in 1801 went over to France on a secret mission from that body to the French Government. In this mission his companion was De Lany, of Kildare, an ex-officer in the Austrian service, who had been deeply engaged in the rebellion. Under feigned names they found their way from Ireland to Yarmouth, whence they crossed to Hamburg, and thence, with passports from General Augereau went on to Paris, where Emmet remained in communication with the French Government until the signature of the truce of Amiens. He then returned to Ireland, going *en route* to Brussels to visit his elder brother, who had been released from the imprisonment to which he had been subjected for his share in the " '98." Within a short time of his return to his native land the death of his father left him in the possession of about 3000*l*., with which he at first engaged in trade, but appears to have soon withdrawn his capital and projected a visit to America, whither his brother had already gone, but was stopped by the rupture with France.

[3] The following details of the movements of Emmet and his confederates are taken from the letter, marked "most secret," written by Mr. Wickham, the Chief Secretary for Ireland, to Mr. Speaker Abbot, given in Lord Colchester's " Diary," vol. i. p. 444 et seq. The preparations made by Emmet in Dublin, and his various changes of name and residence, were proved on his trial and on that of the rebels.

About the time of Emmet's return to Dublin the French Government was permitting, if not conniving at, a serious expedition for the invasion of Ireland, under the guise of one for a settlement in Louisiana. In this project the Irish in France were invited to join, under their old commander General Humbert, who was recalled from St. Domingo, induced to resign his commission in the French army, and, nominally as a private adventurer, lead the officers, soldiers, and refugees who were to form the new colony. Assembling at Havre, the expedition was to find its way to the coast of Connaught, where the ground would be prepared for it, to effect a landing, and form the nucleus of a serious insurrection. In this expedition several of those who were afterwards found engaged in Emmet's affair were actively engaged, though it is doubtful whether the secret of it was revealed to Emmet himself. As early, however, as February, 1802, Emmet was recognized as a leader, and one of his subsequently most active allies (Quigley) was sent over to him at that time by one McCabe, who was deep in the Louisiana plot, as to "the man from whom he was to receive their future orders."

The men who now came round Emmet, with the exception of Russel and his relative Hamilton, though men of no social position, were old hands at rebellion, and possessed of considerable influence among the lower classes of their countrymen. Russel, the son of a veteran officer in the army, had served with credit in the American war. After he left his corps, on its being disbanded, he had devoted his attention to the interpretation of the Scripture prophecies, and persuaded himself that the success of such an attempt as was now projected was foreshadowed in the Apocalypse. A Protestant Dissenter of a rigid type, he had little of the common democrat in his constitution, and more of the feelings and sentiments of a gentleman, and a Christian than are usually found in such persons. To him the work in the northern counties of Down and Antrim was committed, where his religious views were not unlikely to increase his influence. Hamilton, by marriage his nephew, and his associate in this mission, held a commission in the French army at the time when their fleet was defeated by Admiral Warren, and being taken prisoner in that action and not recognized, regularly exchanged as a French officer. Of the other comrades of Emmet, Dowdall had been an inferior Customs officer, Redmond a small trader, Allen a broken woollen manufacturer, and Quigley a mechanic. Though in so humble a position, Quigley had been deeply engaged in the "'98," had escaped to France, where he had played an active part among his brother refugees, and now returned from abroad well furnished with money. The special field of his action was Kildare, where he distributed his money and liquor freely among the peasantry. Another intended actor in the drama was Dwyer, who, after the repression of the late rebellion refusing all terms with the Government, had fled with about twenty followers to the Wicklow mountains, and there exercised a widespread influence over the people. Ready, however, as he was to join in the plot, experience had made him cautious. When he should hear that the green flag floated on the castle at Dublin, he said, "he would come in with all his men, but until then he would not leave his secure retreat."

Emmet was far too impetuous and self-confident to pay due regard to the difficulties felt by his more experienced companions, and which they knew must wreck any immediate enterprise. From the moment of his return to Ireland—or at any rate from that of his father's death and his accession to his property—he appears to have commenced his operations. The better to evade suspicion, in the spring of 1803 he left Dublin and took lodgings at Harold's Cross, in the suburbs, where he passed under the name of Hewitt. Here he was often visited by several of those who afterwards took part in his miserable failure.

In the March of that year, fearing probably that his enterprise would be checked by the then impending rupture with France, and, as he himself stated on his trial, convinced that the conciliatory Government of the new Lord Lieutenant would gradually soften the feelings of resentment against the authorities entertained by his followers, and so decrease his power over them, he got possession of a house in Patrick Street, Dublin. Here he at once established a manufactory of hand-grenades, and other explosive weapons calculated to impede the action of the troops in the then narrow streets of the Irish capital. Subsequently he hired a builder's yard, in a narrow thoroughfare known as Marshalsea, or Dirty Lane, where pikes and other offensive weapons were steadily manufactured, and repeated meetings held with his under-leaders for the settlement of their designs. Finding his lodgings at Harold's Cross inconvenient for his work, he took the lease of a house in Butterfield Lane, Rathfarnham, in the name of Robert Ellis, where he resided with Dowdall, under the name of Fraser, and with another person who was never identified.

Passing backwards and forwards from his new house to his depôts in Dublin, Emmet hurried on the preparation of warlike stores and weapons, and held frequent meetings with his sub-agents, who still advised him to do nothing until the French arrived. To this advice Emmet gave but little attention, urging a secret armament, and a sudden rising in Dublin, under the impression that if by this the city could be held only for a brief period, they would be joined by their friends from the country, with whom he was in constant communication. As in Despard's case, no attempt at a regular organization in Dublin was made by Emmet. Uniforms were procured for the intended leaders, and arms steadily manufactured at the depôts, but not placed in the hands of the people, and all was staked on the chance of a sudden outbreak. Though determined to hazard it, Emmet had not as yet definitely fixed on the day for the attempt. He had sent Russel and Hamilton to the north to prepare for early action, and Quigley to Kildare to apprise the people of his intentions and to communicate with the Wexford leaders. These at first agreed to join him, but subsequently refused, when the emissaries they had sent to Dublin reported how few were his partisans, and, that practically, nothing had been achieved but the preparation of ammunition and arms.

Thus the affair lingered until the 7th of July, when

an explosion of ammunition at the Patrick Street factory, exposing the nature of the work there carried on, and necessitating the removal of the stores to Marshalsea Lane, determined Emmet to act without delay, in spite of every objection from his more cautious friends. From that moment he never left this depôt, living there night and day, and allowing only his most trusted followers to leave it, even for brief periods. With an energy worthy of a better cause, he so pushed on the preparations that at the time of the outbreak, only a few days after, a complete armoury was discovered, sufficient for a large body of men. In store he then had, besides numerous boxes of gunpowder and bundles of cartridges for cannon, hand-grenades, and grappling irons for scaling walls, 1700 pikes, 42,000 rounds of ball cartridges, and several very innocent-looking logs of wood, which in reality were hollow tubes, charged with powder and fitted with fusees, intended to be placed across the streets and fired at the approach of cavalry. Here he composed, and from time to time read to his followers, the extraordinary proclamation to the people intended to be issued during the outbreak, a work of marked but sadly misapplied ability. Here, too, he now and then exhibited his gorgeous green and gold uniform, in which he proposed to lead them to victory, and spoke of the great deeds he should perform.

His state of mind at this time was painfully described by him, in a paper in his own handwriting found in his desk at this depôt. "I have little time," he wrote, "to look at the difficulties which lie still between me and the completion of my wishes. That these difficulties will likewise disappear, I have ardent, and I trust rational hopes; but if it is not to be the case, I thank God with having gifted me with a sanguine disposition. To that disposition I run from reflection; and if my hopes are without foundation, if a precipice is opening under my feet from which duty will not suffer me to turn back, I am grateful for that sanguine disposition which leads me to the brink, and throws me down while my eyes are still raised to the vision of happiness that my fancy formed in the air."[4]

The proclamation on which he firmly relied to rally to him the people of the kingdom professed to emanate from the Provisional Government, and commenced by calling on them to show that they were fit to take their place among nations by wresting their independence from England with their own hands. For eight months, it said, the project had been preparing, with a tranquillity mistaken for obedience, and had neither been retarded by the failure of Despard's attempt in England, nor accelerated by the renewal of hostilities with France. A free and independent Republic was to be established in Ireland, and until that was acknowledged by her, no negotiation save for the exchange of prisoners was to be entered into with England. To support these intentions, the proclamation called first on the men of the north, "where the flame of liberty once glowed;" then on the men of Leinster, who were reminded that "six years ago they lost Ireland because their courage was not rightly directed by

[4] Paper found in the depôt, in Emmet's desk, and read by the Attorney-General in his opening speech at the trial.

discipline." With a painful recollection of the conduct of the rebels at that period, they were now called upon to respect the hostages (all Government adherents that might fall into their hands) which they intended to hold for the return of transported rebels, and were warned that the Provisional Government would punish any violation of property, and any refusal to march when ordered. The statement that it was a religious contest into which they were embarking was denounced as a calumny. The men of Munster and Connaught were reminded that they were anxious six months before to act alone, and were called on to show that they only wanted the opportunity now offered to them.

"We war not," continued this clever document, "against property; we war against no religious sect; we war against English dominion; we war not against past opinion or prejudices." The idea of meeting this attempt by a system of terror was ridiculed, and it was boasted that "should such be resorted to by their enemies it would not be imitated by them." "We will not imitate you in cruelty; we will put no man to death in cold blood; the prisoners which first fall into our hands shall be treated with the respect due to the unfortunate; but if the life of a single Irish soldier is taken after the battle is over, the orders issued henceforth to the Irish army are neither to give nor take quarter." That Emmet held these good resolutions in earnest, and believed that he could force his followers to adopt them, no one can doubt who studies his character. How slight his influence really was, and how thoroughly he misunderstood the objects of his followers, is written in the blood of the murdered Lord Chief Justice and his nephew. How little his mad mob regarded the rules of civilized warfare was painfully exposed in the murder of Colonel Browne after he had surrendered himself to his rudely-armed captors.

To this proclamation some thirty decrees of the Provisional Government were attached—abolishing tithes; reclaiming church lands; forbidding all transfers of land, securities, or ships until the National Government was established, and the national will declared; ordering the Irish generals to seize partisans of England as hostages, and to warn the English generals to observe the rules of war, and to do so themselves. All militia, yeomen, or volunteers who within fourteen days should be found in arms were to be accounted as rebels, committed for trial, and their property confiscated. The strictest discipline was to be enforced, and all who disgraced themselves by being drunk in the face of the enemy were to be chased from the ranks. All officers, except colonels, were to be elected by the men. As soon as each county was cleared by the generals, county committees, elected according to the constitution of the United Irishmen, were to take on themselves the civil direction of their county, and to send up representatives to a National Convention in Dublin, the numbers of which were to be 300—the number of those who had sat in the last National Parliament. To this convention, when fully constituted, the Provisional Government would surrender its powers, and become obedient to its orders. Like the paper constitutions of Sieyes, the proclamation read well; it wanted an united nation, not some four score desperate men, to make it work.

A shorter proclamation to the citizens of Dublin, put a less civilized face on the projected warfare. "In a city," it reminded them "each street becomes a defile, and each house a battery. Impede the march of your oppressors; charge them with the arms of the brave, the pike; and from your windows and roofs hurl stones, bricks, bottles, and all other convenient implements, on the heads of the satellites of your tyrant, the mercenary, sanguinary, soldiery of England." These hints were not likely to be lost on the rabble of Dublin. Orangemen were called on, not to add to the catalogue of their follies and crimes, nor to attempt an opposition which would carry with it their inevitable destruction, but to return from the paths of delusion to the arms of their countrymen. All sects were to be embraced in the benevolence of their object, and urged to repress pillage and excesses. They were, however, bid to "remember the massacres of their oppressors for 600 years, and their tortures— their murdered friends—their burned houses—their violated females." A strange mode of inculcating forbearance on so impressionable and passionate a people.

Whatever other reasons may have influenced Emmet not further to delay his mad attempt, there is no doubt that the explosion at Patrick Street depôt, and the consequent discovery of this manufacture of warlike stores, furnished him with good ground for anticipating that the Government would be put at once on his track, and that he must either strike or abandon his enterprise. In reality the Government learnt but little from his accident. The explosion, though fatal to one person, and seriously injuring another, was confined to the interior of the building, not even breaking the windows, or by its report attracting very general attention. The man who eventually died of his hurts, kept his secret with the spirit of a partisan, and the other persisted that he had only been called in the day before the explosion, to build a wall.[5] The Government, however, were aware that ammunition was being stored in Dublin; two of the watch having on the night of the 17th followed two men carrying a cask to a house at the corner of the Coombe and New Street, from which ball cartridges and flints fell when it was accidentally broken as it dropped from the window-sill of the house into which it was being taken. The cask itself was rescued from the hands of the police by an armed party; and though more cartridges were found on a subsequent search in Patrick Street, the police for the time were either baffled or negligent in their inquiries.[6]

Emmet now fixed on Saturday the 23rd of July for the attempt, a day for many reasons suitable for such a project. In addition to its being the time when the neighbouring peasantry and the lower classes of Dublin were wont to resort to the churchyard of St. James's to deck the graves of their rela-

---

[5] Memorandum of Mr. Marsden to Lord Castlereagh on explosion in Patrick Street, dated August 25, 1803. Castlereagh Papers, vol. iv. p. 313.
[6] Marsden's Memorandum to Lord Castlereagh.

tives with flowers, it was market-day, and being Saturday, the working classes were paid at mid-day, and leaving work early, crowded the streets, especially towards evening. It was afterwards noted that the visitors from the country districts were on that day greatly in excess of their accustomed numbers, and that they came in, apparently, in previously arranged groups, and with a concerted action. Even on the morning of the appointed day there was a difference of opinion among the leaders whether the attempt should be risked, as it was known to them that the march of the Kildare men had been countermanded, and that they could rely only on the workmen from the side of Palmerston and the lowest of the rabble of the city. Later in the day Emmet appears to have been inclined to confine his operations to leading those who should come in to the Wicklow mountains, unless they came in greater force than he then expected, and there waiting for a more convenient opportunity. Whether it was only with this object, or that he had again determined to carry out his original design, a little before nine, pikes and a few fire-arms were distributed to about eighty men who could be relied on, and more pikes ranged against the wall in Marshalsea Lane, so that they could easily be taken by other followers. Leading a section of these men, Emmet, with his two generals Quigley and Stockdale, in full United Irishmen uniform, left the depôt, and proceeded down St. Thomas Street towards Francis Street, a route that would enable them to gain the country through New Street without passing any barrack or military post. He soon, however, realized his inability to control the bulk of his retainers, and whether discouraged by the sounds of firing among those in the rear, or disgusted at the evident failure of his attempt, he and about ten followers separated from the rest, and escaped to the Wicklow mountains.

The remainder of the party, practically without a leader, appear to have moved into St. Thomas Street as far as the market-house, attacking on their way any chance victim, and meeting with no resistance. Here Colonel Browne, of the 41st regiment, who had been summoned from his residence in the suburbs, and was on the way to join his men, was murdered after he had surrendered to his assailants, and two unarmed soldiers shared his fate. Another victim was the Chief Justice Kilwarden. After his usual judicial labours he had left for his country residence, and in consequence of the threatening attitude of the persons he met on the road making their way to Dublin, had turned back, with the intention probably of going direct to the Castle. Fatally for himself and his nephew, who, with his daughter, were with him in the carriage, instead of going by a road that would have avoided the scene of the outrage, he drove direct into the city, and in St. Thomas Street came upon the rear of the rebel band. At once his carriage was stopped, himself dragged out, thrown on the ground, stabbed in some thirty places with pikes, and left for dead. His daughter was indeed permitted to escape with her life, and frantic with terror rushed to the Castle, and gave the first news of the insurrection to the officers on guard. Not so his nephew, who was pursued, and killed with all the barbarity that had characterized his uncle's murder.

It is to be hoped that the murder of this upright and humane judge was the unpremeditated act of the rabble. In the discharge of his duties, whether as Attorney-General in the prosecutions of 1795, or subsequently as Judge, the mildness of his conduct had been in strong contrast with the prevailing practice of the crown lawyers and the judges of the day. Even in the throes of death he showed a noble example of firmness and moderation. A magistrate who saw him in his mangled and pitiable situation, but a few minutes before his death, in not unnatural excitement and indignation exclaimed that his murderers should at once suffer for their atrocious acts. " No man," said the dying Judge, raising his mangled head, and with the last exertion of his voice, "must suffer for his death, but by the laws of his country;" and then fell back and breathed his last. A story was current at the time among the lower orders in Dublin, that a relative of one of those who were condemned in 1795 instigated and commenced the attack. The man who then suffered execution was one of fifteen youths under the age of twenty whom Lord Kilwarden, as Attorney-General, had to prosecute. On the day of trial they appeared in the dock wearing shirts with tuckers and open collars like boys, and the Chief Justice of the time, with a heartless pleasantry, addressing the Attorney-General when he came into court said, "I suppose, Mr. Attorney-General, you are ready to go on with the trials of these *tuckered* traitors?" " No, my lord," he indignantly replied, "I am not ready;" adding in a lower voice to one of the prisoners' counsel near him, "If I have any power to save the lives of these boys, whose extreme youth I did not before observe, that man shall never have the gratification of passing sentence upon a single one of these *tuckered* traitors." In redemption of his promise he procured pardons for all, on the terms of leaving the country. One refused, and was executed; and it was by his relative, it was reported, an insurgent of the name of Shannon, that the first blow was struck. Hearing the cry of vengeance when dragged from his carriage, Lord Kilwarden exclaimed, "It is I, Kilwarden, Chief Justice of the King's Bench." "Then," cried Shannon, "you're the man I want," and plunged the pike into his body, when the rest of the brutes crowded round him, and almost fought with one another in their eagerness to join in the assassination.[7] From this dreadful scene the armed mob marched towards the Marshalsea debtors' prison, expecting to be joined by the prisoners. Attacking the small guard, and killing the corporal, they called on the inmates to join them. Far from doing so, the imprisoned debtors demanded arms to resist the attack, and showed so formidable a face that their assailants turned, and hurried away without delay. Soon after this they were met by a few police officers under their chief, Mr. Wilson, who despising their superior numbers called on them to disperse. On their refusal the police fired on the party, shot one of them, and so staggered the remainder by their boldness, that though greatly outnumbered and hardly

[7] "Life of Curran." By his Son. Vol. ii. p. 221, note.

pressed, the police effected their retreat with the loss of only one of their small detachment.

Though the rabble had now been in possession of the streets for above an hour, with the exception of Colonel Browne and the two soldiers, who had been caught unprepared, and murdered, not one of the large garrison of Dublin had appeared. Happily for the safety of the city, Lieutenant Brady, of the 41st regiment, in charge of the guard at the Cork Street Barrack, hearing reports of the attacks on the soldiers, marched out with fifty of his men, with the intention of escorting his colonel from his suburban residence, of whose murder he was ignorant. On his march he came upon the mob in Thomas Street, and in reply to a shot from one of the houses, which wounded one of his men, opened fire on them at once till they fled in all directions, leaving six of their party dead or wounded. About the same time, the light company of the same regiment, under the command of Lieutenant Douglas, encountered the insurgents in the Coombe, and on their resisting, fired, and dispersed them for the moment. Fancying that Lieutenant Douglas had left a neighbouring watch-house defenceless the mob hurried to its attack, were resisted by a few infirm old men left in charge, and turned towards the Coombe guard-house, to which he had retired with his company. They summoned up courage to fire a few shots, wounding two of his men, and then, after receiving a few volleys from his soldiers, fled, leaving several dead and wounded on the ground. All resistance was now over, and by half-past ten the peace of the capital was at least temporarily secured, solely by the promptitude of two subalterns, acting on their own responsibility and without an order from any superior officer. Some time after it had all been over, and not till then, the garrison was turned out, and military possession taken of the city, by the orders of those high officials, military and civil, by whom its safety had been so strangely neglected.[8]

Previously, however, to this action on the part of the authorities, the depôt in Marshalsea Lane had been discovered and seized by Lieutenant Coltman, of the 9th Regiment, who was staying in Dublin on leave. Collecting a few men together, with the aid of a Captain Woodward of the Yeomanry, he moved into the lane, where the sentinels at the depôt, and the lines of pikes, distributed on the way towards it, pointed out the object of their search—a disused malt-house. Here two privates, mounting on the points of the pikes leaning against the wall, made their way in at an upper window, and were soon followed by the captain and his men, who had by this time procured a ladder. In addition to the ample supply of warlike stores already mentioned, they found nearly 7000 copies of the proclamation, and Emmet's desk. In this, and under the rude bed on which he had lately slept, many important documents in his own handwriting were also discovered. In these desultory conflicts twenty-nine of the rebels were killed, and numerous prisoners captured; whilst on the other side, in addition to Lord Kilwarden and his nephew, and Colonel Browne, five soldiers and two private individuals alone lost their

[8] Collated from the evidence given at the trials of the conspirators.

lives. Thus by little more than 100 soldiers, led by resolute officers, not afraid to do their duty without waiting for orders, a daring and dangerous insurrection was crushed at its first outbreak. Left to their own guidance by the early desertion of their leader, the armed mob seemed to have acted without plan, and the Castle, the main object in Emmet's project, was never even threatened—not a single man getting within half a mile of its gates.

The peril of the city—the wanton sacrifice of valuable lives by the neglect of the authorities to use with promptitude the forces at their command, was admitted. Every one agreed on this; they only differed in deciding on whose shoulders the blame should be thrown—the civil or the military authorities of the capital. The opponents of the Government in both countries charged them with culpable ignorance of the plot, or wilful contempt of the means to be employed. As Cobbett wrote "If they were not surprised like a drunken sentinel on his post," they deliberately disregarded the information they had received, looking on the project as too contemptible to require any extra precaution for the preservation of the peace of the city.[9] The cabinet were not agreed in their estimate of the affair. On the news reaching London, a royal message was sent to Parliament, describing the attempt in no measured terms, and

[9] *Cobbett's Register*, vol. iv. p. 255. In another number, August 20—27, 1803, Cobbett alleges that on the day of the rising a general order was issued for ten men from every company of the regular regiments to be allowed to go ten miles from their quarters, to assist in getting in the harvest.

Lord Hawkesbury, in moving the Address in reply, declared "that a rebellion had broken out in Ireland more serious than ever occurred before." A few days after, Lord Castlereagh sneered at the notion of its being regarded in a serious light, and declared that it would have been considered contemptible but for the murder of Lord Kilwarden. Again, in December, on the debate on the renewal of the Irish Martial Law Bill, which had been passed immediately after the event, Mr. Secretary Yorke, the brother of the Lord Lieutenant, boasted that the safety of Dublin was never for a moment in danger, called the rebels a wretched mob, and ridiculed the whole affair as "commencing in Dirty Lane and ending in Cutpurse Row." The truth was, that the evidence of neglect on the part of the authorities grew so strong, that in self-defence the Government could only do their best to reduce the insurrection to the proportions of a street-riot

Who was to be held responsible was all the more bitterly contested, because it involved a personal dispute between Lord Hardwicke as Lord Lieutenant, and General Fox as Commander of the Forces in Ireland, and in that capacity resident in Dublin. The case of General Fox was naturally taken up with his characteristic vigour by Mr. Fox in the Commons, and of course as bitterly attacked by the political friends of Lord Hardwicke. The public journals took their party sides with more than usual bitterness—a Dublin Government journal taunting General Fox with his relationship to Lord Edward Fitzgerald, and suggesting that his apathy might be traced to the family feeling for rebels; Cobbett on the other side heaping unmeasured abuse on the Government, and publishing in the bitter letters of "Juverna," a series of personal attacks on Lord Hardwicke, Chancellor Redesdale, Mr. Under-Secretary Marsden, and Mr. Plunket, one of the counsel on the trial of Emmet. These letters subsequently became the subject of curious and interesting proceedings in the Irish and English courts of law.[1] Was it true, said the friends of the General, that the Lord Lieutenant and his Secretary, Mr. Marsden, had, whilst detailing the information they had acquired of the preparations for, and imminence of, the outbreak, declared to him that they placed no reliance on the information, and urged him not to take steps to rouse public apprehension by his defensive arrangements? Or was it true, as the Government speakers and organs declared, that every information at the command of the Government was revealed to the General —that the imminent danger of a serious outbreak had not been concealed from him—and that he had been trusted by the civil authorities to take the necessary steps for the preservation of the peace and securing the safety of life and property? Was it true that, knowing this, the General had done nothing until at the last moment, when all had been already done by volunteers, and nothing left for the Government to achieve, but the avenging the murders that had been committed, and the punishment of the participators in this insane and wicked attempt?[2]

[1] See the trials of the libels of the "Trojan Horse."
[2] Lord Redesdale to Mr. Addington, August 11, 1803: "We are unquestionably most defective in our military commander.

In both Houses of Parliament the controversy was carried on with ever-increasing political and personal bitterness, all the more increased when General Fox was induced, if not compelled, to exchange the command in Ireland for another military position, and Lord Cathcart appointed as his successor.[2] Since these bitter and fruitless discussions, which of course at the time left each party only more steadfast to their own views, the publication of the diary of Lord Colchester (then Mr. Speaker Abbot), and of Mr. Secretary Wickham's secret despatches to him, as well as of Mr. Marsden's letters to Lord Castlereagh, in the papers of that nobleman, have enabled us to form probably a more correct judgment on this lamentable exhibition of carelessness, overweening self-confidence, neglect, or apathy. Among the latter is the memorandum from Mr. Under-Secretary Marsden already referred to, giving a detailed account of the information of the proceedings of the conspirators received by

---

Lord C. told me long ago he was not calculated for troublesome times. The events of July 23 have occasioned much discontent, and neither the military nor civil officers manifest much confidence." *Same* to *same*, August 19: after stating that information was received before the 23rd, and the details of meeting at the Castle, and General Fox's retirement to Kilmainham, and his sending for Asgill and the other chief officers : " These officers received no orders at Kilmainham, except to return to barracks and wait for the General, who did not come. Marsden, before eleven, sent several messages to the barracks for assistance to guard the Castle, but received none, the officers waiting for the General." Pellew's " Sidmouth," vol. ii.

[2] See Hansard's Debates, House of Commons : December 19, 1803, speech of C. Fox; December 5, 1803, Mr. Addington; December 19, Mr. Secretary Yorke.

him, and of the interview between the Lord Lieutenant and the General, at which that information was communicated to the latter. In the former is a despatch from Mr. Secretary Wickham, marked " most secret," giving complete details, not only of the later, but earlier steps in the concoction of the plot, and the conduct of Lord Hardwicke and General Fox. There is, also, a note in his journal of an interview between himself and the Premier, Mr. Addington, and giving his deliberate opinion on the conduct of both parties, after a perusal of the evidence laid before him by the Government.

From these sources we find that, "through channels in which confidence was placed," the Government knew that Quigley had come over from France to Kildare, had made an unsuccessful attempt to raise the farmers and peasants in that county and in Meath, and was believed, in consequence of his ill-success, to have left Ireland. They could easily have seized him, but did not for fear that such an act " should put notions of rebellion into heads that never dreamt of it." Through similar channels they were aware that Russel and Hamilton, with Allen, Stockdale, and Dowdall, were about some mischief with young Emmet; that they talked of a rising, but all the disaffected said it was useless without French aid; that there was no organization except in Kildare; that Russel and Hamilton were going north to attempt a rising there; and that they were certainly preparing arms in or about Dublin. Other statements by the same parties, as to the movements of Emmet's brother, and other actors in the " '98 " who had been pardoned, proving false, Marsden was led to discredit the whole information given him, and to regard as too contemptible for serious notice the reported acts of Emmet and the minor conspirators. "So," continues Mr. Wickham, "things went on until about the 10th and 12th of July, when Russel and Hamilton went to the north, and our friends have followed them; reasoning *à priori* from the character and known talent of the persons concerned, that these were the two men among the conspirators whom I should have desired to have most closely watched." Three days before the insurrection broke out news came from Belfast that orders had been sent from Dublin to attempt a rising in the north. *Positive information was also given here that an attempt would be made in Dublin at the end of the week.* Marsden on this wished to act with vigour, by getting a suspension of the Habeas Corpus Act; but before his advice could be acted on, the statement was contradicted, from what Wickham calls "a safe source," and nothing was done until on the morning of the day "the information received left no longer any doubt." Though this information reached Marsden before noon, he contented himself with writing to the Lord Lieutenant, (with whom he knew that General Fox had a meeting at two p.m.) to bring him to the Castle, and "on no slight grounds," and requesting the Commander of the Dublin District to call upon him.

Between three and four in the afternoon Lord Hardwicke and General Fox came to the castle, and Marsden, "as he believes," laid the whole of the information before his superiors, and recollects telling them "that *a person who was in the secrets of the disaffected, and with whom he frequently communicated*, had come to him very soon after he reached the Castle that morning, in great alarm, and assured him that the danger was imminent." Similar information had been given by a priest to one of the city aldermen, and communicated to the Secretary. He believes that he also informed his visitors how Mr. Clarke, of Palmerston, had told him that his workpeople had required to be paid off earlier than usual, and had come into the city evidently by arrangement; that an extraordinary number of persons from the country had been moving into Dublin all the day, and that "this circumstance scarcely left a decision with the leaders, however divided they might be as to the opportuneness of an attempt at this time."

Such was the information which the Secretary *believed* that he laid before the authorities. What was the result? The guard at the Viceregal Lodge was doubled, to ensure the safety of his Excellency and his family; later in the evening a small party was sent from the Cork Street Barracks to strengthen the post at Chapelizod, on the Palmerston Road; the Lord Lieutenant returned to the Viceregal Lodge; General Fox drove to Kilmainham,—and the city was left to chance. Though the Secretary had sent in the morning for the Commandant of the garrison, he does not appear to have reached the Castle until about six.

By this time fresh information had reached the Castle, "which had put it beyond a doubt that a riot must happen." The Commandant listened to all that was said, and waited for orders from General Fox, who had assumed the command of the garrison. For several hours he remained listening to the accounts, which hourly became more alarming; and at last, on receiving a message from the General, who on his part had apparently been waiting for him, left the Castle and reached the Royal Hospital at Kilmainham, about the time that the rebels were mustering at the depot, and on the eve of moving into the streets.[1] The alarm increased. "Magistrates and Captains of Yeomanry came to the Castle for orders, and were told to prevent their men from assembling, *lest they*

---

[1] In "Lord Colchester's Diary," vol. i. p. 438, is a letter from Wickham to Speaker Abbot, dated August 12, in which he writes: "Faults were committed on both sides, but by no means those which are reproached to the Government. The Government was not surprised. On the contrary, the greatest praise is due to its vigilance. It was the knowledge that the Government was well informed and about to act vigorously that caused a premature explosion, &c., &c., &c.—if, if, if—not a rebel would have escaped. The truth will come out soon, and when it does you will learn, that the General, who had taken upon himself the command of the garrison of D!! so that Sir C. Asgill and Dunne could not act without his orders, was sent for to the Castle at two, informed that the insurrection would break out that night, and desired to employ his whole force to suppress the insurgents. Sir Charles was also sent for, and M. (Marsden) kept him to a mutton chop at the office, waiting for the General's orders, and would not suffer him to dine out, as he had intended, lest the insurrection should begin earlier than was expected. Between eight and nine the General sent for Sir Charles and Dunne to Kilmainham. Till that moment he had given no orders whatever. On their return they were nearly massacred; they passed along one end of Thomas Street whilst Colonel Browne was massacred at the other. There was not a cartridge at the Castle; the Ordnance, without communication with the Lord Lieutenant, had removed them all away."

should increase the alarm, and because few had arms or ammunition, and relying on the troops at the various posts in Dublin having received warning." And now it was known that the rebels were in the streets. Mr. Clarke on his return to Palmerston had been shot by one of his own workmen. Lord Kilwarden had been murdered. Clarke himself had taken refuge at the castle; and the frantic daughter of the Chief Justice had brought notice of her father's assassination to the Castle guard. No troops had as yet been seen, and the only movement had been an increase of thirty men to the Castle guard—an utterly useless precaution. The yeomen were asking for arms and ammunition. At the Castle there were none worth mentioning of either that could be issued to them. They were sent to the magazine at the Phœnix Park: no one was there who could open it. At last the key was brought, it was opened, and the supply found but trifling—no ball cartridges, no charges for the artillery, and only a few carbines and pistols. The Ordnance authority, without communicating with the Lord Lieutenant, had almost cleared the magazine. Letters and notes were sent in vain to Sir C. Asgill, begging that the troops might be sent into the streets; and no reply came until past midnight—long after the rebels had been routed by the few soldiers and police under Brady, Douglas, and Wilson. By neglect in some high quarters three base murders had been committed, and more than thirty lives lost in a miserable street riot, in the face of a garrison of more than three thousand men.

The civil authorities threw the blame on the

General; the General's friends threw it on the Lord Lieutenant and his Chancellor and his Secretary. It was not denied by the latter that the information then at the command of the Government had been communicated to the General at the Castle interview. It was said, however, in excuse, that "at the same time orders had been given him not to alarm any one." So little was he expected to do, according to Charles Fox's statement in the House of Commons "that on the extra guards being sent to the Phœnix and the Castle, Lord Hardwicke had sent to him to express his surprise, and said 'I suppose by what you are doing you must act on some information unknown to me.'"[5] The friends of the Government did not attempt to deny that at the interview a doubt was expressed whether the attempt would be made that night, and the whole affair was not looked on as serious. They urged, however, that on his hearing the information, however doubted, any one would have supposed that General Fox would have taken every necessary precaution—that it was his duty and not that of the Lord Lieutenant to do so—that the Civil Government had a right to expect that the Commander-in-Chief had done his duty—that the Civil Government was prepared, and the army in a complete state of readiness, and that it was not the fault of the former that the power of the latter had not been used at an earlier period.[6] Speaker Abbot tried to divide the culpability. "It was evident," he

[5] Debate on Army Estimates, House of Commons, December 19, 1803.
[6] Mr. Secretary Yorke and Mr. Corry, same debate.

writes, "that the Civil Government had not given sufficient credit to the information they had received; and that General Fox, though excusable for not taking more prompt and decisive measures of precaution, might, with more activity and a truer judgment of his own responsibility, have easily prevented the whole mischief."[7]

The Government was quick in punishing the offenders whom they had encouraged by their previous dilatoriness. Within a month of the insurrection, seventeen prisoners were put on their trial before a Special Commission for the City and County of Dublin,[8] and within three more weeks Emmet, and those of his followers who had been caught red-handed, had been tried and executed. Six of the

---

[7] "Lord Colchester's Diary," November 23, 1803, vol. i. p. 463. General Fox was transferred to a command in the Mediterranean, and Lord Cathcart appointed as his successor. Addington to the Lord Lieutenant, August 23, when speaking of these contemplated changes, doubts whether a mere military change will suffice, as there is an impression "that some persons in subordinate official situations received the information previously furnished with coldness and distrust, and that these feelings and sentiments manifestly influenced their conduct." Pellew's "Sidmouth," vol. ii.

[8] Commission issued to Lord Norbury, Chief Justice of the Common Pleas, Mr. Justice Downes, King's Bench, Mr. Justice Finucane, Common Pleas, and Barons Denis George and St. George Daly, of the Exchequer. Grand Jury charged by Mr. Justice Downes, August 24, 1803. Bills returned same day against Rourke, Killen, MacCann, Byrne, Clare, Donnelly, Farrel, Begly, Kelly, Bourke, Kearney, Begg, Roche, Maguire, Doran, and Kirwan, and on the 29th against Dennis, Lambert, Redmond. First trial, that of Kearney, August 31, before Lord Norbury and others of the Commission.

prisoners selected Curran for their counsel, most of the rest were defended by Mr. McNally, a man of great experience in criminal trials. For the Crown, of course the Attorney and Solicitor-Generals (Standish O'Grady and M'Lelland) were assisted by Plunket and other leading counsel. Kearney, the first man who was tried, was proved to have been seized pike in hand in Thomas Street, leading a party, and calling on them as Royal Pikemen to charge. In the course of this case, all the details of the insurrection, the murders of Lord Kilwarden and his nephew, the discovery of the depôt, and the proclamations, were proved. For the defence it was urged that the identity of the prisoner was doubtful—due to the confusion which prevailed at the time of his arrest—and the probability of his own story, that he was on his way home from his usual work, got mixed up in the crowd, and was involuntarily an apparent actor in the affair. One of his witnesses admitted that the prisoner did not go straight home, but by way of Thomas Street, and so broke down the little credit that might otherwise have been given to his story. He was found guilty, and executed at the spot where he had been arrested. The next man tried, Roche, a slater, had been taken standing, pike in hand, as an advanced post. At a shout from him a bottle, as recommended by the proclamation to the citizens, was thrown from a window, and a shot fired, by which one of the soldiers fell. In such a case defence was hopeless, it was limited to witnesses to character; found guilty without hesitation, he confessed his guilt before he expiated it on the scaffold.

Curran's first defence was that of Owen Kirwan, who, though only an old clothes' man, had taken a leading part in the attempt. On the firing of a rocket, which apparently he had himself taken beforehand to the depôt, he was heard and seen to call out a number of men that had been congregating at his house, of whom ten had pikes, and then, dressed in a green uniform, and pike in hand, to lead them towards St. Thomas Street. Within half-an-hour of his leaving his house, another body of pikemen, led by a man in a scarlet coat, came there, were supplied with refreshment, and followed in the track of the former body. Curran, in his speech for the defence, full of power, and glittering with eloquent passages, hardly touched on the details of the evidence, and but briefly alluded to the *alibi* which was to be set up in his client's favour. Against evidence so clear against the prisoner, and with only an *alibi* so miserably weak to rely on in his favour, he used a wise discretion in trusting to his powers of oratory.

The main points of the speech were the strong contrast which he drew between the state of Ireland under Lord Hardwicke, and its condition about a year before —one of the reasons, it will be remembered, assigned by Emmet for precipitating his attempt; he was eager to bear his testimony to the firmness and good sense of the Lord Lieutenant; spoke with no feigned horror of the fate of Lord Kilwarden, that most upright and merciful Judge; and ridiculed with his accustomed force and bitterness the idea that "the First Consul would treat Ireland better than he had treated the countries at his very door." "Are you

Protestants?" he said. "He has abolished Protestantism with Christianity. Are you Catholics? do you think he will raise you to the level of the Pope? He has reduced his religion to be a mendicant for contemptuous toleration; he has reduced his person to beggary and to rags." With a really magnificent burst of eloquence he warned the minor actors in the miserable attempt, that if they had succeeded they would be made "the wretched tools of a despicable gang of needy adventurers;" that robbery might make some poor, and but not many rich; and that heavy indeed would have been the tyranny of such governors. With apt ridicule, he declared that the escape of the Government and the Castle, which had never been attacked, reminded him of the young man who escaped being shot at Dettingen, because he had been sent twenty miles off ten days before the battle.

With bitter, but one cannot but feel misplaced, caricature, he pretended to read from the *Moniteur*, the following paragraph, as fairly painting the rise and fall of " this splendid rebellion." " On the 23rd of July last a most splendid rebellion displayed her standard in the metropolis of Ireland, in that part of the city called the Poddle. The band of heroes that came forth at the call of patriotism capable of bearing arms, at the lowest calculation must have amounted to little less than 200 persons. Rebellion advanced with the most rapid steps till she came to the site of the old Four Courts and the Tholsel. There she espied a decayed pillory, on which she mounted to reconnoitre; but she found, to her great mortification, that the rebels had stayed behind. She therefore judged it right to make her escape, which she effected in a masterly manner down Dirty Lane; the rebels in the meantime retiring in some disorder from the Poddle, being hard pressed by the poles and lanterns of the watchmen, and being additionally galled by Mr. Justice Drury, who came to a most unerring aim upon their rear, on which he played without any intermission with his eye-glass from his dining-room window. *Raro antecedentem celestum deseruit pœna pede claudo.* It is clearly ascertained she did not appear in her own clothes, for she threw away her regimental jacket before she fled, which has been picked up, and may now be seen at Mr. Carleton's (a Frenchman, I suppose), at sixpence a head for grown persons and threepence for a nurse and child. It was thought at first to be the work of an Irish artist, who might have taken the measure in the absence of the wearer; but by a bill and receipt found in one of the pockets, it appears to have been made by the actual body tailor of her August Highness the Consort of the First Consul. At present it is but poorly ornamented, and it is said that the Irish Volunteers have entered into a subscription to *trim* it, if it shall ever be worn again." Amusing as this passage may be, it seems sadly misplaced in a trial for life and death, and the more so when the close relation between the leader of the insane attempt and Curran's daughter is borne in mind. It failed, of course, to produce the desired effect. Words, however eloquent, and satire, however severe, could not beat down dry facts. Kirwan was found guilty, and justly suffered for his crime.

The incidents and evidence in the cases of the other

prisoners arraigned in Dublin were so alike, that it would be needlessly monotonous to give them all in detail.[9] One alone, Dennis Lambert Redmond, was of a superior class to the rest, and in his case his almost successful attempts to escape have some of the interest of a romance. A gentleman by birth and education, he had early entered into the plot, and accepted a commission from the professed Provisional Government. He was clearly proved to have held consultations with the notorious Allen who had escaped, and with M'Cabe (an accomplice—probably a Government spy—who had been admitted with others as witnesses for the Crown), as to attacking the artillery barracks at Island Bridge; and in his house and a yard adjoining, a regular manufactory of pikes was found, within a few days after the outbreak. Here among weapons openly displayed, were found what appeared to be harmless logs of woods, but which in reality were rough cases, each holding forty pikes, so concealed as to be easily conveyed to any appointed place, without fear of detection. On the day of the insurrection he left his house, lay concealed in the city for a brief period, and then escaped on board a ship bound for Chester. The elements were against him. Forced by a storm to run for shelter into Carlingford Bay, the ship was boarded by the port officers, and the fugitive being found without the then required permit for leaving Ireland, was detained until he could

---

[9] The following were found guilty and executed in Dublin:— Kearney, Roche, Byrne, Begg, Rourke, Killen, MacCann, Donelly, Farrell, Begley, Kelly, Howley, Mackintosh, Redmond, Clare, a mere youth, was respited.

give some better explanation of its absence than its loss overboard in his portmanteau in the gale. Never denying his real name, he explained his want of luggage by the plea that the guineas in his pocket were far more convenient for the business, the purchase of coals, on which he was bound. At his own request he was permitted to write to a friend at Dublin for proof of his statements, and no reply being received was removed thither in custody. On his way to the capital, at Drogheda, he revealed his real character by the treasonable language in which he indulged, and subsequently by writing a letter to his fellow-countrymen, in which, whilst calling on them to be "patient as lambs and as watchful as lions," he recommended them "not to place confidence in the acquaintance of any man where life and death is depending;" and "when any favourable opportunity occurred," which he intimated might shortly happen, "not as heretofore to take up arms merely to lay them down again, and then to be taken prisoners and die like dogs. Never attempt a revolution of your country, unless you are sober, steady, and determined; then you may expect to conquer, and free your long enslaved country, and be remembered with gratitude by posterity." Against the direct evidence of the accomplice M'Cabe, and misstatements of the prisoner of his acts in Dublin before he tried to escape, no counter-evidence was attempted to be brought. In testimony to character, not of a very satisfactory kind, and in a bitter attack on the King's witness, who stood self-confessed a rebel in "98," and whose only reason for joining Emmet was because he was asked, and who had been taken armed on the fatal 23rd, and saved his own life by turning against his fellow-rebels, the whole defence was rested. Unreliable as was such evidence in itself, it was too clearly supported by other independent testimony to be effectually impeached. Conviction and execution necessarily followed. Before he was sentenced he boldly avowed his position under the Provisional Government, and his fervent desire for the success of the late attempt. Like his leader, he was young in years—but three-and-twenty—though old in treason.

The leader of the insane attempt was brought to trial on the 19th September. The usual counsel appeared for the Crown, and his defence was entrusted to Mr. Burrowes and Mr. McNally. Public expectation was disappointed in Curran not appearing to defend his young friend; and no little indignation aroused, and with reason, by Mr. Plunket, as one of the counsel for the prosecution, exercising the right of reply—though not only no witnesses, even to character, had been called on behalf of Emmet, but not even a word said by his counsel in his defence—and in using that opportunity for a bitter personal attack on the young fanatic. It astonished even those who were accustomed to the sudden political conversions of the time, to hear one so lately the bitterest and most outspoken opponent of the Government, acting as a courtier, and exceeding in the violence of his diatribe against the prisoner the worst specimens of Crown counsel speeches of former days. His reward was not long delayed. Mr. Plunket, the most violent of the opponents of the Union, kissed hands as Solicitor-

General for Ireland within a few months of the execution of Emmet.[1]

To Curran, Emmet had been well known from boyhood. He was a frequent visitor at Curran's house, and unknown to her father had been for some time attached to his youngest daughter. When arrested, letters from Miss Curran and her family were found in his possession, and in consequence Curran's house was searched, in the hopes, no doubt, of implicating him in the designs of his young friend. Curran at once tendered himself to be examined by the Privy Council, and despite the attempt of one of its members to treat him with harshness, thanks to the interference of the Attorney-General was received with deserved kindness, and saved from further trouble.[2] Emmet's conduct towards his old friend was worthy of his best feelings. He offered to plead guilty if the letters to Curran's daughter were suppressed, and it was refused. There was still a wish in some quarters to drag Curran's name into the affair. Emmet again offered, not only to plead guilty, but to furnish the fullest information in his power, short of giving names, if the lives of his followers could be spared. His offer was rejected. The Government would not be satisfied with only one victim—though that victim was the leader. At his trial, though he formally pleaded "Not Guilty," he would not allow a single question to be put in his defence that could by any possibility implicate others; and until the verdict was given he steadfastly refused to say, or to allow his counsel to say for him, a single

[1] See trial of Cobbett for libel on Plunket.
[2] Curran's Life, by his Son, p. 224.

extenuating word. He bore Plunket's unwarrantable speech with patience; and let it be seen, from the first to the last of the trial, that he submitted to it as a mere formality, determined that nothing he should say or sanction should avert the verdict. When called up for judgment he gave a free rein to his pent-up feelings, attempting to justify his conduct and explain his real motives, in overstrained and unnatural language. " Why the usual sentence of the law should not be passed upon him, he had nothing to say. Why the sentence which in the public mind is usually attached to the law ought to be reversed, he had much to say." Repudiating with indignation the charge of being an emissary of France, " I did not wish," he said, " to join this country with France. I did join—I did not create, the rebellion—not for France, but for liberty. It is true there were communications between the United Irishmen and France; it is true that in consequence of them the war was no surprise on us. But the only question with the Provisional Government was— whether France should come to this country as an enemy; whether she should have any pretext for so doing; whether the people should look to France as their only deliverer, or through the medium and control of the Provisional Government attain their object." Bitterly attacking the conduct of France to Switzerland, Holland, and Italy, he called on his countrymen to fight to the last against the French, " to meet them on the shore with a torch in one hand and a sword in the other—to immolate them in their boats before our native soil shall be polluted by a foreign foe." Should they land, " burn every blade of grass before them—

raze every house;" and if driven to the centre of the country, "collect your provisions, your property, your wives, your daughters; form a circle round them; fight while two men are left, and when one only remains, let that man set fire to the pile, and release himself and the families of his fallen countrymen from the tyranny of France." This portion of his address passed unnoticed by the Court; when, however, he admitted that his intention was to effect a separation from England, and avowed that had he power he would repeat his act, he was sharply reprehended by Lord Norbury, and warned to confine himself to urging any point of law in his favour. Emmet would not be silenced; and despite the repeated interruptions by the Judge, in which the language of the one was as bitterly personal as that of the other treasonable, persevered in his justification, until the discussion degenerated to a wrangle. Before, however, he was finally stopped, Emmet repeated that he did not create the conspiracy; that he found it when he arrived in Dublin, and was solicited to join it; took time to consider; was told that whether he joined or not it would go on; and then, finding his own principles to accord with the measure, joined—and under the same circumstances would do so again.

Before his execution, which took place on the next day, in St. Thomas Street, Emmet handed, for transmission to his brother Thomas, a lengthy account of his plans, and the cause of their failure. Briefly, the plans of attack menaced three points in the city—the Pigeon House, the Castle, and the Artillery Barracks at Island Bridge, for each of which a separate division of his forces was appointed. To render these attempts more certain, "Points of check," as he called them, were marked out in the city, where other detachments were to prevent the guards from rendering assistance, and if necessary to occupy these as posts of vantage. Lastly came lines of defence, to be formed by chains, and barricades of carriages and butchers' carts, aided by the loaded beams discovered in the depôt. In addition, the bridges over the Liffey were to be covered with boards full of nails, and with spikes driven through them into the pavement, more effectually to stop the troops of either arm. In these plans every detail was set out with notable care, and evidence given of the completeness of Emmet's designs. Copying old schemes, the attack on the Castle was to have been commenced by the entry of two hackney carriages, in each of which were to have been armed men, who were to rush out and seize the guard; and provision was made for otherwise effecting an entrance in the case of this design failing. What was to be done with prisoners of note in the case of success is not stated; but should the rebels be driven to retreat after only a partial success, "the Lord Lieutenant and principal officers of the Government, with the artillery, were to be sent off under a guard to the Wicklow mountains."

Of these plans, for the execution of which some 2000 men were to be detailed out of the 3000 or 4000 in Dublin alone whom he believed to be acquainted with them, all but the attack on the Castle and the lines of defence were abandoned, for lack of support. The hour of assembly was from six to nine, and at the latter time, instead of 2000, only eighty men assembled. Added to this, from a series of disappointments the preparations were incomplete—scarcely any fire-arms brought up—the man who was to turn the fuzees and hammers for the beams absent in Kildare—the jointed pikes stored in Patrick Street, lost by the explosion—the work impeded by the confusion and crowding of the men on the eve of departure—the cramp-irons still at the smith's—only one scaling-ladder completed—and the money required for the purchase of the fire-arms, without which the people would not move, delayed until five o'clock on the day. To change the day was impossible, because he expected the counties to act, and feared to lose the advantage of a surprise. The Kildare men were coming in for three days, and after that it was impossible to draw back. "Had I," he continues, " had another week—had I 1000*l.*—had I 1000 men—I would have feared nothing. There was redundancy enough in any one part, if complete, to have made up for the deficiency of the rest; but there was failure in all—plan, preparation, and men. It would have given it the respectability of an insurrection, but I did not wish uselessly to spill blood. I gave no signal for the rest, and they all escaped." There is no reason to doubt the truth of Emmet's last words; he was above a falsehood. He may have been deceived by his agents as to the extent to which his design had been adopted by Dublin. It was, however, undoubtedly known to many hundreds, and the secret kept with a fidelity worthy of a better cause. One traitor there was who was in correspondence with Secretary Marsden; and when the scheme came to a sudden and ignominious end, as usual, others aided as witnesses for the Crown in convicting their comrades. Possessed, as we now know the Government officials were, of the fullest information of the presence in Ireland of dangerous men, old offenders, and of their movements in various parts of the country, even if ignorant of the actual preparations in Dublin, they stand condemned on their own admissions of culpable negligence. Even if they had only "the five hours' notice by expresses from Kildare," as stated by Emmet, had those in authority been equal to the occasion the pitiable loss of life would have been prevented, and the city spared the two hours of danger to which it was subjected by their indecision and apathy.

In the brief interval between his conviction and execution, in addition to the document, from which extracts have been made, explaining his plan in detail, Emmet wrote two letters—one to Curran and the other to his son Richard—explaining the grounds on which he had sought the love of the daughter, in tender yet manly language, and affording a striking proof of how little he was affected by his approaching fate. "The same enthusiasm," truly says Curran's biographer, "which allured him to his destiny, enabled him to support its utmost rigour. He met his fate with unostentatious fortitude; and although few could ever think of justifying his projects or regretting their failure, yet his youth, his talents, the great respectability of his connexions, and the evident delusion of which he was the victim, have excited more general sympathy for his unfortunate end, and more forbearance towards his memory, than is usually extended to the errors and sufferings of political offenders." [3]

[3] Life of the Right Honourable J. P. Curran, by his son, W. H. Curran, who adds, " There is reason to believe, that had he attended solely to his safety he could easily have effected his departure from the kingdom ; but in the same spirit of romantic enthusiasm which distinguished his short career, he could not submit to leave a country to which he should never more return, without making an effort to have one final interview with the object of his unfortunate attachment, in order to receive her personal forgiveness for what he now considered as the deepest injury. It was apparently with a view to obtaining this last gratification that he selected the place of concealment in which he was discovered ; he was arrested in a house situated midway between Dublin and Mr. Curran's country seat."

CHAPTER VI.

THE LIBELS OF THE TROJAN HORSE,
AND
THE ANTI-JACOBIN.

FEBRUARY 1804 TO NOVEMBER 1805.

THE conduct of the Irish Government in connexion with Emmet's insane attempt naturally furnished the journalists and pamphleteers of their political opponents with a favourable theme for hostile criticisms, to which the statements in Parliament offered no adequate reply. Many of these attacks were undoubtedly unfounded, and all were bitterly personal. Had they, however, appeared in our time, they would have been treated with silent contempt, and allowed to sink all the more readily into oblivion by being unnoticed. The day has passed for party politicians to bring actions of libel, or for Government to file criminal informations against their political critics. It was not so when these attacks appeared. Successive Attorney-Generals seemed to vie with each other in the ready use of criminal informations—the powers of Parliament over printers and publishers were constantly appealed to, and political libels were nearly as frequently the ground of actions in the Courts as those of a more personal character. It was therefore quite in the usual course that some of the libels in relation to the late lamentable event should be prosecuted by the Government and the individuals who were attacked. On two journals the heavy hand of the law fell—the *Political Register* of Cobbett, the organ of Mr. Wyndham, and the *Anti-Jacobin*, of which Canning was the mainspring.

The position of Cobbett as a political writer was but little understood at a time when such writers were so strictly divided between the friends and the opponents of the Government.

His *Political Register*, though started only the year before, with funds contributed by Dr. Lawrence and Mr. Wyndham, had rapidly risen into popularity, and won considerable influence from the accuracy of its information and the powerful and plain language of its editor, who professed a strong conservative attachment to the Constitution, united with a deep affection for the cause of the people. Over the windows of his shop in Pall Mall were the emblems of the Crown and Mitre; and so bitter was his opposition to the Peace of Amiens, that on the night of the illumination in its honour his house was attacked and his windows smashed by the crowd. Constant in his hatred of Napoleon, and of the French notions of liberty, in July, 1803, he had composed an address to the people of England on the imminent prospect of invasion, which had been accepted by the Government, printed in large numbers, and sent to the parochial clergy, with instructions to place copies on the doors and in the pews of their churches, and to distribute them freely among the poorer members of their flock. For the Cabinet, and especially for its Premier, Mr. Addington, he expressed the most supreme contempt for their folly in trusting the professions of Bonaparte, and lost no opportunity of ridiculing and denouncing their political measures. Hence, therefore, the readiness with which in "The Chronicle of Events" in his *Register* he represented the conduct of the Government in Emmet's affair in the worst light, and admitted communications from Irish correspondents, reflecting with bitter personality on Lord Hardwicke, the Chancellor Redesdale, and the Secretary, Mr. Marsden, and accusing them of making General Fox a scapegoat for their own negligence and incompetency. Some of these letters appeared under the signature of "Hibernicus," others under that of "Juverna." Though both writers were equally pointed in their attacks on the corruption and imbecility of the Irish Government, the letters of the former were allowed to pass unnoticed, and on those of "Juverna" alone informations and actions for libel were instituted against Cobbett and his publisher, and subsequently against one of the Irish Judges, to whom the authorship was imputed.

"Hibernicus" had not confined his attacks to Emmet's matter,* severe, and to some extent unfounded, as some of his criticisms on that affair undoubtedly were. He openly accused the Government of allowing the sale of Commissionerships of

Public Accounts, giving the names of the holders in four successive vacancies, and the price paid by each for his lucrative appointment. Of these accusations neither the parties implicated nor the Government took any notice. "For this shameful increase of the revenue incidents,"[1] continued "Hibernicus," "to the amount of 57,000*l.* a year—for his appointment of the Attorney-General to be a third counsel to the Revenue Board—for his suffering the sale of four Commissionerships—for his supineness and inattention to the state of Ireland, whereby His Majesty's Chief Justice was sacrificed and the capital nearly surprised, not only was his brother made a Secretary of State, a gallant veteran traduced and recalled,[2] but, as is reported, his Excellency himself is to be graced with the highest mark of his Sovereign's approbation—to be honoured with the Garter." These charges were repeated in "Juverna's" first letter, and the further one made, that money intended for the troops in Ireland was wasted on the country residence of Lord Hardwicke and his Secretary. Still neither his Excellency nor the Government interfered to check the scandal. A third and fourth letter from "Juverna" followed, on the 29th October and the 24th December, 1805. In that of October the legend of the Wooden Horse of Troy was applied to

---

[1] "By the accounts laid before the United Parliament it appears," said "Hibernicus," "that the revenue incidents, pensions, and gratuities of Ireland have increased 57,000*l.* since 1800, a sum almost equal to half the expenditure on those heads before the Union."

[2] General Fox removed to a command in the Mediterranean.

the imputed woodenheadedness of the Lord Lieutenant; the Government was accused of having selected the junior Judge on the Bench for the trial of the prisoners in Antrim on account of his known political bias; and a contrast, personally most unfavourable, and from its imputations of official misconduct legally libellous, was drawn between the character of Lord Chancellor Lord Redesdale and the late Chief Justice Kenyon, eulogizing the impartiality and independence of the latter, and condemning the servility and party bias of the former.

The application of the legend of Laocoon, though somewhat laboured, was ingenious and amusing. "*Equo ne credite Teucri*," said the writer, " was the advice which in a dangerous moment Laocoon gave to the Trojans. The author did not mean to confine it to Troy alone; he meant to take advantage of metaphor, by which a certain species of head is called a 'wooden one.' He meant to caution future nations not to put trust or confidence in the apparent innocence of any such wooden instrument, and not to suffer themselves to exalt it into consequence, and not to pay it any respect. He meant to tell that any people who submitted to be governed by a wooden head would not find their security in its supposed innoxiousness, as its hollowness would soon be occupied by instruments of mischief. When I found this portion of the kingdom was threatened by such consequences to our property as the rapacity of Mr. Marsden and his friends, and the pikes of Mr. Emmet and his friends have lately produced—when I could trace all these evils as the inevitable issue from the head and body of such a Government as that of Lord Hardwicke, and I am told of his uxoriousness and firmness, I still reply—The story of the Wooden Horse."

The writer then professes not to impute a wooden head to Lord Hardwicke, though he "fears that were it submitted to a Lavoisier it would be found to contain a superabundant portion of ligneous tendency," and applies to the imputed innocence of the Lord Lieutenant, Burke's words, "They who truly mean well must be fearful of acting ill. Delusive good intention is no excuse for presumption; the Government of a harmless man is not a harmless Government." The writer, however, has inquired for the reasons for his appointment, and the result is that he has discovered that the Viceroy " was in rank an earl, in manners a gentleman, in morals a good father and a kind husband, and that he had a good library in St. James's Square." Further, he has found, "on the authority of one Lindsay, a Scotch parson—since by Divine permission, for it would be impossible to account for it on secondary causes, Bishop of Killaloe in Ireland—that he is celebrated for understanding the modern method of fattening sheep as well as any man in Cambs."

"Juverna" then puts the case of the proprietors of one of our West Indian Islands, threatened with immediate invasion, applying to Doctor Addington for assistance, and describes their consternation on being comforted by the assurance "that he had entrusted the case of their island to a very eminent sheep farmer from Cambridgeshire, who was to be assisted in all his counsels by a very able and strong-limbed Chancery pleader from Lincoln's Inn." Commenting then on the danger of entrusting the government of Ireland at such a crisis to such persons, and promising to speak more at length at another opportunity on the mischief caused by the intermeddling of the "strong chancery pleader," he calls attention to the fact of Lord Hardwicke having had no previous chance of showing his fitness for such a position. "What," he asks, "is he one of the tribe of Hobarts, Westmorelands, and Camdens? Is he one of that tribe who have been sent over to us to be trained up here as politicians, as they train surgeons' apprentices in the hospitals, by setting them at first to bleed pauper patients? Is this the time for the continuation of these experiments? The gift of Lord Hardwicke to us at such a period cannot be compared to anything else than the prank of Falstaff at the battle of Shrewsbury, when the Knight handed over his pistols to the Prince. For indeed, sir, by the present to us of Lord Hardwicke that sentence has proved to us a bloody truth which Falstaff said in a good-humoured jest, "Here is what will sack a city."

In selecting these passages as one of the grounds for the indictment, and omitting others of a graver character, the Crown lawyers acted with judgment. It would hardly have served their cause to have taken legal notice of the contrast "Juverna" drew between the conduct of the King in 1780, "when he came to his Council and told his silent magistrates that if they did not know or would not do their duty, he did know and would do it"—with that of

Lord Hardwicke "at five o'clock in the evening slinking from the meditated scene of action, doubling his guards in a remote spot, consigning the awful night to the wisdom of the little green desk of a clerk, and waiting at a prudential distance till day rose, and then returning with quadruple guards to assemble a council." Voltaire's sarcastic words on the imbecility of the later Roman Emperors were then aptly applied to the Lord Lieutenant, and in the words of the lines of the schoolboy on the miracle at Cana, the writer professed to believe that when first admitted to the presence of his gallant master, "the wood of Lord Hardwicke might exhibit the same consciousness as the waters of Judæa—et erubescat." Did the contrast savour too much of truthfulness to be put before a jury, even in those days, though the verdict were to be controlled by an Ellenborough?

Having thus dealt with the Lord Lieutenant, "Juverna" proceeded to attack Mr. Justice Osborne, who had been selected by the Chancellor to hold the Special Commission for the trial of the prisoners in Antrim; and Mr. Secretary Marsden, by whose influence he assumed this selection had been made, by which the junior Judge was preferred to all his seniors on the Bench. The writer professed to discover the real reason for this preference in that portion of the Judge's charge to the grand jury in which he was reported to have said, "that through the well-timed efforts and strenuous exertions of a wise and energetic Government, the progress of such crimes as lately disgraced the country had been effectually checked." No one, he declared could have stated such an untruth but under the influence of the Castle and the promptings and instructions of Secretary Marsden. "I may, I believe, add," continued the writer, "that men also say, that if it were possible the ermined robe of the most awful attribute of his Majesty should have been wrapped round the acts of Mr. Marsden, in order to screen them from public disgrace, we might then look for another not less fatal end to our liberties and our Constitution than that which rebellion or invasion could produce. And in truth, they say, that except as to momentary effects, rebellion and invasion might be viewed with indifference if it can be supposed that the stained hands of a petty clerk had been washed in the very fountain of justice." In this stilted language a general charge of tampering with the administration of justice is clearly made. What more might be meant was probably more intelligible to those to whom it was addressed than it is to readers of the present day.

"Juverna" now fulfils his promise of returning to the "strong chancery pleader," and in the form of a comparison of what Lord Kenyon would have done had he been Chancellor, brings most serious charges against Lord Redesdale. "Lord Kenyon," he writes, "would have acted with reserve and circumspection on his arrival in a country with the moral qualities of the inhabitants of which, and with their persons, manners, and individual characters and connexions, he must have been utterly unacquainted. In such a country, torn with domestic sedition and treason, and threatened with foreign invasion, and aching since the Union under an untried Constitution, if

Doctor•Addington had required that Lord Kenyon should direct a Cambridgeshire earl in all his councils, Lord Kenyon would as soon at the desire of Lord St. Vincent have undertaken to pilot a line-of-battle ship through the Needles. Particularly the integrity of Lord Kenyon would have shrunk from such an undertaking if a condition had been added to it that no one nobleman or gentleman who possessed any rank, estate, or connexion in the said part of the United Kingdom should be consulted by the Government thereof. His pride would have spurned at the undertaking if he were told that to the Cambridgeshire earl and himself in the cares of Government, a clerk in the Secretary's office (Marsden) and a couple of lawyers (the Attorney-General and the new Solicitor-General, Mr. Plunket), without political habits, political information, or honourable connexion, were to be joined as assessors, and to be the only assessors. His pride and integrity, would have joined in preventing him from being himself the instrument of introducing such men into a cabinet of government."

This general attack on the Chancellor was made apparently only to lead up to the personal attack on Mr. Plunket, of whom Emmet on his trial was made to have spoken " as 'that viper whom my father nourished. He it was from whose lips I first imbibed those principles and doctrines which now by their effects drag me to my grave ; and he it is who is now brought forward as my prosecutor, and who by an unheard-of exercise of the prerogative, has wantonly lashed with a speech to evidence the dying son of his former friend, when that dying son had produced no evidence, had made no defence, but, on the contrary, had acknowledged the charge and submitted to his fate.' To suppose that Lord Kenyon would have recommended such a man was not to be dreamt of, especially when the writer remembered how a noble duke had been struck out of the Privy Council for toasting the sovereignty of the people at a drunken club; and that this man in a grave assembly"—alluding to Plunket's bitter speeches against the Union Bill—"had declared that a law which was disagreeable to the people, however it might have been enacted with all legal and parliamentary solemnity, nevertheless was not binding on them."

Besides thus charging the Chancellor with recommending a base and disloyal man for promotion, "Juverna" accused him of making an order diverting the fees of the secretary of the Master of the Rolls into the hands of his own secretary, "in order that he might discharge the pension of some unknown annuitant on his judicial profits;" "of entering into a combination to sap underhand the independence of the Judges; of suffering the Great Seal to be used for the purpose of garbling the Bench in order to gratify those who might be contented to publicly eulogize that Government which privately they despised;" and of "employing his leisure in searching into offices for practices by which he might harass the domestic arrangements of others, whose pride and whose integrity would not bend to his views, and thus double the vigour of his attack, by practising on the hopes of some and endeavouring to work on the fears of others."

On such paragraphs as these, with others of less personal character, comprising, however, about a third of the whole correspondence, an information was filed against Cobbett, and tried on the 24th of May, 1804, by a special jury, under the direction of Lord Ellenborough and other judges. For the Crown, besides the usual law officers, Erskine, Garrow, Dallas, and Abbott appeared; and the defence was entrusted to Adam and Richardson.

For the Crown the evidence was limited to proof of the publication of the libel within the jurisdiction of the Court, and the identification of the Cambridgeshire earl, the strong chancery pleader, the junior Judge, and the clerk in the Secretary's office, with Lord Redesdale, the Chancellor, Mr. Justice Osborne, and Mr. Marsden. For Cobbett, it was argued that he was a good father, an excellent husband, a virtuous subject of the king, and one who had uniformly in all his conduct, public and private, in this country and abroad, endeavoured to uphold the true Constitution of England, and who for twelve years of his public life had never once till the present time, been questioned for a libel on the Government of any country, or even by his worst enemies accused of being an advocate of misrule. As for the libel itself, it was contended that it was an attack on the political and not on the personal character of any of the parties, and that the remarks on Lord Hardwicke were simply ridicule. As evidence to Cobbett's character, besides the late British Minister in America, Lord Henry Stuart, who had known him in that country, Mr. Wyndham, Lord Minto, and Lord Hardwicke's brother, Charles Yorke, were called, and united in describing him as an ardent loyalist and zealous supporter of the Constitution. Lord Ellenborough in his summing up admitted the right of subjects to exhibit the folly or the imbecility of the members of the Government, but only within reasonable limits. Of the evidence to character, he briefly said that it only went to render a charge doubtful, but that in this case there could be no doubt of publication. If the jury thought the publication to be hurtful to the Government, or individuals of the Government, they must find the defendant guilty; if destructive of the peace neither of the one nor the other, they must acquit him. A verdict of Guilty was of course given without hesitation.[3]

Two days after, an action by Mr. Plunket against Cobbett, for those portions of "Juverna's" letter in which he was specially attacked, was tried in the same court, Erskine leading for the plaintiff, and the same counsel appearing for Cobbett as in the trial of the information. In addition to the passages already quoted, another one was set out in the pleadings, in which, referring to the supposed attack of Emmet on Plunket, it was said "Lord Kenyon would have turned in

[3] Cobbett's trial was held before Lord Chief Justice Ellenborough, May 24, 1804. Attorney-General (Perceval), Solicitor-General (Manners Sutton), Erskine, Garrow, Dallas, and Abbott, for the Crown. Adam, afterwards First Commissioner of Jury Court, Scotland, and Richardson, afterwards a Judge of Common Pleas, for the defendant. In Plunket's case, May 26, the same counsel appeared for Cobbett, but Erskine led for the plaintiff.

horror from such a scene, in which, though guilt was in one part to be punished, yet in the whole drama justice was confounded, humanity outraged, and loyalty insulted. Of Lord Kenyon it never could have been believed that he himself would lead such a character forward to introduce him to the favour of his Sovereign, clothe him in the robes, and load him with the emoluments, of office." Erskine in his opening speech spoke strongly on the absence of any attempt on Cobbett's part to prove the truth of the words attributed to Emmet, or the speech in the Irish Parliament of which Plunket was accused, and put aside as any answer to such a libel, the anticipated defence of the defendant's high character as a father, a husband, and a loyalist.

The defendant's counsel having called Mr. Forster, the Speaker of the late Irish House of Commons to prove that Mr. Plunket was a member, and took part in the Union debates, Adam endeavoured to get from him an admission of some speech of the plaintiff's justifying that portion of the libel. The ex-Speaker refused on the ground of his position to remember any thing that passed in the House during the time of his Speakership. Too persevering to be thus foiled, Cobbett's advocate cited from Plunket's published speeches a passage going far to justify the pretended quotation of " Juverna." " In the most express terms," Plunket had said, " I deny the competency of Parliament to do this. *I tell you that if, circumstanced as you are, you pass this Act, it will be a mere nullity, and that no man in Ireland will be bound to obey it. I make the assertion deliberately. I repeat it*; and I call on any man who knows me to take down my words." It may be possible to attach a meaning to these words different to that which the reported speech was clearly intended to convey. But to say the least, it speaks but poorly for political honour or consistency to find their author a law officer of the Crown under the Union Act, which he declared no one need obey, within but a few years after it had become law.

Following up this home-thrust, Adam justly ridiculed the idea of any personal injury to the author of the published speech from the edition of it published by "Juverna." "He was," said Adam, "his Majesty's Solicitor-General in Ireland at the time of the publication of the libel; and you have it still that he is in the confidence of the Irish Government—that for five years he had allowed his reported words to be sent into every corner of the kingdom, in newspapers and pamphlets, without a complaint or a contradiction; and it was absurd to say that he had been injured by the letter of 'Juverna.'" Adam also, in mitigation of damages, alluded to the narrow means of the defendant, and urged the jury, if they found against him, to consider them in the amount of damages. Lord Ellenburgh of course told the jury that in the absence of any plea of justification they must not pay any attention to the quotation from the published speeches of the plaintiff, and that the reparation due to him, and not the means of the defendant, was the real test of the measure of damages. The result was, that, after a brief consultation, the jury awarded 500*l.* as damages against Cobbett, not one sixpence of which as far as can be discovered was ever paid by the defendant, nor was he ever called up for judgment on his conviction under the Government information.[4]

The truth probably was, that Cobbett had been attacked only as the means of getting at the real author of the letters, the legal phraseology of which, in addition to the grievance made of the nomination of the junior Judge for the Antrim Commission over the heads of his elders, had raised the impression that they were from the pen of a lawyer, and in all probability from that of one of the Judges thus put aside in favour of a junior on the Bench. Cobbett, annoyed at being led into this serious trouble, and as a means, no doubt, of making his peace with Government and evading both the fine and the punishment, gave up the letters. Further inquiry disclosed the strong resemblance of the handwriting with that of Mr. Justice Robert Johnson, one of the Judges of the Irish Common Pleas, for many years previous to his elevation to the ermine Counsel to the Commissioners of Customs in Ireland and a member of the Irish Parliament.

Then it was that the Government determined to proceed against Judge Johnson, but were met by a legal difficulty, which for a time appeared not unlikely to balk them of their intention. The libel had been published in England, though in all probability written in Ireland, and the Judge resided in the latter country,

---

[4] Mr. Smith, the latest biographer of Cobbett, agrees with me in this opinion. Mr. Speaker Abbot, in his "Diary," under date June 9, 1804, says that the Attorney-General (Perceval) protested against any engagement or understanding, direct or indirect, that the surrender of the original MS. of the letters should alter the consequences of Cobbett's conviction.

to which no English writ could run. An appeal was, therefore made to the provisions of an Act only lately passed, which was nominally "to render more easy the apprehension and bringing to trial of offenders escaping from one part of the United Kingdom to another, and from one county to another."[5] It was said, but denied, that the Act was passed to meet the case ; and it is curious to note that it was fathered in the House of Commons by Lord Redesdale's brother-in-law, Perceval, and by Lord Hardwicke's brother, Mr. Yorke. By it power was given to a magistrate in one part of the kingdom to give validity, by his endorsement, to a writ issued in another part. Under this power, on the 24th of November, 1805, Judge Johnson was arrested at his house in Dublin, by a warrant signed by Lord Ellenborough, countersigned by Mr. Bell, a Dublin magistrate, to answer an information of the English Attorney-General's for the publication of this libel.

By this procedure there was a special hardship, as under the Act no one could be bailed until he had come into that portion of the kingdom in which the alleged offence was committed. Judge Johnson, therefore, could not be bailed until he reached Holyhead—even if, as a stranger, he could obtain it there—and though a serious invalid at the time of his arrest, would have to be hurried over at once to the sister country. Apart from this legal difficulty, the Judge, according to his own account, had grave reasons for complaining of the time and manner of his arrest. In the previous summer he had heard that persons were

[5] 44 George III. c. 92. Royal assent, July 20, 1804.

prepared to recognize his handwriting in the "Juverna" MS., and that some charge for a misdemeanour was likely to be made against him in England. He felt, he said, that the letters, libel or not·libel, did not ininvolve any moral guilt ; and that if he were tried in Ireland, where he was known, he must be acquitted.

Four months of severe illness now confined him to his house, during which he heard of the passing of the new Act, and of the report that under its powers he was to be arrested and taken to England for trial. To this report he paid little attention, as he read the Act as applicable only to those who had *actually escaped* from one country to the other, and therefore not to one who, like himself, simply resided in a different part of the kingdom to that in which the offence was committed. In December his illness had become so severe that he was advised to go to Bath for the waters. Fearing that if he did so he should be arrested, he wrote to Lord Hardwicke for an assurance that during his necessary stay there he should be unmolested. Marsden, in reply, curtly wrote him, that if he found sufficient bail the warrant then in force should not be executed ; and three days after informed him, that if bail was not given at once he should be taken. Regarding his giving bail as tantamount to an admission of the legality of the warrant, a request was made by a friend to the Chief Secretary for leave to go to Bath, and for copies of the documents under which he was threatened with arrest, in order that he might take legal advice on their validity. The reply was so evasive that his friends considered the warrant a fiction, and only used to induce him to put in bail ; or as so doubtful in its legality that the Government had been advised not to use it. A further appeal to the Lord Lieutenant brought a letter from the Solicitor to the Treasury, warning him that unless he agreed at once to put in bail and enter an appearance for the next term, the warrant would be executed. To this he merely wrote that his counsel were out of town. On the 17th, therefore, the officers came to his house, tendered the consent for his signature ; and on his stating that he was waiting for a reply to his last letter, and would not leave the house, went away without executing the warrant. On the morrow they returned with peremptory orders, and on his refusing to sign the consent, the warrant was executed, and Judge Johnson taken in his own carriage to the house of a relative in Dublin. There he was told that he must proceed at once to England. On the road to the river side, under the pretence of calling on a friend, by the connivance of his coachman he was driven to Chief Justice Donne's house, and there kept by him until the fiat for the writ of Habeas could be issued, and the first step taken for trying the validity of the warrant.[6]

[6] The case was first heard before the Lord Chief Justice and seven other Judges, and in consequence of the difference of opinion among them adjourned into the Queen's Bench. It was reported that three considered that Mr. Justice Johnson should be remanded, and an equal number that he should be discharged, the other two declining to give an opinion without further argument. It was argued in the Queen's Bench January 26, 1805, and judgment given January 31. In the Exchequer February 4, judgment February 7 ; and subsequently in the Common Pleas, with the same result. The arguments and

The battle over the writ of Habeas was fought out in all the three courts, with the same result, the refusal of the writ by a majority of the judges in each of them. The decision turned on two points : First, whether in the words in the statute, "Felons and other malefactors," the latter word must not be confined to offenders of the same genus as felons, and was therefore inapplicable to misdemeanants. Secondly, whether the operation of the Act was not confined to those who, after being charged or arrested, had escaped from one part of the kingdom to another where the original warrant would, but for this statute, be inoperative, or whether the words "go into, reside, or be," enable proceedings, initiated in England for an offence committed there by a resident in Ireland, to be made available against him in that country. For Johnson, Curran held the leading brief, and to judge from his reported speeches in the King's Bench and Exchequer was quite out of his element in a case requiring a dry legal argument, and in which pathos, wit, and sarcasm, with lively denunciations of kidnapping, including that of the Duke D'Enghien, however attractive and popular, were sadly misplaced. The strict legal acumen and close argument wanting in this brilliant orator were amply supplied by the other counsel for Johnson, and especially by his namesake. They failed, however, to do more than create a difference among the Judges and to protract the decision until an amendment Act was passed by which the

judgments in the King's Bench and Exchequer, with the judgments, are reported apparently verbatim in Howell, vol. xxix. pp. 215—359.

same power of bailing the prisoner was given to the justice who endorsed the warrant, as had by the original Act been limited to a justice in the country or county in which the alleged offence had been committed, and to which place the prisoner was to be conveyed "by the most direct way."[7]

In the debate on this latter Act in the House of Commons, in reply to the charge that the original Act had been passed to meet Johnson's case, it was said that the bill had been drawn for the session preceding that in which it was introduced, and not *pro hâc vice*, and that leave to introduce it had been obtained some days before Cobbett's conviction and some time before his surrender of the MS. of the letters.[8] The explanation was fair to look at, and no more. For it must be borne in mind that from their first publication it was clear that these letters had been written in Ireland, most probably by a local lawyer, and presumably by one in a position to be sensitive at the preference shown by the selection of Mr. Justice Osborn. It may, therefore, be fairly conceived, that one object of the Act was to meet the case of such an offender, if not indeed of that particular one. Thanks

---

[7] 54 George III. c. 186.

[8] On February 8 Mr. Fitzgerald called the attention of the Attorney-General to the defect in the Act as to bail, and repeated it on April 30, when the Attorney-General announced his intention to introduce an amendment Act, which he did May 27. It was on that occasion that the explanation stated in the text was made. June 25, in House of Lords, Duke of Cumberland presented petition from Johnson praying that the Amendment Act might be so amended as not to apply to his case. Bill passed June 27. Royal assent July 10, 1805.

to these delays the case did not begin to get to a hearing in the King's Bench in England until the 29th of June. Then a plea to the jurisdiction, on the ground that the defendant was born in Ireland, and the libels related to events in Ireland whilst he was resident there was put in, and unanimously overruled by the Bench, on the ground that it did not set out any other tribunal by which the defendant could be tried. This step threw the case over the long vacation, so that it was not until the 23rd November that the case really came to trial before a special jury and a full bench of judges with the usual counsel for the Crown, and Adam, most effectually assisted by Allan Park, then in his prime, for the defendant.[9]

From Cobbett, who now appeared as a witness for the Crown, it appeared that previously to the receipt of the first of the "Juverna" letters he had received an anonymous communication from Ireland, asking if he would accept certain useful and true information respecting Irish affairs, and suggesting that the reply, in the answers to correspondents in the next *Register*, should be as if to a correspondent from York. On this being done, the letters themselves came to him *seriatim* in envelopes addressed to his publisher, were regularly printed and published without correction, and in some cases portions of the MSS. accidentally destroyed at the printing-office. Over the envelopes,

---

[9] Before Lord Ellenborough and Justices Grose, Lawrence, and Le Blanc. Attorney-General (Perceval), Solicitor-General (Sir Vicary Gibbs), Erskine, Garrow, Wood (afterwards a Baron of the Exchequer), and Abbott, for the Crown. Adam, Park, Lockhart, and Richardson for Defendant.

which could not be produced, and on which Cobbett swore that there was the Dublin post-mark, a keen battle ensued on the question whether there was sufficient evidence of their destruction to admit of parol evidence being given of the direction and post-mark on them. The struggle was again and again renewed on its appearing that portions of the MSS. themselves had been destroyed in the printing-office. A further contest arose on the absence of any direct proof by independent testimony of a request from Johnson for the publication of the letters, the evidence of which was confined to the references in the later letters to passages in the former ones, and to the promises of further remarks in subsequent communications. In support of the last objection the case of the Seven Bishops was cited, but it was held to be inapplicable, and this with the other points ruled against the defendant.

On the failure of these objections the real defence was raised—a denial of the letters being in the Judge's handwriting, as sought to be proved by the Crown witnesses, and an attempt to prove that a person of the name of Card was the real author, and that he would have admitted the authorship but for the fears he entertained of losing the place he held under the Irish Government. The witnesses on the part of the Crown to prove the Judge's handwriting were persons who had been clerks to the Commissioners of Revenue during the time when Mr. Johnson had been their counsel, and who, therefore, had constant opportunities of seeing his handwriting in legal opinions on revenue cases, and a solicitor who had known him personally as well as professionally for twenty years. These unanimously and unhesitatingly agreed that the portions of the letters shown them were in the handwriting of the Judge.

On the defendant's part, Sir Henry Jebb, who had been his physician and friend for thirty years; Mr. Hodgkinson, the senior fellow of Trinity College, a relation who had known him for twenty years, and a Mr. Archdale, who as a youth had been a clerk in the office of the Commissioners of Revenue, were equally certain that, though not entirely unlike it, the letters were not in the Judge's handwriting. Had the evidence on both sides rested here, the jury might have hesitated on their verdict. On the cross-examination of Sir H. Jebb it transpired that at a meeting at his house, some sheets of paper, after having been marked by him, had been sent out, and after some delay, returned with writing on them closely imitating that of the Judge, and supposed to have been the work of Card. This fact greatly increased the difficulties of the defence, as it landed his counsel in this dilemma. If the letters, as they tried to prove, were not in the writing of the Judge how could they be in that of one who so closely imitated it as Card was said to have done? If they were not in the Judge's handwriting what need was there to try to prove that they were written by one who could so closely imitate it? Why should Card, who so closely imitated the Judge's penmanship, have written the letters in a hand which they tried to prove was so unlike it that no one of his friends could recognize it? The absence of the Judge's brother, who resided in England, was another weak point in the defence, which was further weakened by the absurd conduct in the witness-box of a man of the name of Giffard. Lord Ellenborough, of course, hit all these blots, and the jury after a short consultation found the Judge guilty.

With the naked verdict the case of the Trojan Horse ended. Cobbett, as the reward of his turning king's evidence, escaped imprisonment and fine. Johnson, the real culprit, not only was never called up for judgment, but the proceedings against him were formally abandoned by the Attorney-General who succeeded Spencer Perceval on the change of Government, and Johnson retired with a life-pension from the judicial bench, which, if he was the writer he had disgraced.[1]

One more case arising out of the Emmet Rebellion must be noticed, though, strictly speaking, not a state trial—the action by Dr. Troy, titular Archbishop of Dublin, against the *Anti-Jacobin Review*.[2] On the day after Emmet's attempt, Dr. Troy had issued a pastoral address to his flock, in no way alluding to the event, but apparently anticipating it, and incul-

[1] Sir Arthur Piggott, Attorney-General to the Cabinet of "All the Talents," presumably at the suggestion of Fox, who felt so keenly the conduct of the Government to his relative, the commander-in-chief in Ireland, whose compulsory resignation and removal to a foreign command, was made the ground of one of Juverna's attacks on Lord Hardwicke.

[2] Troy v. Symonds, July 11, 1805, before Lord Chief Justice Ellenborough and a special jury, King's Bench, Westminster. Erskine, Wood, and Talbot for Plaintiff. Garrow, Park, and Richardson for Defendant. For the Fingal and Redesdale Correspondence see Castlereagh Papers, vol. iv. 298—312.

cating obedience to the law, and reprobating violence, as contrary to the principles and teachings of the religion they professed. In a correspondence, most unwisely entered into by Chancellor Redesdale with Lord Fingal, the acknowledged head of the Catholic nobility of Ireland, the Chancellor had lectured the noble lord on his duties as a magistrate, and reflected unfeelingly on the tenderness shown by the priests to those of their flock who were imbued with rebellious notions, and whose complicity with treasonable designs they could not but have known from their penitents in confession. Lord Fingal, in reply, had cited the addresses of Dr. Coppinger to his flock in Cloyne, and that of Dr. Troy, as striking proofs of the loyalty of his co-religionists. In the *Anti-Jacobin* of July, 1804, these addresses were cited as affording the clearest proof of the dissimulation of the Romish priesthood in Ireland, and as sure presages of a deep-laid plot against the Protestant state. It was also noted that the lamentations over secret conspiracy made from their altars were put off until after the conspiracy had resulted in unsuccessful rebellion, " though from the nature of their religion they must have known and might have prevented it." Following up this line of argument, the article averred " that Dr. Troy must have known all the circumstances that preceded the insurrection in Dublin on the 23rd of July, 1803, and yet he did not put the Government on its guard. The present administration," it said, " are convinced of his treachery on that occasion, and yet for many years past he has been treated with the utmost respect, and has even received favours for some of his family.

His exhortation then, to which Lord Fingal alludes, must be considered as a mockery of the state, an insult to the understandings of his Protestant fellow-subjects, and an unquestionable testimony to his want of candour."

That Dr. Troy's address was all that could be wished for by the most loyal Protestant, had it preceded and not followed Emmet's attempt, was not denied. That it was prepared before and handed to the printer to be set up on the morning of the day of the attempt, and that it was printed on the Monday after, and at once distributed to his subordinate priests was proved. For the prevention of the attempt it was useless. It was simply trying to shut the stable-door after the steed had been stolen. So far no doubt the publication of the address was open to adverse criticism. When, however, the critic declared that from the nature of the religion professed by the doctor and the conspirators he must have known that the insurrection was preparing—that with this knowledge he failed to warn the Government of its danger, and contented himself with composing a loyal address, to be issued after the attempt had failed, and that his treachery was known to and actually rewarded by the Government, any justification of the libel was impossible from the known relations existing between the priest and the penitent, and there could be no legal defence to the action. It became a mere question of the amount of damages.

Garrow, who was counsel for the publisher of the paper, no doubt fully satisfied his client and his client's Protestant friends with the defence which he was allowed to make. Disclaiming anything personal to

Dr. Troy, and urging that he was attacked solely as one bound by the principles and practice of his Church as to confession, he criticized with just severity the breach of confidence that had been committed by the publication of the Fingal correspondence. Then by a series of extracts, cleverly but most unfairly selected from Plowden's "History of Ireland," he endeavoured to prove that it was impossible for the confessor not to have known of the designs of Emmet and his followers, the bulk of whom where Catholics, and that if having this knowledge, Dr. Troy did not warn the Government, he was fairly open to criticism as the recognized head of the Dublin priesthood. This warning, he said, might have been given without breaking the seal of confession towards the individuals who had made it, and that by not so doing he had broken his oath of allegiance to the Crown.[1]

To the long and cutting speech of Garrow, Lord Ellenborough did not offer any interruption. Probably he did not regret that such an opportunity had been afforded for so trenchant an exposure of the dangers of confession as enforced by the priests. In his short summing up he left the question with unusual fairness to the jury, and went as far as he could, as a Judge, to recommend them to give only such damages as would purge the plaintiff's character. The jury took the Judge's hint, and gave a verdict for only 50*l.*, though the damages were somewhat ostentatiously laid at 10,000*l.*, and Erskine wisely accepted a verdict for one shilling and costs in the action depending between the doctor and the printer of the review.

[1] See Appendix B.

CHAPTER VII.

LORD MELVILLE'S IMPEACHMENT.

April 29th to June 12th, 1806.

"Quod potui perfeci."
     Lord Melville's Motto.

THE sudden increase of our naval and military power necessitated by the declaration of war against us and the Stadtholder of Holland on the part of the New French republic in 1793, coming after ten years of peace, necessarily offered increased opportunities for the negligence and extravagance then attendant on Government departments. Official management may, at that time, be said to have been in its childhood, and departmental arrangements inadequate, even if honestly and earnestly carried out, to enable officials to cope with the additional duties and responsibilities so suddenly thrown upon them. The heads of the departments, themselves personally above corruption, practically encouraged it in their subordinates, either by doing by deputy what they ought to have done in person, or by exercising only a perfunctory supervision easily satisfied with the appearance of correctness. Hence, in a very brief time, contractors became millionaires through contracts obtained by bribery, and executed under the protection of gratuities to those who ought to have strictly supervised them. Hence, bad food, almost useless clothing, and profitless arms and ammunition often diminished the efficiency of our forces and perilled the success of expeditions. Every commander had, in his time, experienced the baneful influence, and suffered from the dangerous effects of this system, against which individual protest was personally as dangerous as it was practically useless.[1]

Until the appointment of Lord St. Vincent, in 1801, as First Lord of the Admiralty, nothing was done to check this vicious system so far as the navy was affected by it. With all his faults, Admiral Jervis was, to use a modern phrase, "the right man in the right place" for the occasion. A stern disciplinarian on the quarter-deck, he was as stern and

[1] A glaring instance of this neglect of proper supervision of contractors by Government officials was exhibited in the case of the Brothers Hedges, contractors for cooper's work at Woolwich Dockyard, tried before Lord Ellenborough, December, 1803. By fraudulent certificates of quantities of hoops and casks supplied to men-of-war, all apparently regular, but in reality assumed to be so by the various clerks through whose hands they had to pass before payment, these men, in certificates nominally amounting to 2694*l*., cheated Government out of 2415*l*. Though not more than 200 hoops could possibly have been put on one ship's mast between March, 1800, and March, 1801, they had charged 2230, and 29,138 hoops on 3600 press barrels in three years, when the real number of barrels was less than 300. With very suspicious confidence the first clerk by whom the certificates were to be checked assumed they were correct, and on the faith of his signature those successively above him passed them for payment. Howell, "State Trials," vol. xxviii. p. 1315.

as uncompromising as a civil administrator. At his instigation an Act was passed appointing Commissioners to look into the leading departments of our naval administration. Their inquiry was full and detailed, and not completed until the spring of 1805, when their tenth report was presented to the House of Commons. In their previous reports the Commissioners had dealt with the misdeeds and frauds of the storekeepers in our West Indian possessions; the wasteful method of administering the property from which the pensioners at Chatham had been paid; the Prize Agency system, then in the hands of irresponsible individuals; the naval hospital at Stonehouse; the victualling departments at Plymouth, and the receipt and issue of stores in that office. In their last report the department of the Treasurer of the Navy was investigated, and charges of a most serious character made against the then treasurer, Lord Melville, better known as Henry Dundas, the right-hand man of Mr. Pitt.

Henry Dundas, the first Viscount Melville, was one of the most remarkable political men of his day. Though as the younger son of the Lord President of Scotland, he no doubt had the advantages in the commencement of his career due to the position of his father, to a great extent he was a self-made man, and owed his success and his honours to his own abilities and steady perseverance.[2] From his first

---

[2] Henry Dundas was the son of Robert Dundas of Arniston, who was Solicitor-General for Scotland in 1717, Lord Advocate in 1720, Member of Parliament for the county of Edinburgh, 1722, Judge of Session as Lord Arniston, 1737, and Lord President

entrance on life in the Scottish Courts he proved himself a cautious lawyer and a successful advocate, and soon obtained a fair share of the honours and emoluments of his profession. In order to effect this more rapidly he took an active part in the debates of the General Assembly of the Scottish Church, the then favourite arena for the display of forensic talent, and at the same time by his diligence in the preparation of his cases, earned for himself the respect of the Judges before whom he practised. Satisfied, probably, with his professional prospects, he gave up to one of his sisters the small patrimony that came to him on his father's death, and not long after, by his marriage with Miss Rennie, the heiress of the estate of Melville Castle, obtained an income sufficient, had he so chosen, to have made him independent of professional gains. Retirement from his profession never entered his mind. He was determined to rise by it and in it, and he was speedily rewarded for his determination. In 1773, in his 33rd year, Lord North selected him as Solicitor-General in Scotland, and soon after promoted him to be Lord Advocate. A seat in Parliament was now necessary. He was elected for Edinburghshire, a seat he held for ten years.

The political aspect of the times when Mr. Dundas entered Parliament was favourable to a politician of ability and perseverance. The rupture with the American Colonies was steadily developing itself, and

of his court in succession to the celebrated Duncan Forbes, 1748. Henry was his son by his second wife, a daughter of Sir Robert Gordon, Baronet of Invergordon.

the prospect of a hostile collision imminent. The bitterness of party-spirit was at its height, and the difficulties of the administration in the face of an active and brilliant opposition rapidly increasing. Worldly wisdom was Dundas's guiding spirit. Discerning the difficulties of the Cabinet, he prepared himself for the change, which he felt must come sooner or later, by acquiring, and showing in debate that he had acquired, such an intimate knowledge of some of the leading departments of Government as to make him an almost indispensable official to any administration. Whilst loyally and most effectively supporting the measures of the Government of Lord North, he forbore to irritate the leaders of the opposition, who were not unwilling to win to their side, when in office, so practically useful an opponent. Hence, when in 1782 the determination of the Government to continue the war (notwithstanding the successes of the Americans and the increase of popular feeling against any further continuance of the struggle) was censured by the House of Commons, and on the resignation of Lord North and his cabinet, Lord Rockingham and Mr. Fox formed their administration, Dundas remained as Lord Advocate, and gave as hearty a support to his new leaders as he had done to their predecessors in office. He also continued to retain his place in the subsequent and short-lived Government of Lord Shelbourne on the unexpected death of Lord Rockingham in the same year.

In the negotiations preceding Lord Shelbourne's acceptance of office, the Lord Advocate played a busy part. It was at his house, as on neutral ground, that the leading rival politicians met and discussed future arrangements over the dinner-table, and tried in vain to persuade Lord North to join one or other of the sections into which the Rockingham Cabinet were divided on their leader's death.[3] By Lord Shelbourne's administration peace was made with America, and its terms approved in the House of Lords by a narrow majority, but condemned in the Commons, and with this vote Lord Shelbourne's administration came to an untimely end. It was during this administration that Mr. Dundas, still Lord Advocate, acted as chairman of the secret committee on the causes of the war in the Carnatic, and began to acquire that intimate knowledge of Indian affairs which subsequently qualified him for the Presidency of the Board of Control, of which he was the creator.[4] Within a few days after the new cabinet —the coalition between Lord North and Fox—came

[3] "Auckland Correspondence."—Mr. Eden to Lord Loughborough, July 24, 25, 1782, and Lord Loughborough to Mr. Eden, no date, vol. iv. p. 41. July 24, Eden writes, "The Advocate was expected yesterday, and will certainly join Lord Shelbourne if they will give him the Scotch office for life;" and again, July 25, "The Advocate dined with General Conway yesterday, and with Lord Shelbourne the day before. They will give him his own terms." Lord Loughborough to Eden, giving accounts of dinners at the Lord Advocate's, at which Lord Shelbourne and Lord North were guests, and others of the rival sections. Lord Loughborough and Eden were urging North to join Fox, and Jenkinson, Dundas, and Robinson pressing him to join Lord Shelbourne.

[4] August 9, 1782. April 4, 1784, brought in the Bill creating the Board of Control of Indian Affairs, of which he was the first Chairman.

into office, as chairman of that committee he brought in its report, and moved resolutions condemning the conduct of Warren Hastings. In this report criminal charges were made against Sir Thomas Rumbold, the late Governor of Madras, a member of the House, that a Bill of Pains and Penalties was at once brought in, partially proceeded with, and only dropped when the Coalition Cabinet was dismissed by the king in consequence of Fox's India Bill.

In December, 1783, Mr. Pitt became the youthful Premier, and at once recognized the value of Mr. Dundas by appointing him Treasurer of the Navy, in addition to his position as Lord Advocate.[5] The amount and variety of work undertaken by Dundas at this period was remarkable. In addition to that incident to his ostensible official positions, he not only continued his practice at the Scottish Bar in appeals to the House of Lords, but assumed the responsibilities and the labour of the Government share of the affairs of India. His opposition to

[5] "Called to the Bar," writes Lord Holland, "at an early period, Member of Parliament for Mid-Lothian, he obtained the command of the Corporation of Edinburgh. Made Lord Advocate by Lord North, whom he deserted on the decline of his power. In the changes and intrigues of that period his versatility was extraordinary, and his want of principle notorious [*a popular failing among the politicians of that day*], but his talents and courage showed him an useful man. He continued to remain Lord Advocate with Lord Rockingham and Lord Shelbourne, and was supposed to be among the foremost in urging Mr. Pitt to set up for himself, and thus, after the short interval of the coalition, he found himself higher in station and confidence with the new Premier than he had ever been with his predecessor."—" Memoirs of the Whig Party," i. 238.

Fox's India Bill had given him great influence with not only the Directors of the East India Company, but all the various commercial interests connected with that portion of the empire. Their support proved most useful to Mr. Pitt in his appeal to the nation when repeatedly defeated by the coalition in the Commons, and enabled Dundas to introduce that check on the Government of India by the Company provided by the Board of Control, of which he was naturally the first chairman. It is curious to note that as Treasurer of the Navy he brought in the bill on which the bulk of the charges against him were eventually based, by which the funds for naval outlay were henceforth to be placed at the Bank of England, and only drawn out as required for the different services, and future treasurers were prohibited from making any use for their own benefit of the monies imprest to them for the naval service. In these varied and laborious offices, with the exception of the Board of Control, he continued until Mr. Pitt resigned in 1801, when he retired with his firm friend and leader.

During the whole of that anxious period he took a leading part in defending the Government, speaking in a much stronger party-spirit than on previous occasions. Such in an especial manner were his speeches in opposing Lord, Surrey's resolutions in 1783, affirming the absolute necessity for a Cabinet that had the confidence of "this House and the public;" on the projected Regency in 1789; in defending the action of the Ministry at the critical period of 1792, in the temporary absence of Pitt; on the declaration of war by France in the following year; in bringing in the measures to meet the action of the Corresponding Society in the same session, and in opposing Sheridan's motion for so amending the Oath of Allegiance as to enable Roman Catholics to serve in the army and navy. It was no doubt this increased party colour of his speeches which prompted the attempt of the opposition in 1794 to vacate his seat on the ground of his having accepted a third Secretaryship of State, and gradually created against him that personal feeling which showed itself so plainly during the impeachment and in the discussions by which it was preceded.[6]

Since Mr. Pitt's acceptance of the premiership, Dundas had been looked upon as the minister for Scotland,[7] and shown his affection for his countrymen

---

[6] " By the combined influence of his own and the Duke of Buccleugh, whom he governed, he acquired great ascendency in Scotland. His parliamentary merits consisted chiefly in outward appearance, spirit, and readiness; an unblushing countenance, a manly figure, a sort of grotesque hoaxing eloquence, conveyed in a loud voice and a provincial dialect, which was neither pleasantry nor invective, and yet reminded one of both. He never hesitated in making an assertion, and without attempting to answer an argument, he either treated it as quite preposterous, or, after some bold misstatements and inapplicable maxims, confidently alleged that he had refuted it. . . . Mr. Fox used to say that he never failed to speak with effect unless, by some strange fatality, he happened to thoroughly understand the subject. . . . He had much frankness and good-humour in his countenance, and no man was more implacable in his hatreds."
—Lord Holland, " Memoirs of Whig Party," i. 238.

[7] 1784, brought in bill for restoring the estates forfeited in the Rebellion of "'45."

in the distribution of his patronage with a national but inconsiderate zeal. In this patronage his family and himself had shared largely, his patent offices as Privy Seal and Keeper of the Signet for Scotland assuring him "considerable income, whether in or out of office in the administration of the country." With the friends of the Prince of Wales, whatever may have been his earlier relations with them, he thoroughly broke, when, in 1795, he contradicted Sheridan's statement, made, as Sheridan declared, on the Prince's own authority, that the Prince had never seen that passage in the royal message recommending the payment of his debts, in which it was stated that he had promised and arranged to retrench his extravagance. Hence when he retired with Mr. Pitt he did so as the devoted follower of his leader, and as one who had staked his future on that leader's fortune.

He was too well acquainted with the difficulty of the political situation not to see that Mr. Addington's ministry was simply a temporary stop-gap to prevent the accession of the opposition, and to be pushed aside so soon as the return of his political patron and personal friend could be safely made. Whether in or out of office, in Mr. Addington's opinion, he was worth conciliating at the price of a peerage for himself and several good situations for his friends and relations.[8] During the Addington administration he took but little part in public affairs. He

[8] Chancellor Loughborough created Earl Rosslyn, and Dundas Viscount Melville, on formation of the Addington Ministry.

bided his time, and when, in 1804, Mr. Pitt returned to office, the new peer came into the Cabinet as First Lord of the Admiralty. His undeviating good fortune had now apparently deserted him. By this time Lord St. Vincent's Commissioners, in their laborious investigations, had reached the office of the Treasurer of the Navy. They had inspected not only the public, but the private banking accounts of Lord Melville during the two periods in which he had held that office, and inquired closely into his financial relations with one Alexander Trotter, who had been his Paymaster-General during the greater portion of his second treasurership. In their opinion the evidence they had obtained proved that there were deficiencies between the balances as returned by the noble lord and those really remaining in his hands at various dates, and that he had applied money imprest to him solely for navy services to the purposes of other departments. They also reported that in the face of the statute which he had himself introduced and carried, he had either personally applied unused navy balances to his own use, or had, by allowing them to be transferred from the Bank of England to the account of Mr. Trotter at Coutts's, connived at his paymaster using portions of them in the payment of bills and the purchase of securities for Lord Melville's benefit. In making these serious charges, however, it was admitted that the misappropriation had been only temporary, and that in the end the whole of many millions that had passed through his hands as treasurer had been fully accounted for.

When examined before the committee, Lord Melville had not denied that two sums of 10,000*l.* and 11,000*l.* had been for a time appropriated to other services than those of the navy, but had refused under the protection of a clause in the Act which he had introduced, to disclose the nature of the services for which they had been used.[9] To the charge of misusing balances for his own benefit, he gave a direct denial. To those of allowing or conniving at any such use of them by his paymaster, he declared that it was done, if done at all, without his knowledge. He also asserted, that he was not aware until the inquiry had elicited this fact from Mr. Trotter, that any of the public balances had been paid to and mixed up with the private account of Trotter at Coutts's, or that any advances made to him had been made from other than Trotter's private means.

Trotter had been a very successful man. When first raised to the paymastership, he was a clerk in the Navy Office at 100*l.* a year, and his pay as paymaster had never exceeded 800*l.* Before the committee, however, he admitted that he was worth more than 60,000*l.*, only about a tenth of which had come to him from private sources, and he did not deny that he had used the balances in his hands in discounting navy bills and otherwise dabbling in the funds with invariable success. In any payments of accounts or purchases of funds which he had made for Lord Melville, he declared that they were made either from private funds of his lordship's, to whom he acted as agent, or if taken from the navy balances, were uniformly represented to Lord Melville as

---

[9] 43 George III. c. 16, sec. 5.

having been procured by other means. And he again and again repeated, that when he had once suggested to Lord Melville to use a comparatively small amount of public money, which could not be required for a long time, for his own benefit, his principal had so decidedly objected to such a course that he not only never hinted at such a step again, but took care that Lord Melville should not know that he was so misusing them. For some time Mr. Trotter refused to give this evidence, though threatened by the House with commitment, and it was not until an Act of Indemnity was passed in his favour that he admitted the full nature of his transactions with the public funds.[1]

In consequence of these revelations, Mr. Whitbread, on Monday, the 8th of April, 1805, moved a series of resolutions condemnatory of Lord Melville's conduct. Of these the ninth commenced with a recital of the increase of the treasurer's salary in 1782, in order to compensate for that use of the unrequired balances by the responsible heads which had previously been the custom in all the depart-

[1] Trotter's Indemnity Bill, when in the House of Lords, July 9, was objected to by the chancellor, because it declared that the acts charged against Lord Melville were illegal, and proposed to indemnify witnesses against civil actions either by the Crown or individuals. In consequence it was amended on third reading, and that delayed in order to take the opinion of the Judges (for which an Act of Parliament was required) whether a person is compellable to answer questions which may not criminate himself, but serve to establish that he owes a debt for which he might be sued in a civil court. When it went down to the Commons it was rejected, because the Lords' amendments infringed their privileges, and new Bill brought in and passed.

ments, and the passing of the Act of 1785 requiring the navy monies to be deposited at the Bank of England. It then assumed that the required transfer to the Bank was postponed by Lord Melville for a year, and that from that time until June, 1800, " large sums of money were, under pretence of naval services, and in scandalous evasion of the Act, at various times withdrawn from the Bank, and invested upon Exchequer and Navy Bills, and upon the security of stock employed in discounting Navy Bills, or purchasing Bank and East India stock, and used in various ways for the purposes of private emolument." The tenth resolution stated that Trotter was the person by whom and in whose name the public money was so employed, and "that in so doing he acted with the knowledge and consent of Viscount Melville, for whom he was at the same time private agent, and for whose use or benefit he occasionally laid out from 10,000*l.* to 20,000*l.*, without considering whether he was previously in advance to his lordship, and whether such advances were made from his public or private balances." The eleventh resolution affirmed that Lord Melville, " having been privy to and connived at the withdrawing from the Bank of England for purposes of private emolument sums issued to him as Treasurer of the Navy and placed to his account in the Bank in accordance with the statute, *has been guilty of a gross violation of the law and a high breach of duty.*" The next resolution referred to Lord Melville's statement that he had no materials now for making up an account of his receipt and repayment of the sums so misapplied, and that " if he had the materials he could not do it without disclosing delicate and confidential transactions of Government, which his duty to the public must have restrained him from revealing." This conduct the last resolution declared to be "inconsistent with his duty, and incompatible with those securities which the Legislature had provided for the proper application of the public money."

How these resolutions should be met was a subject of serious dispute in the cabinet. Pitt clung closely to his valuable political and personal friend, and for some time after the Commissioners' report had been presented, refused to reveal his intentions, much to the dissatisfaction of the general supporters of the Government in the House of Commons. The old Addington section (Sidmouth, Buckinghamshire, and Hawkesbury), "expressed their opinion that Lord Melville should either stand an inquiry or resign altogether," and Lord Sidmouth plainly warned Pitt of the danger of defending his friend, and told him that if he did so he would resign. Eventually it was agreed that Pitt should move to refer the tenth report to a select committee, which was agreed to by Melville, who was made to understand that he must resign during the Easter recess.[2] To Whitbread's resolutions, therefore, Pitt moved the agreed amendment, which if carried would have prevented them from appearing on the journals of the House. To avoid this, on Fox's suggestion, Pitt agreed to move the previous question, reserving the motion for reference to a committee to a further stage in the discus-

---

[2] Lord Colchester's "Diary," vol. i. April 6, 7. Pellew's "Life of Lord Sidmouth," vol. ii.

sion. Though the debate which ensued was of a bitter and strictly party character, the division showed a tie—216 on each side, and the decision fell to the Speaker. At four o'clock in the morning, in a house extraordinarily crowded for the times, Speaker Abbot, showing in his countenance the responsibility he felt in deciding so grave an issue, gave his vote with the ayes. His reasons for this step, as he records in his diary, were that on the first two charges (violation of the statute, and connivance at Trotter's profits) any further inquiry was needless ; that they were ripe for the judgment of the House, and that the plea that further material information might be obtained could apply only to the charge of personal participation in these profits. Whatever we may think of this distinction and of the Speaker's justification for his vote, it was approved by Lord Melville's son, and the Premier wrote to the king that the Speaker " necessarily voted for the question."[3]

One further attempt was made by Pitt to lessen the force of the censure, but it failed. The resolutions were carried, and the House adjourned at five in the morning till the following Wednesday.

On that day Pitt announced the resignation of his colleague, in the vain hope, probably, that the opposition would be satisfied with the sacrifice, but it was not so. Mr. Whitbread at once proposed an address to the Crown to dismiss Lord Melville " from all offices held by him during pleasure, and also from his councils for ever." This motion, which was entirely

---

[3] Lord Colchester's " Diary," April 8, 1805.

without precedent, was, after a bitterly personal debate, abandoned in favour of a simple resolution, that the resolutions of Tuesday morning should be presented to the king, and further proceedings against Lord Melville commenced without delay. On the reassembling of the House, after the Easter vacation, the discussion on the further proceedings was at once resumed. At first it was decided that a civil suit should be brought against Lord Melville and Trotter.[4] On this Mr. Whitbread, on the 6th of May, proposed to renew his motion for Lord Melville's removal from all his places not held by patent, and from the Privy Council, when he was met by Pitt's announcement, given with painful reluctance, that his Majesty had been advised to strike Lord Melville's name out of the list of the Privy Council. A month now passed without any further action on the part of the opposition. Sir Charles Middleton—afterwards Lord Barham—an octogenarian, was appointed as Lord Melville's successor at the Admiralty, and the resignation of Lord Sidmouth and his personal friends prevented by an agreement, that the appointment should be only temporary; that all further abuses should be effectually prevented, and "Lord Sidmouth and his friends in both Houses, should be at liberty to

---

[4] April 29, on the motion of Mr. Stanhope for suit by Attorney-General for ascertaining and recovering any sum of public monies applicable to naval services used by Lord Melville and Mr. Trotter subsequently to January, 1786. Amendment by Mr. Banks, "That a criminal prosecution be instituted."
    For original motion, 223
    For amendment . . 128—95

act in the matter as they pleased without affecting the state of parties." [5]

On the 11th of June Lord Melville, by permission of the peers, attended the House of Commons, to be examined as to the statements in the Commissioners' tenth report. Standing behind the chair which was placed within the bar for his use, he spoke for upwards of two hours. According to Speaker Abbot, his speech was "boldly delivered, chiefly hardy assertions and flat denials." As to the 10,000*l.* applied to other state purposes than those of the navy before

[5] Lord Colchester's "Diary," April 25 and 28, on the authority of Hatsell and Vansittart. From Lord Sidmouth's letter to Pitt, April 22, it appears that having failed in his discussions with the Premier to get either Lords Hood, Castlereagh, or Hawkesbury appointed in Melville's place, or his offer to take the Home Office accepted, he wrote Pitt that Middleton's appointment would weaken and lower the Government at a time when it was most important to raise its character, "and that he was convinced that his continuance in office would be neither useful to the public or honourable to himself, an opinion to which I have long been compelled to incline." In a subsequent letter, April 27, to Lord Hawkesbury, he speaks of "the influence of an individual possessing neither the confidence of Parliament nor of the public (Canning ?), personally hostile to me, instead of being diminished, as you know I had reason to believe, is apparently increased. My friends are accordingly compelled to think that the reconciliation with Pitt is not on his part cordial and sincere, and that they and I are only made use of for purposes of political convenience." After a week's discussion, on the assurance of Pitt that he had full confidence in Sidmouth and his political friends, and that Lord Melville had no longer any influence with Pitt, and that every allowance would be made for his friends on the Melville case, the threatened resignation was withdrawn. Lord Sidmouth to Hiley Addington, April 28. He really wanted Lord Buckinghamshire to be appointed.—Pellew's "Life," vol. ii.

Trotter was paymaster, and the 11,000*l*. after his appointment, he said "that being entrusted with the confidential management of the king's interest in Scotland, he had applied the money in a way that no consideration should induce him to reveal." He was heard with the utmost attention and silence, but, adds the Speaker, "he certainly did not appear to improve his cause. There was a tone of defiance and a want of moral feeling which evidently hurt his own friends and gave support to his enemies."[6] On his withdrawal Whitbread at once moved his impeachment, to which, by arrangement with the Sidmouth section of the cabinet, Mr. Bond moved an amendment for a criminal prosecution, which on a subsequent night was carried by a majority of nine only, in a House of 464 members, and thirteen days after rejected in favour of an impeachment in a much thinner House without a division.[7]

The effect of the final decision of the House on the Premier was much disputed at the time. Even his bitterest opponents admitted that "his defence of his friend and colleague was the most amiable passage in his life," but whilst Wilberforce thought that

[6] Lord Colchester's "Diary," June 11, 1805.
[7] For Mr. Bond's amendment, 238
 For Mr. Whitbread's motion, 229—9, June 12.
June 24, Mr. Leycester gave notice of intention to substitute impeachment for criminal prosecution. June 25, motion to that effect by Mr. Leycester, opposed by Mr. Bond and Fox, the latter of whom moved "the orders of the day"—Ayes, 143 ; Noes, 166 —23 Fox then moved a call of the house—negatived. Motion for impeachment carried without division, and Whitbread appointed manager.

it did not affect his health, his political friends considered it to be one of the more immediate causes of his early death. When the king first heard of the first division caused by the Speaker's casting vote, which was told him as he was getting ready for hunting, he said, " Is that all ; I wonder how he slept after it." When, however, a few days after, Lord Melville tendered his resignation, George the Third is said to have written his fallen minister that "he was sorry that his incautious conduct had rendered it necessary for him to retire from his situation as First Lord of the Admiralty, and he hoped posterity would do justice to his character"—a consolation of a very Delphic character.[8] He had but little love for him since his report, as chairman of the Indian Select Committee against Warren Hastings.[9]

Public opinion, as exhibited in the journals of the day, took sides with more than usual party rancour. Bishop Porteus was attacked as having preached a sermon at Curzon Chapel in Lord Melville's defence, and Canning's paper, the *Oracle*, was summoned to the bar of the Commons for a libel of the bitterest kind on some of the leaders in the prosecution. The poor bishop, it seems, had selected a twenty-four-year-old sermon on not censuring our neighbours rashly and uncharitably, simply because it had never been preached at that chapel, and some of his hearers perhaps felt that the cap fitted them.[1]

[8] "Auckland Correspondence," vol. iv. p. 233, note, and Lord Henley to Lord Auckland, iv. p. 235.
[9] "Auckland Correspondence," vol. iv. p. 282. Bishop Porteus to Lord Auckland, May 29, 1806.
[1] At the votes of Lord Sidmouth's friends in the minority on

For the attack in the *Oracle* no such excuse could be found. The writer declared that Lord Melville's condemnation was "an instance of the strong effects of prejudice," that he had fallen a victim to confidence misplaced, to prejudice misjudged, and to indignation misapplied." That "he had been condemned without a trial," and that his appeal to be heard "had been met by a presumptuous negative directed and enforced by the violence of the times." On the 25th of April, 1805, Mr. Grey moved to call the printer and publisher of the obnoxious paper to the bar, and succeeded, though Pitt, whilst admitting the libellous character of the article, deprecated any action unless libels on the other side were treated with like punishment. During the discussion Mr. Robert Ward persisted in reading the conclusion of the article. In this, a strong contrast was drawn between the conduct of those great officers of state who had not paid over the balances of public money, and that of Lord Melville, whom "his most implacable and bitter enemies," it said, "had not dared to charge with such an act ;" and then, " Can so much be said," con-

Mr. Leycester's motion, Pitt took offence, and hesitated to find the positions he had previously promised for Mr. Bond and Hiley Addington. At a meeting between him and Lord Sidmouth on June 30, Lord Sidmouth writes Hiley Addington "that it was not satisfactory. Pitt said such conduct must be marked, and the injustice, and, I must add, the arrogance, of that sentiment convinced me that there was no hope of preserving the connexion but by an implicit conformity little short of unconditional submission." After a second interview on July 4 or 5, Lord Sidmouth resigned, and was followed by Lord Buckinghamshire. Pellew's "Sidmouth," vol. ii.

tinued the writer," of the follies of some men? If the public were paid its pecuniary claims, long since indisputably proved, certain famous patriots instead of living in splendour would be put on the parish. In the future resolutions of the House of Commons, in the future resolutions of all public meetings, we hope that an immediate attention be paid to the enormous debts still due to the public by certain noisy individuals will be strongly recommended." Fox, feeling the application of the remarks to his father, asked "Is this any palliation?"[2] "It affords," truly replied Mr. Ward, "a good and sufficient reason for the whole inquiry being prosecuted with temper, and especially by those whose families might appear to have been defaulters to a considerable amount."

The printer's apology was too bold and singular not to be noticed. After the usual expressions of regret and admission of his indiscretion, he boasted of his journal having uniformly supported the character of the House against the Socialists which were its enemies, and added " in any observations which your petitioner may have published on the conduct of Lord Melville, he could not but bear in mind that the views of those societies abetting domestic treason and assisted by the co-operation of the revolutionary power of France, would, he verily believes, have effected the destruction of the British Constitution, had not the wise and efficient measures brought forward by that administration, in which Lord Melville

[2] Henry Fox, first Lord Holland, 1757, Paymaster-General of the Forces, in which situation his conduct as to the balances in his hand was very much commented on.

held so conspicuous a situation been adopted and this Honourable House would not in that case perhaps, have been now in existence, either to censure your petitioner or crush Lord Melville." Over this extraordinary apology a sharp debate ensued, in which Canning flew to the rescue of his friend, and eventually obtained his discharge by a narrow majority of twenty-one votes.[3]

On the 26th of June, 1805, Mr. Whitbread and a large number of members attended the Lords and handed in the vote for the impeachment, and on the same day a committee, with him as chairman, was appointed to draw up the articles on which the trial was to be held. These, at that time, ten in number, were sent to the Upper House on the 9th of July, and as the prorogation of Parliament was imminent, a bill, to keep alive the impeachment over any prorogation or even dissolution, was pushed through both Houses, and received the royal assent immediately before the royal speech.

Within a few months the political situation of parties was changed by the death of Pitt and the accession to a brief tenure of power of the Cabinet of " All the Talents."[4] If the junction of a variety of party

[3] By a majority of 162 to 121. Canning, if not the editor, was certainly closely connected with the *Oracle*.

[4] Pitt died January 23, 1806, and on February 5 the Cabinet of "All the Talents," in which Lord Sidmouth's party joined those of Grenville and Fox, came into office, Lord Ellenborough, though Chief Justice of England, having a seat, but without office, an appointment seriously canvassed at the time, and happily never repeated. Speaking of this incident, Lord Rous described Sidmouth and the Chief Justice " as the old steward

interests and equal variety of talent could have formed a strong Government, that of "All the Talents" must have succeeded. To the old and new oppositions of Grenville and Fox, and the party of Lord Sidmouth united, any opposition on the part of the friends of the old cabinet, shorn of their strength by their leader's death, seemed hopeless. There were, however, powers beyond the precincts of Parliament which the Cabinet had not taken into account. The bulk of the journals and the pamphlet writers were on the side of the Pittites. The Crown servants who had been appointed by the late Cabinet were conspicuous by their absence from divisions. The monetary and commercial classes looked doubtfully on Fox and his opinions. Rapidly, therefore, the belief arose that the Cabinet was but a makeshift, and that it must fall to pieces from the want of cohesion in its discordant materials. But for the change of Government, probably the management of the impeachment would have been controlled, if the impeachment itself had not been conducted by men of discretion and judgment and not left so entirely to the indiscreetness and virulence of Mr. Whitbread. The jokes of the day were more true than party witticisms are wont to be when they described Lord Melville as "Whitbread's Entire butt;" and said that the manager's "eloquence, like his beer, was bitter stuff and bad taste,"[5] and de-

with his mastiff, watching new servants, lest they should have some evil designs against the old family mansion." Lord Rous to Lord Sidmouth.—Pellew's "Sidmouth," vol. ii. p. 147.

[5] Speaker Abbot's "Diary," vol. ii. pp. 62 and 63. Another joke of the day recorded by the diarist was, that the archbishops and bishops, walking in the daily procession from their house to

VOL. I. O

scribed the managers as "mismanagers and imaginers."

Soon after the re-assembling of Parliament (January, 22, 1806), Lord Melville put in his plea of Not Guilty, and Mr. Plomer, Mr. Adam, and Mr. Hobhouse were named as his counsel. Report said that he would not avail himself of professional aid, deterred by the heavy preliminary sum asked by the solicitor who had defended Warren Hastings. Whether this rumoured 10,000*l.* was found or the sum was a fiction, the same solicitor acted for him.[6] From then until the end of April but slow progress was made. The Commons presented an eleventh article, to which the same plea of Not Guilty was put in, and the Lords occupied the time in searching for precedents and arranging with the Cabinet for the formal preliminaries of the great inquest, of which Westminster Hall was, as usual, the selected scene. On the 29th of April the stately proceeding was commenced. Preceded by the Clerks of Parliament, Chancery and the King's Bench, the Masters, Sergeants-at-Law, and Judges, the peers marched in, fully robed, beginning with the youngest and lowest order and ending with eight princes of the royal blood; Erskine, the Chancellor, being Lord Steward for the occasion. When the articles of impeachment, the plea in defence, and the replication of the Commons had been read, Erskine, in order to hear more readily, moved

the hall, were described to country spectators as Peeresses in their own right.

[6] "Auckland Correspondence." Lord Buckinghamshire to Lord Auckland, December 17, 1805.

into the body of the Court, and Whitbread opened the case of the managers in a speech that occupied the remainder of the day. Nominally the case was entrusted by the Commons to three-and-twenty members, among whom were Fox, Lord Howick, Sheridan, Lord Henry Petty, besides Jekyll, Best, and Morris, with the Attorney and Solicitor-General to furnish legal aid: in reality it was managed by Whitbread and a Mr. Giles. Romilly contented himself with a very brief summing-up of the evidence, the Attorney-General, Sir Arthur Piggott, confining his part to a few words on cases cited by the defendant's counsel.[7] The articles formed a lengthy

[7] The trial of Lord Melville was miserably conducted by the Commons. Though there were five or six managers, the articles were so ill drawn that it was difficult to ascertain to which act of Lord Melville each respectively referred. Sir S. Romilly made a good sarcastic speech, but the only person who did himself credit was Sir A. Piggott (Attorney-General), who spoke in the authoritative tone of a representative of the people, and though he combated the technical objections of the counsel with the learning of a lawyer, he handled them judiciously and successfully, never lost sight of the great principle, that the Commons of England, in impeaching a delinquent, were not to be fettered by the strict rules of inferior courts. Mr. Whitbread, though he had pursued the subject with prodigious diligence, and understood the whole transaction, was so occupied in displaying his wit and eloquence, or, as the lively Duchess of Gordon expressed it, "in teaching his dray-horse to caper," that his speeches convinced nobody; and even in cases of complicated accounts, left the Lords to draw the facts from the evidence as well as they could, without assistance from him, This management no doubt contributed to secure an acquittal. but other circumstances contributed to it. Lords Grenville and Spencer absented themselves after the third day of the trial.—

bill of indictment, which it would be tedious to reprint, the substantial charges in which may be briefly stated.

The preamble to the charges detailed with minuteness the inquiries and proceedings relative to the custody and use of public moneys from the time when the Commission, appointed in 1782 to investigate the state of the national accounts, reported in favour of all such moneys being issued only to the custody of the Bank of England. It then cited the resolution of the House of Commons of June 19, 1782, approving this recommendation of the Commissioners, and laying down that the Treasurer of the Navy should not henceforth apply any money imprest to him for navy services for any other purpose or for his own advantage or interest. Referring then to the Royal warrants of June 22nd, 1782, and August and October in the same year, augmenting the pay of the Treasurer to a clear 4000*l.*, "in lieu of all wages, fees, or other profits, or emoluments," previously enjoyed by these officers, it noted Mr. Dundas's tenure of that office from August, 1782, to April, 1783; his subsequent reappointment on the same conditions in January, 1785, and his continuance as such until May, 1800. It called particular attention to the fact of Mr. Dundas having in February, 1785, introduced the bill to carry out these resolutions of the Commons, and quoted those sections of the Act (1, 3, 4, and 5), by which after July 31st in that year all such monies were to be passed direct to the Bank of England, and

Lord Holland's "Memoirs of the Whig Party," vol. i. 190, *et seq.*

not drawn out except by drafts specifying the particular heads of the navy services for which they were demanded. This Act, it was said, had been neglected or evaded by the noble defendant, by his not opening the required account at the Bank until the 13th of January, 1786. Trotter's appointment as Paymaster in January of the same year, with full power of attorney to act for his principal was also recited. The preamble to the original indictment then concluded with two averments, first, that it was the duty of the Treasurer at *all times* to abstain from applying funds imprest for navy services to his own advantage, or that of others, either directly or indirectly, and to prevent others from so doing, or to divert them to other than navy services; and secondly, after the passing of the Act of 1785, to observe and pursue the directions of that statute, and that the defendant, disregarding this duty, had committed the following specific overt acts :—

By the *first* article it was charged that in his first Treasurership, previously to the Act of the 25th George III., he had applied 10,000*l.* to other than navy services, and that he refused to reveal the nature of the application. By the *second*, that after the Act he connived at and permitted Trotter to transfer navy moneys from the Bank of England to Trotter's own account at his own bankers, Messrs. Coutts, and subject there to his sole control. By the *third*, that with his privity and by his connivance and permission, Trotter mixing these monies with his own, applied them to his own advantage and exposed them to the risk of loss. By the *fourth* that among the moneys so misused was a sum placed in the hands of one Sprott. By the *fifth*, that in the face of the Act Lord Melville frauduently and for his own profit drew from the Bank of England 10,000*l.*, and converted it either to his own use or to some other corrupt or illegal purpose. By the *sixth*, *seventh*, and *eighth*, that Lord Melville procured advances from Trotter, partly at interest and partly not, made from public moneys in his paymaster's hands, and that in February, 1803, in order to conceal these transactions, he agreed with him that they should give each other a mutual release, and destroy the vouchers of the various payments. By the *ninth* it was charged that Trotter acted gratuitously as Lord Melville's private agent, and as such made him advances from time to time of from 10,000*l.* to 20,000*l.* in consideration of his being allowed to illegally use the public monies, and with a knowledge on his lordship's part that he could not have made such advances from his own private means. Lastly, by the article added on the 10th March, 1806, it was alleged, in extension of the charge in the first article, that between January 5th, 1784, and January 1, 1786, he had taken 27,000*l.* from the navy moneys for his own use or for other purposes unauthorized and illegal, and had continued so to use them after the passing of the Act of 1785.

Assuming for the present the truth of these charges, three points of law arose—(1) Whether previous to the Act of 1785, notwithstanding the terms of the royal warrants, by which the pay of the Treasurer was from time to time increased, it was a misdemeanour on his part to apply any of the moneys for navy services to any other use, public or private, without specific authority for so doing. The Judges to whom this question was referred were unanimously of opinion that it was not. This decision entirely covered the *first* and *tenth* charge. Lord Melville, had he pleased, might, until 1785, have used the navy balances as much for his own private profit as the balances in other departments had been wont to be used by their respective custodians. As for the temporary transfer of portions of these balances to other public uses, whatever the uses were in his case, the custom had long been prevalent, and extended even to our own times.

During the debate introductory to the impeachment, Mr. Pitt revealed the object for which, in 1796, he had applied to Lord Melville for such a temporary use of 40,000*l.*, the disclosure of which could no longer be prejudicial to the public service. At that time, when the Irish insurrection was impending, cash payments suspended at the Bank of England and a serious run made on the Northern banks, the second instalment of a loan for 18,000,000*l.* became due from the contractors, Messrs. Boyd and Benfield. At that juncture, though they had ample securities on which to have raised the amount they required to meet the payment, had they gone into the public market with them or sold stock of the loan in their hands, undoubtedly great discredit would have been thrown on them, and public credit would have been injured by the public failure of its financial contractors. To save this Mr. Pitt authorized the advance, on security, of the sum of 40,000*l.* from navy funds, which was all repaid, and the difficulty tided over. Mr. Whitbread moved resolutions somewhat reflecting on the conduct of the Premier, but was defeated, and a motion made by Mr. Lascelles affirming "That the loan was made for the purpose of averting consequences which might have proved highly injurious to the financial and commercial interests of the country, and though not conformable to law, appeared at the time to be called for by the peculiar exigences of public affairs." This was carried without a division, and a bill indemnifying Mr. Pitt at once brought in and carried.[8] According to Lord Hawkesbury, Melville had applied his advances in a more mysterious and less defensible way, "partly during the king's illness" in 1789, "and partly on Scotch elections."[9]

The second and third points referred to the removal of portions of the navy funds from the Bank of England to Coutts's, and their deposit there to the account and at the disposal of Paymaster Trotter till required to meet bills and other navy accounts. The Judges were asked whether such monies could be drawn, before these accounts became due, "and lawfully lodged and deposited in the hands of a banker, other than the Bank of England, for and until the payment of these bills; and whether such an act was an offence or crime at law; and whether, until such payment, they might be "deposited in the hands of a private banker in the name and under the immediate sole control and disposition of some other person or persons than the Treasurer himself." To the second question, the Judges unhesitatingly replied

[8] Hansard's "Debates," June 14, 1805.
[9] Lord Colchester's "Diary," May 25, 1805.

that, notwithstanding the Act of 1785, "it was in law a crime or offence." Upon the third question they drew this distinction, whether the drawing of the money in anticipation was solely for the purpose of making such private deposit, or whether it was done " *bonâ-fide* as the means, or supposed means, of more conveniently applying the money to navy services." The transfer in the first case would be unlawful, but not so under the second state of circumstances.[1] This opinion covered the ground of defence to the removal of the money from time to time to Trotter's account at Coutts's, which, it was said, was partly to avoid the danger of sending drafts for gold by messengers to the Bank of England after the Navy Office had been removed from the City to Somerset House, and partly to accommodate the west-end holders of navy bills to whom Coutts's was a far more convenient house of payment than the Bank of England.

The remainder of the case against the ex-Treasurer depended solely on the amount of knowledge he might be assumed, if not directly proved, to have had of the private uses to which Trotter put such of the balances in his hands as were not required at the time, and, as a special instance of this misuse by him of these funds, the application of portions of them to payments of bills and purchases of stocks for him by Trotter as his private agent. Trotter, in his repeated examinations, uniformly declared that not only were such dealings with the public monies never sanctioned by Lord Melville, but each transaction in which they

[1] For questions to and opinions of Judges, see *post*, p. 217.

were misused was so represented to him as to lead him to believe that the money was found from other and legal sources. On this evidence, looking at Trotter as a witness called by the prosecution, forced under the threat of severe penalties to give his evidence, with every temptation to save himself by turning on his principal, there is much to warrant the Lord Chief Baron Macdonald's statement, that he should at once have shut up his notes, had he been trying the case criminally, and directed an acquittal of the defendant. On this view of the case, no doubt, Lord Eldon, in the discussions on the verdict, struggled hard for an entire acquittal. It must, however, be remembered that an impeachment is not like an indictment, limited to crimes and misdemeanours, but extends in such a case as that of Lord Melville's to "proceedings contrary to the duty of his office, and in breach of the great trust reposed in him." The Lords, therefore, were fully justified in not at once closing the case, even if they believed Trotter's evidence, and in considering how far the defendant had exceeded his official duty, or committed a breach of the trust confided to him. A judgment against him on these points would legally, however, have only the value of an expression of opinion, and could not involve any punishment. A comparatively brief analysis of the evidence given on the second and third class of charges—the transfer of the balances to Trotter's account, and the payments and purchases made by him on Lord Melville's behalf—will justify us in forming an opinion on the verdicts of his lordship's Judges.

The bare fact of the transfer to Coutts's, and the payments and purchases for Lord Melville not being denied (though they could not well be so far admitted by the defendant's counsel as to preclude the necessity of their being formally proved by the prosecutors), the only evidence of importance in explanation of them was that of Trotter. That, in an examination extending over the greater part of two days, and comprising nearly eight hundred questions, he should have been caught tripping in minor facts was only to be expected, especially when accounts and disputed figures formed so large a portion of the subject-matter of his examination. Still, though so minutely and rigorously examined, not only by the managers and his own counsel, but by some dozen noble lords, several of whom were fully capable of putting any witness to the test, he gave a very consistent and clear statement. He exposed a careless system of management in the duties of the office, an entire disregard of the spirit, if not a legal violation of the letter of the Act of 1785, a painful carelessness on Lord Melville's part of his own private affairs, due probably to the multiplicity of the public duties which he had taken on himself, and a most misplaced confidence in his busy, laborious, crafty, and scheming paymaster.

According to Trotter's own account he had entered the Navy Office as an under-clerk, at a salary of 50*l.* a year, subsequently doubled, and had soon shown his aptitude for the business of the department by a set of regulations which he had put before his principals, who had readily adopted them.

After a year's absence from the office, by the influence of Mr. Pitt, obtained through his relatives, the Coutts's, and the good opinion which Lord Melville had entertained of him when previously in the office, he was in 1784 appointed Paymaster, at a salary of 500*l.*, subsequently increased to 800*l.* a year. On his return, as before he left the office, he found the navy balances, with the exception of those in the sub-accountant's hands for small payments, in the custody of the Bank of England, and utilized as required by sending drafts by messengers to the bank, bringing back cash to the office. As Paymaster, according to established custom, he received from the Treasurer the fullest powers of dealing with these monies without reference to his principal, only referring to him in the few cases of doubt or difficulty that arose. At about this time the office was removed from near the Bank to Somerset House, and in consequence he represented to Lord Melville the risk run in sending into the City for large amounts of money by messengers, and suggested and obtained his approval of the removal from time to time of portions of the balances to the neighbouring banking-house of his relatives, the Coutts's. Not only, he said, would it be safer to do this, but it would offer greater facilities for the payment of the West-end holders of navy bills than by giving them drafts on the Bank of England. From the first he assumed that he had the right to deal on his own account with such balances as were not likely to be required for some time, and he declared, that it was not for his greater convenience in such transactions that he advised the transfer. Of these balances a portion consisted of Exchequer fees, which would not have to be accounted for until the Treasurer had left office, and of the amounts due on uncalled-for navy bills to the extent, on the average, of 140,000*l.* a month. He did not, however, consider himself limited to these, but entitled generally to the use of any balances not likely to be immediately required.

With these sums of money, undoubtedly to a large amount, he discounted navy bills, speculated in the stocks, and lent money on short account to friendly stock-brokers. So uniform had been his success that in a comparatively short period he had realized a fortune of 65,000*l.*, and built a mansion in Edinburgh, though his accessions of property by his marriage and from his family had not amounted to more than 13,000*l.* Taking this view of his right over the public money, he had not opened a separate navy account at his own bankers, but mixed his own and the public money in one account, and thus became one of their best customers, apparently as a private client. Whether right or wrong in so doing, he could boast, without fear of contradiction, that of the 120,000,000*l.* which he had administered, not a penny was lost to the public, and that no one had even to complain that the portion of public money due to him was not paid when duly demanded. From the first, without a thought of remuneration, he had acted as Lord Melville's private agent, receiving his salary as treasurer, and his dividends, meeting his various engagements, and for that purpose keeping a regular account with him, which he from time to time laid before Lord Melville, and to which that nobleman paid little or no attention.

In the capacity of agent, Trotter admitted that he lent Lord Melville, in 1786, 4000*l.* on the security of a bond which on the face of it did not bear interest, asking no interest for the loan, and employing for this purpose the Exchequer fees' fund. In 1789 he suggested to Lord Melville, who had expressed his opinion—well founded, no doubt, as he was then Chairman of the Board of Control—that India stock would steadily rise in value, to use some of the uncalled-for balances in purchasing India stock on his own account, and received such a rebuff that he never mentioned the subject again, and feared that he had incurred the displeasure of his chief. Then it was, he said, that he represented to Lord Melville that he could borrow the amount required for the purchase—some 23,000*l.*—on the security of the stock, and finding that impossible, advanced from his own "mixed account" at Coutts's the requisite funds for the purchase, placing the stock at his bankers on trust for himself, but duly accounting to Lord Melville for the difference between the interest on the loan and the dividend on the stock. The amount of this loan was afterwards reduced by a payment of 3000*l.* by Lord Melville, and ultimately sold at a similar profit when, on his retirement, the balances at the Bank of England had to be made up. His chief never troubled himself to inquire how the money for the purchase was in reality obtained, content apparently with Trotter's statement that it could be found on the security of the stock itself.

In 1792 he made a further purchase of 2000*l.* stock,

as a qualification for Lord Melville as a voter at the India House, paying for it as before from the " mixed account," and subsequently in 1789 found, from the same source, the instalment on Lord Melville's subscription of 10,000*l.* to the loyalty loan, and for the purchase of 7000*l.* three per cent. reduced. For some of Lord Melville's engagements to bankers he believed that he had private funds remitted to him from Scotland, but generally he admitted that the advances on his principal's behalf came from that account of his own at Coutts's, in which the navy balances were mixed up with his own funds. The accounts of and the vouchers for all these intricate transactions had apparently been preserved until 1803. In that year, Trotter, as he swore, knowing Lord Melville's carelessness about papers, and fearing, as the noble lord was then in ill-health, that he might have trouble with his heir, instructed his own solicitor to draw up a release of all transactions between them. Of this no draft was sent to Lord Melville, before the engrossed copy was forwarded to him in Scotland for his execution. In this document, which was signed by Lord Melville, apparently without any careful perusal, was a clause reciting that previously to the execution or immediately after it, both parties would destroy every document or voucher which could throw any light on these transactions. Trotter denied, indeed, that he had done so before he was first examined by the Navy Commissioners. He could not, however, deny that the release was not thought of by him until after the Commissioners had called upon him for a detailed return of the balances from time to time at the Bank of England during Lord Melville's term of the treasurership, and consequently after special attention had been directed by them to the conduct of his official duties under the provisions of the Act of 1785. He was still Paymaster under the various successors of Lord Melville, and his attention had been forcibly called to the provisions of that Act by Mr. Bragge Bathurst, one of his masters, who had required him to return the balances then at Coutts's to the proper place of custody, notwithstanding the reasons he assigned for their retention at his private bankers'. The inference from these admissions is irresistible. He felt that the impending examination by the Navy Commissioners could not but condemn his dealings with the public money, and he determined to throw every difficulty he could in the way of their tracing these transactions with the Treasurer.

These explanations of Mr. Trotter's were in every way consistent with the statement made by Lord Melville to the House of Commons, and in his previous examination by the Commissioners. "I never knew," he said, "that Mr. Trotter had drawn any money for the purposes of private emolument from the Bank. I never knew that he had invested money in Exchequer or Navy Bills. I never knew that he lent on the security of stock. I never knew that he had employed public money in the purchase of Bank or India stock." He denied most implicitly that he directly or indirectly participated in Trotter's profits. He explained, as already stated, his grounds for the promotion of Trotter to the paymastership. He had no reason to believe that money was drawn from the bank for other than navy purposes, and as directed by the Act, and contended that when it was so legally drawn he was justified "in permitting Trotter to lodge it at his private bankers until it was demanded for public services." He believed that the sole advantage that would thus accrue to his paymaster "would arise from an understanding between Trotter and his bankers, as to the advantage they might derive from the customary use of money in their hands, and that such an arrangement would not prevent his paymaster from drawing, at any moment, any sum requisite for the discharge of any claim for which the deposit was liable." Until the examination of Trotter by the Commissioners, he was entirely ignorant that these navy moneys were not placed to a separate account, but mixed up with Trotter's private balances. It was only then that he learnt that Trotter's advances to him had been drawn from this mixed account, and that though the Commissioners had in 1786 recommended the increase of the Paymaster's salary, it was not until 1800, on the eve of his leaving office, and then only in consequence of the extra work thrown on the department, that he carried out their recommendations in that and other cases.

As to the transfer to Coutts's, he was satisfied at the time with the reasons assigned in its favour, and still believed them sufficient. He admitted that when he put down his name as a subscriber to the loyalty loan, he had not the money in hand, but believing it to be his duty as a public man to encourage the proposal, he borrowed the first instalment in Scotland, and whether Trotter paid the others from his own or other sources, he was entirely ignorant. Having subscribed solely for this reason, he placed a power of attorney in Coutts's hands for its sale at their own convenience, and received no profit but the dividends from the transaction. From his intimate relations with Trotter officially, he regarded him as fitted to act as his agent for minor transactions, and believed that, during the fourteen years that he so acted, nearly 70,000*l.* of his own private money passed through the hands of his paymaster. As for his use of navy money for other confidential Government purposes, Trotter had nothing to do with them. In the whole, including the 40,000*l.* to Paul and Benfield, 60,000*l.* had been so temporarily applied, and he repeated his regret that in the public interest he could not even then reveal the objects of those advances. Finally, referring to the release, he said that he believed it came to him in a blank cover from London, when staying at his son's in Scotland; that there was nothing to call his attention to the clause providing for the mutual destruction of documents and vouchers, and, that had he done so, it would not have struck him "as anything unusual, or meaning more than a clause of common form, expressive on the parties not to keep in their possession any receipts or other vouchers which could be made the ground of a claim by the heirs of either party on the other. If," he added, "the charge means anything, it must mean that Mr. Trotter and myself, being conscious of some foul transaction, had resolved to destroy the evidence of them. If this were so, what," he continued, "prevented their meeting at any period, and doing so, instead of embodying their intention in a deed that must have been known to the solicitor who prepared and his clerks, and of which, as it was proposed to be registered, a copy would have been deposited in the public office."

As the charges rested on numerous financial details, which had to be traced not only through the various navy accounts and the books of Lord Melville's and Mr. Trotter's private bankers, but to be ferreted out of the papers of Trotter's predecessor in office, the bulk of the evidence was of a most minute and uninteresting character. Practically, however, the case rested on the evidence of Trotter, and the statement of Lord Melville to the House of Commons. On the tenth day of the inquiry the case of the Commons was summed-up by Romilly, in what Lord Holland calls "a good sarcastic speech," and the ground was cleared for the defence, which was most ably made by Plomer and Adam. Grouping the charges under three heads, they contended that, as to the charge for the use of navy moneys before the Act of 1785, there was no law, common or statute, to prohibit it. Traversing the history of the management of the navy balances set out in the preamble to the charges, they reminded the Lords how, in the discussion on the report of the committee on public accounts in 1781, Fox had defended the right of public accountants to the use of uncalled-for national balances. When Lord Holland ceased to be Paymaster of the Forces in 1778, and went out of office owing some 450,000*l*., Charles Fox was indignant at the attacks on him as a defaulter. "It was true, no doubt," he said, "that Lord Chatham had never made any profit out of the balances in his hands," but he was willing to confess that his noble relative had pursued a contrary course. "I am here," he said, "ready to throw down the gauntlet and to argue it against whoever maintained a contrary opinion, that if a public accountant held himself liable at all times, without possibility of check or prevention, to produce the whole of the public money whenever he was called upon so to do, it was in that case a matter of indifference to the public whether he used it or not for his own advantage." On the same occasion the Attorney-General had said that all he required was, that the balances should be correctly stated, and that the party should be called upon to pay interest for the money left in his hands subsequent to his resignation. The resolutions of 1782 were not, as put in the preamble, declarations of what the law was, but only introductory to a new law, a sort of pledge to Parliament for the adoption of those principles at a posterior date, and which never became law until the statute of 1785. As to this charge, the only obligation rested on the warrant increasing the salary, and that at the utmost involved only a civil right.

On the second group of charges, based on the transfer of the balances to a private banker after the passing of the Act of 1785, they urged that its provisions referred only to the primary place of deposit. They insisted, therefore, that under such circumstances as had been shown in this case the navy money could be transferred from thence for convenience' sake to a private depository, subject to its always being ready to meet the claims to be made upon it. On the third group of charges, those imputing personal corruption with and connivance at Trotter's misdeeds, Lord Melville's voluntary resignation of his salary as a Secretary of State, and his acting for nine years as President of the Board of Control without pay, were relied on as proofs of his liberality and evidence against the likelihood of his demeaning himself to make such petty gains from public moneys. Trotter's exculpation of him was strongly urged, especially as he was a witness brought forward by the prosecution, on whose evidence it was alleged by the managers every reliance could be placed. Lord Melville's refusal to disclose the use of the money diverted for a time for other public services, was illustrated by the Act of Mr. Pitt in the case of the advances to the loan contractors. Lord Melville's inability to explain the payment of the two sums of 1000*l.* each paid by Trotter's predecessor to his private account from moneys drawn in the name of the chief cashier of the victualling office, was ascribed to the length of time that had elapsed since the transaction, and Lord Melville admitted carelessness in the management of his own money-matters.

Sir A. Piggott's reply was confined to the interpretations put on the statute of 1785, and the civil obligation said to be involved in the warrant. The former, he said, made the statute a sham, the latter was in direct variance with the dictum of Lord Mansfield in the case of Bembridge, "that if a man accepts a place of trust and confidence, especially when attended with a pecuniary trust, he is amenable to the king for the faithful discharge of his duties. There is a breach of trust between subject and subject, in which the party would be liable to a civil action, but with the Crown he is indictable."² It was well replied by Plomer that the circumstances of the two cases were different. The charge against Bembridge was the fraudulent abstraction of a loan, and clearly an indictable offence, and the opinion of Lord Mansfield a dictum inapplicable to the facts of this indictment.

The case was now ripe for judgment, and further speaking might well have been spared. The vanity of Whitbread, however, could not be repressed. Though he had from the first movement in the case pursued the subject with prodigious diligence, and understood the whole transaction thoroughly, he was bent upon displaying his own wit and eloquence, rather than explaining the complicated accounts on which the charges rested. Hence, for the greater portion of two days, he wearied the Lords with recriminations on the counsel who had attacked him in his double position of prosecuting counsel and witness, and laudatory remarks on the purity of the principles and exalted motives of the managers. These he illustrated by personal recollections of his own and his father's career in business, which deservedly laid him open to the witticisms of contemporary satirists and caricaturists.

One instance of his oratorical bathos, immortalized by Canning's lines, may be mentioned. When, as a witness, he attempted to give his version of Lord Melville's statement to the House of Commons, he had been sharply cross-examined by Plomer as to his reasons for recollecting the date of the 11th of June. "My lords," he now said, "there are in the history of

² Bembridge's case, Howell's "State Trials," vol. iii. p. 120.

every man, however obscure, certain *dies notandi*. Some, indeed, bring to the minds of the children the gallant exploits of their ancestors; others have their memory impressed, like myself, by more humble events. Now, my Lords, the 11th of June is to me a *dies notandus*. On the 11th of June my father set up in business. On the 11th of June he annually balanced his accounts, and on the 11th of June his son was required to assist him in his laborious business. On the 11th of June he knew the progressive increase of his substance and the generous fruits of his honest industry. On the 11th of June my father died, and the day on which a good man dies is not to be forgotten."[3] Such a staid and decorous assembly as the

[3] Versified by Canning in the well-known lines in the *Oracle*, beginning,—
" If you ask why the Eleventh of June I remember
Far better than April, or May, or November,
On that day, my Lords, with pride I assure ye,
My sainted progenitor set up his brewery.
On that day, in the morn he began brewing beer;
On that day, too, commenced his connubial career;
On that day he renew'd and he issued his bills;
On that day he clear'd all the cash from his tills.
On that day he died, having finish'd his summing,
And the angels all cried, ' Here's Old Whitbread a-coming.'
So that day still I hail, with a smile and a sigh,
For his beer with an ē, and his bier with an I.
And still on that day, in the hottest of weather,
The whole Whitbread family dine all together.
So long as the beams of this house shall support
The roof which o'ershades this respectable court,
So long as the light shall pour in at these windows,
Where Hastings was tried for oppressing the Hindoos,
My name shall shine bright, as my ancestor's shines,
Mine recorded in journals, his blazon'd on signs."

House of Lords, had they not been then sitting as the highest Court of Justice, could hardly have refrained from laughter at such a specimen of bathos. That he did more harm than good by his orations, is admitted by one of his political friends, who tried his best to repair the mistakes the fluent speaker had committed.[4]

After a short adjournment, to allow of the voluminous evidence being printed, the Lords reassembled to consider their future course of procedure. Though, as the House sat with closed doors, no authorized report was taken of their debates, the account given by a contemporary writer who had the best opportunity of obtaining information, may be accepted as substantially correct.[5] At the commencement of the discussions, an attempt was made by the Chancellor and Lord Ellenborough to set aside the old custom for the Lords to decide on their verdict in their own house, and then adjourn to Westminster Hall, merely to go through the form of giving judgment. The defective and confusing form of the Articles was severely criticized, and after a long debate the form of question to be put to each peer on each Article was settled, and a further adjournment to the 2nd of June decided upon. On that day the usual motion was made, and discussed at considerable length, and with much feeling on both sides, "that the Commons had made good their first article of charges," and

[4] Lord Holland, see note *ante*, p. 195.
[5] Account of trial in "Annual Register," written by Allen of Holland House notoriety, presumably from Lord Holland's information.

adjourned for the opinion of the Judges on points of law raised by Lord Eldon.

The first of the questions put to the Judges was, whether the transfer of the navy funds to a private banker was illegal. To this they answered unanimously, that the mere transfer from the Bank of England to a private banker was lawful, and was not, in law, a crime or offence. To the second question they said, "if for the purpose of being deposited in the hands of a private banker," it was to be understood that such was the object of the transfer, then they held it illegal, though the moneys so transferred were ultimately applied to their proper use. If, on the contrary, the transfer was " made *bonâ fide* as the means, or the supposed means of more conveniently applying the money to navy services," then it was lawful.[6] Sir James Mansfield declared " the words of

[6] Questions to the Judges. First, "Whether moneys issued from the Exchequer to the Governor and Company of the Bank of England on account of the Treasurer of H.M. Navy, pursuant to 25th George III. c. 31, may be lawfully drawn from the said bank by the person duly authorized by the Treasurer to draw upon the bank, according to the said Act: the drafts of such person being made for the purpose of discharging bills actually assigned upon the Treasurer before the date of such drafts, but not actually presented for payment before such drawing; and whether such moneys, so drawn for such purpose, may be lawfully lodged and deposited in the hands of a banker other than the Bank, until the payment of such assigned bills, and for the purpose of making payment thereof when the payment thereof shall be demanded, or whether such act in so drawing moneys and lodging them as aforesaid is in the law a crime or offence."

Second Question. "Whether moneys issued from the Exchequer to the Bank of England on account of the Treasurer of the

the statute were so wide of their intention, that had Lord Melville spent the money entrusted to him at the gambling-table, and yet paid the demands when made upon him he would have incurred no liability, but only such as the laws annexed to gaming." Similar motions, affirming the charges of the Commons on the other articles, were subsequently made, but all adjourned without decision ; and of many further questions proposed to be put to the Judges one alone was eventually allowed on the 6th of June. The question then put covered the most important portion of the articles. The Judges were asked whether before the passing of the Act ordering the deposit of the navy funds in the Bank of England, and after the warrant increasing the salary of the Treasurer in lieu of all other emoluments and profits, it was lawful for him " to apply any sum of money entrusted to him for navy purposes to any other one whatsoever, public or private, without express authority for so doing, and whether such application would have been a misdemeanour punishable by information or indictment." They were again unanimous that such an act was not " unlawful so as to constitute a misdemeanour punishable by information or indictment."

Navy, pursuant to 25th George III. c. 31 may be lawfully drawn therefrom by drafts drawn in the name and on behalf of the said Treasurer, in the form prescribed in the same Act, for the purpose of such moneys being ultimately applied to navy services; but in the meantime, and until the same shall be required to be applied for the purpose of being deposited in the hands of a private banker or other private depository of such moneys in the name, and under the immediate control and disposition of some other person or persons than the said Treasurer."

It is to be regretted that no record of the numerous speeches made during these discussions has as yet been discovered. Lords Holland and Lauderdale, with the Chancellor and the Chief Justice, exerted themselves for a conviction, but Erskine's ignorance of the forms of the House to which he was so new, and Ellenborough's intemperance, undoubtedly weakened the effect of their exertion. On the other side Lord Melville's old colleagues, with the exception of Lord Sidmouth, headed by Lord Eldon, were far more than a match for the supporters of the impeachment.[7] Resting his defence, on the points of law, on the answers of the Judges, Lord Eldon directed all his ability and influence to repel the charges of personal corruption. He acknowledged that " he would rather cut off his right arm than be guilty of such culpable negligence " and criminal indulgence to his paymaster as Lord Melville had, and admitted, that had the Commons thus confined their charges, he must have pronounced him guilty.[8] On the 12th of June the Lords

[7] Third Question to the Judges. "Whether it was lawful for the Treasurer of the Navy, before the passing of 25th George III. c. 31, and more especially when, by warrant from his Majesty, his salary as such Treasurer aforesaid was augmented in full satisfaction for all wages, fees, and other profits and emoluments, to apply any sum of money entrusted to him for navy purposes to any other one whatsoever, public or private, without express authority for so doing, and whether such application by such Treasurer would have been a misdemeanour punishable by information or impeachment."

[8] " In the Lords, Lord Erskine's ignorance of forms, and Lord Ellenborough's intemperance, threatened to confirm the impression so unfavourable to the prosecution produced by the mismanagers in Westminster Hall. Lord Lauderdale and

gave their verdict, by substantial but varying majorities, acquitting Lord Melville on all the charges.[9]

The charges were clearly divisible under three heads. First, comprising the first and tenth articles, that previous to January, 1786, he had, contrary to the intention of the warrant increasing the Treasurer's pay, applied public moneys to his own private use. After the opinion of the Judges on the third question put to them, it is surprising to find that any votes were given for a verdict of guilty. The second class of charge, that contained in the second article of the impeachment, involved the question of his guilt in allowing his paymaster to transfer the navy moneys to his own bankers. As the legality or illegality of this act turned on the intention for which it was permitted to be done, there was reasonable scope for such a difference of opinion as was shown in the narrow majority by which he was acquitted. The remaining charges imputed his connivance at the use by Trotter of the money transferred to his private bankers for the profit of Lord Melville as well as his own. On those imputing that he knew and allowed Trotter to misapply the public moneys in loans to and other payments on Lord Melville's behalf, the majorities were as decided as could be expected in a bitter party contest. On one charge, indeed, that in the fourth article, myself exerted ourselves in the intermediate discussions. We perhaps did not obtain a vote from any lords who were not already convinced, but we drove away some who were disposed to acquit Lord Melville, and we harassed the consciences of many who were determined at all risks to save the associate of Pitt."—Lord Holland.

[9] Lord Holland, *vide supra*.

that he knowingly permitted Trotter to place navy moneys in a broker's hands for purposes of profit, the Lords were unanimous in acquitting him. On the next article, that charging him with fraudulently applying the 10,000*l.* to his own or some other corrupt purpose, the minority against him fell to three. On the other articles in which personal connivance and knowledge were not charged the majorities were sufficient, and no more.[1]

The failure of the impeachment was a blow to the Government of Lord Grenville. The public, we are told, imputed the acquittal either to the fear of the political party to which Lord Melville belonged, or to tenderness for the species of guilt in which he was involved. By his friends it was hailed as a triumph over party rancour, and so satisfied was Lord Melville with the result that he at once resumed his place in the House, and took part in the discussion against Lord Lauderdale's appointment to India. Considering how much a strict interpretation of the words of

[1] Question put on each article, "Is Lord Viscount Melville Guilty or Not Guilty of the high crimes and misdemeanours charged against him in the —— Article?"

			Guilty.	Not Guilty.	Majority.
Result, Art.		1.	15	120	105
"	"	2.	54	84	27
"	"	3.	52	83	31
"	"	4.	0	135	Unanimous.
"	"	5.	3	131	128
"	"	6.	47	88	41
"	"	7.	50	85	35
"	"	8.	14	121	107
"	"	9.	14	121	107
"	"	10.	11	124	113

statutes had served him on his trial, it is characteristic of his boldness that in discussing this appointment he insisted "that Acts of Parliament were not to be literally and technically construed, but their sense or spirit collected from the temper of the times, the resolutions of the House of Parliament in which they originated, and the speeches and intentions of those who proposed them." Though from time to time he spoke in the House of Lords, and his name was restored to the list of Privy Councillors, he had lost much of his former political influence. His friends in Scotland, however, were faithful, and by their parliamentary support made him worth conciliating by any weak minister. Hence when, in 1809, Perceval succeeded to the Premiership, on the retirement of the Duke of Portland, though he refused to readmit Lord Melville himself to office, he was anxious to have the assistance and countenance of his eldest son. For a time Lord Melville refused his sanction, though offered an Earldom as a consolation for his own disappointment. Eventually he consented, and Mr. Dundas joined Perceval as head of the Board of Control.[2] From that time Lord Melville gradually sank out of sight as a public man, living for the most part in retirement in Scotland, where he died in 1811, within five years of his impeachment.

[2] See correspondence in October, 1809, between Perceval, Lord Melville, and Mr. Dundas, in vol. ii. of Walpole's "Life of Perceval."

CHAPTER VIII.

THE GREAT COMMISSARIAT FRAUDS.

ALEX. DAVISON AND VALENTINE JONES.

DECEMBER, 1808, AND MAY 26TH, 1809.

DURING the closing years of the eighteenth century and the period included in the present criminal records, there were few private persons more useful to the ministers of the day than Alexander Davison. In Bloomsbury he was apparently only one of the many army and navy clothiers and contractors who were daily amassing fortunes through the heavy demands for military and naval stores and equipments created by the long and difficult wars with France and Spain, which at that period tried to the uttermost the resources of our country. In another place he was a banker and financier, ever ready to seize the advantage which the financial pressure on the country offered. At the West-end, and at his country seat, he was the liberal patron of art, and the amphitryon not merely of commoners in high places, but of peers and royal princes, offering the splendour of his hospitality even to the heir of the Crown. Many a party quarrel was made up at his dining-table, and many a party difficulty evaded by his shrewd counsels. Not only ostensibly, but in reality his means were immense, and as he made money easily, so he spent it liberally. From the outbreak of the great war he had taken a leading share in the contracts offered by Government, and, apparently, until tempted by over-greed, had furnished his supplies with as much honesty, and from his great capital, with more punctuality than his rivals in trade.

In his eagerness to get a seat in Parliament for Ilchester, with his characteristic energy he stopped at nothing to secure his election. So openly and lavishly did he bribe, that the election committee which sat on the case unhesitatingly reported that such a gross system of corruption and of individual acts of bribery had been carried on by him and his colleague Parsons, that the House of Commons, after a brief discussion, ordered both of them to be prosecuted. The result was their conviction and imprisonment for twelve months. So lightly was this offence then regarded, that as soon as Davison came out of prison, Lord Moira obtained permission of Mr. Pitt to be allowed to appoint him Commissary-General of the Forces, which he then commanded, and subsequently, with Lord Grenville's full consent, made him Treasurer of the Ordnance. Nominally this last office was unremunerative. To Davison, as a banker, it could not but be a mine of wealth, as from three to four millions of money annually passed through his hands, and, according to the dangerous custom of the time, he had full power over, and full use of the unemployed balances. It has been seen, in Lord Melville's case, how large these balances could be made by the prevailing system of drawing on the Treasury greatly in advance of the real wants of the department to which the moneys were issued, and the length of time likely to elapse before the amounts advanced were accounted for. To the last, Davison so ingeniously contrived his frauds that even when his deceptions were clearly proved, leading officials in several state departments testified not only to the goodness and punctuality of his supplies, and his liberality on several occasions towards the Government, but to the correctness of the accounts which had come under their special cognizance. Like all ingenious rogues, until he was found out, his character was exceptionally good, and apparently trustworthy. His real character and mode of doing business only came out when his accounts were investigated by the committee on military expenditure.

In the third report of that committee, the Master General of the Barracks in the Channel Islands—a General De Lancey—was reported to have been in the habit of drawing through Greenwood, the army agent, immense sums of money before they were in reality required for the public service. In that portion of his accounts which the committee had been able to examine, they reported that he made overcharges to the extent of 90,000*l*. With De Lancey, Davison was a favourite contractor for stores at a commission on the market price, but for coals as a merchant. Whether he charged the stores supplied on commission at fictitious prices, and thus reaped a merchant's profit in addition, could not be proved. That he did so may be fairly assumed from the facts disclosed on his trial for a similar subsequent offence, and that he did so in the case of the coals was not denied. By the contract he was bound to supply at market prices and to give certificates of persons of respectability in the trade that these prices were fair. The character of the persons whose certificates he sent in may be conceived from the fact, that one of them was his sub-contractor and agent on commission, and was convicted and suffered death for perjury. De Lancey did not trouble himself to inquire, and took all for granted. The result was that Davison not only took to himself the extra chaldron on the score allowed him by the coal-owner, but so timed his deliveries to Government as to enable him to charge the highest winter prices for what he had purchased at summer rates. It was calculated that the entire cost to Government thus incurred was not less than thirty per cent. on the real market price. When asked by the Commissioners for his cash account, he had the effrontery to refuse it, on the excuse that "it was too mixed up to enable him to give a clear view." This impudent fraud was brought before the House of Commons, and proceedings ordered for the recovery of the overcharges. Thus put upon the track of this man's misdeeds, the law officers soon obtained information sufficient, despite the legal difficulties surrounding such prosecutions, to put him on his trial for similiar frauds in other contracts with De Lancey, and to lay bare the ingenious and impudent system by which they had been effected.[1]

[1] Information by Attorney-General, Sir Vicary Gibbs, filed Hilary term, 1807. Trial before Lord Ellenborough and special

In 1794, General De Lancey, as Barrack-Master-General, invited Davison to act as buyer of military stores for the Government on a fixed commission on the amount of the purchases. He was to appoint a proper packer, to whom the goods were to be sent by the contractors, and to furnish the department with receipts from these contractors for each consignment. Davison, by letter, accepted the office on a commission of two and a half per cent., including all percentages on making insurances, recovering losses, averages, and replacing all damaged or unserviceable articles delivered at the barracks. A man of the name of Lodge was appointed as packer, and the goods were sent to him with a delivery-note in the form: " Mr. Lodge receive from A. B. [naming the supplier] such and such goods," Lodge sending to Davison weekly returns of the goods received, and subsequently a half-yearly return of his receipts and deliveries. From these Davison professed to make out a similar return for Government, adding the amounts professedly paid for the articles supplied. For several years apparently the duty was honourably performed by Davison. In 1798, however, he made a plausible but entirely unfounded representation to De Lancey, that in consequence of the increased pressure on the trade, caused by the greatly increased armaments, there was a difficulty in getting some classes of stores from the other makers, and requested permission to supply them from his own workshops. Without any inquiry De Lancey granted the required permission, and from

jury, December 7, 1808. Attorney-General and Garrow for the Crown. Dallas for Defendant.

that time in reality, but as yet not openly, the bulk of the stores came from Davison's Bedford Street warehouse, and in his account with Government he charged his commission as buyer as well as his prices as the seller. That the authority to supply stores did not carry with it the right to charge commission as buyer, might, one would suppose, have been assumed. It was almost unnecessary for the Barrack-Master-General to deny that he ever gave Davison such an authority, or to repudiate any such intention as a gross breach of his duty as an officer. That Davison did not believe that he had such an authority is evident from the scheme he devised for supplying these stores from his own warehouse in the names of fictitious salesmen.

In the delivery-notes sent to Lodge, the goods were represented as sent in by Mungo Shedden, who was Davison's manager at the Bedford Street store. When, however, the half-yearly returns for the department had to be made out, Davison saw the danger there was of Mungo Shedden's name being known at the barrack office, and the deception discovered. The name of an inferior clerk—one Watson—not likely to be recognized, was therefore substituted for Sheddon's in the bills of parcels, and another junior clerk signed receipts for the amounts professedly paid for them, in the name of the fictitious seller. His book-keeper offered himself as the scape-goat. He swore that he had suggested to Davison the impropriety of making out the bills of parcels in his own name, and that in consequence of his remonstrance the trick was played. If he had authority to sell from his own stores, why should he not do so openly, as he did subsequently in 1803? Because before then the inquiries of the Commissioners had commenced, and Davison's accounts had been the subject of discussion—because then it would be suicidal to charge commission, and the advice of his clerk to refrain from so doing was seen by his master to be indispensable.

The book-keeper swore that on his giving this advice Davison ordered him to get the accounts back and make the proper alteration, saying, " If I am to err, I would rather err on the other side,"—that he then applied to the accountant in the barrack department to have the accounts back for correction, and on his refusal went to De Lancey, who replied that it was beyond his power to do so, but that any errors might be corrected in a supplemental account. A supplemental account was indeed sent in, in May, 1806, in which it was admitted that items to the amount of 15,000*l.* had been improperly charged, and Davison instead of claiming a balance in his favour of more than 9000*l.*, confessed himself a debtor to the department to the extent of 6000*l.*

Though the accounts were asked for, if the book-keeper is to be believed, with the object of correcting the charges for commission illegally taken, and the supplemental account was suggested to cure all errors, no overcharge for commission appeared in it. The book-keeper said " he forgot to insert it!" It may seem strange that General De Lancey did not discover this illegal charge of commission when he countersigned the half-yearly accounts forwarded to him from the accountant's department. But the truth was, that in these accounts, the only ones seen by that officer, no separate charge for commission appeared, the amount charged on each consignment being included in its professed cost. The accountants to whom the bills of parcels and the charge for commission were sent had, therefore, no knowledge of any leave having been given to Davison to supply stores from his own warehouse, and, even if they had known it, would have been deceived by the bills being made out in Watson's name, and apparently bearing his receipt for the nominal cost. These receipts—forgeries of the clerk Allen—it was admitted by the book-keeper, were signed in batches of several half-years subsequently to the delivery of the goods, and used as required.

At the trial, which came on before Lord Ellenborough, on the 7th December, 1808, the charge was confined to one half-yearly account, that ending December, 1800. In this, stores to the amount of 52,000*l.* had been supplied by Davison himself, but nominally by Watson, and a commission of 1323*l.* had been included. In addition to the evidence already detailed, the Attorney-General put in the letters constituting the contract with De Lancey, the terms of which could admit of only one reasonable interpretation. In his examination by the Commissioners of Military Inquiry, Davison declared that this was the *only* agreement he had entered into with the Barrack-Master-General; and, in the same examination, Davison had given the following account of his mode of executing this contract :—

"Q. 11. I received the order from the Barrack-Master-General ; the goods were procured wherever they could be had the cheapest and the most expeditiously. The examination of bedding was by the packer, who was responsible; the examination of other articles was had at the barracks, and if not satisfactory to the Barrack-Master, they were returned at my own expense. I was responsible for the articles until I got the Barrack-Master's receipt. My account with the Barrack Office was a regular half-yearly one, *vouched by the original bills of parcels and the receipts of the parties from whom purchased."*

"Q. 15. The bills of parcels were sent half-yearly with the half-yearly accounts, *and of course the names of the tradesmen appeared thereon."*

"Q. 31. There were some articles that were furnished from my own clothing warehouse, *upon these no commission was charged."*

For the defence, Mr. Dallas relied mainly on proving that in 1798 General De Lancey had varied the agreement to the extent of allowing Davison to supply stores, when absolutely necessary, from his own warehouse;—that the charge of commission on these was made either under the erroneous notion that, as he had other duties to perform under his original agreement (such as seeing that the stores were good and safely conveyed), he was entitled to his commission in addition to his profit as the seller, or that he was not conscious that commission had been charged. He urged on the jury, that in his examination by the Commissioners as to the existence of a second agreement, as the question put to him related only to the agreement then under consideration, his answer referred to that and that alone; and that the making out the bills of parcels in the names of his clerks was done with such publicity that it was absurd to suppose that he could have done so fraudulently, and, besides, it was never done until after the date of the second agreement with De Lancey.

The excuse for Davison's denial of the second agreement to the Commissioners was too weak to need further comment. Dallas evidently expected to prove that the second agreement was meant by De Lancey to include the commission, but he failed miserably, and with this failure the whole fabric of his defence collapsed. His own witness, Bowring, the book-keeper, on cross-examination, only made his case worse. In the end he had nothing to rely upon except the improbability of a man in such a position risking his place and character for so small a sum, an improbability made the greater by the high testimonies to his previous character by men of the most unexceptionable character, who, as heads of public departments, had known Davison and his previous dealings with Government.

In his charge to the jury, Lord Ellenborough called their attention in an especial manner to the admission of Bowring, the book-keeper, that the bills of parcels were deliberately made out by Davison's direction in false names, and false receipts given for the amount charged "as a matter of form." "How," said the Chief Justice, "can a man, who wishes to have any estimation in a Court of Justice, state that the falsification of an important document upon which so much is to be paid, is 'only a matter of form,' the circumstances under which it was framed being thereby concealed from the persons to whom it was tendered? Bowring says, I communicated Mr. Davison's directions to Mr. Watson and Mr. Shedden. I remember that the accounts came back from the barracks to have the accounts put up in a different form ; the first receipt by Allen was signed at a subsequent period to 1801, I think, in consequence of the accounts coming back. Several of them, that is to say, three or four half-yearly receipts were made out all at the same time to comply with the form of the barrack-office. *Mr. Davison seeing the inconsistency of bills of parcels Alex. Davison bought of Alex. Davison,*' said the voucher is of no consequence because the prices are agreed on." " But," said the Judge, " it was extremely material whether it should be reported by the barrack-office as a purchase by him as agent or seller upon which commission was due or not. A change was made in 1802, and then Alex. Davison was made debtor to the Bedford Street house ; now, if it was possible to make that charge in that way, and make him buyer and seller, why it was not done at first seems to puzzle all human ingenuity." As for the evidence to character, that, he reminded the jury, " was valuable only when the evidence was in even balance. In such a case character would preponderate for the defendant ; but to let it have that character the case must be reduced to that situation." During the brief period of the jury's absence an attempt was made by Dallas to show that there was a variance between the agreement set out in the indictment and that proved in the case ; the latter, as he read it, giving a commission on insurances as well as on prices, the former confining it to a commission on prices only. The point met with no encouragement from the Judge, and, on second thought, was deemed too doubtful to be raised when the prisoner was called up for judgment on the verdict of guilty.

When, after the lapse of a month, the defendant was brought up for judgment, in addition to affidavits in mitigation, by Lords Moira and Chatham and Sir Even Nepean, detailing previous good and liberal services of Davison as a Government contractor, Mr. Stanbank and General De Lancey, who had apparently refreshed their memory, endeavoured to put a better colour on the transaction. Stanbank now remembered that Davison called his attention to the charge of commission in 1803-4—that he or Bowring mentioned the intention of repaying it—that in consequence he thought it was included in the supplemental account, and told De Lancey so in 1808. This conversation with Stanbank, De Lancey now recollected. Lord Ellenborough simply read out Stanbank's previous statement, utterly inconsistent with this late recollection, and made no further comment on these very suspicious after-thoughts.[2] In his speech in aggravation

[2] Stanbank, the chief accountant in the barrack department, in his examination in chief, referring to Bowring's visit to him, and request to have the accounts back, swore, "I think he said it was for the purpose of making some correction. I don't know that he mentioned the part of the account he wished to correct, nor the reason why he wished to correct it. I did not give him the account back, because it was settled and signed by General De Lancey. I think I told him that, if there were any corrections to make, he might give credit in a supplementary account. I don't remember his saying anything about commission improperly charged."

the Attorney-General spoke, evidently with an object, of the total amounts by way of commission so fraudulently received, and of the duty of the culprit to repay them, or of the Government to proceed for their recovery. Davison appears to have taken this allusion as an opening in his favour. By agreement apparently, ostensibly on the ground of pressure of business in the Court, judgment was again deferred until the end of April, and in the interval 18,000*l.* were repaid by Davison to the Exchequer. In the end his act of contrition was of no benefit to him. The sentence passed was twenty-one months' imprisonment, making, with the time he had been in prison since his trial, the full penalty for such an offence as that of which he had been convicted.

The frauds of Valentine Jones, which were among those brought to light by the West Indian Commission of 1802, had been perpetrated by him as far back as 1796, in his capacity of Commissary-General of our forces in the West Indies, a position to which he had risen by his previous good services. For ten years he had acted as Public Secretary at Barbadoes, an office of great confidence, with a high character for diligence and integrity, and when in 1794 he was appointed Deputy Commissary, he appears in the discharge of his onerous duties to have maintained his former character. It was due to this, that he was in the following year sent out as Commissary-General, and the whole of the enormous expenditure required for the supplies of the 30,000 troops in our garrisons in the West Indies, and the conveyance of the detachments from place to place was placed under his sole superintendence. Early in 1795 the home government issued fresh instructions to all commissariat servants in the hope of checking the vicious system of private profits which had hitherto prevailed in that and indeed in all branches of the public service. Additional pay was given, sufficient to make these officers fairly independent of irregular gains, and special instructions issued forbidding them from "deriving the smallest advantage in any shape whatever from their situations beyond their pay and the actual allowances for provisions and furniture supplied from the other departments." Instant dismission would follow on a breach of these orders, and the offending party be prevented from ever again being employed in any public situation. These instructions appear, at first, to have made a deep impression on the new Commissary-General, as he lost no time in transmitting them to his assistant in the West Indies, and in impressing on him the necessity for their strict observance, and calling his and his subordinates' attention to the fact that the increased pay had been granted solely to prevent any further attempt at illegal profits. Yet within a few weeks afterwards the writer had agreed to the fraud by which, within less than a year, nearly 90,000*l.* were abstracted from Government.

Though his warrant of appointment is dated in September, 1795, Jones does not appear to have arrived in the West Indies until the following May. On his arrival he found the Commander-in-Chief, General Knox, temporarily acting as Commissary-General, and one Matthew Higgins, a local merchant, supplying the troopships. For some reason or other this contractor fancied that the new Commissary-General would not confirm him in his contract. Under this impression, and in all probability believing in the existence of the old system of gratuities, he took counsel with a Mr. Hugh Rose, an acting deputy-paymaster, who had already shared his Government contracts (a friend if not a connexion of Jones's), how, through his influence, the loss of his contract might be avoided. Rose's interference was as effectual as it was profitable to himself and his friend, the Commissary-General. According to his tale he had arranged that not only should Higgins keep his shipping contract, but should have a preference in supplying the troops with spirits and provisions on surrendering *three-fourths* of the profits. Of the total profits Jones was to have *one-half*, and the go-between Rose *one-quarter*. In the brief space of ten months the share of the Commissary-General amounted to 87,000*l.*, and the contractor was no doubt well paid with his profit of nearly 44,000*l.*, and would gladly have supplied Government at that rate of profit, if these harpies had not interfered and carried off their portions of the plunder. "You see in every way," said the Attorney-General in his opening speech, "this injures the public, who are unprotected and undefended from the fraud. In the first place he takes this sum from the public; in the next, he divests himself of all possibility of correcting abuses, creating in himself an interest to raise these charges to the highest possible amount, in order that his profits may be raised in proportion."

The arrangement of the contract, as told by the contractor, is simple. When at St. Lucie, on board one of his ships, with Mr. Rose and the Commissary-General, " Rose told me that he had arranged the business with Mr. Jones, or settled it for me, and that I was to continue the contract. I told him I was very much obliged to him. He replied to me that he was obliged to make terms with Mr. Jones. I asked what terms? He said that Mr. Jones must have a moiety of the emoluments arising from the contract, and the other moiety was to be divided between him (Rose) and myself. I told him that I would have nothing to do with it. Rose said I was very wrong; that I should think of it; that there were many people very ready to take it, and willing. Rose said that the vessels might be discharged, for Mr. Jones had commenced purchasing vessels; that the intention, he thought, was to buy for Government, and to navigate them, and let them be the property of the Government. I told him I thought he would find that impossible. Rose used further arguments, and said that sooner than I should not go on with the contract, I might keep his part of it. I then told him that I should go on with it, and I would not accept his part."

"Afterwards he stated to me that for the loss I should sustain on giving up so much of the contract it would be made up to me in the supplies—that whatever supplies were wanting for the use of the Government, I would be applied to for furnishing them. It was mentioned that the profit arising from the supplies was to be divided in the same manner with the profits arising out of the vessel contract. This was on ship-board." "Mr. Rose told me Mr. Jones was in the cabin, and desired me to go down to him, which I did. The conversation with Rose was on the quarter-deck. *I went down to Mr. Jones, and I repeated to him the conversation that had passed between Mr. Rose and myself, as far as regarded the terms of the agreement and my acquiescence. He assented to it, as far as my memory goes,* by an inclination of his head, rather than by any expression."

"Q. You stated the terms to him?—A. I did.

"Lord Ellenborough: Did you state them distinctly and audibly?—A. I did. After this I went on with the vessel contract, and the supply of stores to a considerable extent for nine or ten months."

The result of this Jovian nod was, that, when the account of these ten months' contracts was closed, it appeared from the books of the contractor, into which more than once the Commissary-General had looked to see how the account went on, that a profit had been made of 306,547*l*. 15*s*. 8*d*. currency,[3] and that he was paid by Jones only half this sum, the remainder going into Jones's own pocket. Of these accounts there could be no suspicion, as they were made up in 1797, and closed years before even a rumour arose of these transactions, or before any inquiry had been instituted. But for the searching inquiries of the West Indian Commission the fraud would have slept securely, and Higgins, when he had his accounts made out, could not have done so

[3] Equal to about 174,000*l*. sterling.

to trump up a charge against an innocent man in order to cover some iniquity of his own.

But this plunder, large as it was, was not all that fell to the lot of the Commissary-General. Higgins, Jones, and Rose had an "American adventure" of this kind. When payments had to be made in the West Indies, Rose, as deputy-paymaster, drew bills on the Treasury, which had to be brought into the market for sale, and the proceeds credited to the Treasury. As these were issued they were given to Higgins to discount, who, to do so with greater profit to himself and partners, established a house in Philadelphia, where he could buy provisions at lower rates, and make a further profit by debiting the Government with a greater rate of discount than that at which he was thus enabled to negotiate these bills. The fact that the accounts of this transaction could not be closed with the other account in 1797, but formed a subject of future inquiry and settlement in 1800, furnished a piece of evidence strongly corroborative of the entry of the greater fraud, as it appeared in Higgins's books. The actual profit on the "American adventure" amounted to 3068*l.*, of which Jones's share would be 1534*l.* When, however, that account was ripe for settlement, it had been discovered that there were errors in the former settlement of profit on the contract to the extent of 1411*l.*, one-half of which would fall on Jones. His share, therefore, of the "American adventure" was reduced to a little over 829*l.*, for which sum a receipt "in full of all accounts between him and Matthew Higgins," dated February 26th, 1800, was produced. "Let me suppose," said Sir Vicary Gibbs, "these gentlemen to have acted honestly. Mr. Jones was the Commissary, Mr. Higgins was the merchant. Higgins was to supply the Commissary with stores, he was to pay for the hire of the vessels—money might be due from Jones to Higgins—it was impossible, in the ordinary course of things, that any could be due from Mr. Higgins to Mr. Jones. Will Mr. Jones explain this balance—will he give an account how this debt arose?"

No explanation could be ventured on, beyond the assertion that the "American adventure" was entirely independent of the contract, and that the errors in some previous account referred to in the settlement might have been equally a purely private matter. Such an assertion, unsupported as it was by evidence, was worthless, and any further defence was mainly rested on the fact of Higgins being an accomplice in the fraud, and therefore requiring more confirmation than such as was furnished by the accounts and the statements of the accountant who had checked them. The idea of the fraud, it was urged, originated with Higgins, and though, if proved, legally it was a fraud in the case of a public officer, yet that no exorbitant charges were proved to have been made, and that the stores would have cost as much without the fraudulent agreement.

One person, Hugh Rose, who could, had he pleased, have explained the whole secret, was not called by either side. The Crown refused to call him because he had declined to give any information, and might eventually be subjected to prosecution for his part in this and former contracts. The counsel for the prisoner declined on the ground of his refusal to answer questions. He was far too dangerous a person to be put in the box by either side. In fact, as Lord Ellenborough said, the whole case rested on the credibility of Higgins, who was not legally an accomplice under this indictment and whose testimony, even if he were so, was to some extent confirmed by the books and the receipt for the balance of the final settlement. The previous good character of the defendant was not contested. Up to the time of this fraudulent transaction, it had been of the best, and if that was not his first fraud, he had been sagaciously adroit in not being found out. A verdict of Guilty was of course at once returned, and when called up for judgment the only additional excuse that was urged, was that he had been continued in office for a year after rumours had been circulated of his misconduct, and that during that period he never made any illegal profit. The full punishment awarded by the statute —three years' imprisonment and deprivation of future employment by Government—was passed upon him.

CHAPTER IX.

THE DUKE OF YORK AND MARY ANN CLARKE.

JANUARY 27TH TO MARCH 30TH, 1809.

FREDERICK AUGUSTUS, the second of the numerous sons of George the Third, and his father's favourite, born on the 16th of August, 1763, as a child shared in the good looks of his elder brother, and as a man grew to be known as one of the handsome sons of the aged monarch. Like most of his brothers, willing and sharp in acquiring the learning which then went to make up a liberal education, he shared with them the family failing of an utter incapacity to understand the value of money or to calculate the extravagance of his mode of life, and readily became the youthful votary of sensual pleasures and victim of his passion for gambling and of his unthinking extravagance. From his first manhood the companion of the Prince of Wales in the immoralities of the fashionable life of the time, from his easy and generous temper he all the more easily became the prey of women notorious as much for their craft as for their personal attractions and licentiousness. From lack of thought, or misplaced confidence in the objects of his pleasures, he allowed them to mix up his name with transactions the mere idea of which were utterly at variance with his frank and manly character. Intended for a military career, he went in his seventeenth year to Germany to study war in the school of Frederic at Berlin. There he not only acquired a thorough theoretical knowledge of the art of war, but learnt to appreciate the claims of soldiers as well as officers to a just and honest administration of military affairs, and to being regarded as something better than mere machines for mutual slaughter. After various honorary steps in the army, he was created Duke of York and Albany in 1784, and, three years afterwards, on his return from abroad, took his seat in the House of Lords. Soon after this, in 1791, he was married to the eldest daughter of the King of Prussia, a political alliance which brought no comfort to either party, leading almost at once to a practical though not an avowed separation. At Oatlands the Duchess followed her amusements, content apparently with the few formal visits paid her by her husband, whilst the Duke, now in one part of London, now in another, sometimes in more than one quarter at the same time, and not unfrequently within sight of Oatlands itself, kept establishments for what society called his "favourites," and was bled unceasingly by a succession of mistresses, whose sole object seemed to be to coin money out of their regal protector.

Raised to the Commandership-in-Chief of the army in 1793, the Duke, unfortunately for England, took the command of our forces in Flanders, whence he was, after some hard-fought battles creditable to the courage of the troops, driven out by Pichegru in 1795, and only too glad to be able to re-embark the remnants of his shattered army. Again, in 1799, when the expedition sailed to the Helder, he took the command. Some successes were at first obtained, but in a few months, he was convinced that the Dutch were too cowed by the power of Bonaparte to actively join the allies in the protection of their fatherland. Thus left without active support and pressed by the steadily increasing armies of the French, he was obliged to sign a Convention, by which, on the surrender of his prisoners, he was enabled for the second time to re-embark an army so unfortunate under his command.

Though a failure as a general in the field when opposed by the new school of military tacticians, as Commander-in-Chief he was a decided success. During his reign at the Horse Guards he tried, and with effect, to regulate the promotions in the army in strict accordance with the regulations framed for that purpose, and to give a just place to merit and long services. By him the food and clothing of the common soldier were greatly improved, a better provision made for the relief of those whom wounds or sickness rendered unfit for further service, and, for the first time in the history of the army, a school established for the education of their orphans.

"In respect to the state of the army," said the most competent authority of the time,[1] "I can say

[1] Sir Arthur Wellesley, also General Norton. "His Royal Highness, I believe, was the means, through the medium of this House, of giving bread to the soldier, when he had little or nothing to eat," stating the case of the 33rd regiment, when offered either

from my own knowledge, as having been a Lieutenant-Colonel in the army when his Royal Highness was appointed to command it, and having a very intimate knowledge of it since, that it is materially improved in every respect ; that the discipline of the soldiers is improved ; that owing to establishments formed under the directions of his Royal Highness the officers are improved in knowledge ; that the staff of the army is much better than it was ; that the cavalry is improved ; that the army is more complete in officers ; that the system of subordination among the officers is better than it was, and that the whole system of the management of the clothing of the army, the interior economy of the regiments, and everything that relates to the military discipline of the soldiers and the military efficiency of the army has been greatly improved since his Royal Highness has been appointed ; and this improvement," he added, " was greatly due to the personal superintendence and exertions of the Duke in seeing that the regulations he had established were carried out by general officers."

Despite, however, the regulations, and the best intentions of those who had to carry them out in practice, the establishment of the system of purchase,

to remain abroad or come home, unanimously accepted the former offer, on the ground that " where they were they had sufficient to eat, and that if they came to this country they should not have a dinner. His Royal Highness first got an allowance of bread to the soldier, and afterwards of beer, and then their pay increased." He also instituted the York Hospital for wounded men, as an addition to that of Chelsea, the want of such an institution being severely felt by the soldiers during the war with America.—Trial, twelfth day, February 22.

now some five-and-thirty years old, offered every facility for counteracting them. In order to provide a pension fund for retiring officers, in 1762-3, a Board of General Officers fixed the sum each officer, according to his rank, should receive on his retirement, and thus established purchase in the army under what was known as "The regulation price of Commissions."[2] This system, though apparently guarded from abuse by the declaration of each officer on applying to be allowed to retire or to purchase a step, that he had given only the regulation price, opened the door to an almost incredible amount of deception and fraud. Not only were there secret traffickers in commissions at twice and three times the regulation prices, but offices were publicly opened for the sale of places, the system of corruption extending far beyond the army. If the officer himself did not find the additional price there were always friends to find it for him. Now and then a more notorious case than usual was detected and the attempt failed. So varied, however, in their social position were the subordinate actors in the plot, and so cleverly masked their proceedings, that it might be almost assumed that the payment of only the regulation price was the exception and not the rule in military promotions. How this baneful system of bribery, under the name of commissions or presents pervaded almost every department of State we have seen in previous cases.[3] The present investigation

[2] Lieutenant-Colonel Gordon, military secretary to the Duke.—Trial, fifth day, February 10.
[3] See the cases of Davison and Valentine Jones.

will disclose its prevalence in the army, and will bring prominently forward the influence exercised by the female "favourites" of men in power and position in the State—an influence to which the Royal Princes, from their martial engagements, were notoriously subject.

One of these creatures, the Mary Ann Clarke of the present case, appears to have been connected with the Commander-in-Chief as early as the year 1803, and to have lived with him in ostentatious adultery for rather more than three years. The daughter of one Farquhar, a printer's reader, as a mere girl of seventeen she married the son of a builder in London, and lived with him in apparent respectability until 1802. With whom she commenced to sin is not clear, probably with an army agent of the name of Ogilvie, by whom she became initiated into the corruptions of army purchase—presumably with others in good social positions, but nominally living separate from her husband, with her mother. That she was agreeable, after the fashion of "favourites," clever, and crafty, was proved by the success which attended her early career in that character. To judge from her portrait she had the licentious attractions required for her position, whilst the boldness, cunning, and ability with which she met the repeated and vigorous examination to which she was subjected at the bar of the House of Commons, made it evident that her natural abilities had been improved and sharpened by the instructions she had received from her successive protectors.

For this woman the Duke openly kept a most extravagant establishment in Gloucester Place, with carriages and horses, cooks, men and women servants, which he must have known could not be maintained for less than five times the amount of the allowance he nominally made her, and also a country house within sight of Oatlands. With her he really made his home, living with her in the most open shame, and entertaining his and her friends at her dinner-table. Though no doubt, in the way of presents, and the purchase for her house, of plate[4] and other luxuries, he threw away between 10,000*l.* and 12,000*l.*, her mode of life involved her in serious pecuniary liabilities, the means for meeting which she failed to extract from her royal lover. The position she held with the Duke was notorious, and every one believed in the extent of her influence over him. Well aware of this reputation, she soon turned it to her own use, professing to be able to influence his patronage, and establishing a regular scale of bribes, varying with the value of the appointment to be obtained through her interposition.. By this system, undoubtedly, she obtained considerable sums of money from officers and their friends, and to the last day of her connexion

---

[4] The plate of the late Duc de Berri was bought for her of Birkett, the silversmith, at the cost of 1500*l.*, and paid for by bills of the Duke's, with the exception of a sum of 500*l.* in cash from Mrs. Clarke herself, the date of the payment of which in May, 1804, tallies with that on which she received 500*l.* from Colonel French, for assisting him in obtaining his letter of levy.—Evidence of Captain Huxley Sandon, third day, February 7, and T. Dockeray, sixth day, February 13.

with the Duke carried on the trade in commissions, all the more successfully because some promotions followed, if they were not effected by, her promised interposition.

In 1806 she received her *congé*, ostensibly because she had, by a plea to an action for debt of being a married woman, placed the Duke in danger of being brought into court as a witness to her real position; and, in consequence, her husband had threatened to take proceedings against him. There was some truth in this charge; a subpœna had certainly been issued, with this result, that the debt was settled in all probability by the Duke.[5] Another reason assigned was, that as a witness at a court-martial she had described herself as a widow.[6] The truth, however, was that the attorney in this case, for decency's sake, had so described her at the head of her deposition, which was never read or heard read by her, or a single question put to her as to whether she was a wife, a widow, or a spinster. Mr. Adam,

---

[5] See evidence of John Few, glass dealer, and James Cowrie, Mrs. Clarke's solicitor, second day, February 3. Few being defeated by the plea of coverture in 1804, issued a circular warning tradesmen against dealing with her, and also served the Duke with a subpœna as a witness, immediately after which his debt was paid by Cowrie's clerk.

[6] At court-martial on Captain Thompson, 1808, for circulating presumably forged bills in the name of Mary Ann Clarke's mother, her name was given to the Deputy-Judge-Advocate by her solicitor as of Loughton Lodge, widow, but it was admitted that she was never asked the question, or had the description in any way brought to her knowledge.—Evidence of Deputy-Judge-Advocate Sutton, fourth day, February 9; Rowland Maltby, solicitor, sixth day, February 13.

the Duke's private agent, gave as another reason that she had raised money on the Duke's credit. When, however, the attorney who had been set to find out what she had done in money-matters was examined, not only had he never heard of her having done so, but all he could say was that he believed that from the repute of her connexion with the Duke, she had obtained more credit from her tradesmen than she ought to have received on her own account. As the Duke at once consoled himself with a new "favourite," the true reasons were, as Mrs. Clarke hinted, that either he found her a too expensive luxury, or, like many another rake, had got tired of his leman. Whatever were the true reasons, or the ground of those so assigned, Mr. Adam saw the woman, and briefly informed her that the connexion must cease, and that so long as her conduct was *correct*, her late protector would allow her 400*l.* a year, but would not put his promise in writing, so that "it might rest entirely on his word." It was soon discovered that her behaviour was not such as the Duke and his advisers considered "*correct*" in an ex-mistress, and the annuity was discontinued.

That she should try to avenge her desertion was only to be expected from one in her position, and there were not wanting persons ready to take advantage of her irritated feelings. Rumours about the fraudulent sale of commissions had long been rife, and Mrs. Clarke's name as a trafficker in such things had been more than hinted at in the newspapers and pamphlets. In one of these pamphlets, that by a Major Hogan, it was deliberately asserted that he had paid Mrs. Clarke money for her supposed interference in his favour with the Commander-in-Chief, and the connivance of the Duke in such transactions was distinctly asserted. These attacks upon the Duke were prompted if not actually written by a man of the name of Macallum, connected with one of the daily papers. This man entertained a grudge against the Commander-in-Chief for the support he had rendered to General Picton during the hostile proceedings against him, with whom Macallum had quarrelled during the General's governorship in the West Indies. So long, however, as the case was only in such hands, the accusations were allowed to pass with but little notice. Public opinion began to veer to the Duke's side, when Major Hogan, the author of the most pertinent of these pamphlets fled to America, on the excuse of "urgent private affairs," but really to escape prosecution by the law officers of the Government. When, however, the case passed into the hands of an active and intelligent member of the House of Commons, a man of good family and repute, and an officer of acknowledged merit, a public investigation became a necessity.

Colonel Wardle, by whom this investigation was forced upon the House of Commons, was a Cheshire squire, who during the rebellion in "'98" had served as Lieutenant-Colonel of the Antient Britons, a volunteer regiment raised by Sir Watkin Williams Wynne. Until his election for the borough of Oakhampton, in 1807, he was known more as a convivial companion and an ardent sportsman than as a politician. Save for the part he took in this affair and the manly consistency and ability with which he persevered in working out its details, in the face of abuse and threats from the partisans of the Duke and of the Cabinet, he would probably have passed unnoticed as a silent member of the opposition. In the reports of the abuses prevalent in the army and the undue influence exercised in obtaining promotion, as a military man, he naturally took a deep interest. When, cotemporaneously with these revelations, he heard of Mrs. Clarke's complaints of the Duke's conduct to her, he obtained an interview, and induced her to give him the information on which he eventually founded the charges against the Commander-in-Chief, and the whole system of promotion in the army.

Thus instructed, on the 27th of January, 1809, Colonel Wardle moved for the appointment of a committee "to investigate the conduct of H.R.H. the Duke of York, in his capacity of Commander-in-Chief, with regard to appointments, promotions, exchanges, the raising new levies, and the general state of the army." He justified his motion by citing six cases in which money had been paid to Mrs. Clarke for her supposed influence with the Duke, and that influence appeared to have succeeded. There were other cases, he intimated in which the Duke alone was implicated, such as promising to use his influence to obtain an important appointment, if a much-needed loan was obtained for him by the friends of the party interested. The evidence he affirmed would prove not only that "Mrs. Clarke possessed influence to obtain promotions and effect exchanges, as well as the power of augmenting the military establishments of the country, for the use of which she was allowed to receive pecuniary remuneration; but also that the Commander-in-Chief endeavoured to procure pecuniary advances to himself, both in conjunction with, as well as independently of Mrs. Clarke."

During the debate that followed, Colonel Wardle extended the charge of corruption to the Premier and Lord Chancellor, and denounced an office in the city where commissions were openly offered at Mrs. Clarke's prices, and the agents declared that they were employed by the new favourite, a Mrs. Carey. The appointment of the committee was welcomed by the Secretary at War and Sir Arthur Wellesley, confident that it would result in the vindication of the Duke's character, and the disproof of the charges against the authorities at the Horse Guards. Mr. Adam, who described himself as for twenty years the unpaid professional agent of the Duke, craftily proposed that the inquiry should be by a committee of the whole house, in which he was supported by Perceval. The only right course was that advocated by Wilberforce, the appointment of a committee with power to take evidence on oath, and to be guided by the well-known rules of law, excluding the hearsay and gossip of which so much of the so called evidence eventually consisted. Lord Castlereagh, with his accustomed violence, declared that a conspiracy existed to traduce the Duke, and excused the lack of prosecutions of the libellers on the ground of the difficulties caused by the ingenuity with which the libels were framed; and Mr. Yorke denounced the attempt as a Jacobin conspiracy against the House of Brunswick, and insisted that the issue must be " infamy to the accuser or the accused."

In such a temper the House, on the 1st of February commenced the inquiry. For twelve days witness after witness was examined, and subjected to the most rigorous and often most irregular cross-examination by members; Mrs. Clarke herself was called up at least a dozen times, either to tell her own story of each case, or to meet the statements of other witnesses. Colonel Wardle had repeatedly to give his account of his dealings with Mrs. Clarke, and Mr. Adam to explain his conduct. Ministers themselves were asked, in more than one instance, for explanations of the parts they had taken; and as the inquiry wandered away from the strict issues, the details of the whole of the promotions for many past years were canvassed, and the whole machinery of the Horse Guards thoroughly overhauled by eager inquirers.

In the first case,[7] that of an exchange between Lieut.-Col. Brook of the 5th Dragoons, and Lieut.-Col. Knight of the 56th Foot, it was not denied that

[7] Knight's case. Evidence of Dr. Thynne, Mrs. Clarke's doctor, who, at Knight's request, offered 200*l.* to effect the exchange. Knight's brother, who suggested the offer to Dr. Thynne, and found the money. Mrs. Clarke admitting receipt of the money, and declaring that she spoke to the Duke on the matter and "informed him that she had received a compliment," and showed him the note for 200*l.*, and sent it to be changed by one of his servants. Colonel Gordon producing official papers and protesting that there was no delay, but not explaining satisfactorily the endorsements on the letters.—First day, February 1. Subsequently several servants and tradesmen were called to disprove Mrs. Clarke's statement about sending the note to be changed, throwing doubts on it, but not entirely disproving it.—Evidence of Orasmin, second day, February 3; David Pierson, Mrs. Clarke's butler, third day, February 7, and sixth day, February 10.

about the middle of July, 1805, Knight's brother gave Clarke's medical man notes for 200*l*., which the latter handed to Mrs. Clarke to induce her to expedite the exchange, the request for which had been sent in on the 1st of July. It appeared by the office records that the exchange was approved on the 23rd, and in due course gazetted on the 30th of that month. According to the military secretary, all went on without any difficulty or delay, yet when the original application was produced, there appeared written upon it, in pencil, "Cannot be acceded to, H.R.H. does not approve of the exchange ;" and then a later endorsement, dated July 23rd, "H.R.H. does now approve the exchange." Clarke's story was that she spoke to the Duke about it, told him she had received a gratuity, and sent one of the notes to be changed by one of the Duke's own servants. The second endorsement was certainly after the date of the bribe, but that it was due to her interference rested solely on Clarke's evidence.

The second charge,[8] the promotion of a Mr. Maling, who had but lately been a clerk in the office of Greenwood and Cox, the army agents, was so satisfactorily explained that it was finally dropped. The African corps into which he was posted was so largely composed of convicts, that the authorities were only too glad to get respectable men to accept commissions in these regiments.

The third charge[9] related to a letter of licence for

[8] Evidence of Colonel Gordon, second day, February 3.
[9] Evidence of Domenico Corri, that 2000*l*. was offered for the levy, introduced several persons to Mrs. Clarke, destroyed his

raising a levy of 5000 men, chiefly in Ireland, obtained by a Colonel French. In this transaction, Corri, Mrs. Clarke's music-master, appears to have hinted to French's intended partner, one Captain Huxley Sandon, who was undoubtedly a trafficker in promotions, that he had a powerful friend at the Horse Guards, whose influence would be worth purchasing. Through this convenient agent, who got a douceur of 200*l*. for himself, French was introduced to Clarke, and a bargain struck by which she received 850*l*., in addition to the fee to Corri for his introduction. Had she got such amendments of the terms of the letter, as to have ensured its success, Mrs. Clarke's pay would have amounted to 2000*l*. As it was, the recruiting was so scandalously carried out, that instead of producing 4000 men in nine months, not more than 219 were raised. In consequence the letter of levy was recalled in April, 1805, and the few recruits found fit

letters at her request, as there was a great noise, and she told him the Duke was watched by Colonel Gordon, and she by Greenwood. Captain Huxley Sandon, " The levy was for 5000 men, at thirteen guineas a head, afterwards increased to nineteen. Paid Mrs. Clarke 850*l*. French believed in her; I did not. Did not think she expedited it." William Dowler said "that he repeatedly discussed the terms of the levy with French and Sandon at Mrs. Clarke's house in Gloucester Place, and urged her to have nothing to do with it, and offended her by so doing. Paid her 1000*l*. for his appointment in the Commissariat, and believed he got it through her." Dowler subsequently proved to be either her husband or paramour.—Third day, February 7. Mr. Huskisson, Secretary to the Treasury, that five additional Assistant-Commissaries were appointed at the request of the Commissary-General, and among them Dowler; everything regular as far as he knew. — Fourth day, February 9.

for service drafted into regiments on service. If Mrs. Clarke was to be believed, she was constantly worrying the Duke on the matter, and trying to get better terms for her *protégé*, from whom and his partner she was as frequently pressing for more money. She claimed the credit of the few improvements which were made in the terms, but in that she was not corroborated, and indeed the favourable changes appeared to have been made generally for all recruiting parties. She of course asserted that the Duke knew of the gratuities she received, and a Miss Ann Taylor, whose brother had married a sister of Mrs. Clarke, and who was a frequent guest at her house, was called to corroborate her statement. "One day," she swore, "she was dining at Mrs. Clarke's when the Duke was present." The Duke it was not denied was very free in his conversation with his mistress, and, according to his own admission, might at times have spoken to her on military matters. Miss Taylor's account of what passed on this occasion must be given as detailed in the evidence published by the House of Commons:—

Mr. Wardle—Did you ever hear the Duke of York speak to Mrs. Clarke respecting Colonel French and his levy?

Miss Taylor—Once only.

Wardle—Relate what passed.

Taylor—The Duke's words were, as nearly as I can recollect, " I am continually worried by Colonel French; he worries me continually about the levy business, and is always wanting something more in his favour." Turning to Mrs. Clarke, I think he said, " How does he behave to you, darling?" or some such kind of words as he used to use.

Wardle—Do you recollect anything further passing than what you have stated?

Taylor—Mrs. Clarke replied, " Middling—not well ;" that was all she said.
Wardle—Was that the whole of the conversation ?
Taylor—No.
Wardle—Relate the rest.
Taylor—The Duke said, " Master French must mind what he is about, or I shall cut up him and his levy too." That was the expression he used.[1]

On this witness a most unmanly attack was at once made by the Attorney-General.[2] She was examined again and again as to the real name of her father, whether she knew where he was, what was her employment, her residence, her connexion with Mrs. Clarke, her knowledge of Mrs. Clarke's real position, her opinion whether she regarded her as an honest woman, in questions so framed and put with such an emphasis as to raise the idea that she was as bad as Clarke herself, and probably connected with her in concocting the whole story. The truth was, that in consequence of difficulties on the Stock Exchange, her father went under an assumed name, and she and her sister maintained their mother and themselves by keeping a small school in Chelsea. So far as an attack on her character the attempt

[1] Evidence of Mrs. Clarke, confirming Sandon's, and that she paid the 500*l.* to Birkett on account of the Duc de Berri's plate. The Duke allowed her 1000*l.*, and gave her presents besides. Establishment at Gloucester Place, two carriages, six to eight horses, and eight men servants, besides female. Used to stay with the Duke at his house at Weybridge from Saturday to Monday. Had numerous applications for her interest, and always gave the Duke their names. Once pinned them inside the bed-curtains. Miss Ann Taylor's brother, married to Mrs. Clarke's sister, had known her ten years.—Fourth day, February 9.

[2] Sir Vicary Gibbs.

signally failed. It, however, brought ruin on herself and her family. She was at once pressed for a small debt, her furniture seized, the school broken up, and she and her sister left to the kindness of friends and a small subscription raised by the public. The torturing of this witness went far towards increasing the public feeling against the Duke and his friends, and had little if any effect on the value of her evidence. Indeed, it led many to attach to it far more credibility than it would have possessed, if its improbability, and the fact of her never having heard any more such words from the Duke during her many visits, had been alone relied on.

How far it is probable that the Duke should have made such a compromising statement in the presence of a comparative stranger, may be judged from the tone and temper of the two love-letters produced during the investigation, the authenticity of which was not seriously contested. Among the numerous persons applying to Mrs. Clarke for her influence with the Duke was a General Clavering, a mixture of fool and knave, who offered her 1000*l.* if she would persuade her keeper to give him authority to raise a new battalion.[3] With this explanation the following

[3] General Clavering, when called on the fifth day to contradict a statement of Mrs. Clarke's, that she had asked him to influence the vote of Lord John Campbell on the Defence Bill at the close of 1805 or beginning of 1806, declared that, except in the case of a Lieutenant Summer, he had never had any communication with Mrs. Clarke on the subject of promotions in the army. Subsequently, on the eleventh day, he explained that he meant "epistolatory" communications relating to others than himself, and admitted his offer of 1000*l.* for his own promotion. Motion to

disgraceful epistle, directed,[4] according to an arrangement between her and the Duke, nominally to her brother, tells its own tale. The Duke was away on a tour of inspection.

"*Sandgate, August* 24, 1804.

" How can I sufficiently express to my darling love my thanks for her dear, dear letter, or the delight which the assurances of her love give me? Oh, my angel! do me justice and be convinced that there never was a woman adored as you are. Every day, every hour convinces me more and more that my whole happiness depends on you alone. What a time it appears to me since we parted, and with what impatience do I look forward to the day after to-morrow; there are still, however, two whole nights before I shall clasp my darling in my arms.

" How happy am I to learn that you are better; I still, however, will not give up hopes of the cause of your feeling uncomfortable. *Clavering is mistaken, my angel, in thinking that any new regiments are to be raised; it is not intended; only second battalions to the existing corps; you had better, therefore, tell him so, and that you were sure there would be no use in applying for him.*

" Ten thousands thanks, my love, for the handkerchiefs, which are delightful; and I need not, I trust, assure you of the pleasure I feel in wearing them, and thinking of the dear hands who made them for me."

Then follows an account of his various inspections, the letter concluding in the same sensuous language.

" Adieu, therefore, my sweetest, dearest love, till the day after to-morrow; and be assured that to my last hour I shall ever remain yours, and yours alone."

The second letter is dated nearly a year later, written apparently from Weymouth, where he was standing godfather to Lord Chesterfield's infant

commit him for prevarication postponed by influence of Perceval until the investigation closed.—See *post*, p. 280.

[4] Sixth day, February 13, letters put in

Besides being a love-letter, it evidently answers an application which she declared she made to the Duke, to use his influence to get a Dr. O'Meara, an Irish clergyman, appointed to a bishopric, and shows, unmistakably, the use Mrs. Clarke made of her royal lover. As she was at the time staying at Woking, the necessity for addressing the letter in her brother's name did not exist.

"*August* 4, 1805.

"How can I sufficiently express to my sweetheart, my darling love, the delight which her dear, her pretty letter gave me, or how much I feel all the kind things she says to me in it. Millions and millions of thanks for it, my angel! and be assured that my heart is fully sensible of your affection, and that upon it alone its whole happiness depends.

"I am, however, quite hurt that my love did not go to the Lewes races; how kind of her to think of me upon the occasion; but I trust that she knows me too well not to be convinced that I cannot bear the idea of adding to those sacrifices which I am too sensible she has made for me."

Then, after a few lines about the life he is leading at Weymouth, and the absence of news, he continues:—

"*Dr. O'Meara called on me yesterday morning, and delivered me your letter; he wishes much to preach before royalty, and if I can put him in the way of it I will.*"[b]

---

[b] From paragraph in the *Morning Post*, October, 1805, "The Rev. Dr. O'Meara preached on Sunday an excellent sermon from Rom. xii. 5, on universal benevolence. The reporter adds, "That sweet charm, that celestial unction which Christian oratory demands, this gentleman possesses in an eminent degree. The king was very attentive, and stood for nearly the whole sermon, and expressed his high approbation to the Earl of Uxbridge and others; whilst the queen and princesses, and the whole audience, were melted in tears." The date of the sermon confirms the power Mrs. Clarke had over her protector.

The conclusion is in apparently the stereotyped style of these ducal love epistles.

"What a time it appears to me already, my darling, since we parted; how impatiently I look forward to Wednesday se'night!

"*God bless you, my own dear, dear love!* I shall miss the post if I add more. *Oh! believe me ever, to my last hour, yours and yours only.*"

In addition to these undisputed letters, which were received by the House with peals of laughter, was one containing little more than a dozen words of pregnant import, if they were really in the Duke's handwriting.

A Captain Tonyn,[6] in the hope of expediting his promotion to a majority, to which he was fully entitled from his services, had been persuaded by Captain Huxley Sandon, undoubtedly Mrs. Clarke's agent in the majority of these transactions, to promise her 500*l*. The promotion being delayed, Tonyn asked Sandon to get back the memorandum promising the money. On Sandon applying to Clarke, she called Tonyn a shabby fellow, urged Sandon to persuade his friend to wait a little longer, and in order to convince him that she really had the influence to which

[6] Evidence of Lieutenant Donovan of the Veteran Battalion described by Colonel Wardle, "as not being a trafficker in places, but having a certain tendency to negotiate them, and take a pecuniary advantage for them," admitted trying to buy writership of East India Company for 3000*l*. through Tahourdin, a solicitor who trafficked in them, and a deanery for Dr. Glasse, through Mrs. Clarke, and had other negotiations with her for appointments of Landing Waiters, and in the Commissariat.— Fourth day, February 9. On second examination, February 10, said he negotiated Tonyn's matter with Mrs. Clarke, through Captain Sandon, and that Gilpin, an army clothier, had agreed to pay the money. Confirmed by Sandon and Mrs. Clarke.

she pretended, gave her go-between this letter and the envelope of another to show to Tonyn. If this letter was the Duke's, it clearly proved the truth of Mrs. Clarke's statement that she had spoken to the Duke on Tonyn's matter, and that his being gazetted followed within a few days after she gave the disputed note to Sandon. The note, like one of the previous letters, was addressed, "George Farquhar, Esq.," and was not dated. It briefly said :—

"*I have just received your note, and Tonyn's business shall remain as it is. God bless you.*"

The history of the production of this note exposes the manner in which the friends and advisers of the Duke and of the Ministry were not ashamed to conduct the defence of their princely client. Ten days before the letter was produced, Perceval and Adam had seen a copy of the note, which Sandon had shown to the colonel of his regiment and of which he allowed him to take this copy. Colonel Hamilton had begged Sandon to carefully preserve the original, but was soon after informed by him that he had lost it. The letter was mentioned to the Duke. "He had no recollection of it."—"It must be a forgery." When, however, he was told that a second letter subsequent to this had been shown to Tonyn by Sandon, saying that Tonyn should be gazetted that night, he admitted that "he might have written this had a simple inquiry been made whether he would be gazetted or not." In his examination Sandon had never mentioned this letter, and though the copy of it had been several days before in Perceval's hands, he allowed the witness to leave the bar without a question as to its existence.

No sooner, however, had Colonel Wardle concluded his case, than the story of the note was sprung upon the House by Perceval on the lame excuse that he and Adam and the Duke's advisers thought that it would be less embarrassing to the promoters of the inquiry to introduce it then, than in its natural position in the course of Sandon's cross-examination.[7]

The truth was at length admitted by Perceval. They believed the note was destroyed, and no doubt expecting to get Sandon to confirm this, they would have produced the copy and with undoubted effect have urged that had such a note not been a forgery it would have gladly been produced by the Duke's accusers. As it was they were "hoist by their own petard." Sandon, on being recalled, prevaricated so about the note and its destruction that he was sent in custody to search for it at his lodgings. There it was found and produced to the House, and Sandon justly rewarded for his conduct by being committed to Newgate. Mrs. Clarke, on being shown the mysterious paper, declared it to be in the Duke's handwriting, and that the seal on the note was the Duke's, of which she had many impressions on other letters, and though she had forgotten that she ever gave it to Sandon, presumed that she must have done so, as it was in his possession. She also identified the direction on the envelope, and its seal as the handwriting and seal of the Duke. By

[7] Nearly the whole of the ninth, tenth, eleventh, and twelfth days were occupied in getting at the history of this note, and the explanations by ministers and Mr. Adam of their reasons for holding it back, and the attempt to prove that it was not in the handwriting of the Duke.

pletely it not only failed to make out their case, but strengthened that of their opponents. Both the inspectors of franks concurred in thinking that the note and the letters were in the same handwriting. One of the inspectors of the powers of attorney considered that the handwriting was not the same, the character of that of the note being smaller and neater and not showing the same freedom as that of the letters. He was, however, bound to admit, that, as his constant practice had been to verify signatures only, he did not consider himself a competent witness. The other inspector from the Bank took a different view, and should have passed both powers of attorney if one had been written in one hand and the other in the other handwriting. One other witness, an inspector of notes at the Bank, whilst admitting that his duty was to look at the paper, the date, the engraving, and indeed the whole note, and that nothing on a note was in writing but the date, the number, and the signatures, would have supposed the letters and the note to have been written by the same person. The Duke's statement, according to Mr. Adam,[9] was "that if he had ever written to Mrs. Clarke on any military matters it must have been in answer to some question put in a letter of hers, and that when, once, early in the con-

[9] Adam, when first examined about the disputed note (eleventh day), reported the Duke as saying that "he was perfectly certain he had not written such a note—that he had not any recollection of it. To the best of his recollection he had never written to Mrs. Clarke on the subject of military affairs, and that if he had done it, it must have been very rarely." Shortly after, on the same day, he gave the latter portion of the Duke's reply as inserted in the narrative.

nexion she spoke to him about a promotion, he said that was business, and he could not listen to it, and heard no more about it."

The fifth case, that of Samuel Carter's commission, even assuming Mrs. Clarke's story to be the strict truth, was not so much to the Duke's discredit. The natural son, apparently, of an officer of merit of the name of Sutton, he had undoubtedly been in Mrs. Clarke's service, and when appointed by her influence to a commission, was indebted to her liberality for his outfit. In 1801 Captain Sutton had applied to the Duke on Carter's behalf and received the usual reply of that time, when the reduction consequent on the temporary peace almost stopped promotion, that the request would be noted for a future opportunity. It is noteworthy that, though at the outbreak of the war within a year afterwards, commissions were abundant, no notice of Carter was taken until March, 1804 —a year after the Duke's connexion with Mrs. Clarke had commenced and the lad himself been for some time in the service of the reigning favourite.

The case of Major Turner brought another "favourite" on the ground—one Lucy Sinclair Sutherland. Though she had been long since deposed in favour of Mrs. Clarke, her influence with the Duke was still sufficient to impede for the time the sale of his commission by an officer against whom no one but this woman could say a word. In September, 1808, Major Turner's agents, with the approval of his commanding officer, sent in his request to be allowed to sell his commission to the senior lieutenant at the regulation price. On the same day

this ex-favourite wrote the Duke, asking him to delay his acceptance until March, as Major Turner "had behaved with unkindness towards a lady who merited different treatment; and it was of importance to her to know where to find him for the next six months; and that if he quitted the regiment he meant to secrete himself from her. Major Turner," added the Duke's frail correspondent, "depends on Colonel Gordon to expedite his resignation; I depend on your Royal Highness to prevent his obtaining it for some months. I flatter myself such a trifling and just request you will not refuse." Instead of treating such a communication with the contempt it alone deserved, the Duke had it filed with Major Turner's papers, and the whole affair "put by" whilst inquiries were made as to the truth of this woman's statement.[1] As might be expected, whether it was Mrs. Sutherland or some other artful woman of a similar character by whom Turner had got entrapped, there was nothing in the connexion to justify any obstacle being made to his request. Eventually, but not until Major Turner had threatened to expose the whole affair, the exchange was gazetted.

On the ninth day of the inquiry a case was brought forward by Lord Folkestone, entirely unconnected with any female favourite, showing how the pecuniary straits into which he had been driven by his mode of life led the Duke astray in the exercise of his official duties.[2] In the summer of 1804 a proposal was made

[1] According to Colonel Gordon, it was the invariable custom of the authorities at the Horse Guards.—Seventh and eighth days, February 14 and 15.

[2] Evidence of Archibald Duff, solicitor to Commission of

to the Duke by a Mr. Kennett to raise for him a loan of 70,000*l*., and cotemporaneously with it an application from the same party begging him to use his influence with Mr. Pitt for the purpose of procuring an appointment to which he had been recommended by Sir Horace Mann. To this request, without making any inquiries into the antecedents of Kennett, the Duke readily acceded. His private secretary, Colonel Taylor, wrote Kennett to this effect on the 22nd of July, and a week after referred him and his loan project to Mr. Adam, the Duke's financial agent. Leaving the loan matter in Adam's hands, the Duke, through Taylor, pressed Kennett's case on the Premier, and when he found that the post in Surinam was given away, applied for two other posts for his friend. All this time the loan business was in Adam's hands, and in Kennett's letters to Colonel Taylor that and the Surinam promotion were openly spoken of together in such a way as made it impossible to doubt that the loan and the promotion were to be one transaction.

During all these negotiations, which extended over several months, no inquiry was made into the antecedents of Kennett. When, however, damaging reports of his character at last reached the private secretary, the exertions in his favour ceased, and cotemporaneously the loan proposal seems to have been considered as too wild for further consideration by the Duke's financial agent. Kennett, in truth, was a notorious vagabond. He had twice been a bankrupt.

Bankruptcy against Robert Kennett, and Lieutenant-Colonel Taylor, private secretary to the Duke, Mr. Adam, and Mr. Greenwood, the army agent.—February 16.

Formerly he had been an upholsterer in Bond Street; but when, in 1803, he was made a bankrupt for the second time, he lived in Lincoln's-Inn-Fields, ostensibly curing toothache by the use of a smelling-bottle, but in reality a touter for disreputable money-lenders. Since the second commission of bankruptcy he had been prosecuted for a conspiracy to defraud his creditors, found guilty, and put in the pillory. Such was the man who narrowly escaped being appointed to a position of trust under Government. Such the transaction in which, under the pressure of pecuniary difficulties, the Duke's name and character had been implicated.

The pecuniary difficulties of her royal friend were well known to his "favourite," and one attempt was undoubtedly made by the Duke to obtain a loan of 10,000*l.* through Mrs. Clarke's private solicitor, and only dropped, ostensibly, from the inability or the unwillingness of the Duke's solicitors to answer the queries put by the solicitor of the party who proposed to advance the money.[3] If Mrs. Clarke, when not confirmed by other evidence, is to be believed, the bribe of a loan of 5000*l.* was held out by Colonel French to induce the Duke to assist him in getting some arrears due from other offices than the Horse Guards, and only refused because he had no power

[3] Evidence of Cowie, that at request of Mrs. Clarke he had interviews with the Duke and Adam as to a loan for 10,000*l.* on the Duke's property at Oatlands; that abstracts of title were sent to him by the Duke's solicitors, and the money was ready to be advanced, but the queries on the abstracts were not replied to by the Duke's solicitors, and the loan dropped.—Second day, February 7.

over these departments.[4] Anyhow, it is clear that the pecuniary wants of the Duke were taken advantage of by those who, either through his "favourite" or other friends, expected not only to influence the distribution of his own patronage, but to have his personal influence exerted for them with other high officers of State.

In considering the cases relied on by Colonel Wardle, the evidence of Mrs. Clarke, unless supported by that of other reliable witnesses or documents, has not been pressed into the argument. It may be, as one speaker said, that she had contradicted herself or been contradicted by others in two dozen instances. Still, the story of the mutual confidences between her and her keeper on the subject of military promotions and of the presents she was receiving from applicants for exercise of her presumed influence with him, is to a great extent confirmed by the tone of his love-letters, and the admissions he made of having talked to her on military matters, and having, though rarely, written to her in reply to questions in her letters on official business. Rightly or wrongly, the world assumed that the "favourite" had an influence in high places well worthy of their purchase. In addition to the application for a bishopric for Dr. O'Meara and a deanery for a Mr. Glasse (for the latter she was to receive 3000*l*.), Baroness Nollekens[5] did not think it either

[4] Evidence of Mrs. Clarke.—Fourth day, February 9.
[5] Letters from Baroness Nollekens to Mary Ann Clarke, and from Mr. Elderton. One of the letters from Elderton, addressed to the Duke, thanking him for confirming his leave of absence, was produced by Mrs. Clarke, not sealed, and apparently left for

discreditable or useless to ask her for the Duke's influence with the Premier and the king in increasing her husband's pension ; a Mr. Elderton begs her to help his son to a paymastership; Mr. Dowler, nominally her husband, undoubtedly one of her paramours, admits that he paid her 1000*l.* for his appointment in the Commissariat Department; Mrs. Hovenden, a rival in the business, deals with her for Major Law's promotion ; and Maltby, a solicitor holding the responsible position of clerk to a great City Company, "though his memory was suspiciously defective," was obliged to admit negotiations with her, on a pecuniary basis, for her supposed influence in at least half a dozen cases. Can all these persons—some of them jobbers themselves, and all shrewd men of business, have all wilfully deceived themselves ?[6]

The method in which these proceedings had been carried on, and the nature of the tribunal which had now to decide on the effect of the statements that had been allowed to be made, were due, as we have seen, to the suggestion of the Duke's financial agent, when the proposal of Wilberforce, to have the evidence taken on oath, had been rejected by the Cabinet and

her to give to the Duke or not, as she deemed advisable.—Eighth day, February 15.

[6] Evidence of Mrs. Hovenden (fifth day), a very doubtful person, who did not remember how long she had lived in any one of her numerous lodgings, admitted negotiations with Mrs. Clarke in Shaw's matter, the price to be 700*l.* Could remember the names of only two others for whom she negotiated. Rowland' Maltby (sixth day), Clerk to the Fishmongers' Company, admitted numerous negotiations with Mrs. Clarke for appointments, and deposit of money for payment.

the Duke's friends. No sooner, however, had the investigation dragged its weary length to an end, than the Duke repudiated the form which they had forced on the House, and begged the members not " to deprive him of the benefit and protection which was then afforded to every British subject by those sanctions under which, alone, evidence was received in the ordinary administration of the law." The step taken by the Duke, doubtless by the advice of the Cabinet, was at once offensive to the House, if not a direct breach of its privileges. It was, moreover, a most unwise attempt, not to use a harsher term, at the last moment to arrest proceedings to which he ought to have objected at their initiation, and to do so, only on the ground of his own consciousness of his innocence. . This tardy interference came in the shape of the following letter to the Speaker, which was read to the House on the day on which it bore date :—

"*Horse Guards, February* 23, 1809.

"SIR,—I have waited with the greatest anxiety until the committee appointed by the House of Commons to inquire into my conduct as Commander-in-Chief of his Majesty's army had closed its examinations, and I now hope that it will not be deemed improper to address this letter, through you, to the House of Commons.

" I observe with the deepest concern, that in the course of the inquiry my name has been coupled with transactions the most criminal and disgraceful, and I must ever regret and lament that a connexion should ever have existed which has thus exposed my character and honour to public animadversion.

" With respect to my alleged offence, connected with the discharge of my official duties, I do in the most solemn manner, on my honour, as a prince, distinctly assert my innocence, not only by denying all corrupt participation in any of the infamous transactions which have appeared in evidence at the bar of the

House of Commons, or of any countenance at their existence, but also the slightest knowledge that they existed at all.

"My consciousness of innocence leads me confidently to hope that the House of Commons will not, upon such evidence as they have heard, adopt any proceedings prejudicial to my honour and character; but if upon such testimony as has been adduced against me, the House of Commons can think my innocence questionable, I claim of their justice that I shall not be condemned without trial, or be deprived of the benefit and protection which is afforded to every British subject by those sanctions under which alone evidence is received in the ordinary administration of the law."[7]

This letter had been originally drawn at much greater length by Perceval, and judiciously curtailed on the advice of his colleagues. The nature of the resolutions to be proposed by the friends of the Duke was a matter of most serious consideration. Lord Melville, who, though not in the Cabinet, had great influence with its leading members, sent the Duke of Portland a draft address which spoke very plainly of the lives of others of the Royal family than the Duke of York. After giving the opinion of the House on the direct charges, it proposed to conclude with the following pregnant remarks :—

"Your faithful Commons feel it their indispensable duty to

---

[7] The Prince of Wales told Earl Temple that "he considered this letter a most ill-advised measure, and that it was a breach of privilege. He knew the circumstances of it. The Cabinet had written a letter for the Duke, notifying to the House of Commons his resignation, but the Duke had positively refused to sign it; that he sent another form to the Cabinet, which they refused to agree to, and in their turn sent a third, which was presented."—Duke of Buckingham's "Courts and Cabinets of George III." vol. iv. 326. Earl Temple to the Marquis of Buckingham. See Canning's letter to Perceval, p. 279.

state that these charges have originated from an unfortunate and unworthy connexion which his Royal Highness had permitted himself to form with one of the material witnesses, who seems to have availed herself of her intimacy with his Royal Highness, to have converted it to the most nefarious and corrupt practices ; and it is the earnest prayer of your faithful Commons that the circumstances of the unfortunate transaction may produce a salutary effect of convincing all branches of his Majesty's illustrious family, that nothing can conduce so much to the prosperity of his Majesty's reign and the welfare of the people, *as that those connected with the throne should exhibit in their own persons the same bright examples of decorous and regular conduct which has characterized his Majesty's reign.*" [8]

---

[8] Of the indecent parade of their mistresses by the royal princes the following account from the *Courier* of August 3, 1806, on the occasion of the birthday dinner at Bushey Park of the Duke of Clarence, affords a glaring instance. After describing in the usual newspaper style the grand hall and dining-room, the arrival of the bands of the Dukes of York and Kent, and the music from "The Creation" played by them, and the means taken to enable the people who crowded the grounds to witness the ceremony, the account proceeds as follows :— "About five p.m. the Prince of Wales, Dukes of York, Kent, Sussex, and Cambridge, and Colonel Paget arrived from reviewing the German Legion, and after dressing for dinner walked in the grounds, accompanied by the Lord Chancellor, Earl and *Countess* of Athlone and *daughter*, Lord Leicester, Baron Hotham and *lady*, Baron Eden, Attorney-General, and a number of other persons. At seven o'clock another bell announced dinner, when *the Prince took Mrs. Jordan by the hand, led her into the dining-room, and seated her at the head of the table. The Prince took his seat at her right hand, and the Duke of York at her left, &c.* . . . *The Duke of Clarence sat at the foot of the table.* . . . *The numerous family were introduced and admired by the Prince and the royal family and the whole company.* An infant in arms, with a most beautiful white head of hair, was brought into the room by a nursery-maid." Enough of this sickening exhibition. Well might Cobbett, in quoting this

Lord Melville further urged on the Duke of Portland the necessity for the king acting up to the spirit of this address. "*The Princess of Wales,*" he wrote, "*must no longer reside in any other apartments than those belonging to her in Carlton House. The public must never again hear of a Mrs. Clarke, or* . . ." It is not difficult to fill up the asterisks which the author of the life of Perceval has here inserted.

The Duke sent this draft to Perceval, who was at the time engaged in drawing up the letter from the Duke of York to the Speaker. Thinking highly of the suggestion, he circulated the document, with his draft of the proposed letter to the Speaker, among his colleagues. The Premier, with Lord Liverpool and Lord Castlereagh, appear to have approved the suggestion, when Lord Mulgrave interposed. "It would be," he wrote, "an unequivocal pledge on the part of the other branches to accept the conditions, and should they fail,"—Lord Mulgrave knew them too well not to anticipate failure,—"the House of Commons would have been urged to a solemn and fruitless charge against the whole body of the Royal family—the public murmurs would then be sanctioned and inflamed by the deliberate and formal declaration of the popular branch of the constitution, conveyed in a distinct and indiscriminate complaint to the sovereign. Such an imputation, conveyed by the Commons, without an immediate, exemplary, and steady reform of conduct, would authorize clamour

disgraceful scene, say, "How about the royal proclamation for the suppression of vice? Why pursue poor women with these daylight lanthorns, and not put up one at Gloucester Place?"—Cobbett, *Register*, February 18, 1809.

and discontent, and extend to the mass of the people in the most distant quarters of the empire, where the impression may have been yet but slightly, if at all, received of the scandal arising here." Lord Mulgrave's advice prevailed; the proposed letter from the Duke was cut down to what it now appears, and the only allusion to the public life of the Duke, in the proposed resolutions, was the moral tag hereafter quoted, expressing the confidence felt by the Commons that for the future he would keep in view the uniformly virtuous and exemplary conduct of his father.[9]

[9] "Perceval Papers," quoted by Spencer Walpole in his life of Spencer Perceval, vol. i. p. 316, *et seq.* From a letter of Canning's, March 5, 1809, to Perceval, it appears that the Duke was a very obstinate and shifty client. "What," he writes, "is the relation in which we, the Government, stand to the Duke of York? Has he put his defence into our hands, and therewith the regulation of his conduct, with a view to that defence, also? Or has he only stated his expectation that we shall defend him, but reserving to himself to act as he thought proper? . . . When we were discussing the letter to be written to the Speaker, I certainly thought we were advising him (perhaps thought mistakenly); but it is the essence of advice given by persons *responsible* for giving it, that it should be either accepted or rejected *in toto*. Otherwise there is no safety for the advisers, and will probably be no consistency in the conduct which is partially guided by their advice. Yet on Wednesday, at Lord Camden's, I learnt, to my surprise, that there were certain things which the Duke was determined not to do, *if* advised, and certain other things which he was inclined to *expect* would be advised in supposable cases." Canning then reminds Perceval how he thought that the letter should have ended with the statement that the Duke resigned *till he was cleared;* that he gave way when the majority of the Cabinet were against him, but " did not understand the decision to be founded in any degree on a notion that the Duke *would not* resign, if the Cabinet thought right."—" In the way in which we are now

After some few days' delay, during which the question of punishing General Clavering for his prevarication, and the advisability of enforcing a call of the House were discussed, and, for the present, adjourned, on the 8th of March the struggle for the verdict commenced in earnest. As the promoter of the investigation, Colonel Wardle, assuming that his case had been proved up to the hilt, proposed a resolution affirming the Duke's knowledge of the existence of the corrupt practices which had been clearly proved to every one's satisfaction, and the necessity for his removal from the command of the army. The debate which ensued, conspicuous for the ability and earnestness with which it was conducted, and in which nearly every member of note took part, continued during six protracted sittings of the House, the last concluding only between six and seven o'clock in the morning of the 15th of March. Perceval met Wardle's verdict of guilty by a sort of special verdict of qualified acquittal. His resolutions were to the effect (1) that as the evidence on the charges against the Duke had been before the House, it felt it its duty to pronounce a distinct opinion. (2) That there was no ground for imputing personal corruption or criminal connivance. (3) An expression of regret that, despite the excellent mode in which business was conducted in the Duke's office, the House could not but regret the connexion with Mrs. Clarke, and that, though disgraceful frauds had been committed, coupled with

going the Duke will be turned out of office, probably by a vote of the House of Commons, but most assuredly by the voice of the country."—"Life of Perceval," p. 321-3.

the Duke's name, it was a great consolation to observe his deep concern thereat, and, on the expression of this regret, the House was confident that the Duke *would keep in view the uniformly virtuous and exemplary conduct of the king* since the commencement of his reign, which had endeared his Majesty to all his subjects."

The absurdity of such a resolution, in the face of the admitted fact that another favourite reigned in Mrs. Clarke's place, and that her name was freely mentioned in connexion with fraudulent purchases of commissions, was too evident to need proof. The last paragraph of this laboured apology at once fell to the ground, and the verdict in the end was taken on an amendment of Mr. Banks.

He characterized Perceval's resolution—which was in the form of an address to the Crown—as the echo of the letter, received under such circumstances that it would be so like a humble obedience to the declaration of the Duke, that it would not convince the country that they had proceeded on pure and honest grounds. By his resolution he acquitted the Duke of personal corruption, connivance, or participation in any of the profits, but expressed an opinion, the soundness of which cannot be doubted, that these corrupt practices could not have existed without exciting the Duke's attention, and, if that was so, submitting whether the Crown could longer continue him in his present position. Though the whole power of the Government was brought to bear against it, and on a division it was defeated by 93 votes, in a House exceptionally large for those parliamentary days, it was supported by more than 200 members, including several who, on any other occasion, would have been unhesitating supporters of the Cabinet.[1]

There were men on both sides of the House who took extreme views. Mr. Yorke, with his wonted violence, denouncing Wardle's resolutions "as a mean and slavish deference to a popular cry;" Croker, in a violent speech, which was ill-received by the House, declaring that they should first acquit the Duke of every charge, and then address his Majesty with condolences for the flagrant attack on his son, and congratulations on its miserable failure. Burdett commented with severity on the Cabinet appearing for the defence, and not as prosecutors of a public delinquent. Whitbread spoke with marked effect on the purchase of the Duke de Berri's plate for this woman. "I cannot," he said, "help thinking it an awful recollection, and one peculiarly applicable to the present case: it recalls a revolution brought about not by philosophers but by corruptions." Wilberforce, with admirable temper, urged on the House

[1] For Mr. Banks' amendment, 199
Against it 294

Majority, 93
On Perceval's first resolution—Ayes, 364
Noes, 123

Majority, 241

This motion really only affirmed that, having heard the charges, the House should pronounce an opinion on them. The House adjourned at half-past six.

that the Duke must have known of the report of these practices, and that "the mistresses of princes were in fact the most likely persons to keep an open shop for the sale of offices. The Duke," he added, " did not seem to confide in his military advisers, and kept even Colonel Gordon at a princely distance. If an ex-mistress, as Mrs. Sutherland, had still such power with the Duke, as to temporarily delay Turner's well-earned promotion, what must have been the power of the woman whom the Duke addressed as 'his own dear love—his darling—his angel?'"

Perceval, having defeated the more moderate censure conveyed by Mr. Banks' amendment, easily disposed of that of Colonel Wardle, carrying his own first resolution by a majority of nearly two to one. When, however, the House resumed the debate, with an unwise confidence in his late victory, Perceval endeavoured, by altering one word in his first resolution, to obtain such a thorough acquittal of the Duke as to render his removal from the command of the army unnecessary. As no one now appeared to press " charges," he proposed to substitute the word " statements." Tierney at once opposed this verbal correction with indignation. He admitted the Duke's ability in his command, and the reforms which he had introduced, but declared that, however much his removal was to be regretted, it became a necessity after the disclosures, and that he should vote against the amended resolution, unless an addition was made " that there were other circumstances and transactions disclosed in the evidence on which the opinion of the

House must be declared." General Ferguson, whose services and political views gave especial importance to his opinions on such a subject, agreed with Tierney in the practical value of the Duke's administration, and expressed his thanks for personal favours. He, however, declared " under an imperious sense of duty, that whilst a cloud of suspicion had been collecting and settled upon the Duke's character ; while that cloud remained, until it had been dispelled, his opinion was, that it was not for the honour of the army that the chief command should remain in the hands of the Duke of York."

The marked attention with which this declaration was received convinced Perceval of the error he had made. With the consent of the House he withdrew the new resolution, and at once brought forward his second resolution, " that there were no grounds to charge his Royal Highness with personal corruption or connivance at the infamous practices disclosed in the evidence." By 'no grounds," he explained, that he meant no such grounds as would justify an impeachment. Treating these words as equivocal, Sir Thomas Turton raised a definite issue by an amendment, " that there were grounds to charge his Royal Highness with a knowledge of these practices, with connivance at them, and consequently with corruption." The same struggle was thus renewed as had already been fought out on Colonel Wardle's motion and Mr. Banks' amendment, and with the same result. Sir Thomas Turton's amendment was defeated by an overwhelming majority, and the resolution of Perceval carried by nearly the same majority as had defeated the amendment of Mr.

Banks.[2] One notable speech was made during this portion of the protracted debates — that of Lord Henry Petty. He for one could not say that there were "no grounds"— loose as the evidence was there were documents that bore on it, the authenticity and importance of which could not be doubted, and by which the evidence was on many points supported. There was not cool and deliberate connivance, but was there not what was equally criminal, "a sort of voluntary blindness and negligence"? Perceval's resolution was equivocal, and he would not vote for it. Taken together with the address to the Crown, by which it was to be succeeded, it meant "we find you accused unjustly of corruption, but we brand you with adultery."

Before the subject was resumed by the House, the inevitable resignation of his office had been made by the Prince, in a letter to his father, in which he assumed that he had been acquitted, and that the patience and firmness with which he had met the accusation "arose only from a conscious feeling of his innocence." When he had read this extract, Perceval left it to the House to say whether any further steps should be

[2] Friday, March 17.
 For Sir Thomas Turton's amendment, 135
 Against it 334

 Majority, 199
 For Mr. Perceval's motion, 278
 Against it 196

 Majority, 82
The House adjourned at half-past four.

taken, trusting evidently that the sacrifice so tardily made would induce it to let the whole matter drop.[3] But it was not so. Bragge Bathurst seized the opportunity of reviving the resolution of which he had given notice on the early nights of the debate. Admitting the practical benefits of the Duke's administration, it expressed the regret of the House, "that in consequence of a connexion most immoral and unbecoming, a communication of official subjects and an interference in the distribution of military appointments and promotions, had been allowed to exist, which could not but lead to discredit the official administration of his Royal Highness, and to give colour and effect, as they actually had done, to transactions most criminal and disgraceful." This motion, which only revived the amendments twice previously defeated, was eventually negatived without a division, and the final issue taken on one made by Lord Althorp, that as his Royal Highness had resigned the command of the army, the House did not *now* think it necessary to proceed further in the consideration of the evidence—so far as it relates to him." The word "*now*" formed the object of this last struggle. Interpreting it as meaning the Duke's perpetual exclusion from office, Perceval in-

[3] He was temporarily succeeded by Sir David Dundas. As early as February 6 the king had written a note from Windsor, in the course of which he said " he laments the disgraceful connexions which appear to have been formed by the Duke of York, but acquits him (even in suspicion on his part) of criminality of his official conduct."—W. H. Fremantle to Marquis Buckingham, "Courts and Cabinets," iv. 315. By letter from *same* to *same*, March 24, it would appear that the evidence taken from day to day was kept from the knowledge of the king.

sisted on its omission, and eventually the pregnant little word was removed by the strength of the Ministerial party, and the Prince and the Cabinet left in the enjoyment of their narrow escape.[4]

Notwithstanding the resignation of the Duke of York, an attempt was made to continue the investigation into the corrupt practices which had been so clearly proved to exist in almost every department of State. Lord Folkestone, in bringing forward this motion on the 17th of April, guarded himself from appearing even to desire to revive the charges against the Duke, resting his case on the corruption admitted to exist apart from his case, — on the notorious existence of an office for the sale of places under Government, and on the disclosures with reference to the purchase of letters of levy, in the last report of the Commissioners of Military Enquiry.[5] Conscious

[4] Monday, March 20.
    For omitting the word "Now," 235
    Against it 112
                     Majority, 123

Strangers were not admitted after the division, but it was understood that Lord Folkestone gave notice for April 17, for further inquiry into the minutes of evidence in the case of the Commander-in-Chief.

[5] In this report it was shown that out of 211,000*l.* paid on these letters of service, 90,000*l.* had been drawn by fraud and imposition. Lord Folkestone's motion was "for a committee to inquire into the existence of any corrupt practices with regard to the disposal of offices in any department of state, or any agreement, negotiation, or bargain, direct or indirect, for the sale thereof, and of any corrupt practices relative to the purchase and sale of commissions in the army, and also to examine into the terms on which Letters of Service have been granted, for

of the disgraceful disclosures which must result from such an inquiry, and anxious rather to stop than to further expose the corruption that prevailed, Perceval opposed the motion on the plea that a bill for prohibiting such transactions was already before the House, and that further exposure could only keep up the agitation, without affording a remedy for the admitted evil. With this view the House eagerly agreed, and Lord Folkestone's motion met with but little support from even his former friends.[6] The prohibitory bill was accordingly passed without opposition, and except in some of the most outrageous cases bygones were allowed to be bygones.

The necessity for this measure had been made evident, not only in the disclosures during the Duke's case, but from the previous investigations that had taken place in relation to the appointments to cadetships and writerships by the Directors of the East India Company. As far back as 1793, in consequence of rumours of these appointments being purchasable an oath had been framed to be taken by each director on his accession to office, that he had not personally taken any bribe for his nomination, and a bye-law passed imposing a penalty of double the amount of the bribe in the event of discovery. Each person appointed as a "writer" had to make a declaration that nothing had been paid by him or for him, and a similar declaration was required from the next-of-

raising men for the army by way of levies, and the manner in which such levies have been conducted."

[6] Division—Ayes, 30; Noes, 178.

kin of an applicant for a cadetship. There was also a notice in the preliminary instructions to a cadet that any such payment would ensure his immediate dismissal, and incapacitate him from serving the Company in any capacity.

These precautions proved so ineffectual that five years afterwards a Committee of the Directors was appointed to inquire into the known existing abuses, and each Director called upon to deny any connexion with or connivance at such transactions. Still the abuses continued, and the well-intentioned regulations were successfully evaded. In 1799 an attempt was made to get at the facts, which, however, had no practical result, by offering an indemnity to those who had been so fraudulently appointed if they would make a clean breast of the transaction, and declaring their places void if this condition was not complied with. On the change of Directors in 1800 various attempts were made to eradicate these abuses by exacting a declaration from each Director on oath. On this provision the discussions were frequent, and the doubt which arose as to the legality of such a condition, enabled the party, which did not care to push these inquiries to the uttermost, to prevent the reappointment of the Committee on the change of Directors in 1801.

In this position the matter rested until the existence of this traffic in a most bare-faced form was disclosed during the investigation into the charges against the Duke. A Select Committee was at once appointed to inquire into the real state of matters. From their report it was clear, that three writerships in the gift of

Mr. Thelluson, one of the Directors, had been sold through his cousin, and a solicitor of the name of Tahourden, for from 3000*l.* to 3500*l.* each, and twenty-one cadetships for from 250*l.* to 500*l.* each, mostly through a person of the name of Shee, and two through one of the chaplains of the Duke of Clarence. Many other cases of the same nature could not be traced by the Committee, from their inability to bring the parties before them, and in some of these ladies of rank were clearly implicated. In one case a cadetship had been purchased for a mulatto, who paid another person twenty guineas to appear and pass the examination in his name. In this inquiry, as in the previous one by the Board of Directors, the declaration of the Directors was found to be sufficient, and no case of corruption or abuse of patronage could be traced against any members of the court. As in the Duke of York's case, it was "a sort of voluntary blindness and negligence." It is gratifying to find that Thelluson was rejected when next standing for re-election.

The Duke's resignation was only temporary. It had served its purpose, and having done so, was soon forgotten. No sooner was his brother Regent, than the Duke was restored to his former command.[7] His

[7] On May 23, 1811. On June 4 a motion was ineffectually made by Lord Milton, reflecting severely on the Duke's re-appointment. Referring to this, Lord Temple states that he was asked by Lord Yarmouth, one of the Regent's household, whether, in consequence of the views he had held on the Duke's conduct, he should refuse to join any Cabinet which permitted the Duke to hold the command of the army. Not able to screw his courage to this point, Lord Temple stayed away from the debate, to the satisfaction apparently of the other Grenvilles. The temptations of office were too great to allow him to commit

mistress's career was of a less prosperous character. Within a few months after the close of the investigation, Colonel Wardle was sued by an upholsterer, whom she swore he had authorized to furnish a house for her in Chelsea, as one of the inducements offered for her information of the alleged misdeeds of her royal lover. Though the woman herself made but a doubtful appearance in the witness-box, the confirmatory evidence, in the absence of any to rebut it, ensured a verdict against the colonel. In an intemperate letter " to the public " he charged his former witness and her friends with deliberate perjury, and

himself.—Letter from Lord Temple to Lord Milton. " Regency," vol. i. p. 98. During an early stage of the inquiry the Prince had sent for Lord Temple, who found him as usual selfish and undecided. At first he would be neutral, then Adam had nearly talked him into actively supporting his brother. Then Temple " used very strong language " to him of the danger of such a course. The Prince said the Duke had behaved shabbily to the woman ; that "a gentleman's word was sacred, and he could not talk of his honour as a prince who could not keep his promise as a gentleman. He was no party to his irregularities, *he did not like such society, and thought his taste better than the Duke's.*" " My conviction," writes Temple, " is that his alarm is very great, that he thinks extremely ill of the Duke's case, and is ready to give him up if he could think he would be supported in doing so, and that the fall of the Duke would not necessarily include the victory of the republican party."—Earl Temple to Marquis of Buckingham, February 26. " Courts and Cabinets of George III." iv. 329. The Prince afterwards told Earl Temple that the queen had written him that the king's health and life depended on the issue, as well as the honour of the family. " Still he would make no change, except to send McMahon down to vote for the Duke, and prove he did not condemn him, but all the others to remain as before. Such," adds Temple, " is the nature of the man."

professed his intention of proving his charge "so soon as the forms of law allowed." On second thoughts he forgot his promise, preferring to pay his money and avoid further publicity.

Her next appearance was as an authoress. She threatened to write her own life, and give with it the letters not only of the Duke but of all those who had dealt with her for her supposed influence. On offering this collection to Sir R. Phillips for publication the honour was declined, but so dangerous did the proposal appear that, though he offered to introduce her to a publisher, he at the same time suggested a negotiation with the Duke for their suppression. That the publication was suppressed is a fact, but for what consideration there is no reliable evidence. Rumour reported that it was bought off for 7000*l.* in money, a permanent annuity of 400*l.* to herself and annuities of 200*l.* to each of her daughters. Anyhow the book, to the extent of 18,000 copies, was destroyed at its printer's, 200*l.* paid him as an indemnification, and no less than ninety letters given up, to the great regret of the lovers of scandal in high places.

Not content with this, in a pamphlet entitled "The Rival Princes,"[8] she attacked the Duke of Kent, asserting that the fall of his brother of York was due to his intrigues, and desire of succeeding him as Com-

---

[8] "The Rival Princes; or a faithful narrative of facts relating to Mrs. Mary Ann Clarke's political acquaintance with Colonel Wardle, Major Dodd, &c., &c., who were concerned in the charges against the Duke of York; with a variety of authentic and important letters, and curious and interesting anecdotes of several persons of political notoriety." By Mary Ann Clarke, 1810.

mander-in-Chief. That this imputation was utterly false and unfounded, was proved in the pamphlet entitled, "The Royal Dukes," and by the affidavit of the Duke of Kent, who refused to prosecute her for libel, treating her accusations with the contempt they deserved. Again, in 1814, she indulged in a libel on the Right Honourable William Fitzgerald, formerly Chancellor of the Exchequer, and M.P. for Ennis, for which she was severely punished. Her accusations against him were of the most malignant character—that he had seduced his friend's wife, getting her husband sent to an unhealthy climate was the least offensive of them, the others being of a character unfit for publication. In mitigation of the impending sentence, she told a long story of her intimacy with Fitzgerald's father and of his having negotiated with her for his promotion. She asserted that she had given up to his son his father's letters, seriously implicating him, which she had laid before the committee in the Duke of York's affair, and been advised by it not to make public, as they might injure his and his father's prospects—that she had also given other letters from a "person in high authority," assuring her of his intention to provide for the son, and that when he refused to return them and ceased to be a friend she had published the libel, in which she declared she had exposed no one who did not deserve it, and threatened to deal with others shortly. After such a defence it is not surprising—except for its leniency—that a sentence of nine months' imprisonment was passed on her and that she was bound over to keep her tongue quiet for at least three years. Beyond the incidents in her troubled life already noticed, nothing further is known for certainty about this clever disgrace to womankind. It is believed, however, that she eventually returned to Paris, and died there, leaving a fair fortune to her daughters, whom, to her credit be it said, she had studiously trained in the paths of virtue, resisting more than one attempt on the part of aristocratic roués to purchase their seduction.

CHAPTER X.

TRIALS OF GENERAL PICTON FOR AUTHORIZING THE INFLICTION OF TORTURE WHEN GOVERNOR OF THE ISLAND OF TRINIDAD.

JANUARY 1804 TO FEBRUARY 1810.

THOMAS PICTON, the younger son of a Pembrokeshire squire, was born in August, 1758, and at an early age sent to the military academy of a Frenchman of the name of Lachée. From his youth he exhibited the determination and perseverance which characterized his whole career, taking eagerly to his military studies, and when only a subaltern at Gibraltar employing his spare time in offering suggestions and making designs for the improvement of the defences of the rock and in obtaining a competent knowledge of the Spanish language. Though not without family influence in the army, his promotion was not rapid for those times.[1] His only opportunity in early life

[1] Gazetted ensign 12th regiment, 1772; joined, 1774, at Gibraltar; captain 75th regiment, 1783; on half-pay till 1794; deputy-quartermaster-general and aide-de-camp to Sir J. Vaughan, 1794; major 68th regiment and aide-de-camp to Sir Ralph Abercrombie, 1795; governor of Trinidad, 1797.

of proving his courage and true military spirit was in 1783, when, at the reduction of the army on the peace, his regiment mutinied at Bristol, he seized the leading mutineers with his own hand and quelled the outbreak by personal audacity and firmness. For this timely act he received the approbation of the king, and the promise of a majority—a promise conveniently forgotten until, ten years afterwards, by his services in the West Indies, he extorted the long-deserved promotion. When his regiment was disbanded, he returned to Pembrokeshire, where he had inherited a competence from his mother, thoroughly enjoying a country life without relaxing his military studies. On the outbreak of the war in 1793, after trying in vain for employment, he sailed for the West Indies, where he was welcomed by his friend Sir J. Vaughan, the commander-in-chief, and at once appointed to a captaincy and as aide-de-camp to the General, and subsequently deputy-quartermaster-general and major of the 68th.

On the death of General Vaughan and the arrival of General Knox as Quartermaster-General, Picton had determined to return to Europe, when his career was changed by the advent of Sir Ralph Abercrombie, who retained him as his aide-de-camp. Under Abercrombie, Picton bore his part in the captures of St. Lucie and St. Vincent, returning with him to Europe for a couple of months, and then going back with him to the West Indies in 1797. In that year Trinidad was captured from the Spaniards, and Picton made governor of the new possession. The task thus imposed on Picton was of a most arduous character.

"I have placed you," wrote Sir Ralph, "in a most trying and delicate situation, nor to give you any chance of overcoming the difficulties offered to you, can I leave you a strong garrison. But I shall give you ample powers. Execute Spanish law as well as you can—do justice according to your conscience, and that is all that can be expected of you." Again, when contradicting a rumour of having been influenced in making the appointment by a General Maitland, Abercrombie wrote, "If I knew any officer who, in my opinion, would discharge the duties annexed to your situation better than you, to him I should have given it. No thanks are due to me." It is important to consider these opinions of Sir Ralph, when treating of the subsequent attacks on Picton, as "*un homme antique en scélératesse*," and to remember that in subsequent despatches, after revisiting the island whilst under Picton's rule, Abercrombie recommended him as "an officer in every respect qualified to fill the important situation of governor," and to the day of his death was never heard to express himself disappointed or deceived, or to censure the acts of his nominee.

At the time of its capture, thanks to the neglect of the Spanish governor and the maladministration of the existing laws, there was little respect for life or property. "Murder and robberies were committed with impunity, widows and orphans despoiled, inheritances plundered; creditors and debtors equally ruined in affairs of the most simple nature."² The population, according to a most competent authority, was composed of "refugees and desperate characters who

² Address of inhabitants to Picton.

had been implicated in the rebellions and massacres of the neighbouring isles; their principles incompatible with all regular government, their inveteracy to the English irreconcilable—Spanish Pæons, or people of colour—a set of vagabonds who usually come over from the Continent and are ready to join in any disorder that affords a prospect of plunder, and a great proportion of slaves who have been sent here from other islands for crimes dangerous to their safety—only waiting a favourable opportunity to show themselves—studying you and your garrison."[3] So notorious was the character of the Trinidadians that in the laws of the Isle of Grenada it is provided "that whereas Trinidad is a spot which holds out a retreat for fraudulent debtors and stealers of slaves, and where no redress or justice can be had," any one coming from thence should give a bond for 1000*l.* to be of good behaviour, or be declared a vagabond.[4]

To keep in order such a dangerous population and, at the same time, to watch the intrigues of the governors of the Spanish settlements on the mainland and guard against the raids of French privateers, Picton was left with a garrison nominally a thousand strong, one 64-gun ship and a small brig. Disease and desertion soon reduced the garrison to half its nominal strength, one hundred of which were Germans of Hompesch's brigade, little to be relied on, and an equal number of negroes, chiefly picked up on the

[3] Report of Don Christoval de Robles, who for fifty years had held responsible positions in Trinidad, to General Picton.—Robinson's " Life of Picton," vol. i. p. 54.
[4] Laws of Grenada, iii. 232, clause 8.

island, even less reliable than their German comrades.[5] By the establishment of a local militia and an efficient town police, subsequently extended to the rural districts ; by the fitting out of armed launches, to watch the coast, and the most determined and speedy exercise of the powers entrusted to him as governor, Picton rapidly reduced the island to quiet, and enforced implicit obedience to the order of the authorities.[6] Within six months after the capture of the island, Picton could report that "perfect tranquillity existed throughout the colony—that the beneficial effect of the influence and protection of the British Government was acknowledged by all classes—commerce protected by the armed launches—the market for British manufactures daily increasing, and the general condition of the island so improved that it was able to supply Grenada and St. Vincent with provisions, at the time when these islands were seriously distressed from the failure of their accustomed supply from the American main."[7]

[5] Picton's Report to Commander-in-Chief. The Germans were so greatly given to desertion that a reward was offered of $16 a head for their capture, alive or dead. Picton's defence, put in to the Privy Council, December 8, 1803.—Privy Council Record Papers.

[6] Picton's Report, April 4, 1797. Letter from Gilbert Petrie, twenty years' resident in Trinidad, of December, 1803, testifying to the general opinion of the meritorious conduct of Picton as governor, the condition of the population before the capture of the island, filled with French refugees and banditti from Martinique, Guadaloupe, and St. Lucie, and giving the character of Picton by the French officer in command at Tobago, as *Il est sévère, mais il est juste.*—Picton Papers, Privy Council.

[7] Picton to Right Hon. H. Dundas, July 26, 1797.

Until the year 1799, with the exception of an abortive attempt at revolution on the part of some of the French inhabitants, the island appears to have gone on steadily progressing, especially in its commerce with the neighbouring islands, and exciting the jealousy of the Spanish settlements on the main. A letter from the English Government to Picton instructing him to carry out the English trade and navigation laws,[8] having been intercepted by the Spaniards, endeavours were made by their emissaries under the guise of traders to seduce the garrison. With this object a regular scale of prices for the encouragement of desertion was issued by the neighbouring Spanish governors, ranging from one hundred dollars for "a corporal alive or his head," to twenty thousand dollars for the head of "Don Thomas Picton." "Your Excellency," wrote Picton to one of these governors, "has highly flattered my vanity by the very handsome value which you have been pleased to fix upon my head. Twenty thousand dollars is an offer which would not discredit your royal master's munificence. As the trifle has had the good fortune to recommend itself to your Excellency's attention, come and take it, and it will be much at your service."[9]

[8] Letter of April 8, 1797, from Mr. Secretary Dundas to Picton, with instructions for his conduct in command of the forces in Trinidad, and as to maintaining and encouraging trade with the other Spanish settlements.—Picton Papers, November 29, 1803. Instructions for carrying out the trade laws under penalty of fine and removal from government.—"Plantation Register," 1789 to 1801, p. 516.

[9] Proclamation of Governor of Isle of Margarita, by order of the Captain General of Province and Council of War, offering the

Satisfactory as was Picton's rough and ready style of dealing with offences to the majority of the inhabitants of the island, it was not so to those who had profited from the weakness of his predecessors, the Spanish governors. To such, his unhesitating severity and promptitude in punishment, his prohibition under pain of death of the wearing of daggers, his amelioration of the condition of slaves, and his reformation, partial though it was, of the Spanish judicature, were most unwelcome. It was impossible that a man of Picton's character and temperament, holding, as he believed, as full and autocratic powers as any of his Spanish predecessors among such a population and under such circumstances as those in which he was placed, could avoid making numerous and bitter enemies. Bitter indeed they were alike in acts and words. "Excepting Danton and some of Robespierre's coadjutors," they declared, "there were no instances in modern times of similar atrocity." And when Abercombie's approval of his conduct was cited, they protested that "by a long course of duplicity he had deceived his patron into a belief of his efficiency, and

following rewards :—Soldier with arms, $25; without, $16; with extra musket, $8. Person bringing in (alive or his head) corporal, $100; sergeant, $300; sub-lieutenant or lieutenant, $2000; captain, $3000; lieutenant-colonel, $5000; brigadier- or major-general, $8000; Don Thomas Picton, $20,000. If captor Indian, perpetual exemption for self and heirs from capitation tax; if slave, freedom. Copies in English to be distributed in the English islands.—Minutes of Council of Trinidad, March 31, 1803.—Picton Papers. Letter to Don Pedro Carbonelli, Governor-General of Caracoa, January 25, 1799. Similar letter to Governor of Guagna.—Robinson's "Picton."

thereby abused his generous confidence." By their acts his enemies kept him in perilous and costly litigation for seven years, which would have crushed any less determined man than Picton.

So long as Pitt lived and Dundas had charge of the West Indian department, Picton's enemies failed in their attempts against him. In 1801 his full appointment as Civil Governor of the island was gazetted, and instructions based on those of Abercrombie passed by the Privy Council.[1] By those instructions he was to administer the government "according to the terms of the capitulation, as nearly as circumstances would admit, in conformity to the ancient laws and institutions that subsisted within the same previous to the surrender, subject to such directions as he might hereafter receive from our Privy Council or to such sudden and unforeseen emergencies as may render a departure from them necessary or unavoidable." He was to retain the Courts of Judicature and the laws existing at the time of the capture, and "all judicial powers exercised by the Spanish governors were to be exercised by him as the same were exercised previous to the surrender, but to allow appeals to the Privy Council in Civil Cases of over 500*l*.[2]

---

[1] In 1800 a charge was sent home against him of exporting colonial produce in foreign ships, to the detriment of British shipping, which was found to arise from private ill-will and personal disappointment, and so clearly disproved that Secretary Dundas wrote him that he and his colleagues were perfectly satisfied with the explanation, and convinced that the charges were without foundation.—Robinson's "Picton."

[2] "Plantation Register," 1789 to 1801, commission to Picton, dated "41st of our reign." Instructions, p. 505, Clauses 5, 7,

On the accession of Mr. Addington to power an important change was made in the government of Trinidad. The appointment of Picton was revoked, and a commission issued to William Fullarton, a colonel in the East Indian service, Picton and Captain Hood, R.N., to administer the government. The ostensible plea for this change was, that "from the union of civil, military, and naval talents, combined in the persons selected, advantages must arise which could not be expected from the labours of one person."[3] If the evidence of a medical man of the name of Lynch is to be believed in the face of the contradiction to his statements made by the then Under-Secretary of State, one object of this commission was to investigate the charges lately made against Picton, and to ensure his being sent home in disgrace within a very few months of the arrival of the first commissioner in Trinidad.[4] Anyhow, Picton

and 8: transmitted to Picton, with letter from Lord Hobart, dated June 29, 1801. By clause 15 freedom of worship was granted to all creeds, and the education of the negroes ordered to be seen to.

[3] This commission is entered in the "Plantation Register" for 1803-6, and the instructions to accompany it at p. 387. From the recital of the revocation of this commission in that subsequently issued to General Hislop, November, 1835, it appears that it was really dated October 13, 1802. The instructions to these commissioners, with the exception of varying the numbers and the power of the council, were identical with those issued to Picton.

[4] See affidavit of F. T. Lynch, M.D., who had letters of introduction to Picton, that Under-Secretary Sullivan had recommended him to get letters of introduction to Colonel Fullarton before sailing for Trinidad, "as in all probability Colonel Picton would be ordered home before expiration of

took offence at his removal from supreme power, and after a very brief interval of apparent friendliness between him and the colonel, the quarrel commenced which resulted in his resignation of his appointment, and the preparation by Fullarton of numerous charges of tyranny, cruelty, and extortion against him during his past government. Without assuming that Fullarton went out predetermined to get up charges against Picton, it is clear that, from the moment of his arrival, he readily accepted the statements of Picton's enemies. It is admitted that he assisted them to the utmost of his powers in concocting a series of the most atrocious accusations against him, taking advantage of the absence of Captain Hood to exercise autocratic powers in opposition to the opinion alike of the Council and Picton.[5]

Colonel Fullarton arrived in the island on the 4th January, 1803, and immediately on the arrival of Captain Hood, Picton sent in his resignation, and in June left for Barbadoes. Thence he returned to England in the October of that year, where he found

six months, as Colonel Fullarton was instructed to investigate Colonel Picton's past conduct;" and affidavit of Right Honourable John Sullivan, distinctly denying this statement, and quoting letters of Colonel Fullarton to the effect that he had been well received by Picton.—Trial of Colonel Draper for libel on Mr. Sullivan. Howell's "State Trials," vol. xxx. pp. 1034-39.

[5] Captain Hood was so disgusted with Fullarton's conduct previous to his own arrival in the island, that he publicly in the Council expressed his opinion of his conduct and "his intention of requesting to be relieved as soon as possible from so disagreeable a situation with a colleague in whom he could have no further confidence."—Lord Hood to Lord Camden, September 1 1804.

himself described in newspapers and pamphlets as "the blood-stained governor," and warned that the "friends of humanity were preparing to bring him before the bar of offended justice."[6] Previously to his arrival in England the minutes of the reported dissensions between the commissioners had been referred to a committee of the Privy Council, and within a few days after Colonel Fullarton transmitted to that tribunal the abstracts of eight cases, seven of which imputed illegal punishment of death, and the eighth the infliction of torture under the orders of Picton. In six of these charges he said that he was ready to proceed by documents and witnesses then in England. In the remaining cases he could not proceed, unless he was allowed to bring with him from Trinidad certain witnesses who he declared were prevented from leaving by the interference of the

[6] At the Westminster election Picton's case was used as a political engine against Sir S. Hood, who had lately been acquitted by the Privy Council of any share in the acts imputed to the late Governor. Among the poetical squibs then circulated with effect, was "The Picton Veil, or the Hood of Westminster." In this the Cabinet was represented as throwing its shield over Picton and Hood, each stanza ending,—
"It bodes our country little good
When murder's cover'd by a Hood."
And ending,—
"Oh! Fullarton, the brave and good,
With noble firmness you withstood
Torture and waste of human blood.
Long may a God of mercy spare
Thy life unto thy country's prayer,
'Gainst tyrant foes to prove her shield,
Either in council or in field."

authorities as soon as he had surrendered his government to General Hislop.[7]

The first of these cases was that of a Spaniard named Celestino, hanged without trial, for making a disturbance in the house of Josepha Perez in St. Joseph. He was said to have been sent to the Governor by the Assistant-Commandant of the district with a request to deport him from the island, but hanged by Picton without any evidence except that of the officer who arrested him. Then came the case of an artilleryman named Gallaghan, hanged without court-martial for the robbery and rape of a negress, though Nihill, the Chief Justice, was said to have looked on the charge as frivolous, and recommended that he should be confined for a few hours in the guard-room. On coming to Picton, according to Fullarton's statement, he was asked if he had seen the sun rise, and on his replying in the affirmative, the Governor told him that he should not see it set, and at once ordered him for execution. It was not, however, denied that three other artillerymen were tried by court-martial as accessories, and sentenced to 1500 lashes each for their share in the matter. The next case was that of Pierre Warren, a negro, sentenced, as a runaway slave, to have his ear cut off, though his master interfered on his behalf, from which punishment he died. In April,

---

[7] September 19, Secretary Lord Hobart to President of Privy Council, enclosing minutes of dissensions and correspondence. September 28, order of Privy Council to refer the same to a committee. October 29, letter from Colonel Fullarton, with details of eight cases in which he is prepared to proceed, under provisions of 3rd Henry VIII.—Picton Papers, Privy Council.

he characterized Fullarton's conduct as incited solely by "personal hatred and vengeance," and his witnesses as "wretches raked out of the most despicable classes of the colony, without property or character, a mixed and spotted breed, to whose evidence little or no attention would be paid by the magistrate of the colony from which they came, and under the tuition of two despicable fellows, Juan Montez and Pedro Vargas." The severities with which he was charged, he repeatedly declared, "were required by the extraordinary circumstances in which he was placed requiring powerful remedies and unusual means; but such as were given by the laws under which he was to act, and used only by necessity and sound policy."

In support of this defence, he laid before the Council the state of the island and the character of its population, and the dangers from Spanish intrigues, which we have previously quoted, and cited the repeated memorials in favour of his government, and the request to the Crown not to remove him, already alluded to. In the case of Celestino, he justified his immediate execution for attempting to stab the sergeant of the Convalescent Hospital, situated seven miles from any military force, and on the representation of the Spanish commandant of the quarter that he was dangerous to the peace of the island. He claimed to have thus put a stop to the use of the dagger, which the Spanish law forbade to be carried under pain of immediate death.

from Picton to Privy Council, September 2, 1804; ditto September, 1804.—Picton Papers, Privy Council.

Gallaghan had not only deserted his post, but seduced his comrades to join him, and had actually held the poor negress whilst they outraged and robbed her. From the state of the garrison it was impossible to hold a general court-martial, and he was obliged to act on his own responsibility.[1] The patron of the trading schooner had already carried off eleven of Hompesch's regiment, and had returned to carry off another when seized, and his engagement with the Spaniards was found on him. The negress was taken in a camp of Maroon negroes, whom she supplied with provisions and ball cartridge purchased from the soldiers, and executed without trial, according to the Spanish law.[2] In Alarcon's case, three of the crew of a launch had risen on the captain with the object of stealing the vessel, and made the one in charge of the helm change its course. Getting drunk, two of the mutineers had, in their drunken sleep, been killed by the captain, who, with the help of the helmsman, brought the third

---

[1] Bound into the volume of the Picton papers is a portion of a leaf of a diary, with entries of May 26, 27, and June 8. That of May 27 relates to Gallaghan's case. "Hugh Gallaghan, R. Irish Art., hanged for ravishing a negro woman, holding her whilst two others did the same, and for robbing her of eight dollars. The fact was clearly and satisfactorily proved, and from the state of the garrison it was impossible to assemble a general court-martial." On June 8 is the curious entry that from "a small privateer preventing the launches coming from the main, therefore a scarcity of beef, the contractor requested leave to supply the troops once a week with turtle."

[2] These Maroons had murdered a Spanish settler, and Picton gave the widow thirty Joes (about 50*l.*) out of his own pocket.— Letter of Attorney-General Gloster, July 20, 1803, with details of this case.—Picton Papers, Privy Council.

mutineer into port and delivered him to the governor. Picton, feeling the importance of protecting the trade with the other islands which had so largely developed under his rule, and satisfied of the truth of the story of the captain and the other sailor, from the answers given by the prisoner, had him executed without further trial, thus crushing the boat-stealing that had previously prevailed. He passes Goliath's case with a reference to the cross-examination of his master, and the remark "that it is needless to speak further on it as Colonel Fullarton has since accused another person, a respectable magistrate of the island, with this crime.

The supplementary charges were three in number— execution of deserters in 1797, without trial, justified by the state of the garrison; that of an owner of a launch who had given a passage from the main to three persons hostile to Government; and numerous cases of natives convicted of sorcery by local tribunals, unlawfully appointed by Picton, and ordered to be tortured, mutilated, hanged, or burnt, or to assist at the execution of others, and then banished. It does not appear from the Council records that any attention was paid to the first and second of these charges. The third, however, was considered sufficiently serious to warrant the issuing of a Commission to Trinidad to inquire into the cases of sorcery, and whether the offenders were punished in accordance with Spanish law.[3] At what date this Commission reached the

---

[3] July 19, 1804, case for opinion, Attorney-General (Perceval) and Solicitor-General (Manners Sutton), as to legality of pro-

island, and what was the nature of its report, does not appear in the records of the Council. That it was favourable to Picton's exercise of authority in that case must be assumed, as on the 5th of January, 1807, the Committee of the Privy Council in its Minute, after recording its issue and return, reports that it is not advisable that proceedings under the statute of Henry VIII. should be instituted against the late governor.[4]

Though relieved from the fear of any proceedings on the part of the Government, Picton was by no means free from litigation of a most dangerous and vindictive character. Aware, probably, that he was not gaining ground with the Privy Council, and calculating that criminal proceedings in the torture case, already made so popular by pamphlets and pictures, might strengthen his case before that

---

posed Commission. February 22, 1805, draft commission to Mr. Dean and others to inquire as to the sorcery cases. Signed, Perceval and Vicary Gibbs.—Picton Papers, Privy Council.

[4] Register of Privy Council, January 5, 1807, reciting that they have been engaged for a considerable time on charges against Colonel Thomas Picton, as Governor of Trinidad, and submitting " that on the charge of the trial of various Mulattos, &c., for sorcery, divination, and poisoning by charms, it was desirable to obtain the original or copies of the commissions issued by Colonel Picton, and to inquire into the existence of other commissions of the same tenor during Spanish rule, the issue of the commission, and its sentence." Confirmed by King in Council, January 7. Letter from Clerk of the Council to Colonel Fullarton, that the report having been approved, their Lordships have not directed any further communication to be made to him on these proceedings.—Register, February 14, 1807.

NARRATIVES OF STATE TRIALS. 313

tribunal, in January, 1804, Colonel Fullarton [5] caused an indictment for misdemeanour for torturing Louisa Calderon to be sent up to the Grand Jury of Middlesex. This tribunal found a true bill, and th:s initiated the proceedings which in one form or other occupied the King's Bench for the next eight years.

In the first instance commissions to Trinidad to obtain copies of the proceedings in the case, and to examine resident witnesses, not only with reference to the facts of the case, but as to the laws and usages prevailing in the island at the time of its surrender delayed the trial for two years. The arguments, on a motion for a new trial, adjourned from time to time, were not concluded until February, 1808. The second trial resulted in a special verdict, and the details of its settlement occupied so long a time that the arguments on the case did not commence until February, 1810, and were not concluded until the 25th of June, in that year. Practically, however, the case ended with the close of the arguments, as the Court never gave judgment, and in January, 1812, respited the recognizances of the defendant until further order. During this protracted litigation Fullarton had died, Picton had been sent on the dangerous service of the Walcheren expedition, and been earning his well-deserved laurels in the Peninsula under Wellesley, and, except to the legal profession, all interest had

[5] So infatuated was Colonel Fullarton by the case of Calderon, that in 1805 he was introducing her in his own county (Ayrshire) as "the blessed innocent."—Letter from J. Dowie from Ayrshire, December 8, 1805.—Robinson's "Picton."

ceased in the case, and Louisa Calderon had been forgotten even by the newspapers.

The returns made by the commissioners were very voluminous. They included not only the original evidence in the case in which Louisa Calderon had been put to the torture of the piquet as a false witness and probable accomplice of the culprit, but further evidence taken before the Governor and Council, explanatory of the original proceedings. To these were added the testimony of several landed proprietors and magistrates to the condition of the island at the time of its conquest, and to the character and conduct of Picton as its Governor. Though, amid a mass of doubtful and conflicting testimony from witnesses, many of whom were not to be believed, one must fail to extract the exact truth, the following facts appear reliable.[6]

On the 7th of December, 1801, a trader and shopkeeper of the name of Pedro Ruiz, residing on the Marine Parade at Port of Spain, almost opposite to the Government House, laid a formal complaint before Picton that he had been robbed of two thousand

[6] The documents occupy two hundred and twenty-four of the closely printed columns of Howell's "State Trials." It was admitted by the Escrivano de Castro, whose duty it was to make the official record of the proceedings, that there were many omissions in it, namely, the non-appointment of a defensor, Louisa Calderon being a minor; that five days had not elapsed between the order for, and the infliction of, the torture, and certain extra-judicial examinations, and her confession, after previous denial, of illicit intercourse with the prisoner. No order for the appointment of a defensor was made until February 20, 1802.

dollars, accusing Louisa Calderon and her mother, his partner Perez, and one Carlos Gonzales, of the robbery. These parties were at once arrested, and the case formally handed over by the Governor to the local tribunal.[7] Of the women whom he accused, Louisa, then about fifteen years of age, had been his mistress for two years and a half, and her mother his domestic servant.[8] Both the mother and daughter were illegitimate, and the latter was at last compelled to admit that Gonzales was her paramour. The box from which the dollars were stolen stood in the middle of one of three rooms, along one side of which ran an outward passage, and a plank from its wall had been broken out, to give the idea of a robbery from the outside. Gonzales, it was proved, knew where the dollars were kept. He had been seen to enter the house immediately before the robbery, following Louisa, and to leave it after a short stay. A neighbour, who was in bed with palsy during the time Gonzales must have been there, also heard blows, as of breaking open a box.

Louisa Calderon, who, though charged with the theft, was examined as a witness, denied any knowledge of the robbery, and any connexion with Gonzales. "Though suspecting that she was concealing

[7] Louisa Calderon swore at the first trial in the King's Bench that, when first taken before Picton, he told her that if she did not confess she should be turned over to the hangman.

[8] A deliberate attempt was made to prove her only ten years old when first living with Pedro Ruiz, but the falsity of the register of baptism was clearly proved, and, according to Burmudez, who was appointed her defensor, her mother admitted to him that she was over fourteen at the time of the trial.

the truth, the Alcade was persuaded that by means of a slight torture she would discover it." He, therefore, applied to Picton (in whom, as Governor, he believed, resided the same power of ordering torture as in Spanish times had been exercised by the superior tribunal at Caraccas), to authorize its infliction. Picton, assuming that he would not be asked to exercise such a power without good reason, gave the required order, "*Inflict the torture on Louisa Calderon.*" In no other way did he interfere in the case, leaving to the Alcade to carry out, in accordance with Spanish law and custom, the order for which he had applied. After three admonitions and warnings of the danger in which she stood, and her repetition of her denial of any knowledge of the robbers, she was put to the torture of the *piquet* in the presence of the judge, his alguazils, and the scribe by whom the proceedings were to be recorded. The instrument of torture was a round-headed piece of wood, fixed in the floor, above which the victim was suspended by one wrist from a beam overhead, her other arm being tied to her side, and the great toe of the opposite foot resting on the head of the *piquet*.

For nearly an hour she was kept in this position of suffering before she agreed to confess. Her confession was evidently not the truth. "Carlos," she said "was her paramour, but only once; he stole the money, and she saw him do it. When she came home and let herself in with her own key, she heard blows, and on lighting a candle and retiring out of sight, she saw him break open the box, take out the bags of dollars, and leave the house. She did not know what he had done with it. He had not given any of it to her mother." Adhering still to her story that she had had no communication with Carlos about the money, and did not know where it was, she was again put to the same torture for about twenty minutes. She fainted, or appeared to faint, and on being recovered by a glass of wine, repeated that Carlos had the money in the way she told the Judge the day before, but did not know where he had placed it—he was, she said, the cause of her sufferings. "He thinks to get off in this world, but will not in the next; God reward him!" When a few days afterwards she was confronted with Carlos, she still maintained her confession, whilst Carlos at length admitted his intimate connexion with her, which before he had repeatedly denied. She was then remitted to prison, and there she remained, treated apparently better than her fellow-prisoners, for nearly seventeen months, and then released, as she was considered to have expiated her share in the robbery by her torture and her long imprisonment. The trial itself was not completed until July of 1802, when the lengthy proceedings were transmitted to the Governor, and Carlos adjudged to pay to Ruiz 1800 dollars and the full costs of the trial, and to be banished the island.[9]

At the first trial before Lord Ellenborough, Garrow, who had been one of the legal advisers of Colonel

---

[9] During the proceedings, on the petition of his wife, the trading-vessel of Gonzales was worked for her benefit by a person appointed by the court, a debtor and creditor account with whom is attached to the original proceedings, showing a profit of 634 dollars. The costs on taxation amounted to 2830 rials.

Fullarton during the previous proceedings, opened the case for the prosecution with his usual bitterness.[1] Adopting the popular views of his client's case, he dwelt on the details of her sufferings under the torture, "the bloody order for which Picton had," he urged, "written with his own hand"—rechristened "Piqueting" as "Pictoning." Displaying one of the coloured pictures of the girl hanging in a half-dying state by her wrist, whilst her torturers sat by unmoved (by which popular feeling had been so widely raised against the defendant), he laid it down, as law, that even if Spanish law, at the time of the capture authorized the infliction of torture—which he denied—it would be no justification for a British Governor. Nothing but imperious necessity could justify its infliction—it was abhorrent to English law and practice, and Picton was bound to have known that from the moment of its capture and its reception under British rule, torture would be for ever banished from the island. As the real question was that of law and not of fact, the evidence was taken shortly, Louisa Calderon giving her version of the affair, supported by the alguazils, Chando and Montez, and the voluminous depositions from Trinidad being referred to by both sides.

Dallas, for the defendant, rested his defence on three grounds. First, that by the Spanish law, which, under

[1] February 24, 1806, special jury. For prosecution, Garrow, afterwards Baron of the Exchequer; Adam, afterwards Lord Chief Commissioner of the Jury Court of Scotland, and Harrison For defendant, Dallas, afterwards Lord Chief Justice of the Common Pleas; Lawes, and Abercrombie.

the instructions of General Abercrombie, Picton was bound to administer, the infliction of torture was lawful on the request of the Judges of first instance to whom the case had been referred; secondly, that even if unlawful it was not in the sense of the indictment malicious. Lastly, that even if unlawful, yet if Governor Picton had been misinformed on that point, and led to believe that the request made to him by the judge was strictly legal, the case resolved itself into one of mere error of judgment, for which no criminal responsibility attached. After a slight struggle with the Chief Justice the second and third points were left for the consideration of the Court above, and the case before the jury rested on the question whether in such a case torture was applicable by the laws of Spain, under which her Indian possessions were governed.

To prove this contention on the part of the defendant, three books of Spanish law were relied upon—the "Bobadilla de la Politica," the "Curia Philippica," the commentaries of Colom, and a sort of Crown circuit companion by a Dr. Elizondo.[2] These authorities agreed that "in cases of high treason, homicide, theft, and robbery, and crimes of an atrocious character, suspicions being strong, and the accused hardened, not only torture, but unusual torments might be applied,"—that when torture was applicable to the delinquent it was also applicable to a witness "who varies and prevaricates in his evidence, or who denies the truth, or who refuses to declare it, there being a presumption that he knows it," and also to an accom-

[2] "Bobadilla de la Politica," the "Curia Philippica," "Colom," "Elizondo Practica Universal."

plice—and that the only persons who are to be present at its infliction are the judge, the executioner, the scribe, and the victim. In Spanish days the order for its application was made by the superior tribunal, the Audiencia at Caraccas, whose power, it was contended, had, on the capture of the island, descended to the Governor under the authority of General Abercrombie's instructions.

To meet this evidence, the correctness of which, as exhibiting the old law of Spain, was hardly contested, the prosecution produced a skilled witness—one Pedro de la Vargas—a native South American advocate, who had practised in several of the Indian Spanish possessions. He swore that these colonies were governed under a new code of laws contained in the "Recopilacion de las Leges de las Indias," a compendium of the laws for the Indies made by order of Charles II. of Spain, and published in the year 1681. He added that he had never heard of torture being administered during his time in the Spanish Indies; that the only law authorizing it even in Spain was one dating back to the year 1260,[3] but that its infliction in the Spanish settlements was held in abhorrence, and that though there was nothing in the compendium forbidding the application of torture there was nothing that authorized its infliction. Other witnesses, filling magisterial appointments, one of whom had known Trinidad for thirty-two years, and the other for more than twenty, swore that they had never heard of torture being administered, especially such as that

[3] One of the laws of the "Seven Partidas of the sapient King Don Alonzo."

of the *piquet*, which it was admitted was introduced by
Picton. The evidence of Vargas appears to have come
upon the counsel for the defendant somewhat by surprise. No attempt was made to examine the book
which he produced, and beyond eliciting that he was
employed by Colonel Fullarton in getting up evidence,
his statement of the law was left practically unchallenged.[4] The jury, therefore, had no hesitation in
finding that no law allowing the application of torture
in such a case existed in the island at the time of its
capture, and in pronouncing a verdict of Guilty, subject to the opinion of the full Court on the points previously reserved.

Before the motion for a new trial came on the value of
the evidence of De La Vargas had been severely tested.
Copies of the " Recopilacion," and of another book of
authority, " The Politica Indiana," had been obtained,
and carefully examined, and two treatises on the laws
of Spain, by Spanish advocates of undoubted position,
had been discovered in the library of Lord Holland.
From these latter treatises it was shown that, according
to the views of these experts, as late as 1776, the application of torture on the petition of the prosecutor, if
the evidence was insufficient, was in the discretion of

[4] Vargas admitted that he came to England in 1799, passing
under the name of Smith, and that he was Fullarton's assessor
in preparing evidence. From copy of minutes of the Council of
Trinidad, produced before the Privy Council, June 3, 1803, containing examination of Juan Pla and Francisco Salazar, it appears
that Fullarton privately interrogated these men, under oaths of
secrecy, as to their knowledge of the cases of the Guarani Indian
and Celestino, in which proceeding Vargas assisted.—Picton
Papers, Privy Council.

the judge, and that, except in cases merely involving the penalties of fines, it might be repeated. From the "Recopilacion" it was clear that, whether wilfully or through ignorance, Vargas had entirely misrepresented this compendium. It was true, no doubt, that there were no instructions which in so many words authorized the infliction of torture, but again and again it enjoined that "the laws of Castille should be followed as well for substance, determination, and decision as for the form and order of the proceedings,"—"that the laws for the Indies should be as far as possible conformable to those of Spain," and that "the ceremonies of the Chancery of Castille should be observed in the courts of the Indies, unless there was special provision to the contrary." The same opinions were enforced in the "Politica Indiana," published by royal authority in 1776. "The courts in the Indies were invested with the same powers as those in Spain, and were to govern according to Spanish law, unless there was some special provision to the contrary."[5]

Again, after the motion for a new trial had been formally opened, and whilst it stood over for argument news arrived that the question of the legality of the infliction of torture in the island, at and before its

---

[5] "Recopilacion de las Indias," by order of H.C. Majesty Charles II., printed at the Royal Press, Madrid, 1681. "Politica Indiana," by Don Juan de Solerauno and Paregra, one of his Majesty's Councillors of the Supreme Court of Castille and the Indies, Royal Press, Madrid, 1776. "Instituciones del Direchio Civil de Castille," fifth edition, 1792. "Instituciones del Direchio Publico General de Espana, fifth edition, Madrid, 1802.

capture had been the subject of investigation by the councils of the island and the result transmitted by the Governor to the home Government. At that investigation, held in the preceding May, evidence was given by professional men who had practised in the island for several years previously to its surrender that the laws regulating both the civil and criminal justice were the old laws of Castille, as modified by the "Recopilacion," and as explained by the "Curia Philippica," and the treatises of Bobadilla, Colom, and Elizondo. They agreed that by these laws torture was legally applicable in such a case, and referred to a case in 1791, when it had been ordered to be applied to a negro slave accused of murder. That it was not then applied was due to his escape from prison during the time that the order for its application, made by the judge of first instance, was being referred to the Audiencia of Caraccas in which, during Spanish rule, the supreme civil and criminal power resided. These opinions were confirmed by the affidavit of the Chief Justice of the island, who, on the advice of its general assessor and auditor at the time of its surrender, had always regulated his practice by the explanatory treatise of Doctor Elizondo, and who pointed out that that author "cited the law for the infliction of torture very clearly, and pointed out the cases in which it was to be inflicted."

Technically, this evidence was inadmissible in the form in which it was then offered. The necessity for its being brought before the Court in a legal form was at once admitted, and the action further adjourned, whilst a new Commission was sent to Trinidad to take evidence on the disputed question.[6] The concurrent opinion of all the skilled witnesses examined under this second Commission may be taken in the words of one of them, who had practised as an escrivano under the Spanish law. "The same laws," he said, "are in force in Trinidad at this day with respect to torture as were in force at its capture in 1797. These laws are the laws of Castille, the laws of the Indies, the Seven Partidas, as appears by the Spanish authors of the "Curia Philippica," Colom, Febrero, Elizondo, Herrera, Bobadilla, and other authors who have written on the subject of torture. All those laws recognize and authorize the torture to be inflicted in case of robbery, or other heinous crimes, on the principal, the accomplice, and witnesses to come at the truth."[7] Included in the return to the mandamus were the full proceedings in 1790 in the case of the negro slave charged with the murder of another slave and sentenced to torture by the presiding judge. In this case, after judicial proceedings before him ex-

---

[6] The inquiry by the Council of Trinidad was held in consequence of the report of the doubt on the point of law raised at the first trial, the existence of the law of torture having been assumed when the first Commission was opened in the island. The witnesses examined by the Council, and subsequently by the second Commission, were, with one exception, identical, and included several escrivanos of from fifteen to twenty years' standing, two alcades who had held that and similar offices for many years previous to the capture, a practising king's counsel, and the Chief Justice, Mr. John Nihell, who had resided for twenty years in the island. By the Council the Syndic Proctor General of the Cabildo, who had resided twenty years in Trinidad, was also examined.

[7] Evidence of Joseph de Orosco, escrivano.

tending over twelve months, the judge ordinary decreed "that as everything had been done and executed in this process and nothing left to be done, his Honour assented that on the consideration of the proceedings and events resulting therefrom, and circumstantial evidence with the symptoms that augment and establish it to be more than semiplenary or half proved, his Honour being *pro Tribunali secreto* pronounced and decreed that it was his duty to condemn, and he accordingly does condemn the aforesaid negro Francisco to be put to the torture, and which shall be put in force in the mode in which his Royal Highness may be pleased to determine and to whom it is reserved to specify the nature and degree of severity of the said torture, and the order or stated time at which the same is to be inflicted." To obtain this authority the file of the whole proceedings were sent to the Royal Audiencia at Caraccas. Before, however, the confirmatory order arrived the wily negro had gone off with "John the Englishman," the sentinel in whose charge he was placed, leaving the jailer and the remainder of the guard to bear the brunt of his well-planned escape.

On this evidence a new trial was ordered, and came on in June, 1808, when the evidence as to facts given at the previous trial was briefly repeated, the examinations of the skilled witnesses lately taken in the island read, and numerous quotations made from the Spanish law-books supporting their opinions, and proving that under Spanish law a judge who acted without malice was not responsible for any errors of judgment. Pressed with the conclusive nature of the new evidence as to the Spanish law at the time of the cession of the island, Garrow, though still formally denying its effect, rested his case against Picton on three points :—*first*, that Louisa Calderon was under the age at which torture could be legally inflicted : *secondly*, that a defensor ought, by Spanish law, to have been appointed for her at an early stage of the proceedings, and *thirdly*, that even if the right to inflict torture existed at the capture of the island, it ceased on its coming under British rule. "Whatever," said Garrow, the law might have been before the cession, the moment the islanders had the benefit of British law, I insist that the punishment of torture virtually ceased ;" resting on the dictum of Chief Justice De Grey, in the old case of Fabrigas *v.* Mostyn,[8] that "every English

---

[8] Fabrigas *v.* Mostyn.—Cowper's "Reports," 161. Howell's "State Trials," vol. ii. Action by resident in Minorca against the Governor for assault and imprisonment justified under the law prevailing in Minorca at the time of the capture. The Governor, informed by old Minorquins that he had such authority, without trial, sent Fabrigas to solitary confinement in the prison, and afterwards on board ship, with the intention of banishing him to Carthagena. On trial in Common Pleas before Justice Gould, verdict for plaintiff, 3000*l.* On motion for new trial before full Court, Chief Justice De Grey, after commenting on the unnecessary cruelty used to Fabrigas in prison, added, "He is then confined on board ship, under the idea of banishment to Carthagena. I do believe Mr. Mostyn was led into this under the old practice of the island of Minorca, by which it was usual to banish. I suppose the old Minorquins thought fit to advise this measure ; *the Governor knew that he could no more imprison him for a twelvemonth* THAN HE COULD INFLICT TORTURE ; yet the torture, as well as banishment, was the old law of Minorca, *which fell of course when it came into our possession. Every English governor knew he could not inflict*

governor knew he could not inflict torture ; the constitution of this country put an end to that idea."

It being agreed that this point and the question how far Picton, as a superior judge, was protected if his judgment was only erroneous and not malicious, should be reserved for the full Court, Lord Ellenborough left only two points to the jury, those of the existence of the law of torture at the time of the cession, and the imputation of personal malice in ordering its infliction. That the girl was of full age to undergo torture he declared to be well proved, and the neglect of appointing a defensor at the commencement of the proceedings was, he said, that of the alcade who tried the case, and not the duty of the Governor, as representing the superior tribunal at Caraccas. On both these points the verdict of the jury was in Picton's favour, and the findings turned into a special verdict to enable the Superior Court to determine the points reserved.

The settlement of the special verdict, in which the facts we have related were fully set out, was so protracted that it was not until February, 1810, that the arguments on it were commenced. It is to be regretted, seeing how important were the points raised, that no judgment was ever pronounced. The case, apparently by consent on both sides, slept until early in 1812, when Picton's recognizances were respited until further order, and the prosecution virtually ceased. It was the opinion of the legists of the day "that the judgment would have been against

the torture; the constitution of this country put an end to that idea."

Picton, but that, upon a consideration of the merits, it would have been followed by a punishment so slight, and so little commensurate with the magnitude of the question embraced by the case as to have reflected but little credit on the prosecution."

Whilst the Court was deliberating, Picton had been fighting his country's battles in the Peninsula, and earning wreath after wreath of glory under Wellington. After the great day of Vittoria, on his return to England from ill-health, he was elected member for his native county, appointed colonel of the 77th Foot, made a Knight of the Bath, and in November of that year received the thanks of the House of Commons for his services at Ciudad Rodrigo, Badajos, and Vittoria. After a very brief rest he returned to the field, though by no means fully recovered in his health, and bore his part in the battles of the Pyrenees, for which he again received the thanks of Parliament, and within a year fell at Waterloo " gallantly leading his division to a charge of bayonets, by which one of the most serious attacks made by the enemy was defeated." [9] The monument in St. Paul's, erected to his memory by an unanimous vote of the House of Commons, marked the esteem in which, despite all his errors of temper and judgment, he was regarded by his country. His character exhibited a strange mixture of failings and virtues: "Stern of countenance, robust of frame, austere in demeanour, inclined to harshness, rigid in command, prone to disobedience

[9] In the well-known picture of Picton's death, he is represented as being carried off the field by Highlanders, instead of, as was the case, by two grenadiers of the 32nd Regiment.

yet exacting entire submission from inferiors, ambitious and craving of glory," and generous to a fault. Though sorely pressed by the cost of the litigation in which he was involved, he declined the Duke of Queensborough's offer of 10,000*l.*, and when the inhabitants of Trinidad sent him 4000*l.*, he returned it on hearing that a disastrous fire had destroyed their principal town, content with the sword of honour which they had voted him, and which the Commander-in-Chief gladly presented to him with justly deserved words of praise and commendation.

Truly has it been said, " How often is it the case that naval and military men, who know no party than that of the country for which they are recklessly staking their lives, are made a sacrifice to the caprice, pique, and vindictiveness of faction. No one ever suffered from this more than Picton. They not only attempted insult, but they inflicted injury." [1]

[1] Captain Marryat's *Metropolitan Magazine*, Dec., 1835.

CHAPTER XI.

PRESS PROSECUTIONS.

JAMES PERRY, COBBETT, LEIGH HUNT, AND OTHERS.

OCTOBER 1809 TO NOVEMBER 1811.

THE Press fared badly during the Attorney-Generalship of Sir Vicary Gibbs, whose readiness in using the extraordinary powers of his office in filing criminal informations became notorious.[1] Cobbett, Leigh Hunt, James Perry, and other less known editors and proprietors of journals fell under his legal lash within the present decade. Juries, with rare exceptions, found the accused guilty, and judges inflicted on them severe punishments. Of these, four may be selected as well worthy of report, from the literary position of the parties accused, and the subjects about which the alleged libels were written. In the first case, that of John Lambert, the printer, and James

---

[1] The Marquis of Buckingham's anonymous correspondent, who was certainly a most industrious picker-up of news, writes to the Marquis, December 11, 1809, "There are now on foot two prosecutions against the *Morning Chronicle*, two against the *Times*, one against the *British Press*, one against the *Examiner*, and two against Cobbett."—"Courts and Cabinets of George III." vol. iv. p. 399.

Perry, the sole proprietor of the *Morning Chronicle*, the person and government of the king were alleged to be libelled, and the drift of the article—a short paragraph taken out of a long leader—was charged as tending to alienate and destroy the affections of the people towards their Sovereign, and to bring into discredit his person and the government of the kingdom. In those of Cobbett, Leigh Hunt, and a country editor of the name of Drakard, the inhuman severity of the military punishments of the time, and the use of German troops in repressing the outbreaks of native soldiers, formed the subjects of the alleged libels.

In the *Morning Chronicle* of the 2nd October, 1809, at the end of a political article on the negotiations for the accession of the Grenville party to the Cabinet, appeared this paragraph :—

"What a crowd of blessings rush upon one's mind, that might be bestowed upon the country in the event of a total change of system ! Of all monarchs, indeed, since the Revolution, the successor of George the Third will have the finest opportunity of becoming nobly popular."

Sir Vicary Gibbs was content not to quarrel with the first sentence. He would assume that it applied only to a change of Ministers, and according even to his view of " the just latitude which the press ought to enjoy, he could not quarrel with them on this branch of the record." In the other sentence lay the deadly libel,—" it fixed the era for the enjoyment of these blessings to be the death of his present Majesty." " It stirs up," he said, " and influences the minds of the people against the king's person, and is, in other words (joining the two parts of the sentence together) neither more nor less than this, that a total change of system would bestow a crowd of blessings on the country; but this is not to be expected, except by the removal of his present Majesty." If such was the real meaning of the paragraph, it savours of most unwonted mercy on Sir Vicary's part, that he did not charge them with intending the king's death.

Perry, who out of delicacy to his usual counsel, Mr. Jekyll, the Solicitor-General of the Prince of Wales, defended himself and his co-defendant in person, rested their defence on the unfairness of picking out one paragraph from the article with which it was connected, and claimed to explain its apparently questionable phrase, by the context of the leader to which it was attached. The article was a narrative of the negotiation in September, 1809, between Mr. Perceval and Lord Liverpool and Lords Grenville and Grey for the adhesion of the latter to the Ministerial ranks. The obnoxious paragraph had appeared in the *Examiner* of the previous Saturday, and "finding it to harmonize with the essay he had written, he had appended it as a just corollary to his own propositions." After stating the fact of Lord Grenville's arrival in town, the article alluded to the report of his refusal, "consistently with his principles, to have any interview with Mr. Perceval, or to enter into any discussion with him, as he considered their measures to be most objectionable in every respect, and he could never approve the principles of their formation." "It is understood" continued the writer, "that when he said this, he begged to express his most invariable and profound sentiments of respect for his Majesty ; that his conduct and principles, he trusted, had always been calculated to heal, not to foment, the divisions of the Empire, but that he could not view what was proposed as tending to that end." On this the writer argued that nothing short of a total change of men and measures would suffice for the occasion, and that however willing and ready to devote themselves to the service of their king and country, the noble lords could not, " consistently with their principles, permit Lord Liverpool and Mr. Perceval to be the persons to communicate their thoughts and views to the king." To these reflections followed a paragraph commending the Prince of Wales for not interposing his high influence in the formation of an administration, and for " his firm and unalterable determination to preserve the same course of neutrality which he has maintained, and which from every feeling of dutiful attachment to his Majesty's person, from his reverence of the virtues, and from his confidence in the wisdom and solicitude of his royal father for the happiness of his people, he is sensible ought to be the course that he should pursue." To this eulogy on king and prince the obnoxious paragraph formed a not unnatural appendage.

Notwithstanding an ingenious attempt on the part of the Attorney-General to show from other portions of the article that it was really a bundle of independent paragraphs, Lord Ellenborough felt bound to admit that the latter portion of it might fairly claim to be taken as a whole. It, therefore, was for the jury to say whether "upon the fair construction of these words, the writer meant to calumniate the person and character of the Sovereign." "If," he added, "you don't see that it means distinctly and fairly to impute any maladministration to his Majesty, or those acting under him, but is at all reconcilable to the imputing only an erroneous view of public administration, I am not prepared to say that is a libel,"—"the greatest of monarchs who ever sat on the thrones of Europe, and who have been the promoters of the greatest blessings to their country in some respects, and who have contemplated its welfare with the greatest solicitude, have had their errors, but can a statement of that be considered as disparaging them?" With this view of the Lord Chief Justice the jury immediately agreed, pronouncing a verdict of Not Guilty, on which the information against the Hunts for the original paragraph in the *Examiner* was withdrawn, and this attempt to distort a political criticism into a personal libel frustrated.

We come now to a series of prosecutions for libellous criticisms on the employment of the Hanoverian troops in England, and the savage punishments by which, at that period and for long after, it was sought to maintain discipline in our army. On the 24th June, 1809, a regiment of militia mustered for training at Ely. On the alleged grievance of stoppages for knapsacks, it broke out into a mutiny, in such force and with such violence, that it was not quelled until some squadrons of the German Legion, quartered at Bury St. Edmund's, were called in to repress the rising. For this outbreak five of the ringleaders were sentenced to 500 lashes each. On this text Cobbett, in his *Register*, quoting the account of the scene given in the Government paper, the *Courier*, wrote the following characteristic criticism, contrasting the barbarities of our military discipline with that by which Bonaparte maintained his armies, and bitterly attacking those writers and speakers who denounced the cruelty of the conscriptions by which he recruited his legions. We give the diatribe in full.

LOCAL MILITIA AND GERMAN LEGION.

"See the motto, English reader! See the motto, and then do pray recollect all that has been said about the way in which Bonaparte raises soldiers. Well done, Lord Castlereagh! this is just what it was thought your plan would produce. Well said, Mr. Huskisson! It was really not without reason that you dwelt with so much earnestness upon the great utility of foreign troops, whom Mr. Wardle appeared to think of no utility at all. Poor gentleman! he little imagined how a great genius might find useful employment for such troops. He little imagined that they might be made the means of compelling Englishmen to submit to a sort of discipline which is so conducive to the producing in them a disposition to defend the country at the risk of their lives! Let Mr. Wardle look at my motto, and then say whether the German soldiers are of *no use*. FIVE HUNDRED LASHES EACH! Ay, that is right! Flog them! Flog them! Flog them! They deserve it, and a great deal more! They deserve a flogging at every meal-time! Lash them daily! Lash them daily! What! shall the rascals dare to mutiny, and that, too, when the German Legion are so near at hand? Lash them! Lash them! Lash them! they deserve it! Oh, yes! they want a double-tailed cat, the base dogs! What! mutiny for the sake of the price of a knapsack! Flog them! flog them, base rascals! Mutiny for the price of a goat-skin! and then, upon the appearance of the German soldiers, they take a flogging as quietly as so many trunks of trees! I do not know what sort of a place Ely is, but I really should like to know how the inhabitants looked one another in the face while this scene was exhibiting within their town. I should like to have been able to have seen their faces and to hear their observations to each other at the time. This occurrence at home would, one would hope, teach *the loyal* a little caution in speaking of the means which Napoleon employs (or rather which they say he employs), in order to get together and to discipline his conscripts. There is scarcely any one of these loyal persons who has not, at various times, cited *the handcuffings* and other *means of force* said to be used in drawing out the young men of France. There is scarcely one of *the loyal* who has not cited these means as a proof, a complete proof that the people of France *hate Napoleon and his government*, assist *with reluctance in his wars*, and would *fain see another revolution*. I hope, I say, that the Loyal will hereafter be more cautious in drawing such conclusions, now that they see that our gallant defenders not only require physical restraint to certain cases, but even a little blood drawn from their backs, and that, too, with the aid and assistance of *German troops*. Yes, I hope the Loyal will be a little more on their guard in drawing conclusions against Napoleon's popularity. At any rate, every time they do, in future, burst out in execration against the French for suffering themselves to be chained and forced, at the point of the bayonet, into military duty, I shall just republish the passage which I have taken for the motto to the present sheet. I have heard some pretty little things of the same sort; but I rather take my instance (and a very complete one it is) from a public print notoriously under the sway of the ministry."

For this article Cobbett, with his printer and publishers, were prosecuted on the 15th of June, 1810, and sentenced to a most severe punishment. In the opening speech in the case, Sir Vicary Gibbs, excusing the flogging to which the mutineers at Ely had been subjected, said "the aggressors were not dealt with as Bonaparte would have treated his refractory troops," alluding no doubt to the readiness with which the punishment of death was awarded in the French army, and inferring that the lash, however brutally applied, was preferable. Of this sentence the editors of the *Examiner* took advantage, heading with it an article in which a series of instances of barbarous military punishment were collected from various journals, and commenting on them in terms more likely to injure than to advance, the cause of humanity in the support of which they were professedly written. It was not to be expected that the Government would not attempt to repress such attacks, and even a less prosecuting Attorney-General than Sir Vicary Gibbs might be excused for the proceedings he instituted against their authors. The trial of Leigh Hunt and his brother John came on before Lord Ellenborough on the 22nd of February, 1811, and is chiefly noteworthy for the elaborate and successful defence made by Brougham to the intense dissatisfaction of the Chief Justice. Nominally, it was before a special jury; in reality only two special jurors appeared, and the list had to be made up from the common jury panel, much to the advantage of the defendants. To those acquainted only with the leader-writing and criticisms of the press of the present time, the article, which we produce in full, must be a startling novelty. No journal of any credit would now admit such a composition into its columns, however bitterly opposed it might be to the Government of the day. Such an article would now have to take refuge in the lowest of the public prints.

ONE THOUSAND LASHES.
(*From the " Stamford News."*)

" The aggressors were not dealt with as Bonaparte would

have treated his refractory troops."—*Speech of the Attorney-General.*

"Corporal Curtis was sentenced to receive ONE THOUSAND LASHES, but *after receiving two hundred* was, on his own petition, permitted to volunteer into a regiment on foreign service. William Clifford, a private of the 7th Royal *Veteran* Battalion was lately sentenced to receive ONE THOUSAND LASHES for repeatedly striking and kicking his superior officer. He underwent part of his sentence by receiving *seven hundred and fifty lashes* at Canterbury, in the presence of the whole garrison. A garrison court-martial has been held on board the 'Metcalf' transport at Spithead, on some men of the 4th regiment of Foot, for disrespectful behaviour to their officers. TWO THOUSAND SIX HUNDRED LASHES were to be inflicted among them. Robert Chillman, a private in the Bearstead and Malling regiment of local militia, who was lately tried by a court-martial for disobedience of orders and mutinous and improper behaviour while the regiment was embodied, has been found guilty of all the charges, and sentenced to receive EIGHT HUNDRED LASHES, which are to be inflicted on him at Chatham, to which garrison he is to be marched for that purpose."—*London Newspapers.*

"The Attorney-General said what was very true; these aggressors have certainly not been dealt with as Bonaparte treated his refractory troops; not indeed as refractory troops would be treated in any civilized country whatever, save and except in this country. Here alone, in this land of liberty, in this age of refinement, by a people who, with their usual consistency, have been in the habit of reproaching their neighbours with the cruelty of their punishments is still inflicted a species of torture, at least as exquisite as any that was ever devised by the infernal ingenuity of the Inquisition. No, as the Attorney-General justly says, Bonaparte does not treat his refractory troops in this manner; there is not a man in his ranks whose back is seamed with the lacerating cat-o'-nine-tails; his soldiers have never yet been brought up to view one of their comrades stripped naked, his limbs tied with ropes to a triangular machine, his back torn to the bone by the merciless, cutting whip-cord, applied by persons who relieve each other at short intervals that they may bring the full, unexhausted strength of a man to the work of scourging. Bonaparte's soldiers have never yet, with tingling ears, listened to the piercing screams of a human creature so tortured; they have never seen the blood oozing from his rent flesh; they have never beheld a surgeon, with dubious looks, pressing the agonized victim's pulse, and calmly calculating to an odd blow how far suffering may be extended until, in its extremity, it encroach upon life. In short, Bonaparte's soldiers cannot form any notion of that most heartrending of all exhibitions on this side hell—*an English military flogging*.

" Let it not be supposed that we intend these remarks to excite a vague and indiscriminating sentiment against punishment by military law. When it is considered that discipline forms the soul of an army, without which it would at once degenerate into a mob; when the description of persons which compose the body of what is called an army, and the situations in which it is frequently placed, are taken into account, it will, we are afraid, appear too evident that the military code must still be kept distinct from the civil, and distinguished by greater promptitude and severity. Bonaparte is no favourite of ours, God wot, but if we come to balance accounts with him on this particular head, let us see how matters will stand. He recruits his ranks by force —*so do we*. We *flog* those whom we have forced—*he does not*. It may be said that he punishes them in some manner; that is very true. He imprisons his refractory troops—occasionally in chains —and, in aggravated cases, he puts them to death. But any of these severities is preferable to tying a human creature up like a dog, and cutting his flesh to pieces with whipcord. Who would not go to prison for two years, or, indeed, for almost any term, rather than bear the exquisite, the almost insupportable torment occasioned by the infliction of seven hundred or a thousand lashes? Death is mercy compared with such sufferings. Besides, what is a man good for after he has had the cat-o'-nine-tails across his back? Can he ever again hold up his head among his fellows? One of the poor fellows executed at Lincoln last Friday is stated to have been severely punished in some regiment. The probability is, that to this odious, ignominious flogging may be traced his sad end; and it cannot be doubted that he found the gallows less cruel than the halberts. Surely then he Attorney-General ought not to stroke his chin with such complacency when he refers to the manner in which Bonaparte treats his soldiers. We despise and detest those who would tell us that there is as much liberty now enjoyed in France as there is left in this country. We give all credit to the wishes of some of our great men. Yet, while anything remains to us in the shape of free discussion, it is impossible that we should sink into the abject slavery in which the French people are plunged. Although we do not envy the general condition of Bonaparte's subjects, we really (and we speak the honest conviction of our hearts) see nothing peculiarly pitiable in the lot of his soldiers when compared with that of our own. Were we called upon to make our election between the services, the whipcord would at once decide us. No advantage whatever can compensate for, or render tolerable to a mind but one degree removed from brutality, a liability to be lashed like a beast. It is idle to talk about rendering the situation of a British soldier pleasant to himself, or desirable, far less honourable in the estimation of others, while the whip is held over his head, and over his head alone; for in no other country in Europe (with the exception, perhaps, of Russia, which is yet in a state of barbarity) is the military character so degraded. We once heard of an army of slaves, which had bravely withstood *the swords* of their masters, being defeated and dispersed by the bare shaking of *the instrument of flagellation* in their faces. This brought so forcibly to their minds their former state of servitude and disgrace, that every honourable impulse at once forsook their bosoms, and they betook themselves to flight and to howling. We entertain no anxiety about the character of our countrymen in Portugal, when we contemplate their meeting the *bayonets* of Massena's troops; but we must own that we should tremble for the result, were the French general to despatch against them a few hundred drummers, each brandishing a *cat-o'-nine-tails.*"

After an attempt on Brougham's part to rescue Leigh Hunt from the indictment, on the ground that John Hunt's name alone appeared on the *Examiner* as the printer, which was easily defeated by reference to the joint affidavit of the brothers as proprietors when the paper was first registered, the formal proof on the part of the Crown closed. The text on which the defence rested was the intention of the writers. " If that," said the advocate, " has apparently been good, or whether laudable or not it has been innocent, if it has been innocent and not blameworthy ; then, whatever you may think of the opinions, you must acquit those who published it." To show the innocency of their intentions—the language of their criticisms he could not defend—Brougham pressed into their service the published opinions of military men of repute against the existing system of life-service which then prevailed, and the barbarity of the lash as a punishment for grown men. Quoting from a pamphlet of Sir Robert Wilson's, who every one would admit had the good of the service at heart, he laid great stress on his condemnation of "enlisting for life as repugnant to freedom, and to the particular character of the British constitution," and to the strangeness of its "being continued after every other nation in Europe had abandoned it as impolitic, and as too severe an imposition upon the subject."

"If in those countries," General Wilson said, "where the inferior orders are born in vassalage, and where the will of the sovereign is immediate law, this power has been relinquished in order to induce men voluntarily to enlist, surely there is strong presumptive evidence that the general interests of the service are improved instead of being injured by this more liberal consideration. . . . What is the inference to be now fairly drawn from the perseverance of enlisting for life ? Is it not that the British service is so obnoxious and so little conciliating that, if permission to retire were accorded, the ranks would be altogether abandoned and the skeleton only remain, as an eternal and mournful monument of the wretchedness of a soldier's condition? Is it not a declaration to the world, that the service is so ungrateful to the feelings of the soldiery, that when once the unfortunate victim has been trapped, it is necessary to secure his allegiance by a perpetual state of confinement."

Passing from this point to the question of flogging, Brougham quoted from the same source, how Sir Ralph Abercrombie, Lord Moira, General Simcoe, and almost every general officer in the army expressed his aversion to corporal punishment, and the pride with which Sir Robert Wilson contrasted his own regiment—" the 15th Dragoons, before which corps the triangles were never planted"—with those in which it was the almost daily occurrence.

"There," said Wilson, " each man felt an individual spirit of independence ; walked each as if conscious of his value as a man and a soldier; where affection for his officer and pride in his corps were so blended that duty became a satisfactory employment, and to acquire for each new distinction the chief object of their wishes. . . . There is no maxim more true than that cruelty is generated in cowardice, and that humanity is inseparable from courage. . . . Corporal punishments never yet reformed a corps, but they have totally ruined many a man who would have proved, under milder treatment, a meritorious soldier. . . . Instead of upholding the character of the soldier, as entitled to the respect of the community, this system renders him despicable in his own eyes, and the object of opprobrium in the state, or of mortifying commiseration."

Similar opinions of another eminent officer were quoted not so much as enforcing those of General Wilson, as for the bold comparison he drew between the English and foreign systems of army discipline. If an eminent officer like General Stewart could praise the discipline of the French army in contrast to that in our own without its being imputed to him that his object was to disgust the English soldier with his service, and sow dissension in the ranks, why not these writers?

"In the French army," wrote Stewart, "a soldier is often shot, but he rarely receives corporal punishment; and in no other service is discipline preserved on truer principles. I know the service: I have had occasion to see it in practice, and therefore I quote the example of the French, whose discipline is preserved on principles, too true, alas! for our ill-fated allies. It is therefore that I quote the French army, in order to show that the change I recommend is necessary for the perfection of discipline, and to save us from the fate of our allies."

The reply of the Attorney-General and the summing-up of Lord Ellenborough drew the distinction between a fair and honest discussion by men capable of giving an opinion, and such an article as that now under prosecution, the mere form, let alone the language of which excluded it from such a parallel. The jury, however, took the view, that what Wilson and Stewart might write, and Abercrombie say, might be said by journalists in their own way—a way which the then unbounded licence of the press had made familiar to their ears. Though the Chief Justice under the suggestion of the statute gave it as his opinion that the article had been published with the intention imputed to it in the information, after some delay the jury acquitted the defendants.

A country editor was not so fortunate as the Hunts. On the 13th March in the following year John Drakard, of the *Stamford News*, was tried at Lincoln before Baron Sir George Wood for repeating the article in the *Examiner* with some special additional remarks materially adding to its bitterness. Again

Brougham quoted his military writers, and again urged the arguments he had used with such effect to the London jury. Whether in this case, the local special jurors answered more freely and composed the bulk or perhaps the whole of the jury, is not clear. At any rate the men of Lincolnshire did not agree with their brethren of London, and John Drakard was found guilty of the self-same libel of which the Hunts were acquitted.

The case of one more editor brought to trial for criticisms on our military discipline must close this series of press prosecutions. On the 1st of November, 1811, H. White, of the *Independant Whig*, fell under the lash of Sir Vicary Gibbs for an article charging gross partiality and injustice towards common soldiers in confining the distribution of honorary medals in celebration of victories to officers, and contrasting this treatment of our soldiers to that of Bonaparte towards his, and concluding with the usual common-place invectives against the Government. This editor did not attempt to justify his criticisms, but excused himself on the ground that at the time when the letter, which formed the subject of the information, was published, he was in gaol, 120 miles off at Dorchester, and compelled to have his work done by a deputy, who had offered to surrender if the Attorney-General would consent, which he had refused. At the trial he called a son to prove that he heard his father say that the libel was written by a brother who had a discretion and latitude with respect to the insertion of articles headed "London" during his father's imprisonment.

Lord Ellenborough, as usual, addressed the jury strongly for a conviction, but they found him guilty only of publishing and printing through his agent, and on account of his peculiar situation at the time strongly recommended him to mercy. The Chief Justice refused to receive this verdict, and the jury thereupon found White Not Guilty, and so another of Sir Vicary's Press Prosecutions failed.

CHAPTER XII.

THE BERKELEY PEERAGE CASE.

HOUSE OF LORDS, 1799 AND 1811.

FREDERICK AUGUSTUS,[1] fifth Earl of Berkeley, succeeded to his title as a youth, and received the education usual for one of his position. Falling in early manhood into the vicious circle of which the Royal Princes were the leaders, he soon became notorious, even in those days, for his immoralities and the pursuit of the gratification of his pleasures among the lower classes. More than one female favourite had reigned at Berkeley, and been cast aside for a new mistress, when, in 1784, he became acquainted in Gloucester with the daughter of a small tradesman, the future mother of a numerous family, and to whom he was undoubtedly married twelve years after. Until then, and for more than a year after that marriage, she was known at Berkeley and Cranford, and the other residences of the Earl, only as Miss Tudor; and though not associated with by the ladies of her neighbourhood, was regarded as

[1] Frederick Augustus, fifth Earl of Berkeley, born May 24, 1745; succeeded his father, January, 1755; died, August 8, 1810.

remarkable, in her presumed position, for the prudence and propriety of her conduct. Over the Earl she soon acquired undisputed influence. If she was not, in law, his wife, she behaved as such to him and her children, and used the power she had obtained with the best effect. Whatever may have been his previous life, from the time when Miss Tudor came to Berkeley, a marked change for the better was noted in the habits of the Earl. Previously to the public marriage in 1796, four sons and one daughter had been born, each of whom was baptized as the child of the Earl of Berkeley and Mary Cole[2]—the

---

[2] Extracts from Register of Baptisms of the parish of St. George's, Hanover Square, produced by the Windsor Herald at examination by Committee of Privileges, 1799.

"(a) January, 1787, William Fitzhardinge, son of the Earl of Berkeley and Mary Cole.

"(b) March, 1788, Morris Frederick Fitzhardinge, born January 3, son of Right Hon. the Earl of Berkeley and Mary Cole.

"(c) Augustus Fitzhardinge, son of Right Hon. Lord Berkeley and Mary Cole; baptized, March, 1789; born, February 26."

From Register of St. Martin's-in-the-Fields :—

"(a) July, 1793, Henrietta Fitzhardinge, daughter of the Right Hon. the Earl of Berkeley by Mary Cole, born June 23. She died December 6, 1793.

"(b) Francis Henry Fitzhardinge, son of the Earl of Berkeley, by Mary Cole, born December, 1794 ; baptized, March, 1795."

Produced by Garter King-at-Arms. Extract from Register of St. Martin's-in-the-Fields :—

"November, 1796, Right Hon. Thomas Fitzhardinge, Lord Dursley, son of Right Hon. Frederick Augustus, Earl of Berkeley, and Mary, Countess of Berkeley."

Subsequent entry in 1796 by Mr. Carrington in Register of Berkeley Church :—

"Thomas Morton Fitzhardinge, son of the Earl and Countess

original name of Miss Tudor. In the affidavit sworn by the Earl, for the purpose of obtaining a licence for the marriage, in 1796, he had described himself as a bachelor, and Mary Cole as a spinster. The next son, Thomas Moreton, was born in 1796, and in his baptismal register described as Lord Dursley, the son of the Earl and Countess of Berkeley.

Miss Tudor's was a painful history. The youngest of the three daughters of William Cole, a butcher at Wootton-under-Edge, on the death of her father she had removed in 1784, with her mother, to the house of an elder sister, who had married one Farren, in the same trade as her father, and who kept a shop in Gloucester. From there she and her sister Susan went into service in London, and afterwards in Kent, where she bore an excellent character. Whether, after a short stay in Kent, she returned to Gloucester, and went at that time to her sister Susan in London, or she had already become known to Lord Berkeley, must remain moot points. Anyhow, she was at her sister's, in London, in 1784, and there, if the evidence of one witness is to be believed, she was repeatedly brought into the society of the Earl and men of his set, and then "as much sold as a lamb that goes to the shambles" to her future husband.[3] Finding her sister Farren ill, she had gone up to Susan, who professed to be married, but in reality was under the protection of a rich man.

---

of Berkeley, born October 19, 1796; baptized at Berkeley Castle, December following, by C. Carrington, chaplain to the Earl of Berkeley."

[3] Rev. John Chapeau.

What followed must be told in the words of the witness to whom she told her tale.

"'I took up the knocker; but recollecting that my mother had given me strict orders never to speak to my sister Susan any more, I laid it down again and took a turn to reflect upon my disobedience; but when I thought of returning to all that misery at my sister's... I faced about, went to my sister's once again, took up the knocker, and gave a loud rap. Who should come to the door but (as if it had been on purpose) my sister Susan herself, dressed out in all the paraphernalia of a fine lady going to the opera. She took me into her arms, carried me into the parlour and gave me refreshment, began to tear a great many valuable laces, of sixteen shillings a yard, to equip me for the opera, and when I was so dressed I looked like the devil. I went to the opera and was entertained with it, and at night returned again to my sister's, and there I found a table well spread. At that table were Lord Berkeley, Sir Thomas Kipworth, I think a Mr. Marriott, and a Mr. Howarth; the evening went very dull, and they soon left the place.... When they went away I requested my sister to give me a cheerful evening, that we might recount over our youthful stories; the day was fixed, and our supper consisted of a roast fowl, sausages, and a bowl of punch. In the midst of our mirth a violent noise was heard in the passage, and in rushed two ruffians, one seizing my sister by the right hand, and the other by the left, trying to drag her out of the house, in order to carry her to a sponging-house.' She told me the men would not quit her sister unless they received a hundred guineas. She fainted away; then, when she came to herself, she found Lord Berkeley standing by her sister Susan, who was not there before. Miss Tudor fell on her knees and desired my Lord Berkeley to liberate her sister; that she had no money to do it, and if he would, he might do whatever he would with her. He paid down the money, the ruffians quitted their hold, and my lord carried off the lady.

"Q. In conclusion, did her ladyship say anything?

"A. Yes; she said, 'Mr. Chapeau, I have been as much sold as any lamb that goes to the shambles.'"

The witness, a sporting parson, undoubtedly an

intimate friend of the Earl's, the first of whose children he baptized, and to the second of which he was godfather, and a constant visitor at his house, may have painted up the scene. Still, however, it reads like the truth; it is accepted as the truth by one of her sons,[4] and the Marquis of Buckingham "had a faint recollection of Lord Berkeley saying something of paying money for her, but could not undertake to say the precise sum." It can hardly be supposed that Chapeau would have dared, even if he had wished, to invent such a story. He repeated the story soon after to friends, and the servant-maid, whose conduct had formed the occasion for the reported statement by Lady Berkeley, was present when it was made. The conduct of the sister is too consistent with her life and character, and the story too much in accordance with the manners of the time in which it is supposed to have occurred, not to be accepted as true, despite all the embroidery which may have been added by its relator.[5]

[4] "Grantley Berkeley's Life," vol. i., Marquis of Buckingham's evidence.

[5] The reason for this statement to Chapeau is thus given in his evidence:—"In October, 1787, when I came into the parlour at Spring Gardens, I believe to shelter myself from rain, Miss Tudor was discharging a servant she had had out of the country, and persuading her to return to her friends, telling her she would pay her stage-coach if she would. She refused, saying she liked to stay in London better. Upon which Miss Tudor asked me if I did not think the girl extremely obstinate; and that a girl with a good countenance, and dismissed from service without money, would be sure to fall a prey to some man or other. 'In this situation,' said she, 'I was once myself; but having a friend of my mother's, whose name I recollected, and

So notorious were these incidents, and so consistent with them had been the life of the principal actors, that society was as incredulous as astonished, when, in 1797, it began to be rumoured among Lord Berkeley's friends that a secret marriage had been celebrated in 1785. The reason for its concealment was equally untrustworthy. The officiating clergyman, it was said, had destroyed the register of the marriage, and Lord Berkeley had kept the secret solely out of kindness to the clergyman, and to screen him from the punishment of his serious offence.

The new tale, whether true or not, could not for long escape the severe test of a public examination. At the union, in pursuance of an old standing order of the House of Lords, it became necessary not only to prove the pedigree of the then Earl of Berkeley, but to put on record the birth of his descendants. On the 27th of May, 1799, therefore, the Committee of Privileges met to consider the pedigree of the Earl and the statement of his present descendants, which he had forwarded to the Garter King-at-Arms. Then it

whose house I found out, very luckily was received with kindness; but that kindness did not last long, for he came to me and said, "Mary, you must not stay longer under my roof. I have lived in good esteem among my neighbours, and the young people will laugh at me if you continue, and the old will despise me; therefore, child, you must go down to your friends at Gloucester."' I said to her, 'I hope that he did not turn you away without some money.' 'No,' she said, 'he did not; he gave me a very handsome present, and with that I quitted his house and went to my sister Farren, whom I found ill, and two or three children diseased and dirty.'" Having got medical assistance for her, and paid an old servant to attend on her sister, she left for London as is stated above.

was that the Peers were so little satisfied with the account the Earl had given, that they called for evidence and partially sifted the story. Eventually, after eight sittings, at which numerous witnesses were examined—all produced by and in the interest of the Earl—they adjourned without admitting the statement, Lord Berkeley, it is believed, declining to pledge his honour to the truth of the documents produced in the case.[6] The missing register of the marriage and of the publication of the banns was now produced. According to these papers, the banns had been published in Berkeley Church on the 28th of November and 5th and 12th of December, 1784, by the then rector, Mr. Hupsman, and the marriage celebrated by him on the 30th day of March, 1785, in the presence of William Tudor and Richard Barns. As to the identity or existence of Richard Barns no evidence was offered. No one had ever heard of him, either before or after the marriage. The clergyman, Mr. Carrington, Mr. Hupsman's successor, had never asked who he was, nor ever made any inquiry whether he was dead or alive. William Tudor, however, was forthcoming, the brother of Mary Cole, a dependant on the bounty of his sister. His whole career, and his assumption of the name of Tudor, became one of the most interesting points in the evidence, and the little reliability which might otherwise have attached to his account of the transaction

---

[6] Minutes of evidence before Committee of Privileges, House of Lords, 1799, May 27, 28, 30, June 3, 5, 13, and 20, and July 8; reprinted with the minutes of the inquiry in 1811.

faded rapidly under his cross-examination as to his assumption of the name of Tudor.

The history of the discovery of the lost documents was dramatic in its incidents. In March, 1799, Mr. Scriven, a conveyancer, was sent by the solicitor of Lord Berkeley to search for the documents which the Earl had declared had been destroyed years before.[7] Going to Berkeley with the Rev. Caleb Carrington, the then rector, he found that the usual register-box was empty; that the registers were at the curate's, whence they were brought to him and his companion in the Muniment-room of the castle. All the books were gone through at first without any discovery. They then exchanged books, when Carrington called his attention to two leaves in one of the books which were pasted together and between which, when opened with a penknife, the register of the banns was found. Induced from this to resume their search,

"We observed," said Mr. Scriven, "and I think it first occurred to me that there was a puckering at the end of one of the books; and, if I rightly recollect, there was an appearance of the cover of a letter, or some such thing, wafered upon that which appeared to be the cover of the book. I again took my penknife and opened a corner of it, and soon found that it was the registry, and then, perhaps rather carelessly, tore it up; and I think Mr. Carrington made a copy of it, and it proved to be the registry of the marriage." According to Mr. Carrington's evidence it was "concealed in the inside of the cover of the book upon the pasteboard; it appeared to have been written between lines ruled with ink for the purpose upon the last blank leaf of the book, but the wrong side upwards, which made me suppose that at the time of the entry the book might be reversed, and this

---

[7] Examination of John Scriven and Rev. Caleb Carrington, 1799 and 1811.—Minutes of evidence.

appears to be the first entry in it. The leaf appeared to have been divided in a line from side to side without separation from the binding. Another marriage was entered upon the upper side of the same leaf, on the part left uncovered. The piece of the leaf covered which contained the entry was turned down upon the pasteboard cover of the book like a strap, and the whole seemed the original cover of the book, over which an old paper was stuck with wafers. We happened to open the bottom of the book first, by which means we tore the entry from the book, of which I am certain it had been part, by comparing the parts separated, and the indents fitted each other. The date of the other marriage is of June 24, 1790."

Mr. Carrington identified the signature of Mr. Hupsman, and in this was confirmed to a great extent by his curate, a Mr. Lewis. He believed that Lord Berkeley, who, it may be remembered, always said that the register was destroyed, told him that it was concealed with his consent, and he admitted, that, until more than a year after the second marriage, Miss Tudor was never addressed or spoken of as Lady Berkeley, or the eldest son as Lord Dursley.

To complete the evidence of the first marriage, William Tudor was put forward. As a boy of about sixteen, he had once come over to Berkeley church to hear the banns read—he believed by Mr. Hupsman; he could not say how long before the marriage, beyond this, that his sister was not then at the castle. He had also come over to the marriage, which was celebrated early in the morning, no one being present but the parties, the clergyman, and the witnesses. The body of the register was made out before he signed. He could not say in what part of the book it was, "but it appeared to be regular entered, as such a thing should be. There was not a piece of paper cut and turned up to write it upon. It was a common open entry in the course of the book." "Had only a feeble recollection of its being one of the outside leaves, but could not say whether the whole leaf appeared to be ruled." "Understood from the Earl that the marriage was to be kept secret for a short time."

As to the second marriage, he not only had been present at it, and signed as a witness, but under the advice of counsel had urged its celebration, believing that the first marriage could not be proved in consequence of the destruction of the register, as he supposed, by the Earl's desire. Neither his sister nor Lord Berkeley had intimated to him that the register was only concealed, and not destroyed. He was then pressed with the following questions, to which his replies must be given in full :—

Q. Had you, in point of fact, in communication with your sister, a letter soon after the first marriage, in which she signed herself Berkeley?

A. I have not at this moment a letter from any one person whatever during my residence abroad, which was seven years. My sister signed Maria. I directed to her under cover to Lord Berkeley in general. I cannot be positive by what direction, and do not recollect directing to her as Countess Berkeley.

Q. How could you be surprised that the marriage was not declared on your return home, when, by your own account, you avoided directing to her as Countess Berkeley?

A. I certainly did expect the marriage would have been published sooner; but I cannot exactly recollect how I felt at the moment, except that I was extremely hurt. I had not corresponded with her twelve or fifteen months before I returned home. I do not know the reason why she was not called Lady Berkeley at once after the second marriage, or for not declaring the first marriage as soon as the second had taken place. Have never seen Mr. Hupsman again, or asked him what had become of the register. I dare say I might have found him out. It was at Lord Berkeley's request that the matter should not be brought forward in Hupsman's lifetime. I did not ask counsel's opinion whether Hupsman's evidence would not be material.

Q. What did you mean to say about the register being destroyed?.

A. I was given to understand it was, by my sister and Lord Berkeley. Understood it was done by his consent, first from my sister, and then afterwards from Lord Berkeley. Cannot say whether he never addressed his sister as Lady Berkeley. At first did not by desire of both parties.

Tudor further explained, as his reasons for urging the second marriage, that "at that time he was not certain of bringing forward specific proofs of the first marriage, and because counsel had told him that persons might marry as often as they liked, and that the second would not invalidate the first marriage— it was only a confirmation."[8] Forgetting that he had

[8] Tudor had verbally consulted Mr. Bearcroft as to the necessity for a second marriage, and Carrington, in February, 1799, had obtained a written opinion from Mansfield (subsequently Chief Justice of the Common Pleas) on the proof of the first marriage, but without disclosing the names of the parties. In his opinion, Mansfield says, "the single witness now surviving may be sufficient to prove the marriage. The parties in a case so circumstanced may also prove the marriage, but this can hardly happen in the lifetime of the husband, because the only question which can produce an inquiry into the truth of the marriage must be owing to some claim made by the children as legitimate. After his death his wife might be examined in support of such claim." Carrington appears to have also asked as to the value of a declaration of the first marriage being made in the register of the children's baptisms; and though Mansfield did not think it could be of any use, "it cannot," he wrote, "I think, do any harm. If made, it should express not only the first marriage, but the reason why it was supposed not to be

professed entire ignorance of the reasons why the
first marriage was not published, he subsequently
admitted that on his return from abroad "he particularly
requested to know the reason, and was
informed there were private and very urgent reasons
which Lord Berkeley had why it should not be made
public, and after pressing both his sister and the Earl
on the subject, was given to understand that the
register had been destroyed.

Not less unsatisfactory was William Cole's account
of his taking the name of Tudor. When first examined
he swore that he was christened William Tudor
Cole, and took the name of Tudor from that cause
and the request of his relatives; that he never went
by his father's name that he could recollect, and
never signed himself by any other name than Tudor.
When, however, he was subsequently recalled he
admitted that until his father died he had always
borne his father's name, and that it was not until
after his father's death, when he went to London,
that, at the request of an aunt of the name of Tudor,
who had some property to leave, and of his sisters,
he dropped the name of Cole and took the more
aristocratic one of Tudor. His previous answer, that
"he had never gone by his father's name," was then
read to him when he replied :[9]—

A. I beg leave to point out that, by the question alluded to, I
did not say so, as I said I *took* the name of Tudor. No particular

---

valid. The same sort of declaration should be made where the
baptism of the children born since the second marriage is
entered, to explain the difference in the registrations prior to it."
[9] Examination in 1799.

time when I did take the name. Those who knew my father naturally called me *Cole*.

The examination was continued.

Q. You were asked, did you ever go by any other name? Your answer there is absolute, I never signed myself otherwise than Tudor?

A. As I understood, according to my own idea, that I had been sufficiently clear as to the statement that I had not always borne the name of Tudor, I thought the lord that put the question meant whether I had ever borne a third name.

Q. The question is very plain : Did you ever go by any other name? Your answer is, I never signed myself otherwise than as Tudor. It had reference to the preceding question, reference to the name of Cole. What do you say to it now?

A. I say I took the name of Tudor.

Q. The question was simply what name you bore?

, A. I am very sorry ; I think it is clear I meant otherwise.

To subsequent questions he said, " I was generally called Cole, and never took the trouble to contradict people. There is not any act or writing except as Tudor; whenever anything of consequence I write Tudor. Until the time I took it up entirely, and dropped Cole, I might sign Cole." This most unsatisfactory evidence was rendered more so, when the register of his baptism, as "William" only, was produced, and it was sworn by two residents in the same village that he had passed for years as "Cole," had never said a word about this "Aunt Tudor," and that as far as any one knew, that name was unknown in Gloucester.[1] After such evidence it was only natural

[1] John Allen, of Norton, who lived near Wootton, and had known the Coles some seventeen years, produced copy of register of baptism of William, son of William Cole and Susannah his wife, April, 1769, at Wootton. Theodore Gwinnett, of Barwood, in which parish part of Wootton is, schoolfellow of William Cole. No attempt was made to dispute the certificate

for the Lords to have a strong impression that the name of "Tudor" was not assumed until years after the professed marriage—probably only when, in 1794, Cole became a clerk in the Commissariat Department—and that in signing the certificate he at the time forgot that circumstance, and by using the name which he then bore proved that the certificate had been forged years after the date which it pretended to bear.

Before the case closed, a witness was produced to identify Hupsman's writing, who told a tale which probably astonished all parties equally. After giving the witness who had produced the baptismal register a bad character, and "not to be attended to, anything he said or did," she not only gave her opinion that both documents were in Hupsman's writing, but swore that, in 1786, she had heard him say that whenever Lord Berkeley died, she (Miss Tudor) would be Countess Berkeley. Had heard him say so fifty times." In the face of the admitted secrecy enjoined about the matter, and of the entire absence of any public recognition, the bold assertion of the witness was as destructive of her veracity as of the case.[2] It is not surprising that my Lords declined to proceed further with the inquiry, adjourning its consideration *sine die*, and that an attempt to revive the Committee, in June, 1802, was negatived without a division.[3]

of baptism. A witness, Mary Routh, was called to give Allen a bad character; and Tudor, when confronted with Gwinnett professed not to know him, or to remember a boy of that name at school with him.

[2] Mary Routh. See previous note.
[3] Calendar of Journals of House of Lords, June 3, 1802.

Foiled in the House of Lords, Lord Berkeley proceeded by bill in Chancery to get the evidence of these documents perpetuated, so as to be capable of being used, in any future proceeding for establishing the legitimacy of his elder sons.[4] In this proceeding the incidents already described were set out, the first marriage boldly asserted, and the supposed destruc-

Moved that the entry in the Committee of Privileges Book, June 20, 1799, touching the said Earl's pedigree, be read ; and being read accordingly, motion was made that the Committee of Privileges appointed to consider the pedigree of the said Earl be revived, and that the Committee do meet to consider the same Thursday next ; but the same, upon the question, refused.

[4] The original bill, now in the Public Record Office, was filed April 17, 1801, and subsequently amended May 7 and July 20. The parties were :—Plaintiffs, Hon. William Fitzhardinge Berkeley, commonly called Lord Dursley, and his three brothers, Frederick, Augustus, and Francis, by Lord Craven, as their next friend. Defendants, Thomas Moreton, calling himself Lord Dursley, and his brother Grantley, by Lord Grantley, their guardian, and the Hon. George Cranfield Berkeley (the Earl's brother), and his son George Henry, by his father. Demurrer by the Hon. George and his son, for remoteness of interest. The other defendants awaited the result of demurrer. Decision of Lord Eldon, July 7 and 9, 1801.—vi. Vesey, 251. In overruling the demurrer, Lord Eldon's remarks on the next friend of the children by the second marriage showed his opinion of the whole transaction. " I do not know who is the next friend of the children claiming under the second marriage, but I must say that, whoever he is, no man ever took upon himself a more solemn and more delicate duty. If he, for any reasons of connexion with any part of the family, does not exert himself for those children as zealously as if he were supporting his own claim to the dearest interest in life, he does not do his duty. It may be an instrument of mischief and oppression, or what would require a harsher name, to the children claiming under the second marriage."

tion of the certificate and difficulty of proving it, assigned as the reason for the second marriage. The discovery of the missing documents was briefly alluded to, and then it was gravely asserted as evidence of the truth of these statements that "*the said Earl did previously to the said first marriage consult with Hupsman as to the best manner of celebrating his intended marriage, so that the same might not be known to his friends, and that Hupsman recommended a marriage by banns in Berkeley Church.*" Lord Eldon's criticism of this singular device was unanswerable.

"Upon the whole," said the Chancellor, "enough has been stated of the circumstances upon this bill to raise as questionable a case as could be put on record ; for it states that a marriage was for certain reasons intended to be kept secret for some time, and the means of accomplishing that object are very singular : the marriage being attended with as much publicity and notoriety as could be given to it; a marriage in the parish church of Berkeley, and, according to this bill, attended with a due publication of banns ; with all the circumstances that belong to a marriage ; a due registry and signing by all the parties present, and it alleges that the thing was quite notorious ; that the clergyman and parties were constantly talking about it and it became the habit and repute of the place." Referring to the second marriage, Lord Eldon sarcastically remarked that "however prudent it might be as to future issue, it was not marked with singular prudence to marry again under the maiden name of the lady to prove the legitimacy of four children born antecedent to it."

The bill was allowed, the testimony was perpetuated and never used. Whatever was sworn then is now sealed up in the Record Office. From the subsequent proceedings in the House of Lords we learn that one portion of this evidence was an affidavit of the Earl himself, presumably to the truth of the first marriage and the execution of the certificate. Had he made a declaration on his honour as a Peer to the truth of these events, when his pedigree was under examination in the Lords years before, it would have spared him the necessity for the present attempt to support "the questionable case." What he feared to do then, when it would have been publicly known at once, he dared to do, when he knew that his statement could not be divulged until the succession was contested after his death.[b]

Though further legal proceedings to clear the difficulty could not be taken during the Earl's lifetime he did his best to impress public opinion with the truth of his "questionable case" by repeated assertions to friends that the first marriage had taken

[b] On May 3, 1811, Serjeant Best proposed to put in evidence the declaration of the late Earl upon the bill filed in Chancery, to which the Solicitor-General for the infant offered no objection, "as he felt it would conduce more to the truth and justice of the case" to admit it, but confined himself solely to the admission of this document. The Attorney-General for the Crown objected. The Committee informed the petitioners that they must produce the whole proceedings or none, to which they offered no objection. The question, however, was referred to the Judges, and, on their opinion, the evidence was rejected.—See proceedings in 1811. For the purposes of this bill, on June 29, 1801, the officer of the House of Lords was ordered to attend the Court of Chancery with the disputed documents, which, when reproduced in 1811, bore the endorsement of their production in the cause.

place, and by the public recognition of his eldest son as Lord Dursley and heir to his estates and his honours. He made no secret of having executed a will settling all his property on his eldest son, and leaving to those who were undoubtedly legitimate only small portions of his wealth. To make the case, as he thought, more secure, he had added a penal clause that if the sons of the second marriage claimed the title they should forfeit all interest under his will. On his death—August, 1810—the question of the succession could no longer be evaded.

In October, 1810, the Lord Dursley petitioned the king for his writ of summons as his father's heir; it was referred to the Attorney-General, and by his advice referred to the House of Lords in consequence of the doubt raised by the second marriage and his inability to decide, having no power to examine witnesses.[6] As the eldest son of the second marriage was a minor, the Lords addressed the Regent to appoint one of the law officers of the Crown to take care of his interest, and in consequence the Solicitor-General appeared on his behalf. Best and Romilly were counsel for the claimant, and the Attorney-General, as customary in all such claims, attended on the part of the Crown. The case commenced on the 7th of March, 1811, and did not terminate until the 18th of June, during which period no less than seventy-six witnesses were examined, very many of them on points of very minor importance.[7] This voluminous evidence may for convenience be divided under the following heads:—

[6] The petition was signed by Best, Romilly, and A. Moore.
[7] Such as, whether the militia under Colonel Berkeley were out

(1.) THE CERTIFICATES OF BANNS AND MARRIAGE.

It will be remembered that at the inquiry in 1799, Scriven and Carrington spoke of finding the certificates of the Banns and the Marriage on the 7th of March in that year in the cover of one of the volumes of the parish register. This evidence they now repeated. A solicitor of the name of Pitt, however, proved, and no attempt was made to contradict him, that when he most carefully examined the books on the 15th of April "he found the upper part of the last leaf remaining, but the lower part not visible. He was led to suspect from that circumstance that in that particular part of the book there might have been some trick played. He therefore was more minute with respect to his attention as to that part, and that notwithstanding all that minuteness—he saw nothing like an entry of Lord Berkeley's marriage—he found no pucker whatever which he was convinced would have led him to make a further search as to the cause of it." Simmonds, the Earl's steward, was present and confirmed his statement. When, however, he examined the book again a month after, there was the register in full view and certified as having been found by Scriven and Carrington. Bryan Donkin, a papermaker of long experience, proved that the cut leaf at the end of the Register Book and the cut leaf on

for training in Gloucester in 1783 or 1784, and whether at that time Lord Berkeley was a visitor at Farren's shop, where Mary Cole was living. Another point of but little value was the terms of Lady Berkeley's intimacy with a Mrs. Bell and her husband at Cranford. The evidence now given, it is believed, gives a correct view of the case without encumbering it with minor details.

which the register of marriage was written had formed
one sheet, the shifting of the water-mark, due to careless workmanship, being visible in both its portions.[8]
The evidence as to the handwriting of Mr. Hupsman was very contradictory. Dr. Jenner, a local
medical man at Berkeley, was clear as to the signature,
but doubtful about the writing of the rest of the document, which if signed by Hupsman would according
to his custom be entirely in his handwriting. Lady
Berkeley and Mr. Tudor, of course, swore to seeing
him sign, and a Mr. Bloxome, the deputy clerk of
the peace for the county, under William Tudor,
believed Hupsman's name to the banns and marriage-
certificate to be his, but the rest of the entry Lord
Berkeley's. One Nicholas Hicks, too, also a solicitor,
but of very doubtful antecedents, swore to the vicar's
signature, but as he got committed to Newgate for
prevarication, we need trouble ourselves but little

[8] It is impossible, on inspecting the fac-similes of these
certificates, not to be struck with the appearance of their being
in one handwriting, with the exception of the names of " Mary
Cole" and "William Tudor," and the great likeness of the
writing in the body, especially of the marriage-certificate, to the
signature of "Berkeley." The signature of Hupsman, and
especially of the "Augustus" in it, if not real, is a very admirable imitation, capable, no doubt, of being made by a tracing
from other real signatures of his in the books. How or when
these certificates were concocted must remain a mystery.
Grantley Berkeley's anecdote about the tracing-machine with
two pens, which he saw the surgeon of his father's regiment
using when, a mere child, he was playing on the floor, can have
no relation to this event. Grantley was not born until 1800,
and the certificates were in evidence in the House of Lords in
1799.—See " Grantley Berkeley's Life," &c. i. 25.

FAC-SIMILES of the BANNS, and REGISTER of MARRIAGE, of the EARL of BERKELEY and MARY COLE.

[*Extracted from the Parish Books of Berkeley.*]

(The Year 1) Page

No. 43

Banns of Marriage between Frederick Augs. Earl of Berkeley of this Parish Bachelor, and Mary Cole of Rewant spinster were published on the three Sundays underwritten:
That is to say, On Sunday, the 28 November
On Sunday, the 5 Decr.
On Sunday, the 12 Decr.

1785 Augt. Thos. Hupsman Curate

NOTE.—The theory of the claimant's case was, that the whole of both these registers, with, of course, the exception of the signatures of Berkeley, Mary Cole, and Wm. Tudor, was in the handwriting of Hupsman. The likeness of the B's to that of Lord Berkeley's signature must strike the most casual observer.

No. 74 Frederick Augustus Earl of Berkeley of this Parish — Bachelor — & Mary Cole of the same Spinster — Married in this Church by Banns this Thirtieth day of March in the year one thousand seven hundred and Eighty five — by me Aug.t Tho.s Stephenson Vicar

This marriage was solemnized between us { Berkeley
Mary Cole

In the presence of { W. Tudor
The mark X of Richard Barns

about his testimony. On the other hand, the widow and daughter of Mr. Hupsman declared that the words, "The mark × of Richard Barns," were "not a bit like Mr. Hupsman's writing," and the Marquis of Buckingham, (on another point, a most important witness,) who, as an intimate friend and connexion of the Earl's, had seen him write a hundred times, believed both to be in the handwriting of Lord Berkeley. As for the publication of the banns, the widow and daughter of the vicar, constant attendants at the church, had never heard them read, and to every one in the parish they were unknown. We are even now too accustomed to the negligent way in which banns are read in our churches, not to admit the possibility of this proceeding having been so performed in Berkeley Church (especially if it was intended that they should not be heard) as to escape observation. It is a large church and no doubt at that period cumbered with high pews and furnished with the old three-decker erection of pulpit, reading-desk, and clerk's seat.[9] Still, the

[9] The old church of Berkeley was restored by Sir Gilbert Scott in 1865, at the expense of Lord Berkeley, and is now furnished with a reading-desk within the rood-screen on the south side of the chancel, and pulpit and eagle in the nave. The present dimensions are, nave, 94 ft. by 65 ft., and the chancel, on the south side of which is the Berkeley vault, 43 ft. by 24 ft. A relative resident in the neighbourhood, to whom the author is indebted for these measurements, reports that an old inhabitant, who was confirmed in the church some forty-five years ago, believes that then the reading-desk—a three-decker pile—stood in the nave, some 12 or 15 ft to the south-west of the rood-screen. The ecclesiological probability is, that it had occupied that place for many a long year before, and that little if any alteration had been made in its structure.

probabilities of such banns being thus published in the church, the congregation of which lived on and by the castle and its lord, without being recognized, verge on improbability. Besides, it must be remembered that Tudor swore that he heard the names distinctly—of course if he spoke the truth he was expecting them—that "there were persons between him and the clergyman" who read them; that "there was silence in the church when they were read," and "that there was a congregation, though he had no recollection of the numbers attending the service." He never went to Berkeley Church but that time, about which he could only say that it was some time before the marriage; that he could not remember in what part of the service the banns were published, and had no recollection of the appearance, height, or size of the clergyman. Yet if it was Hupsman, as the certificate states, he saw him again at the marriage ceremony in the early morning in March.

(2.) SOCIAL POSITION OF LADY BERKELEY PRIOR TO SECOND MARRIAGE.

Mr. Carrington, vicar of Berkeley since 1799, and for five years before tutor to the elder boys, admitted that "previously to 1799 he never heard of the first marriage, or that any of the children were legitimate. It was a dubious matter. Lady Berkeley was called Miss Tudor. Sometimes, perhaps, written or spoken to as Lady Berkeley, but not by himself. Lord Berkeley called her 'Mary,' and asked for her as 'the lady,' or 'your lady'—well-bred persons called her 'madam,' and inquired after her as 'the lady, the 'lady of the mansion,' but never positively as 'Lady Berkeley.' The eldest son was called 'Fitz,' the others by their christian names. The eldest was never called Lord Dursley during the five years he was there." Chapeau, the sporting parson, who had baptized the eldest son and stood godfather to the second, and had given a certificate in which the child was described as the "Natural Son,"[1] related anecdotes, which, if true, were decisive on the point. "One day in October"—he was very uncertain as to dates —"when shooting at the castle, a servant said to Lord Berkeley, 'My Lady Berkeley is in the pleasure grounds,' when Lord Berkeley replied, 'You fool, whom do you mean by Lady Berkeley, I have no Lady Berkeley belonging to me but my mother.' Again, at the house in Spring Gardens, when he asked Miss Tudor to let her eldest son go out—she had shut him in a room for disobedience—she said, 'Go thank Mr. Chapeau for your liberation. Now, you little dog, though I am not your father's wife, I will make you know that I am your mother.'"

Whatever doubt there may be as to the strict credibility of the evidence of this gossiping parson, to that of Mrs. Lumley, with whom and her family Lord Berkeley had been intimate from an early period, no suspicion

---

[1] According to Chapeau's account, Admiral Prescott wrote the certificate, which Chapeau gave to Lord Berkeley, who read it and left the room, and then went to Dr. Courtenay, the rector. On his return he said it was all right, but when Chapeau saw it next the ugly words were omitted. Prescott, though he did not remember the fact, would by no means deny it.

can attach. It is too important not to be given in full.[2]

"My Lord Berkeley called on me one morning, I cannot say when, in the year 1791, 1792, 1793; it might be previous to that time. Some of our mutual acquaintance had told me that there was, or was to be, a picture of my lord at the exhibition, together with his two children, and that they were very fine children. In the chit-chat of a morning visit, I remarked to my lord that I had heard of the picture and of the children. My lord answered me by saying, 'They are, indeed, lovely children; would to God they were legitimate!' those were the words."

Q. Did you make any answer to that?

A. Yes, I did; I said something like these words—I cannot quite call to mind—I believe these were the words, "It is indeed a thousand pities, but that cannot now be helped;" or "that is now impossible." Something to that purport, as near as I can recollect the words My lord seemed by his manner to feel the subject, and of course I changed it; he said no more to me about the children.

On cross-examination she added,—

"He was leaning against a table between the windows of the room, and he put his hand to his forehead when he made the answer, and he walked down the room and returned to near where I was sitting, and he sat himself down and said what I have stated."

The evidence of the Rev. Robert Ferryman—evidence on which no cross-examination was attempted —was equally decisive. He was an intimate friend of the Earl's since 1787, and at Cranford most days, when the family were residing there.

Q. During this time, by what name did the present Lady Berkeley then go, prior to 1796, from the year 1787?

A She went by the name of Tudor only.

Q. Did you ever hear her called by any other name at that time?

---

[2] Evidence of Maria Lumley.

A. Not at that time. When I first had the honour of being introduced to Lord Berkeley she went by the name of Marie only.

Q. Do you ever remember hearing Lady Berkeley use any expression respecting Lord Berkeley, or the footing on which she lived with him?

A. I recollect, very early in my acquaintance with Lord Berkeley, at Berkeley Castle, one morning after breakfast, Dr. Jenner, I think, was there. I recollect she had one child on her lap, which was Frederick; and the other son was sitting by her, the elder one. She drew him to her and said, "These are my ties; if it was not for these, it could not be supposed I would live with Lord Berkeley on the terms I am living with him," or words to that effect. That was in 1788 or 1789.

With one more extract from the evidence—that of the Marquis of Buckingham—we complete this portion of the case. Its importance will excuse its length. After reminding the House that "he came there in obedience to their orders and not as a voluntary witness, in a matter, for many reasons, so painful to him," the marquis gave the following narrative of his communications with the Earl on the subject of his elder children.

"Somewhere between 1789, when he returned from Ireland and 1793, his lordship told me that he was not married to the mother of some children, I did not then know how many, but boys he told me, whom he requested that I would be guardian to in the contingency of his death. I gave him many reasons which induced me to decline that, but particularly adverted to the circumstance of their illegitimacy, and of their mother being alive, which would be a very awkward circumstance to me in the relation of guardian. He pressed me upon this several times; I declined it uniformly, and for the reason of their illegitimacy, which I assigned as my reason to him. In the course of these conversations he frequently adverted to a matter that dwelt much upon his mind, which he stated as dwelling much upon his mind, namely, the probability that the castle and honour of Berkeley would probably, by the circumstances of his family, be severed from the title, and would not go to his brother, Admiral George Berkeley." [Then he relates how he tried to persuade him to provide well for his children, and not sever the castle from the title, but apparently in vain, and how the Earl hinted at another scheme.] "In about a day or two, I should think the next day, he came to me and told me that he had made up his mind to tell me what his ideas were, particularly as he thought I might assist him, from the influence he supposed me to have from old friendship with his brother, and, to my surprise, he told me that he had a daughter, of whom I had never heard before, but one of these children, and that he was very desirous that his brother should entertain the idea of a marriage between that daughter and the admiral's son. I perfectly remember smiling and saying, 'The young lady is, I believe, three years old,' for I knew that she could not be older, and adverting to the age of the admiral's son, I treated the thing lightly; but he told me if this marriage could take place, he would settle the castle and honours of Berkeley, such as ought to belong to the Earl of Berkeley, upon that marriage."

The marquis then gives in detail the objections to the proposal which he believed Mrs. Berkeley would raise—"the prospect of having a daughter so educated as she was likely to be under a mother not married to him," and the Earl's offer that "she should have the young lady and educate her herself." The marquis, however, saw Mrs. Berkeley, and at his suggestion she raised the difficulty to which he had alluded.

"When," continued the witness, "I gave this answer to Lord Berkeley, he laughed at my having carried a message and brought back an answer, which I told him was one recommended by me, and then said that he would immediately propose to the mother of his girl, or his daughter, the giving up of the child to Mrs. Berkeley; that was the first intimation I had from him that she was no party to the transaction. I told him that, if he had not consulted the mother before, I very much doubted that all the conversation which had passed between us would come to nothing, for that I was persuaded she would never consent to give her daughter to be educated by another person. I ought to say that I stated this from general report of that person, because I never was in the same room with her, and never saw her but by accident, when she was walking with him in the park, at which time I never spoke to him. Shortly after this he was to have called upon me and his sister at Winchester, where I was quartered; he excused himself from it by stating that that daughter was just dead; it is that circumstance which fixed in my recollection positively the exact date at which this conversation must have taken place. After that event Lord Berkeley was much agitated on seeing me the first time at Portsmouth, where he was with his corps; he never renewed the subject of the conversation on that girl, but pressed me once or twice still to be guardian to the boys, which I declined."

In 1797 the Earl called on the marquis, who happened to be away, and left a message to inform him of "what he called his second marriage."

"It was a subject so painful to me that I would not converse with him upon it when we afterwards met, excepting that I told him that if there was any idea, as I had heard from rumour, of setting up a question of a second marriage, this communication which he had made through me to Admiral Berkeley was in Admiral Berkeley's hands, and that I must be bound to give it in evidence if it was ever called for. With these impressions I never attended the Committee of Privileges in 1799, and took no part in it whatsoever, conceiving it was probable that Admiral Berkeley might think it necessary to call for my evidence."

It is to be regretted that the case in 1799 broke down so soon as not to render it necessary for the admiral to call this witness before the peers. One can hardly suppose that in the face of this unhesitating testimony, Lady Berkeley and her brother would have dared to make the statements they did, or to ingeniously put together the tale which they persuaded others to attempt to corroborate. Had it been possible to call the marquis before the case for the younger children closed, it is almost incredible to suppose that the claimant would not have dropped his attempt, and thus saved more than one of the witnesses subsequently brought forward by him from the punishment they so deservedly incurred. What the Earl swore to in the affidavit, still shut up in the Public Record Office, we know not, but this we do know from one who had been his intimate friend for more than forty years, that he dared to commission him to inform the Prince of Wales that the rumour of the second marriage was a truth, and that his eldest boy was rightfully heir to his title and his estates.

"In consequence of a letter from Lady Berkeley when I was at Weymouth in 1797," said Colonel John West, "mentioning that Lord Berkeley had a secret to communicate to me, one morning at breakfast I mentioned to Lady Berkeley, 'You informed me Lord Berkeley had a secret to communicate to me; what was that secret?' It was in the presence of Lord Berkeley; she turned to my lord and said, 'Do tell West the secret now.' He took Lady Berkeley by the hand and said, 'Allow me to introduce you to the Countess of Berkeley.' I said it gave me great satisfaction to know that she was Countess of Berkeley; 'but pray, my lord, will you allow me to ask you one question? When could you have done this? when could you have introduced that lady as Countess of Berkeley to me?' I do not know exactly the number of years, but he says, 'Eleven or twelve years prior to that time.' Then says I, 'My lord, am I to understand that your eldest son is legitimate?' 'I mean that you should understand that positively that it was so.' I then expressed my satisfaction, and begged leave to tell this. 'Will you allow me, my lord, to tell this? to talk of it abroad? Says he, 'You may,' knowing a lady I might tell it to, which was the same as putting it in the papers. I immediately went and informed the Prince of Wales of it; the prince was informed of it that morning at Weymouth."

To another of his most intimate friends, Admiral Prescott, the godfather to his first son, who had been his school-fellow, and had lived with him in London, had been taken by him in 1785 to drink tea with Susan and Mary in Brompton Row, and had hired the house for Lord Berkeley in Park Street, to which Mary came before her eldest son was born, he was strangely reticent—aware, no doubt, that Prescott had seen too much of his life to be easily deceived. It was not, therefore, until 1799 that he assured him that the marriage had taken place in 1785. It was not until about the same time that Miss Tudor, in reply to a letter from him referring to the rumour of the early marriage, replied, "To those who make inquiries after me you may say that your affectionate friend has *for a long time past*," she avoided giving a date, "been Maria Berkeley." [3]

With the king, Lord Berkeley was more guarded. At a *fête* at Weymouth the king asked him which son he should call Lord Dursley. "Your Majesty shall know at the proper time," was the reply. This was in the same year, apparently within a few weeks after he had gone through the scene with Colonel West. Be it put to his credit that he hesitated to deceive the old monarch; naturally he had less hesitation with his boon companions. We do not require the revelations of the Divorce Court of to-day to convince us

[3] It was admitted by this witness that Mrs. Bailey, the favourite at Berkeley Castle deposed by Miss Cole, had been treated in every respect as Miss Cole was.

how utterly unreliable are the statements of the parties inculpated in immoral social relations. For man and woman to perjure themselves seems a part of their code of honour, and the administration of an oath to respondent and co-respondent alike only adds blasphemy to falsehood.

(3.) THE REGISTERS OF THE BAPTISMS OF THE ELDER CHILDREN.

At the investigation in 1799 the Windsor Herald produced the registers of the baptisms of all the children—four sons and a daughter—born before the second marriage. In these the children were uniformly described as the son or daughter of the Earl of Berkeley and Mary Cole. The first son of the marriage in 1796 was, on the contrary, baptized as the son of the Earl and Countess of Berkeley, and described as the Honourable Thomas Fitzhardinge Lord Dursley.[4] Chapeau gave a very graphic account of the baptism of the claimant.

"Till the christening took place he did not know whether any or what lady was living with Lord Berkeley at the time. He then understood that she lived in Park Street, near Park Lane. She was present at the christening, previous to which Lord Berkeley applied to him to christen his child, saying 'he had a natural child, and he should be very much obliged to me if I would christen him.' Mr. Carrington said he could not do it, as it was a natural child, and therefore begged that he would excuse me, for I must apply to the rector of St. George's parish if I did, and I

---

[4] Registers from St. George's, Hanover Square, and St. Martin's-in-the-Fields, produced by Windsor Herald and Garter King-at-arms before the peers, 1799. See previous note, p. 347.

did not think it was a post of honour to apply for any man's natural child."

Q. What passed upon that?

A. I told Lord Berkeley I thought his best plan would be to send the nurse and the child, after morning prayers, to the vestry of St. George's, and there he would find an officiating clergyman that would christen the child and register it at the same time, for I could not register in another man's parish without his leave; then, to my astonishment, my Lord Berkeley called upon me in Piccadilly and produced written leave for me to baptize the child in his parish, signed by Dr. Henry Courtenay. The day was then fixed.

The only explanation offered of these damning entries was the desire to keep the marriage secret, because Susannah the sister was leading an immoral life as a mistress, and a doubt existed, on what ground was not clear, that Hupsman had destroyed the register of marriage, and it would be impossible (though if it was a true register there was, as Lord Eldon pertinently remarked, a living witness to it) to prove its celebration. To prop up this excuse, after the registry was said to have been discovered, a copy of it was deposited in the register of St. Martin's-in-the-Fields with this addition:—

"Although my wife is named in the registering of my children Mary Cole, she was then in fact Countess of Berkeley, my marriage with her (which at the date of this entry was kept secret) having taken place on the 30th day of March, as appears by the register of Berkeley parish, now deposited in the House of Lords, a copy of which is herewith annexed.

"BERKELEY."

And yet this secret marriage, as the bill in Chancery alleged, "was attended with as much publicity and notoriety as could be given to it—was quite notorious—the clergyman and parties were constantly talking about it, and it became the habit and repute of the place."

(4.) THE POSITION OF THE ELDEST SON.

Lord Eldon's suggestion, that "a great deal of consideration ought to be had as to the actual treatment in the family of the children born before and after the second marriage," was not forgotten. Not a word about it had been uttered when the case was before the Lords in 1799, but when it reappeared in 1811 the witnesses were full of it. Lady Berkeley and Mr. Carrington swore that no difference was made between the children of the two marriages, and that the birthday of the eldest was always kept, though he was not introduced as Lord Dursley until 1799. Not one, however, of the friends of the Earl, such as Chapeau, Prescott, West, or Ferryman, were asked to confirm this statement. Could such an incident have occurred yearly without their knowledge? One witness indeed was called to support the assertions of the mother and the curate—Merritt, who had been a tenant of the Berkeley family for thirty years. It must have been amusing to have heard his vague story.

"He remembered the second, if not the first birthday. The name was put up at the gates—Lord Dursley, for us to see coming backwards and forwards—in large letters in front of the lodge, not in pen and ink, nor lamps, but lamps about the place gave light to it. The child was brought into the great hall. Could not tell his age or his dress, whether in petticoats or breeches. Could not say whether he was ten or nine. Put his eyes upon him when the rest went to see him in the upper part of the hall. Could not say whether he was held in arms or put on the table, or whether he was ten or two years old. Drank his health in a bumper. Could not remember who was steward."

And this was the only tenant who could be produced out of the score and more that must, had it been true, have attended this yearly feast, seen these letters, drank his health, and joined in the huzzas the old man swore were given when the heir's health was drunk. It was out of charity probably to his age that my Lords did not send the witness to keep company with Nicholas Hicks and Ellis Farren in Newgate.

(5.) LADY BERKELEY'S STORY.

According to her own account she had known Lord Berkeley from the time she was a girl at school in Gloucester. He had followed her wherever she went, and to avoid him she left Gloucester in 1784, and went into service with her sister Susan at Lady Talbot's, in London, and subsequently alone at Mrs. Foote's, in Kent. James Perry,[5] however, knew her and Susan in London in 1783, when they were lodging near Whitecross Street, in the city; went twice with them to the masquerade at the Pantheon, and was visited by them at his chambers in Clement's Inn, in that year. Mary was as decorous in her dress as in her manner, and they both behaved as decent persons at the masquerade. They both then went by the name of Cole, but soon after he knew Susan by the name of Wright, as the favourite of a nobleman, living somewhere near the New Road, then as Turner, and subsequently living with other protectors, as Mrs.

[5] Apparently this was the subsequently well-known political writer.

Bolton and Mrs. Edge, after which she married and went abroad. According to Chapeau it was when Susan was passing as Mrs. Turner that the scene with the bailiffs—probably duly prearranged—occurred, and the sale to Lord Berkeley was completed.

Whatever may be the true account of this incident it must have been about this time that, according to her own story, she left London by arrangement with Lord Berkeley by coach to Oxford, and thence by chaises to Newport, where she arrived on the 29th of March, 1785. She had previously, in the winter of 1784, written to her brother in Gloucester to go over to Berkeley and hear the publication of the banns, and before now leaving London advised him to meet her at Berkeley Church for the marriage. From Newport she walked to Berkeley, was married between eight and nine in the morning, signed and saw the others sign the register, and then walked back with her brother to Newport ; came at once to London or its neighbourhood with Lord Berkeley, and lived there with him till she returned to Gloucester, in the summer of that year, to her sister Farren's.

It was whilst she was residing with her sister Farren, be it remembered, a young bride, if she speaks the truth, that an incident occurred little consistent with such a position, and showing that this sister as well as Susan had strange notions of the responsibilities of married life. On the 12th or 18th of July, Mr. William Fendall, a barrister on the Oxford circuit, being in Gloucester, and seeing Mary Cole looking out of Mrs. Farren's window, though she was an entire stranger to him, kissed his hand to her, and was so satisfied with the manner in which his salutation was received, that, the door of the house being open, he went up to the room in which he found her with her sister Farren. On this his first visit he stayed tea, and "paid that attention to a very handsome woman whom he found there, which a man might be very naturally expected to pay." As Mary did not appear offended he more than once repeated his visit, always in the evening after dinner, and took what he calls "occasional liberties with her," at which she indeed expressed reluctance, but took no means to prevent. One time he was caught by Farren, the sister's husband, "when by accident she had slipped off her chair." Still he was not apparently forbidden the house. Nay more, she allowed him to correspond with her, and when he wrote for an assignation, she complained, indeed, in her reply, that if his intentions were honourable he would have desired her to be accompanied by a female friend, but still signed herself, "Maria, with equal heart, sits down to answer the letter received." She was not unwilling to receive him on "honourable terms." Strange words these for a bride of four months. Fendall neither saw nor heard of anything to lead him to suppose that she was a married woman, and as "his situation was such as to render it absolutely ruin to him to form an honourable connexion with her," the acquaintance with the young countess dropped.

Previously to, and for nearly a year after her professed marriage, her brother, though a lad of barely sixteen, was her only confidant, and whilst at her sister Farren's she declared that Lord Berkeley's visits were so arranged that no one should see him. Yet Farren's brother swore that he heard his brother and his wife talk of it in 1785, that it was told him as a secret, and that he told it to his mother. As he had made totally different statements to another witness on this point, and the use of the name of Tudor by William Cole, for which he was committed to Newgate, allusion to his evidence is only necessary to prove the way in which, as the case proceeded, daily more and more against the claimant, witnesses were in vain manufactured in its support.

A few weeks before the claimant was born, she had made a revelation to her mother, the history of which as sworn by the old woman, exhibits one of the most painful features in the case. Mary had gone to London in the autumn of 1785, and was followed soon after by her mother, who joined her at her lodgings in Park Street, and remained there with her until the claimant was born, when she returned with them to Berkeley.[6] Before this, however, she had asked her mother to come to her for her confinement.

" She came to me on a Saturday," said the old lady, " and said, ' Mother, will you come and be with me while I lie in?' ' No,' says I, ' my dear, I shall not.'

[6] The mother was treated as a better class of servant, dining in the nursery when the Earl was at the castle, but otherwise allowed to have her meals with her daughter. It is noteworthy that she never saw or heard anything whilst at Berkeley to lead her to believe that Mary Cole occupied any other place than that of her predecessors. Possessed as she swears she was of the secret, one might expect her to have been able to confirm it by observation of the life of the Earl and her daughter at the castle.

'Why, what's your reason?' 'Because,' says I, 'you are not married, and that is the reason I will not go to be with you to encourage vice ; I cannot look upon you as my daughter if you are not lawfully married.' She came up to me and burst out crying, and said, 'Mother, to-morrow is Sunday, and you and I will go to sacrament together, and if you will go with me I will take the sacrament,' but she first said she was married. 'I am married,' said she ; 'but it is a secret ;' and then she said, 'Mother, to satisfy you, we will go together to-morrow and take the sacrament. I will with you, and then I hope you will think that I cannot do such a thing as that without I am a good woman ; I would not do it for the world.' 'Very well,' says I, 'my dear, I will attend on you ;' and we both cried, and then we went to the sacrament, and when she came out she came to me and took me in her arms, and said, 'Mother, do you think I could have done this as I have done, if I was not an honest woman?' 'No,' says I, 'I think and hope you would not.' 'Very well then ; now,' says she, 'I hope you will be content and come and be with me ; I have satisfied you as far as I can.'"

The scene is too awful to bear comment.

(6.) WILLIAM TUDOR'S STORY.

Seriously as the evidence of Lady Berkeley's brother was discredited by his cross-examination in 1799, it fared much worse when he was subsequently called for the claimant in 1811. He had sworn before, and he swore again, that he assumed the name of Tudor when apprenticed to Parker, the surgeon, in Gloucester, and that it would so appear in Parker's books before the date of the professed marriage of his sister at Berkeley Church. Parker's executor now produced the books of his testator, and William Tudor's name was not to be found in them. A brother apprentice knew him only as Cole, as did his school-fellows, who had never heard of his aristocratic name ; and an apprentice, as well as a journeyman of Farren's, corroborated their testimony. According to his own story he must have been in Berkeley Church in 1784 and 1785. Now, there was a Mrs. Price, who had been governess in the family from 1792 to 1799, and whose evidence, though no doubt tainted with ill-feeling from a quarrel with Lady Berkeley, which led to her leaving her position, is in the main reliable. She says that it was in 1796 that she first saw William Tudor, when he was visiting at Cranford, and that he then made such particular inquiries of her as to the castle and church of Berkeley that she advised his coming to see them, if he had not already been there, to which he replied that he had not, but might come soon. In 1797 Lady Berkeley being seriously ill, Mrs. Price, by her wish, wrote Tudor to come to Berkeley, and he came.

"It was on a Saturday," said the witness ; "the precise day of the month I cannot express ; I cannot recollect it. After being in the castle some little time, and seeing his sister, he wished me to show him the church. I did. I think Mr. Carrington was one of the party, the three sons, Master Berkeley, Master Frederick, and Master Augustus. When in the church I observed him looking about very much, which convinced me he had not been there before, on which I put the question, ' Have you ever been here, Mr. Tudor ?' and his answer was ' No.' Next day, in the breakfast-parlour before dinner, I think Dr. Jenner was there—it was a public day, many strangers coming in, I cannot exactly ascertain who was there—they said they were happy to see him, and inquired if he had ever been there before ; his answer was ' No.' "

In anticipation of this evidence, William Tudor had been asked if he remembered this visit to Berkeley Church, or his previous inquiries about it of Mrs. Price, and could only reply that he did not recollect the circumstance—he might—he could not speak positively. Mr. Carrington was not recalled to contradict, and Dr. Jenner could only say that he did not recollect seeing Mr. Tudor at Berkeley in 1797. Mrs. Price's story, therefore, remains unimpeached.

Another incident recollected by this witness—the day of which she was enabled to fix by a cotemporary memorandum in her pocket-book—seems to point to the date of the manufacture of the certificate of the banns and the marriage.

"On February 17, 1799, Mr. Tudor came to Berkeley Castle."

Q. Do you recollect what passed on Sunday, the 17th, after Mr. Tudor's arrival?

A. They were shut up in a centre room, Lord and Lady Berkeley, and Mr. Tudor, for about an hour and a half.

Q. Were there any particular measures taken to prevent interruptions, or anybody hearing or seeing what they were about?

A. The outer doors were locked, a precaution I had never seen used before while I was in the house, and an extra blind was put to the window, to prevent anybody looking over from the other side of the castle. I cannot tell what they were doing.

Q. Had you ever observed that circumstance before, of a blind being put to prevent persons overlooking the opposite side?

A. I do not recollect that I did.

This incident may be capable of an innocent explanation. None, however, was attempted to be given, and it must be remembered that this happened on the 17th of February, and that the certificates were discovered by Scriven and Carrington on the 7th of the next month. The incident must stand for what it is worth.

The most material evidence on the case has now been analyzed, and enough quoted to enable us to judge of the correctness of the decision of the House of Lords, "that the claimant had not made good his claim to the titles, honours, and dignities of Earl of Berkeley." With only this formal verdict the House was not satisfied. On the motion of the Chancellor, a copy of the evidence was laid before the Regent, "in order that his Highness may be enabled to determine whether any measures should be directed with respect to what appeared therein." The Prince Regent, out of friendship for the late Earl, took no steps; and, but for an address by Colonel Berkeley to the Peers, protesting against their decision, the sad tale might have been more readily forgotten, as Moreton, the eldest son of the second marriage, acquiesced in every step his elder brother took to discredit the verdict. On coming of age a writ of summons, as Earl Berkeley, was sent to him by the government of the time, which he treated as an insult, content with his position as a plain, unlettered country gentleman, dependent on his brother's bounty, and feeling too keenly for his mother's reputation to publicly accept a title at the price of her dishonour. The countess herself left England for a time, on the excuse of her health, and her brother, who had married a servant of Susanna's, followed her example.[7] If a pamphlet, published about ten years after this investigation, by William Cole's deserted wife, is to be believed, he was the appropriate tool of his sister and the Earl, and extorted from the former a liberal income as the price of his silence. Grantley Berkeley, the well-known sportsman, had he survived his brother Moreton, would, if he is to be trusted, not only have eagerly claimed the ancestral honours, but endeavoured to set aside those deeds by which he declares that Moreton barred the succession to the estates in favour of his elder brother, and left the title of Berkeley a naked honour. He too is gone at last without heirs, and his personal and political feuds with his eldest brother are only matters of private and local history. Though a possible claim might be raised to the old Barony of Berkeley through the female line when Moreton dies, the claim to the title and honours of the earldom will pass to collaterals on Moreton's death.

For many years the claimant occupied an anomalous position. The decision of the House of Lords negatived his claim to the peerage, and his address to the Peers, in which he adhered to the truth of his case, forbad his exercising the rights of a commoner and retaining his seat in the House of Commons. In 1831, for his political services to the Reform Cabinet, he was consoled with the title of Baron Segrave, and ten years afterwards raised to the earldom of Fitz-

[7] The countess died 1844.

hardinge. Exaggerating the habits of his father, he lived and died a bachelor, and his honours fell with him. In 1861 his next brother, Maurice Frederick,[8] was created Baron Fitzhardinge, having, on his brother's death succeeded by virtue of the deeds before referred to, to the Castle of Berkeley and the estates of the old family.

The improbabilities of the incidents on which it was relied to set up the early marriage, would have fully justified the verdict of the Lords. The address to the Regent seems to indicate that, with Lord Lyndhurst, they regarded the evidence "as a dreadful measure of perjury and guilt."

[8] Maurice Frederick Fitzhardinge Berkeley was born January 3, 1788; entered the navy in 1808, and after distinguished services rose to be Admiral of the White and a Lord of the Admiralty. He died 1867, and was succeeded by his son, the present Lord Fitzhardinge.

CHAPTER XIII.

THE THRESHERS, 1806—THE CARAVATS AND SHANAVESTS, 1810.

THE criminal history of this decade would be incomplete without a notice of the outrages in Ireland by the Threshers in 1806, and their successors, the Caravats and Shanavests, four years afterwards. Though these bands were composed entirely of Catholic peasants, the objects of their confederation were in no way connected with the ever-burning religious question of Protestant ascendency, and their hands were raised equally against their priests and the clergymen, and against rents and wages, whether their landlords or their masters were Catholic or Protestant. Towards the close of Lord Hardwick's tenure of the viceroyship the western counties had been disturbed to some extent by these roving bands of rioters, but not to such an extent as to render necessary any additional exercise of the powers of the executive. With the accession of the pro-Catholic Cabinet of Grenville and Fox, in 1806, and the appointment of the Duke of Bedford to the lord-lieutenancy, the expectations of remedial measures, in accordance with the previously professed views of those statesmen, were naturally revived. Tenants were severely pressed by the rack-rents imposed by middle-men; by the collection of the arrears of tithes by the agents and proctors of the non-resident clergy, and the rates levied by the grand juries of the counties for road-making and other local expenses. At the same time the priests appear to have raised their dues for marriages and other sacraments, and thus added to the widespread discontent of cottiers and smaller farmers.

With the advent of the Bedford administration came no relief from the severe tithe system, and no attempt at redress from the action of, as the people believed, a corrupt magistracy. "The Government," says the Catholic historian of this period, "well knew the progress of the evil; but as it was local no remedy could be effectually applied which they were not called upon to carry into effect throughout the whole nation, and that it appears, by their conduct, they were predetermined not to attempt. They betrayed an uncommon anxiety to suppress the magnitude of the evil from the eyes of the public; and for that purpose resorted to the hackneyed expedient of bribing the periodical publications into silence or misrepresentation."[1] To the credit of the Press, and happily

[1] Plowden's "History of Ireland from 1801 to 1810," vol. ii. p. 408. Though this work, like its predecessor which treats of the history of the Union, is little better than a political pamphlet of the most bitter and prejudiced character, facts cited by him bear out the truth of this passage. This author admits that an alteration in the system of tithes was desired by the majority of the Irish clergy as well as by the people. "The clergy," he writes, "were, in fact, equally aggrieved with the common people

for the peace of the western counties, this attempt on the part of the Government failed, and gradually "true and very alarming accounts of the Threshers were made public." It could no longer be concealed that these men "assembled in bodies of several hundreds, dressed in white shirts or frocks, or other disguises, faced the military for a short time, and then, after a few shots, dispersed in confusion—probably from want of leaders or officers to command or enforce discipline." "They usually assembled early in the mornings, and destroyed whatever tithe corn fell in their way. In the month of November they took eleven tithe stacks from the haggard of a man in the neighbourhood of Ballina, and strewed them along the road up to the very town itself. They made domiciliary visits, both by night and day, in houses and cabins for arms," using the most brutal cruelty to those who did not give them up willingly, or contribute money to Captain Thresher, and not hesitating at murdering any one who dared to inform against them.[2]

The generality of the clergy were not the oppressors, although some instances of oppression from the clergy of the established church might be produced. The clergy, generally speaking, did not levy much above one-third of their dues."—Vol. iii. p. 733. The resistance was really to the tithe-proctors of non-resident clergymen, and the hardship, to a great extent, arose from the inability of the clergyman to grant leases of tithes for a fixed term, and only for that of his incumbency.—See note in Plowden illustrating the operation of this, p. 734.

[2] Mr. Plowden's words are, "They made domiciliary visits both by day and night in houses and cabins for arms, which they took without perpetrating any further outrages." It will be seen from the account of the trial at Sligo and other places where the

To these revelations in the newspapers were added the remonstrances of the leading gentlemen in the disturbed counties, so plainly and strongly expressed that the Government, however unwilling to admit the necessity, were compelled to interfere. One of the castle lawyers was at last sent into the localities, and on his report of the widespread and growing audacity of these associations, a special commission was issued to try the numerous prisoners, which the exertions of the local authorities had succeeded in arresting. The following brief sketch of some of the cases then tried will exhibit the objects and the action of these deluded and too often cruel wretches.

In the case of Peter O'Neil, a small farmer, near Sligo, it was proved that after visiting nine houses in his village, some thirty or forty men with white shirts over their clothes and white scarves over their hats and faces, many of them armed, knocked him up in the night, forced him out of his house, demanding money for "John the Thresher and his men." When he declared that he had no money, they brought up the cards—pieces of flat wood studded with crooked nails—carded him on his naked back, and beat him with sticks and bayonets until he gave them two Irish shillings and promised to send more to a person whom they named. One of his offences in their eyes was that he always paid his priest his dues and refused to

Special Commission sat, that the men who did not at once submit were carded on their bare backs with a fearful instrument of torture, as well as treated with other kinds of cruelty, and that an informer (Thady Lavin) was murdered in a most cowardly and savage manner.

reduce them on the demand of the Threshers. On the score of mistaken identity, the Kearneys, whom he accused of being the leaders in this affair, were acquitted, but little attempt was made to traverse the facts of the attack and the cruelty by which it was characterized.

In another case, a man of the name of Brennan was indicted as one of the party who attacked the house of Brett, a small farmer at Ballyglas, near midnight, on the 11th of November. The attack was resisted and the arms not surrendered until after a stout battle, in which shots were freely fired on both sides, and an attempt had been made to set fire to the house, so bold and open were the proceedings of the Threshers. Others were convicted of supplying arms, and set up as their defence that they had been sworn to do so by Captain Thresher, and that they dared not disobey on fear of their lives. In one of these cases, it was proved that a party, 500 strong, went about administering oaths not to pay tithes to the agents and proctors, to compel the priests to reduce their dues and their employers to pay only certain wages to labourers.[3]

Another class of cases was that of sending persons, under Captain Thresher's orders, to threaten the priests if they did not accept the tariff of dues for sacraments which had been decided on by the rioters.

[3] Case of Fitzsimons, Coyle (farmer), Kilbride, and Coyle (labourer), at Longford Special Commission, December 18, 1806, guilty; and also that of Ferguson, Grant, and Connell, who formed a part of a detachment of 150 tried at Carrick-on-Shannon, December 16, 1806, guilty.

In the following case, which we give, as an example, this duty was discharged in a most open and impudent manner. Thady Thornton, one of the congregation of the chapel at Minola, near Castlebar, gives the following account of the scene :—

"On October 14, I think, I saw the prisoner James McPhadeen, an old neighbour of mine; he came and asked me, was I sworn to go to any place that day. I said I was not, and that if I was I would not go, as it was not proper. He said that a party came to his house in disguise, and swore him to go to the chapel to the town where I live, in Minola, and to go to the clergyman. I said that oath was not binding by laws of God or king, and that if he had a mind he might break it. He said he could not as he was in dread. I then went to mass; and after Mr. Nolan came out to shake the holy water among the people there assembled during the service, the prisoner told the priest he was sworn to come to him. He told the priest that he should marry persons for half a guinea, baptize for nineteen-pence halfpenny, read mass for thirteen-pence, and at any house to which he came to confession, if he got hay and oats for his horse, to take it; but if not, to go away, on pain of suffering for it. The congregation were there at the time. My parish is two miles distant from the prisoner's."

Five more of the congregation—there were nine in court—confirmed this statement. The only defence was compulsion and a good character. The judge did his best to convince the jury that the only restraint or duress that would avail as a defence must be immediately operating at the time when the act is committed —the terror of immediate death, depriving the person of his own free-will and agency. "Here," said Baron George, "this man had three or four days to consider what was right and lawful for him to do—whether he was to obey the law or the Threshers; whether he has to fear the law or the Threshers? and for the choice he has made he is answerable." The jury took a merciful view and acquitted the prisoner.[4] The parties who threatened the priest at Kilcolman were not so fortunate. In their case indeed a notice of the dues to be paid had been posted on the chapel door, and the priest spoke strongly about those who wished to stint him in his prices. The jury hesitated to find them guilty, if they were to be hanged or transported, but when Baron George warned them that they had nothing to do with the punishment, but that if they recommended them to mercy he would send to the Government, they took his advice.[5]

The last case to be cited is that of a Thresher who had informed against a relative of one of those who eventually joined in his murder, and all but killed his wife, who vainly attempted to save her husband's life.[6] Lavin, the victim, had been sworn, like other Threshers "to be faithful and bear true allegiance to Captain Thresher, and not to give evidence against a brother in any court of justice." Repenting him of his oath, on the 13th of September, he gave information against a great number of his accomplices, and,

[4] Castlebar, December 8, before Baron George. James and William McPhadeen. James tried, trial of William adjourned by leave of the Crown to next assizes.

[5] James Mamre, Richard Murphy, and James Clenane, December 12, 1806. Guilty, but recommended to mercy.

[6] Sligo, December 10, 1806. Before Baron George, *Coll Flynn*, Charles Flynn, *Laurence Flynn*, John Callaghan, Daniel Callaghan, James Laydon, Patrick Barrett, John Flynn, Daniel Regan, Thomas Horan. Those in italics found guilty. Edmund Durneen's trial postponed on the ground of having been arrested only the day before.

amongst them, against John Flynn, the son of the prisoner Laurence Flynn, and the near relation of Coll Flynn, who was also in the dock. In the same information he implicated two persons of the name of Durneen, one of them the son, the other the nephew of the prisoner Edmund Durneen. It soon leaked out that Lavin had turned informer, and his stay in the neighbourhood became unsafe. He was, therefore, removed by Government to a village where a military force was stationed, until the Special Assize should sit. On the 10th of November, the prisoners, who were in Castlebar goal, tried to escape, but failed, and four days afterwards, Lavin and his wife came back for a few days to his house at Turneen, with the intention of selling his property and returning with the proceeds to the well-guarded village. Whilst at Turneen with his wife he attended the funeral of a friend, and on his return unfortunately met one of the prisoners, Coll Flynn, who, after a little talking, proposed to purchase Lavin's property on very liberal terms, and to bind it by a drink at the house of Laurence Flynn, another prisoner, the father of one of those against whom Lavin had informed. Thither they went and found there—though it was not a house of public entertainment—the prisoners Charles Flynn, Patrick Barrett, James Laydon, Laurence Flynn, John Flynn, and Edmund Durneen, not then on his trial.

In this society the unfortunate Lavin was persuaded to sit down and drink—strangely suspicious that a company of whom the greater portion were the near relations and connexions of those against whose lives

Lavin had sworn, should, without some secret cause, select that very informer as the companion of their festivity, receive him with friendship, and associate with him on terms of conviviality. Lavin's wife had a prescience of the scene that was to follow, and did her best, by signs and expressing her anxiety to return on account of her children, to induce her husband to leave. To prevent this, Coll and Charles Flynn came one on each side of her, embraced and kissed her, soothed her impatience, offered to send a girl to her house to take care of her children, and assured her that her husband should return home with her shortly. Lavin, probably, already well plied with drink, drank on. Then the prisoner Durneen sent for the prisoners Regan and Horan, with, or soon after whom, came the two Callaghans.

Durneen now left, and was followed at intervals by John Flynn, James Laydon, Patrick Barrett, and John Callaghan, the last two saying they were going fishing—which apparently they did—and taking with them the wives of some of the others who were still drinking in the house. Night grew on and the drinking with it, till in about an hour Callaghan and Barrett returned with some fish, and then suddenly, some fifteen minutes after Callaghan had returned, the door was burst open and five ruffians, with white shirts over their clothes and straw round their hats, rushed in. At their head was Edward Durneen armed with a hatchet, one of those against whom Lavin had sworn, and nephew to the Durneen who had so lately left the house. Four others, armed with pikes and bayonets fixed on poles, followed him. One only of these was recognized, John Connor, also the subject of Lavin's information. The moment he saw them Lavin knew he was doomed, and rushed in vain towards an inner room. He was cut down by Durneen, and when his wife ran to help him, seized Durneen by the hair and brought him to the ground, the other brutes rushed at her husband and despatched him with more than a score of wounds. Durneen shook off the poor wife, cut her to the ground with his hatchet, where his brutal associates stabbed her again and again and left her, as they thought and hoped, for dead.

The murderers fled, no attempt was made to stop them or pursue them. No alarm was given. The corpse of Lavin, together with his sorely wounded wife, were at once removed to their house at Turneen by those who had sat by and witnessed the horrible affair, and on the following morning, when to their dread they found that the wife was yet alive, some of these wretches went through the form of paying her a visit of condolence. The widow's statement could not be shaken on cross-examination. Some distinction was indeed drawn between the cases, and a verdict of Not Guilty returned in favour of those who, however in reality cognizant of the plot, were not actually present at the murder. The others, Coll Laurence, Charles Flynn, Horan, Regan, and Daniel Callaghan were found Guilty, and expiated their crime on the scaffold. " They were not, indeed, his actual murderers, but they brought him to the spot and detained him by dissembled kindness until the murderers were introduced, they were not more deadly to him than those who appeared to be his friends." Except on the supposition of a conspiracy on their part to have this murder effected, it is impossible to conceive human beings looking on such a scene unmoved—sitting by whilst their guest was murdered. Were it related by any novelist that Irishmen sat by unmoved and saw an unfortunate wife mangled when vainly endeavouring to protect her husband from his murderers, it would be denounced as a libel on a nation which so loudly boasts of its manliness and its chivalry towards women. So much more strange is fact than fiction.

Though the strangely named successors of the Threshers did not commit such open outrages until the autumn and winter of 1810, as to require any extraordinary action of the executive, they had assumed their rival names and divided themselves into separate bodies within a very short time after the trials of their predecessors. The origin of their quarrel "was some foolish dispute about May balls;" that of their respective titles was as silly as usual in all party nicknames. The Caravats, the older party, had been called Pauddeen Gar's men, until one of their number, prosecuted by the Shanavests for burning the house of a man who had taken land over his neighbour's head, was hanged, and Pauddeen Gar, their leader, declared he would not leave the place of execution until he saw "Caravat" about the fellow's neck. Their rivals, previously called Moyle Rangers, obtained their name from the old waistcoats which they wore.[7] Bitter as

[7] Evidence of James Slattery, February 6, at Clonmell, in the case of John Corcoran and three other Caravats, when cross-

were their mutual quarrels and faction fights in which deadly weapons were freely used, they attended at their chapel services indiscriminately, and in apparent peace. No respectable person appears to have joined them, no specific local object was in issue between them, they had no political scheme in their association, and certainly no confederation with those who would have exchanged the rule of England for that of France. They were both equally sore at the tithe system, and the increased demands for rents, and showed undisguised hostility to every competitor for the farms of the old occupiers. At first, apparently, their demands for arms were for use in the contests with their rivals. Eventually their outrages assumed an agrarian character, with the object of enforcing a general rate of tithe and rent by threats of injuries to the persons and property of those who should dare to exceed it. As with the Treshers, the cruelties of this paltry banditti were inflicted on men of their own class, the peaceable and unprotected cottager, and their demands, whether of arms or money, levied on those who were least capable of offering resistance and least able to contribute.[8]

To such an extent had these outrages increased in the autumn and winter of 1810, that a Special Com-

examined, and Rev. John Ryan, parish priest of Feathard, when cross-examined.

[8] Disgraceful as were the outrages committed by these bands, the trials before the Special Commission, as reported in Howell, do not furnish any evidence to justify the words of Lord Norbury in his charge that "female chastity was universally violated by licentious brutality—that the shrieks of the violated daughter had pierced the attentive ear of Government."

mission for the trial of the rioters in the counties of Tipperary, Waterford, and Kilkenny, was issued to Chief Justice Lord Norbury and Chief Baron O'Grady in the month of February in the year following. At the trials then held nearly forty persons were tried, the great majority of whom were sentenced to death and executed. A few cases will suffice to exhibit the cruel and dastardly character of these outrages.

David Larny was indicted for firing at one George Moore, a tithe proctor, with intent to kill him. On the 4th September, 1810, Moore, with two other persons, was valuing tithes in the parish of Ballybacon, when he was met by Larny and another man, armed, the one with a shot-gun, the other with pistols. When within twelve yards of them, they were ordered to stand, their books demanded of them, and then sworn never again to value tithes in the parish, nor to follow any business of that sort, and allowed to leave. They had gone barely fifty yards when shots were fired at them, and one of Moore's companions, Malowney, hit in the back and head with slugs. The men then followed them, bid Malowney stand where he was, put Moore on his knees and threatened to shoot him. On this Larny came up, knocked Moore down with his gun, and stamped on him as he lay on the ground. They then allowed them to go, and again fired at them when some seventy yards off. Both Moore and Malowney were again hit with slugs, but this time escaped with their lives. The statement of Moore was confirmed by the deposition of Malowney on his death-bed,[9] and the prisoner, who was clearly identified, convicted and executed.[1]

In another case eleven men were tried for assembling armed, with some eighty or ninety more, assuming the name of Caravats, and sounding a horn as a signal for assembling. It was about two in the morning when the police came upon them, ordered them to stand, when they fled in confusion, some of the prisoners taking refuge in a house near, where the police found arms, and nine or ten persons lying on and under the bed with their clothes on, and another hiding in a potato barn. Happily for these men, they were not indicted on a capital charge, and got off with a year's imprisonment and a whipping. The last punishment was inflicted on another party of Shanavests, who were caught at Coolmoyne racecourse, all armed with guns, pistols, and bayonets, professedly to protect themselves against the Caravats.

At Waterford the details of an agrarian outrage of a most brutal character, with the object of forcing a

[9] Malowney was afterwards, on November 21, killed in a most cruel way, beaten to death with blows on the head from guns and pistols by an armed party, disguised with blackened faces, who first fired on him, Moore, and a police-constable from behind a wall in Ballybacon, and then pursued them to a house in which they took refuge. R. v. Thomas Powers, February 7, Clonmell, for which he was convicted and executed.

[1] Larny called two witnesses to prove that he was some miles from the spot when the shots were fired, but a witness called by the Crown effectually discredited the first of them by the worthless character which he gave him, and so, inferentially, the second who told the same story as his predecessor in the box.

tenant to surrender his farm, will illustrate the darkest phase of this miserable conspiracy. Flahavan, the victim of the attack, had dared to become the tenant of two farms in the county, and though beaten and threatened with further outrage, had persevered in his occupation of these lands at Ballydufe. To protect himself, he had got his nephew Connor to live with him, and procured a pistol and ammunition, with the approbation of a neighbouring magistrate. In this state of imperfect security, on the evening of the 20th November, an armed party of Caravats attacked his house, forced him to open his door in terror of their threats, and then rushed in. In addition to the usual arms, pistols and a sword, these men had Alpine sticks, as they were called—young ash-trees torn up by their roots, from which the fibrous roots were cut off, leaving the knob, and thus forming a most formidable and often deadly weapon in the hands of such ruffians. Thus armed, these men first attacked the nephew, who had snatched up a pistol to defend his uncle and snapped it without effect at his assailants. He was soon disarmed, thrown to the floor, and then barbarously flogged with these Alpine sticks and severely wounded with a spade. Flahavan fled to his bedroom, hoping to escape through the window, but his retreat was cut off by two of the party stationed outside for the purpose. He then tried to conceal himself in the chimney of the bedroom, but was soon discovered, and under a promise that he should not be injured, taken to the outer door and beaten with the Alpine sticks in a most savage manner. To complete his sufferings one of the wretches, who had pledged his honour to Flahavan's protection, kicked and trampled on the body of his prostrate victim. They then dragged the wounded man back into his house and swore him that he would give up both his farms the next morning. During this punishing of Flahavan, Connor seized the opportunity, and by an effort of his almost exhausted strength, escaped through a window and hastened for assistance. As soon as they were aware of this, the assailants fled in alarm, leaving Flahavan half-dead from the serious injuries which he had received; "He had never," he said, "been the same man since." Seven of the gang were caught by the military in one house, clearly identified, and despite an *alibi*, which if true was decisive, found guilty and executed.[2]

The last case to be noted is that of an under-tenant on Lord Besborough's estate, whose sole crime in the eyes of the Caravats was taking from one of that lord's tenants a farm at a fair rent, fourfold of that at which it was ordered to be taken by the conspirators. Lord Besborough was a good landlord, and his agent a fair man. So far from wishing to let his lands to jobbers and middlemen, the noble landlord had parcelled his estate into three divisions, in order to enable the former tenants to continue their holdings. In two of these divisions all had gone well. In the third the old tenants were refractory, and under orders

---

[2] Trial of Thomas Blake and son, and others, under the Whiteboy Acts, 15 and 16 George III., for compelling John Flahavan by threats and menaces to quit his farm, and also under Lord Ellenborough's Act, for an assault on the same with intent to kill. Waterford, February 9, 1811.

from the Caravats, refused to give more than eleven shillings an acre for land which could be let to other persons for two guineas. Lord Besborough was inclined to favour the old tenants by taking a lower rent, but the tenants relied on the system of terror that prevailed, and persevered in their combination. On this, these lands were let for forty shillings an acre; and in consequence, on James Keneally, one of the new tenants, the Caravats vowed vengeance. At midnight, on the 1st of July, his house was attacked by some dozen armed men, who fired shots at the door and window, broke in and penned the occupants in a room, and swore him and his brother to give up the farm. Beyond taking them out of their house to that of a neighbour, whose windows they broke, no personal violence was inflicted, and on the alarm of military coming they dispersed. Of this party, only one, the captain, a stranger to the county, was identified, and with his conviction the Special Commission closed.[3]

The executive having discharged its duty of repressing the outrages—to so great an extent due to the existing mode of assessing and levying tithes in Ireland—it was left to the legislature to provide a remedy for the evil which was admitted to exist. It was in vain, however, that the question of tithes was pressed upon Parliament by Mr. Parnell; not only was the cabinet opposed even to inquiry into the subject, but the Irish members themselves were far from unanimous in supporting the motion for the

[3] Trial of John Quinlan, Kilkenny, February 13, 1811.

committee which Mr. Parnell demanded. Mr. Perceval admitted the existence of the evil, and hoped some day to propose a remedy, but refused for the present on the poor excuse that he regarded the motion as dangerous in awakening expectations, while they were to receive nothing. The small attendance of members marked the little interest the legislature had in the question. By a majority of sixty-nine to forty-eight the motion was rejected, only twenty-seven Irish members voting for it, and thirteen against the proposed committee.[4] But the question, once raised never slept, though put aside year after year, until Parliament itself had been reformed. Then at last it was settled, more than a quarter of a century after these events which so forcibly, and yet for the time so ineffectually, called attention to the magnitude of the evil.

[4] Motion of Mr. Parnell in House of Commons to inquire into the manner of collecting tithes, and such other matters relating thereto as they may consider proper, April, 1810. Though the commutation of tithes for corn-rent was recommended by committees of both Houses in 1832, it was not finally carried out until 1838.

APPENDIX A.

Dr. Troy's Case.
Page 166.

In his defence Garrow had said, "I was lately considering how I might most readily find historical information respecting the conduct of the Roman Catholic clergy as it referred to the affairs of this life. I contemplated this subject as I travelled in a carriage when I happened to have by me and at my hand Mr. Plowden's book. I knew Mr. Plowden, as I dare say you do, to be a man of method ; it occurred to me I was likely to find something useful under the word *Priest*. I looked, and under the title of *Priest*, which I found on p. 716, I found at once a definition of that character as applicable to the Roman Catholic clergy as easy to understand as any commonplace topic in a book of practice in our profession, thus :—*Priests. Some of the Roman Catholic priests always must be found in a rebellion*," and if you want to know his argument for it, you have it thus :—" The almost total dependence of the Romish clergy in Ireland upon their people for the means of subsistence is the cause, according to my best judgment, why upon every popular commotion many priests of that communion have been, and until measures of better policy are adopted, always will be found in the ranks of sedition and opposition to the established Government. The peasant will love a revolution, because he feels the weight of poverty, and has not often the sense to perceive that a change of masters may render it heavier; the priest must follow the impulse of the popular wave or be left on the beach to perish."

These words were not Mr. Plowden's, but those of Dr. Stock, the Protestant Bishop of Killaloe, in his narrative of the events at Killaloe in the summer of 1792. See Plowden's letter to the Editor of the *Morning Post*, printed in vol. iv. of Plowden's "History of Ireland since the Union," pp. 238-9.

APPENDIX B.

THE "FREIHEIT" PROSECUTION. MAY 25, 1881.

Page 96.

AT the Central Criminal Court, Johann Most, the editor and proprietor of a German journal called the *Freiheit*, was placed at the bar, before the Lord Chief Justice, to take his trial on an indictment which charged him with having endeavoured to incite persons in this country and in foreign countries to assassinate their rulers, and also with having published a false and malicious libel concerning the late Emperor of Russia, and with inciting divers evil-disposed persons to murder the reigning sovereign of Russia.

The Attorney-General, with Mr. Poland and Mr. A. L. Smith, appeared for the prosecution; the defence was conducted by Mr. A. M. Sullivan, M.P., and Mr. F. Cooper Willis, instructed by Mr. H. E. Kisbey.

The Attorney-General, in opening the case for the prosecution, said the question to be tried was whether articles of such a nature as that published by the defendant could be published with impunity in this country. The defendant, who was a German, had associated himself with persons of extreme political views, and owing to that connexion, he became the editor of the *Freiheit*. That he was the writer of some of the articles which appeared in the paper was not disputed. Prior to the publishing of the articles in question attempts had been made upon the lives of two emperors in Europe. On the 13th of March the Emperor of Russia was murdered, and no argument could be allowed to maintain the justice of the murder. The prisoner had a right to express his views in relation to political matters, but the question for the jury was whether the prisoner had not exceeded the limit which the law of this country allowed. The *Freiheit* had a considerable circulation abroad as well as in this country, and as soon as public attention was attracted to the publication of the 19th of March the sale largely increased. The article complained of said: " Triumph—Triumph—at last ! The word of the poet is fulfilled—one of the most horrible tyrants of Europe, whose destruction has long been sworn, and before whose withering and revengeful wrath countless heroes and heroines of the Russian people sunk into the grave or the prison—the Emperor of Russia is no more. Could only one such crowned ragamuffin be destroyed per month, there would be slight desire in the future to play at monarchy." There were other articles published in the *Freiheit*, and the assassin Rousakoff was described as a person who ought never to be spoken of but with reverence. It was also stated that the murder of the Emperor Alexander was calculated to have great effect upon the monarchies of other countries, who were represented as suffering from cowardly fear, at which fear the writer of the article expressed his joy. Another article commenced with the expression— " Who could be scoundrel enough to bewail the death of such a beast ?" and it went on to say, " May the bold deed which we commend inspire revolutionary minds far and wide with fresh courage," and said that "the Emperor died like a dog." Another article spoke of the Emperor of Germany as the cruel grape-shot Prince of Prussia, and suggested that he ought to share the fate of the Emperor of Russia. Other crowned heads were mentioned as trembling in fear of a similar fate, and that it was nonsense to suppose that the death of one prince did no good because another took his place; and the thrower of the bomb that killed the emperor was described as being good. The natural inference to be drawn from the article was that the writer regarded the taking of the life of the emperor as an act of virtue, and most persons would suppose that it suggested that complaint ought to be made that murders took place so unfrequently. It was not only expressing the writer's views, but directly incited the readers to murder. Taking the articles as a whole, it could not but be regarded as a direct statement that if the present Czar ruled as his father had done, his life would be taken in the same manner. In the same paper, in connexion with the writing, it was announced that the revolutionary adherents of Most had appointed for the next task "to prepare for the institution of widely ramified and secret boards and clubs" for acts of violence against the representatives of State and social order, through which the execution of the universal revolution was to be introduced. When the prisoner was taken into custody, certain papers were found upon the prisoner and in the house, and amongst them was found a paper in his pocketbook, upon which were the words, "Trieste is a safe address for the storage of dynamite." What, he (the Attorney-General) asked, could have been the object of this information being in possession of defendant unless for some practical purpose? In the article itself dynamite was stated as the means employed for destroying the life of the Emperor of Russia. It was for the maintenance of law and order alone that this case had been brought forward. The doctrine of murder had been preached, and if it had been applied to the humblest persons instead of to emperors, it would have been equally necessary to endeavour to stop the publication of writings which, if acted upon, would have caused the destruction of law and order. There was not the slightest desire to check the free discussion of political matters in the press. On the contrary, it was to preserve that freedom that the prosecution had been undertaken.

Charles E. Marr, examined.—I am a teacher of languages. On the 25th March I went to 101, Great Titchfield Street, and there purchased four copies of the *Freiheit* of the 19th March, one of which I produce.

In cross-examination the witness said,—I went for the paper out of curiosity, owing to a conversation I had had with a friend. When I read the article I sent the paper to Lord G. Hamilton, asking whether the Government would not prosecute.

Philip Joseph Hall, examined.—I am a commission agent, and carry on business at 2, Well Court, Minories. I have been in the habit of selling copies of the *Freiheit*, some of which I obtained from the office of the paper.

Richard Robert Davis, examined.—I am a newsagent carrying on business on Ludgate Hill. I have sold the *Freiheit* for some years. I received fourteen copies per week by post. Some I sold, and a collector called for those remaining. There was a greater demand for the number of the 19th March than for any other. I mostly sold the paper to working men.

Henry Ward, examined.—I am a constable of the Metropolitan Police. On the 29th March I went to Titchfield street and saw the prisoner. I asked him for a copy of the *Freiheit* of the 19th March. He said that there were none left, that they had printed a second edition, but that for the sake of the few they might sell it was not worth while printing any more. I told him that I desired to give one to a friend, and he handed me two printed sheets, which contained the article which he said he supposed was what I wanted.

Cross-examined.—I was in plain clothes when I saw the prisoner, and spoke German to him.

Mr. Henry Ball, examined.—I carry on business as a printer in Great Titchfield Street. I have known the prisoner for two years. I was originally employed to print the *Freiheit* two years ago last Christmas by a person named Weber. I knew the prisoner in connexion with the paper about the time it first commenced. At first we used to set up the type from the MSS. The prisoner began to pay me from the beginning of the year 1880. There were 1200 copies per week printed. At Christmas, 1879, I ceased to set up the type, but it was brought in forms to my office to be printed. I always made out my bills for printing to the prisoner, who sometimes paid me personally.

Mr. W. Bangert, the landlord of 101, Great Titchfield Street, examined.—The prisoner occupied a front room, and a workshop at the back was taken as a printing-office by two gentlemen. When the defendant came to live there he paid the rent of the printing-office.

Police-inspector Charles Hagan, examined.—I went to the house of Most on the 30th March. I first saw him in the printing-office. I asked him whether he was Johann Most, and he said, " Yes." I then told him that I had a warrant for his arrest. He called a man named Martin to him, and took out what he had in his pockets. I told him he could not give these things to Martin, and I took possession of them. Before I read the warrant he said, " I expected this, because I see in the paper there is to be a prosecution. I suppose it is in consequence of my article on the Czar." I then read the warrant to him in German, when he said, " It does not appear from that warrant who is the instigator of this." I told him that the warrant was signed by Sir James Ingham, and that I had to execute it. There was some type already set up, and a quantity loose, which I took possession of. A "pull" was taken from the type in Scotland Yard. When we were about to remove the things the prisoner said, "I beg to call your attention to the fact that they are not my exclusive property. They belong to an association of persons, of whom I am one." The piece of paper produced was in one of the pocket-books. (The slip in which reference was made to dynamite.) . I took Most to the police-station, and when asked what his occupation was, he said, "I am editor of the *Freiheit*, and a literary man."

Cross-examined.—I knew the prisoner by sight, and by hearsay knew that he was editor of the *Freiheit*. I did not give him any caution when I arrested him. There was a large quantity of paper taken possession of, and amongst them many documents. The documents were sealed up immediately. I do not know in whose handwriting the slip found in the pocket-book was. When I took him into custody he had the *Standard* in his hand, and said, " I expected this." We have produced all the papers asked for by the Treasury.

M. Gustave Reinecke, German Master of King's College School, was called to prove the accuracy of the translation of the article from German to English.

This was the case for the prosecution.

Mr. A. M. Sullivan, before addressing the jury, raised several questions of law. On the first count of the indictment he asked his lordship to tell the jury that unless the offence deposed to satisfied them that the prisoner intended to incite persons to kill and slay persons within the Queen's peace, they must find him not guilty. As to the second count (that of intent to incite), he submitted that the prisoner could not be found guilty of intent to justify assassination and murder, or with intent to set up a conspiracy to murder, as the sovereigns of Europe were not within the Queen's peace.

The Lord Chief Justice overruled the objection, in the belief that the case came within the authorities of the few cases which existed on the point.

Mr. A. M. Sullivan.—As to the other counts, he said that this was the first time an attempt had been made to apply the 24th and 25th Victoria to a prosecution of this kind. He submitted that the publication of the newspaper article was not an encouragement to murder "any person" within the meaning of the statute. The Act contemplated some person taking part in a conspiracy of some sort, and that the communication should be addressed to some person with the actual intent and meaning of his carrying out some specific act. The section did not contemplate newspaper invective addressed to no one in particular. The question was one which would affect the press generally of this country.

The Attorney-General argued that where a person endeavoured to encourage or persuade many persons it came within the meaning of the section which dealt with an endeavour to "encourage or persuade any person." The prisoner must be held as bearing the responsibility of what he wrote.

The Lord Chief Justice said that the question was whether the publication was an endeavour to persuade persons to whom the paper was handed. He had some doubt, from the particular words of the section, whether it was ever intended to point to publications. He proposed to direct the jury according to his present impression of the law, and if they found a verdict of guilty, he would like it separately on each count, and reserve the question raised, as after all it only affected the amount of punishment.

Mr. Sullivan, addressing the jury for the defence, said

that the Attorney-General had commenced without alluding to any precedents, and if he had done so he (Mr. Sullivan) would have had to call attention to prosecutions which had not left any favourable impression on the minds of Englishmen. He had a great responsibility in the case, because he was not only defending the prisoner but also the interests of the British press, and his task was made the more difficult from the peculiar circumstances of the case. The jury were called upon to apply an Act of Parliament which had never before been applied to the press of England, and he asked the jury to "beware" how they applied the Act to newspaper publications. If the prisoner were convicted the press would not be safe. For instance, if any one were to write that the Nihilists or the Land Leaguers ought to be swept from the face of the earth, according to the argument of the prosecution that would be inciting the readers to commit murder. The press, he maintained, had a perfect right to indulge in general invectives, but if the Government succeeded in this prosecution, it would be bound to silence all newspaper articles of a dangerous character. In the course of a long and eloquent address, the learned counsel urged that the main question for consideration was whether, according to the spirit of our law, as applied to the liberty of the press, general invectives could be treated as a crime. Shakespeare, Milton, Byron, Shelley, and Disraeli should all have stood in the dock if the doctrine of tyrannicide was to be prosecuted when printed and published. In all previous prosecutions of this kind it had been held to be necessary to put into the witness-box some one from the Foreign Office to say that peace existed between this and the country referred to.

The Lord Chief Justice.—It has been held that proof is unnecessary where the fact is notorious. Notoriety is held to be sufficient.

Mr. Sullivan said that at the present time notoriety as to

where we were at peace and where we were not was of a most hazy kind (laughter). Language more precise than that ascribed to the prisoner in reference to continental rulers were matters of history, and had been permitted without complaint. As instances of this he cited many publications in pamphlet and other forms, including letters of Mr. Gladstone to the Earl of Aberdeen with reference to the Government of Southern Italy, the language of which, he said, was quite as strong as that used by the prisoner, and yet passed unnoticed. The prisoner began political life in Germany, and there commenced open, lawful, and legitimate agitation. Inch by inch they had been driven from their open and lawful resort of honest political life. Although the prisoner had been a member of the legislative body, he had spent many years in the prisons of Prince Bismarck. He consequently came to this country, and it was now sought to send him to prison for his expression of opinion relative to Russia, for words written possibly with a view to promoting a better future for that country. Pent-up voice and utterances would find vent at such times, and it should not be forgotten that the charge referred but to a single issue of the *Freiheit*, published at a time of great excitement.

The Attorney-General said that whilst giving the learned counsel credit for great eloquence, he desired the jury to consider how much of the address was based upon common sense. He protested against it being said that newspapers in general had anything in common with the *Freiheit*, and he thought the liberty of the press would be strengthened by striking off from it such lawless articles as that complained of. He complained of a suggestion that the prosecution had been instituted at the instance of Prince Bismarck, and said that it had been undertaken simply in the interests of law and order. The prisoner might have a perfect right to say that persons had suffered under the Russian

Government, but that had nothing to do with the question for the jury. He, the learned counsel, agreed in the necessity for preserving freedom of discussion, but not in the necessity of extending licence to those who offended against the law of the country. Wherever a publication tended to weaken the bonds of civil society, it became punishable by common law.

The Lord Chief Justice, in summing up, said that in a certain sense he agreed that it was not possible to exaggerate the importance of what was considered the liberty of the press. This country stood almost alone among civilized nations without a censorship of the press. The true censorship of the press in this country was the administration of justice in courts of law. In his judgment, the greatest liberty should be allowed to what he called historical criticisms. It would be a bad day for the country if English writers were prevented from expressing their opinions upon the Government of a foreign country; and even in that particular case, if that particular libel had been merely confined to a denunciation of the late Emperor of Russia, however strong, however coarse, however revolting might be the language used, he would have thought it far better that the press should remain unfettered. However objectionable such comments might be, it would be far better that they should be allowed to pass unchallenged than that the existing right should be injured. It was, however, a very different thing when the writer proceeded from the past to incite to practical acts for the future. Upon the historical examples given by the learned counsel he had but one general observation to make, viz., that they appeared to be apart from the case, because they were passages altered in their bearing by being separated from the context. The prisoner was indicted for having in effect done two things—first, for what was called a common law libel; secondly, for having broken the special provisions of the Act of Parliament, 24 and 25 Vict., c. 100, sec. 4. After referring generally to the subject-matter of the charge, the learned Judge said that any publication which was against public morals, and tended to public inconvenience, or should point to the assassination of rulers of friendly states, was clearly, by the law of England, libel.

The jury retired at half-past five o'clock, and after an absence of twenty minutes, returned a verdict of Guilty upon the whole of the counts, the jury stating that they desired to recommend the prisoner to mercy on the ground that he was a foreigner.

The sentence was postponed, pending the argument on the point of law reserved.

The case of "the Queen *v.* Most" came on, on Saturday, June 18th, before the Court for Crown Cases Reserved. The Judges present were the Lord Chief Justice, Mr. Justice Denman, Mr. Justice Grove, Mr. Baron Huddleston, and Mr. Justice Watkin Williams.

Mr. A. M. Sullivan (instructed by Mr. H. E. Kisbey) was counsel for the defendant, who was out on bail pending the decision of this Court; the Attorney-General, the Solicitor-General, Mr. Poland, and Mr. A. L. Smith (instructed by Mr. Pollard on behalf of the Treasury) were for the Crown in support of the conviction.

Mr. Sullivan, in opening the case, said that Herr Johann Most had been indicted before the Lord Chief Justice at the Central Criminal Court on the 25th of May last, on an indictment containing twelve counts, the first two of which charged him with the publication of a scandalous libel at common law, but these were abandoned. The remaining ten counts charged the defendant with an offence under the 24th and 25th Vict., c. 100, sec. 4, as the writer and publisher of an article in his newspaper, printed in the German language, called the *Freiheit*, which was published in

London, and had an average sale of some 1200 copies weekly. In these counts the defendant was charged with having encouraged and persuaded persons to murder other persons, some of whom were named, while others were not named, and some of these counts charged the defendant with inciting and persuading persons to murder Alexander III., Emperor of all the Russias, and William I., Emperor of Germany. Lord Coleridge directed the jury in the following terms : " If the defendant had incited to or had endeavoured or did persuade other persons to murder any other person, whether the subjects of her Majesty the Queen or not, and whether they were domiciled in this country or not, and that if such encouragement and endeavour to persuade was the reasonable effect of the article, they must find the prisoner guilty." The jury found the prisoner guilty on all the counts. He (Mr. Sullivan) contended that there was no encouragement by the defendant to induce or persuade any person to commit a murder within the meaning of the statute, although he would admit that the defendant was the proprietor, the printer, and the publisher of the newspaper.

Mr. Justice Denman.—We must take it that in this capacity there was evidence to show that he knew the contents of the article charged as libellous.

Mr. Sullivan admitted that as editor of the paper the defendant was responsible at common law for the publication of a libel, but this was totally distinct from the nature of the transaction contemplated by the section of the statute under which he had been indicted.

Lord Coleridge.—If the contents of the libel were scandalous, and its publisher was convicted, we must assume that he was rightly convicted.

Mr. Justice Denman.—Let there be no doubt whatever on this point. We are to take it that the defendant sold the paper well knowing its contents.

Mr. Sullivan.—Yes; I will concede that, my lord. I asked his lordship to tell the jury that this was not such an encouragement as rendered it by this section a statutable encouragement.

Lord Coleridge.—In this Court, Mr. Sullivan, we have to decide a question of criminal law, and your observations must be confined to the point I have reserved.

Mr. Sullivan therefore would submit that the offence was wholly outside the Act under which the prisoner had been indicted, and for this purpose he traced the enactments passed prior to this statute, which came into effect in 1861, under which there were abundant means for punishing any one for inciting to murder. He asked their lordships to hold that the section of the Act under which the prisoner had been found guilty must apply to conspiracy to murder, and not to the publication of a false and scandalous libel.

Lord Coleridge here observed that the Act was to be construed as a consolidation of former Acts relating to offences against the person.

Mr. Baron Huddleston.—The Act contemplates two classes of offenders—the persons who individually conspire, and the persons who persuade and encourage others.

Mr. Justice Denman.—Take this case. A person is anxious to get rid of a foreign sovereign, and there is evidence of his conspiracy with another person to whom, being perhaps a poor person, he may offer a bribe of 1000*l.* or 10,000*l.* to destroy that foreign sovereign by a shell or a bomb, and if that person repudiated the crime as something horrible, would not the person who had incited and encouraged him to commit the act be within this statute?

Mr. Sullivan replied that if a person called A endeavoured to persuade B to murder a sovereign, it would be a conspiracy within the meaning of the statute, but the offence in this case was totally outside the statute. On this point he would cite the case of the "Queen *v.* Faux,"—not Guy Fawkes (laughter), for it was spelt F-a-u-x (renewed laughter). That was a case decided in the Court for the Consideration of Crown Cases Reserved in Dublin, and in which the prisoner was charged with asking a friend of his to murder one Kennedy, but it appeared that the letter got into the hands of another person than him to whom it was intended, and who could not be supposed to have a desire to murder anybody, as he happened to be a policeman in the village (great laughter). At the trial the judge held that by writing and posting the letter the prisoner had made an effort at murder, and he was convicted, but the Court for the Consideration of Crown Cases Reserved had by a majority quashed the conviction. The learned counsel, in conclusion, submitted there was no precedent for giving the statute under which the defendant had been convicted such a wide and dangerous significance as to the responsibility of newspapers, and that the legislature in framing it never intended that it should apply to cases of this description.

The Attorney-General contended that there was no ambiguity about the statute. The section under which the prisoner had been convicted did not deal with a conspiracy, but with a misdemeanour of inciting to crime, and was, in fact, a declaration of common law on the subject. The learned gentleman was proceeding, when the Court stopped his argument as he was observing that the case of the defendant was exactly similar to that of an orator who incited a crowd to murder some one, and which he addressed as individuals, or any given number of individuals in that crowd.

Lord Coleridge gave judgment.—He said he was of opinion that this conviction must be affirmed, and although at the trial he had some doubt as to whether the defendant came within a section of the Act, that doubt had now been entirely cleared away after the arguments now addressed to the Court. It was unnecessary to go into an historical survey of Acts of Parliament from the first Irish Act relating to conspiracy downwards, with which Mr. Sullivan had favoured them, for that was only necessary when some doubt existed as to phraseology, but here there was none at all. He thought that the jury had rightly convicted the defendant on his direction, which he now considered was a right decision, and the conviction should therefore be affirmed.

The other learned judges concurred, and the conviction was affirmed accordingly.

Mr. Sullivan then applied to his lordship to postpone sentence on the defendant.

Lord Coleridge said that sentence would be postponed until the 29th inst.

JUNE 29.

Lord Coleridge, in pronouncing sentence, said,—Johann Most, you have been found guilty by the jury of two separate offences—one for the publication of a scandalous libel, which is punishable by the law of this country, because it is an attack upon the characters of other friendly sovereigns in amity with the ruler of this country, and the natural effect of which might be to interfere with those friendly relations which subsist between the Queen of this country and foreign princes. For that offence the sentence awarded by the law would be imprisonment or fine, or both, within such reasonable limits as in the absolute discretion of the Court it might think fit to impose. You have been found guilty of more than this. After a patient trial and an able defence, you have been found guilty of a wilful, knowing, deliberate intention to incite to murder; and to that offence the

Parliament of England has of late years affixed a graver punishment—it has affixed the punishment of hard labour in addition to imprisonment, or a period of penal servitude. Within my lifetime, in one part at least of the Queen's dominions, the crime of which you have been found guilty would have been punished with death. It is at all times a grave offence. It may be in addition to a grave offence a very cowardly one; because it may be that a man, himself safe under the shelter of a great and free country, sitting at home at ease, may incite others to run into fearful dangers which he himself avoids, and incite them to the commission of detestable crimes which he himself shrinks from attempting. I cannot doubt that in this case you were seriously intending to incite, the more because no one could read what you have written without being certain that you had that intention, because you dwelt with satisfaction—nay, even with delight—upon the horrible bodily torture of one murdered king, and it is manifest that you desired that other kings should share in his torments and in his death. I do not question that you wrote seriously, and that you had a deliberate and real intention that your words should be followed by practical results. I say nothing—it is not for me to say a word—either upon the state of the law or upon the institution of this prosecution. You have been found guilty of a grave offence, and to that offence the Parliament of Great Britain has, as I have said, affixed a grave punishment. I am here to administer the law; and I should repeal the law, and not administer it, if in a case of this kind, and after the evidence that has been laid before us, I passed upon you a slight or trivial punishment. But for the recommendation of the jury to mercy which they made I should have felt it my duty to send you into penal servitude, but I take that recommendation into account. I do not therefore reduce you to the condition of a slave; but I pass upon you a sentence which I believe—

indeed, which I know—to be a sentence very hard to bear. I recollect—as I think I ought to recollect—that by the operation of the Court itself you have already undergone some period of imprisonment, and I order you to be further kept in imprisonment, with the addition of hard labour, for sixteen calendar months.

M. Albert (interpreter) was about to interpret the sentence to the prisoner, when—

Lord Coleridge said that upon the trial he was given to understand that the prisoner was well conversant with the English language, and perfectly comprehended the evidence. There must be no speech after the sentence, but that might be interpreted.

This having been done, the prisoner was taken from the dock, and on leaving was understood to exclaim, " We might as well be in Russia."

INDEX.

	PAGE

ABBOT, Speaker, extracts from his diary and letters to him in
Emmet's case . . . . **124** *et seq.*
Casting vote against Lord Melville 188
Abercrombie in Egypt 6
Appointment of Picton to Trinidad, and character . . 296
Addington, cabinet of, 1801 4
    Resignation, 1804 13
    War policy of Pitt and Addington . . . . 13 *note*
    Created Lord Sidmouth, 1805 13
    Conduct in the case of Lord Melville 186-7, 190
Alarcon, Charge of execution of, against Picton . . . 306
"All the Talents," Cabinet of 16, 192
Ambigu, L', Peltier's libels on Bonaparte in . . . 79
Amelia, Princess, effect of her death on George III. . . 25
America, Peace with 175
Amiens, Peace of 8
Anti-Jacobin, Libels in 142
Armstrong flogged to death at Goree, 1782 . . . 31
Army purchase system commenced 247
Austerlitz, Battle of 15
Austria, Treaty with 15

BANKS, division on his amendment in Duke of York's case . 281
Bantry Bay, Mutiny of the fleet in 44
Bedford, Duke of, Viceroy of Ireland 390
Berkeley, Earl of, public marriage, 1796 347
    Intimacy with Miss Cole 351
    Publication of banns 352
    Facsimiles of certificate of banns and marriage . . 366-7
    Pedigree before House of Lords, 1799 . . . 351
    ,, adjourned *sine die* 359
    Proceedings in Chancery to perpetuate testimony . . 360
    Death, 1810 363
Berkeley Peerage Case. Petition of Colonel Berkeley to House
of Lords 363
    Analysis of evidence . . . . . . 364—386
    The certificates of banns and marriage . . . 364—369

	PAGE
Berkeley Peerage Case. Social position of Lady Berkeley prior to second marriage	369—377
Registers of the baptisms of the elder children	377—379
Position of eldest son.	379—380
Lady Berkeley's story	380—384
William Tudor's story	384—386
Verdict against claimant	387
Berkeley, Colonel, created Baron Segrave, and afterwards Earl Fitzhardinge, and death without issue	388-9
Admiral, created Baron Fitzhardinge, 1861	389
Berlin, Capture of, by Bonaparte	20
Bonaparte, Libels on, by Peltier	79
Bond, Motion of, for criminal information against Lord Melville	188
Bourbon dynasty in Spain, Overthrow of	22
Princes, Expulsion of, demanded	80
Brady, Lieut., disperses the Emmet rebels	115
Browne, Colonel, murdered in the Emmet rebellion	112
Buckingham, Marquis of, evidence in Berkeley case	372

CALDERON, Louisa, Charge against Picton for torturing	309
Charged with robbery	315
First application of torture and confession	316
Second torture and imprisonment	317
Canning's attacks on Addington's war policy	9
Libel on Dr. Troy in *Anti-Jacobin*	166
Duel with Lord Castlereagh	25
Caravats, the origin of name	400
The trial and punishment of eleven	403
Execution of seven, for outrage on Flahavan and Connor	405
Card, pretended author of Juverna's letters	164
Carey, Mrs., succeeds Mrs. Clarke as "female favourite"	254
Carrington, Rev. Caleb, searches for, and discovery of, the pretended certificates of marriage and banns of Earl Berkeley	353
Carter, Case of, Mrs. Clarke's footman	269
Catholics, Concession to, refused, 1807	3, 19
Celestino, Charge against Picton for hanging	306
Chapeau, Rev. Mr. : His evidence in Berkeley case	349, 370
Chenier, putative author of one of Peltier's libels	81
Cintra, Convention of	23
Clarke, Mrs., and the Duke of York, Case of	243—288
Dismissed by the Duke	251
Resolutions of the House of Commons	280—288
Obtains verdict against Colonel Wardle	292
Prints her Memoirs, which are suppressed	293
Libels on Duke of Kent and William Fitzgerald, and sentence, subsequent life, and death	294
Clarke, Sir Alfred, witness to character of Colonel Despard	73

INDEX.   429

	PAGE
Clavering, General : Bribe of 1000*l.* to Mrs. Clarke	259
Coalition Cabinet	17
Cobbett publishes Juverna's letters	143
First trial for the Trojan Horse Libels	153
Second trial for „ ,, „ and fine of 500*l.*	154
Gives up the letters, and is witness for the Crown	163
Trial for libel on military flogging	335
Cole, Mary (Miss Tudor), early history and seduction	349
Evidence as Lady Berkeley	380
Cole, Mrs., Evidence of	383
Cole, William (*alias* Tudor), Evidence of	354 *et seq.*
Coltman, Lieut., seizes the Marshalsea Depôt (Emmet case)	116
Commissariat frauds	14, 223 *et seq.*
Conspiracy of Colonel Despard and trial, 1802	43 *et seq.*
Constitution Society	58
Consul, Bonaparte elected first, for life	9
Continental coalition, End of	15
Copenhagen, Battle of (Nelson)	5
Bombardment of	21
Corunna, Battle of	24
Courier newspaper libels on Emperor of Russia	85
Cruelty practised by the Threshers with "Cards"	392 *note*
Curran, counsel for Irish rebels in Emmet's rebellion	128 *et seq.*
,, „ Judge Johnson in Trojan Horse Libel	161

DALLAS, counsel for Davison	231
„ „ Picton	318
Davison, Alexander, Trial of, for Commissariat frauds	223
Imprisoned for bribery at election	224
Made Commissary-General of the forces and Treasurer of the Ordnance	*ib.*
Sentenced to twenty-one months' imprisonment	235
Debates on Emmet's rebellion	118
De Lancey and Davison	225
Demurrer in the Berkeley Chancery suit	360
Despard, Colonel, Conspiracy of	43 *et seq.*
Previous life and services and character of him by Lord Nelson	45
Arrest and imprisonment in 1793	47
Despard, Colonel, and others, Arrest of, by Stafford, Nov. 1802	52
The plot of	57—59
Preparation of jury, &c., by Government	60
Trial of	62—74
Evidence of Windsor the Government spy and other accomplices against	63—71
Conviction and execution	74-5
Places of burial	76
Donkin, paper-maker, evidence in Berkeley case	364
Douglas, Lieut., fires on Emmet's mob	115

	PAGE
Dowdall, fellow-conspirator with Emmet	101
Drakard, libel on military	343
Dundas, Henry (*see* Lord Melville).	
Durneens, The trial of, for murder of Lavin	398
Dursley, Lord, petition for Earldom of Berkeley	363

EAST India Company, inquiry into corrupt sale of cadetships and writerships . . . . 288—290
Eldon, Lord, Chancellor 5
   Overrules demurrer in Berkeley suit . . . 360 *note*
   Severe criticisms on the proposed evidence . . . 361
Ellenborough, Lord, Cabinet Minister in the Ministry of "All the Talents" . . . . 192 *note*
   Presiding Judge in cases of Despard, 73 ; Peltier, 95 ; Johnson, 163 ; Davison, 230 ; Jones, 239; Picton, 318 ; Leigh Hunt, 357.
Emmet's rebellion . . . . 97—141
   Early life of 99
   Manufacture of arms and ammunition . . . 103—105
   Intended proclamations 106
   Escape to the Wicklow Hills 112
   Capture, trial, and execution . . . . 134—136
   Attachment to Curran's daughter 135
   Detail of his plans 137
Eylau, Battle of 20

FABRIGAS *v.* Mostyn, Case of, *re* Picton 326
Fendall and Mary Cole (Berkeley case) 382
Ferguson, General, speech on Duke of York's case . . 284
Ferryman, evidence in Berkeley case 371
Flahavan and Connor, attempted murder by Caravats . . 404
Flynns, Plot of the, to murder Lavin 399
Fox, C. J., coalition with Lord North . . . 16, 175
   Death of 17
Freiheit, Prosecution of editor of, 1881 . . . 96 *note*, 410
Fullarton, Colonel, appointed Commissioner of Trinidad . 303
   His charges against General Picton . . , 305 *et seq.*
   Death 313

GALLAGHAN, Charge against General Picton for hanging . 306
George III., opposition to Pitt on Catholic question, 1801 . 3
   Negotiations with Addington 4, 5
   Return of illness 12
   Unwilling acceptance of Coalition Cabinet . . . 15, 16
   Refusal to sanction their Catholic Relief Bill . . 18, 19
   Enforced resignation of Cabinet, and appointment of Duke of Portland as Premier 19
   Remark on Lord Melville's conduct 189
   Return of malady, and appointment of Regent . . 25, 26

	PAGE
Germany, Assassination of Emperor of, advocated in *Freiheit*	412
Gibbs, Vicary, Attorney-General, and Press prosecutions	330
Gibraltar: Mutiny of sailors	44
Goliath, Charge against General Picton for flogging, to death	307
Gonzales and others, Arrest and trial of, for robbery of Ruiz	315
Verdict against	317
Gordon, Lord George, libel on Marie Antoinette	85
Goree, Island of, description	28
Trial of Governor Wall of	33—40
Grenville, Lord, Cabinet of	16
HABEAS Corpus Act, Suspension of, in Ireland, 1801	8
Hamilton, colleague of Emmet	102
Havannah, Capture of, 1762	30
Hedges, the brothers, Trial of, for frauds of naval stores	171 *note*
Hibernicus, Letters of, in Cobbett's *Register*	145
Higgins, Evidence of, against Commissary-General Jones	238
Hogan, Major, pamphlet against Duke of York and Mrs. Clarke	252
Hood, Captain, appointed with Colonel Fullarton to Trinidad	303
His support of Picton, and censure on Fullarton	304
Verses on, at Westminster election	305 *note*
Horse, Trojan, The libels of the	142 *et seq.*
Hovenden, Mrs., a negotiator of commissions with Clarke	274
Hunt, Leigh, prosecution for libel	331
And John, prosecution for libel	337—340
Acquittal	343
Hupsman, Vicar of Berkeley, his alleged celebration of secret marriage of the Earl	352
Signature to certificates	366-7
Evidence of his widow and daughter	368
IMPEACHMENT of Lord Melville	192 *et seq.*
Indictment of Gabriel Peltier	9, 78 *et seq.*
Mackintosh's defence of	85
Perceval's reply	95
Inn River, Passage of the, by Bonaparte	9
JENA, Battle of	20
Jenner, Dr., Evidence of (Berkeley case)	365
Johnson, Mr. Justice, suspected author of Juverna's letters	157
Arrested in Dublin, 1805	158
Arguments on validity of his arrest	160
Trial in England	163
Conviction	166
Retirement and pension	*ib.*
Jones, Valentine, Commissary-General in West Indies	236
System of fraud on Government	237 *et seq.*
Trial and conviction	235—240

INDEX.

	PAGE
Judges, Opinions of, on questions, *re* Lord Melville	217—220
Juverna, Letters of, in Cobbett's *Register*	144
Attacks in, on Mr. Justice Osborne, Lord Redesdale, and Plunkett	149—151

KEARNEY, Trial of, in Emmet rebellion 128
Kearneys, Acquittal of, for attack on P. O'Neil . . . 394
Kenealey, Attack on, by Caravats 406
Kennett and the Duke of York 271
Kenyon, Lord, Comparison of, with Lord Redesdale (Juverna) . 151
Kilwarden, Lord Chief Justice, Murder of, and of his nephew by
    Emmet's rebels 112
    His merciful conduct in 1795 114
"King's Friends," The, gained over by Pitt 13

LARNY, Trial and execution of . . . . . . 402—404
Lascelles, M.P., motion on Lord Melville's impeachment . . 200
Lavin, Murder of, by Threshers 396
Law, Sir E. (Lord Ellenborough), Sketch of . . . 33 *note*
Law, Major, and Mrs. Clarke 274
Leigh Hunt (*see* Hunt, Leigh).
Lewis, Sergeant, Evidence of, *re* Governor Wall . . . 33-4
Libels, Trials for, on Bonaparte, by Peltier 78
    On Irish Government, *re* Emmet's rebellion . . . 142
    On Duke of Kent and Hon. W. Fitzgerald, by Mrs. Clarke 293
    On Colonel Fullarton and Hon. J. Sullivan, by Colonel
        Draper, *re* Picton 304
    On King George III., by James Perry 330
    On military punishments, by Cobbett 334
    ,,   ,,   by L. Hunt 337
    On military rewards, by White 344
Lilburne's libels on Cromwell . . . . . . 94 *note*
London, The south of, in 1802, described 48-9
Lumley, Mrs., evidence in Berkeley case 371
Lynch, Dr., Evidence of, in Picton's case 303

MACALLUM's confederate with Mrs. Clarke 252
Mackintosh's defence of Peltier 87
MacPhaden sent to impose terms on his priest . . . 395
Malowney, attempted murder by Larny, and subsequent
    murder . . . . 403 *and note*
Maltby, Rowland, trafficker in promotions with Mrs. Clarke . 274
Mansfield, James (Lord Chief Justice), opinion on secret
    marriage of Earl Berkeley 379
Melville, Lord, career and policy as Henry Dundas . . 172—178
    Raised to peerage by Addington 179
    First Lord of Admiralty 180
    Report of Commissioners of the Navy on him and Trotter . 180-1

INDEX. 433

	PAGE
Melville, Lord, Whitbread's resolutions against, and subsequent debate and proceedings	182—185
Resignation, and name struck out of Privy Council	185-6
Explanations in House of Commons by leave of the Peers	187
The *Oracle* on his opponents	190
Impeachment voted, 1805	192
Trial and acquittal	194—221
Divisions on the articles of impeachment	221 *note*
Subsequent life and death	222
Merritt, Extraordinary story of, about Lord Dursley	379
Middleton, Sir C., appointed, *vice* Lord Melville	186
Militia called out, 1803	10
Moore, Sir John, Death of, at Corunna	24
Moore, G., tithe proctor, attempted murder by Larny	402
Most, Herr, editor of *Freiheit* (Appendix B.), Trial of	410
Mutiny of fleet in Bantry Bay and off Gibraltar.	44
NAPOLEON, War commenced with, May, 1803	10
Unreadiness of England to resist invasion	12
Rapid continental successes	15, 16
Position of England, 1808	21—23
Nelson, Lord, witness to character of Colonel Despard	46
Death of, at Trafalgar	6
Nepeau, Sir Evan, witness to character of Colonel Despard	73
Nollekens, Baroness, and Mrs. Clarke	274
North, Lord, resignation and coalition with Fox	174-5
Northern Confederacy	6
"OAKLEY Arms" Tavern, Arrest of Despard, &c., at	50
O'Meara, Dr., and Mrs. Clarke: Sermon before the King	262 *and note*
O'Neil and the Threshers	393
Oracle newspaper, Libel on House of Commons in	190
Osborne, Mr. Justice, Libels on (Juverna's letters)	149
Otto, M., and the negotiations for peace of Amiens	7
PALMERSTON, Lord, Secretary at War, 1809	25
Paris, Fall of, 1815	10
Parnell's motion in House of Commons on tithes in Ireland	417
Paul, Emperor of Russia, alliance with Bonaparte and assassination	5, 6
Libel on, in *Courier*, 1798	85
Peace of Amiens	7, 8
Peltier, Jean Gabriel, Trial of	9, 18, 81 *et seq.*
Peninsular war commenced, 1808	23
Perceval, Spencer, sketch of early life	33 *note*
Premier, 1809	25

VOL. I.   F f

	PAGE
Perry, James, editor of *Morning Chronicle*, tried for libel and acquitted	331
Evidence in Berkeley Peerage case	381
Petty, Lord Henry (Marquis Lansdowne), speech on Duke of York's case	265
Picton, General, early history	295
Governor of Trinidad	296—302
Price offered for his head	301
Unfounded charges against, in 1800	303 *note*
Resignation on Fullarton's appointment	304
Charges against, by Fullarton	305—311
Commencement of trial	313
Verdict of guilty, subject to points reserved	321
New trial	325
Verdict in his favour	327
At Walcheren and in the Peninsula	313
Gallant services—Death at Waterloo	328
Pitt, W., Premier, 1783	176
Resignation after Act of Union, 1801	3
In opposition, 1804	12
Premier second time, 1804	13
Death, 1806	16
Pitt (solicitor), evidence in Berkeley case	364
Plunkett, W. C., unwarrantable conduct on Emmet's trial	154
Action for libel against Cobbett	154
Extract from speech on the Union	155
Population and revenue of United Kingdom, 1801	2
Porteus, Bishop, Attack on, for sermon, *re* Lord Melville	189
Portland, Duke of, Ministry, 1807	19
Resignation, 1809	23
Portugal, Royal family of, leave for Brazil, 1807	22
Press prosecutions	330 *et seq.*
Price, Mrs., Evidence of, in Berkeley case	385
QUIGLEY, colleague of Emmet	102
REDESDALE, Libels on (Juverna's letters)	150
Redmond, colleague of Emmet, Trial of	102—132
Regency Bill passed, 1811	26
Revenue of United Kingdom, 1801	2
Roche, Trial of (Emmet's rebellion)	128
Rockingham, Lord, Ministry and death	174
Romilly, S., and Best, counsel for claimant in Berkeley case	363
Rose, the go-between in Jones's Commissariat frauds	238
Russel, engaged in Emmet rebellion	107
Russia, Treaty with	15
Paul, Emperor of, assassinated	6
Alexander ,, ,,	411

	PAGE
SANDON, Captain, trafficker in commissions with Mrs. Clarke	263
Committed to Newgate	265
Scriven, John, discovery of the certificates of banns and marriage in Berkeley case	353
Shanavests, origin of name	400
Capture of a large party of	403
Shannon, reported murderer of Lord Kilwarden	114
Shelburne Ministry, The	174
Slave Trade, Abolition of	17
Spain, assumed neutrality exposed	14
Overthrow of Bourbon dynasty	22
Spanish Governor of Margarita offers price for head of General Picton	300
Stanbank, Contradictory evidence of, in Davison's case	234
Stafford's capture of Despard and others	63—65
Stockdale, colleague of Emmet	111
Sutherland, Lucy Sinclair, ex-mistress of Duke of York, interferes to prevent sale of Major Turner's commission	269
THE Threshers, Confederacy of, against tithes, &c., and murderous outrages by	392
Special Commission for trial of	393
Interference with dues of the priests	395
Murder of Lavin by	396
Torture to obtain evidence (*see* Calderon, Louisa).	
Trojan Horse Libels	143
Trotter, Alexander, Early life of	203
Paymaster-General, 1784	204
Acts as Lord Melville's private agent	205—207
Examination of	208—210
Troy, Dr., Libel on, in *Anti-Jacobin*	166—409
ULM, Capitulation of	15
United Kingdom, Population and revenue of, in 1801	2
VIENNA, Entry into, by Napoleon	15
Vincent, Lord St., First Lord of Admiralty, 1801, institutes Naval Commission	171
WALL, Governor of Goree, Trial of	33 *et seq.*
Arrest and escape, 1784	28
Evidence of Mrs. Lacy and others in his defence	37—39
Execution	41
War, Commencement of, with France	96
Ward, M.P., reads article from the *Oracle* to House of Commons, and subsequent proceedings thereon	191
Wardle, Colonel, initiates proceedings against Duke of York	252
Interview with Mrs. Clarke	253
Verdict against him by her upholsterer	291

	PAGE
Warren Hastings, Censure of, by Lord Melville	176
A negro, charge against Picton for his death	306
West, Colonel John, evidence in Berkeley case	375
Reports legitimacy of Lord Dursley to the Prince of Wales	376
Whitbread's resolutions against Lord Melville	182
His reply in the case	214
Canning's verses on it	215
White, prosecution and acquittal for libel	344
Windsor, Government spy in Despard's case	54-5
York, Duke of, early education and life	243
Commander-in-Chief, 1793	244
Army reforms of	246-7
Connexion with Mary Ann Clarke	248
Wardle's motion for committee on conduct of the Commander-in Chief, 1809	253
Case of Lieut.-Colonel Brook	255
,, Mr. Maling	256
,, Colonel French's levy	257
,, ,, Miss Taylor's evidence	258-9
The Duke's letters to Mrs. Clarke	261—263
Captain Tonyn's disputed letter of Duke	263
Lieut. Donovan and Mrs. Clarke	263 *note*
,, ,, evidence of handwriting	266—268
,, ,, committal of Captain Sandon	265
Case of Samuel Carter	269
Case of Major Turner and Mrs. Sutherland	269-70
Kennett and the proposed loan to Duke	270-2
Proposed loan from Colonel French	272
Letter from the Duke to the Speaker	275
Lord Melville's proposed resolution	276—278
Proposed resolutions and debate thereon	279—287
Resignation of, and letter to the King	285
Final division	287
Reinstated by the Regent	290
Buys up Mrs. Clarke's Memoirs	292

See also Clarke, Mary Ann.

END OF VOL. I.

PRINTED BY GILBERT AND RIVINGTON, LIMITED, ST. JOHN'S SQUARE.

A Catalogue of American and Foreign Books Published or Imported by MESSRS. SAMPSON LOW & CO. *can be had on application.*

Crown Buildings, 188, Fleet Street, London,
September, 1883.

A Selection from the List of Books
PUBLISHED BY
SAMPSON LOW, MARSTON, SEARLE, & RIVINGTON.

ALPHABETICAL LIST.

ABOUT Some Fellows. By an ETON BOY, Author of "A Day of my Life." Cloth limp, square 16mo, 2s. 6d.

Adams (C. K.) Manual of Historical Literature. Crown 8vo, 12s. 6d.

Alcott (Louisa M.). Jack and Jill. 16mo, 5s.
—— *Proverb Stories.* 16mo, 3s. 6d.
—— *Old-Fashioned Thanksgiving Day.* 3s. 6d.
—— *Shawl Straps.* 2s. 6d.
—— See also "Low's Standard Novels" and "Rose Library."

Aldrich (T. B.) Friar Jerome's Beautiful Book, &c. Very choicely printed on hand-made paper, parchment cover, 3s. 6d.
—— *Poetical Works. Edition de Luxe.* Very handsomely bound and illustrated, 21s.

Allen (E. A.) Rock me to Sleep, Mother. With 18 full-page Illustrations, elegantly bound, fcap. 4to, 5s.

American Men of Letters. Lives of Thoreau, Irving, Webster. Small post 8vo, cloth, 2s. 6d. each.

Andersen (Hans Christian) Fairy Tales. With 10 full-page Illustrations in Colours by E. V. B. Cheap Edition, 5s.

Angler's Strange Experiences (An). By COTSWOLD ISYS. With numerous Illustrations, 4to, 5s.

Angling. See "British Fisheries Directory," "Cutcliffe," "Lambert," "Martin," and "Theakston."

Archer (William) English Dramatists of To-day. Crown 8vo, 8s. 6d.

Arnold (G. M.) Robert Pocock, the Gravesend Historian. Crown 8vo, cloth, 5s.

Art Education. See "Biographies of Great Artists," "Illustrated Text Books," "Mollett's Dictionary."

Audsley (G. A.) Ornamental Arts of Japan. 90 Plates, 74 in Colours and Gold, with General and Descriptive Text. 2 vols folio, £16 16s.

A

Audsley (G. A.) *The Art of Chromo-Lithography.* Coloured Plates and Text. Folio, 63s.

Audsley (W. and G. A.) *Outlines of Ornament.* Small folio, very numerous Illustrations, 31s. 6d.

Auerbach (B.) *Spinoza.* Translated. 2 vols., 18mo, 4s.

BALDWIN (J.) *Story of Siegfried.* Emblematical binding, 6s.

Bankruptcy : Inutility of the Laws. Lord Sherbrooke's Remedy. Crown 8vo, 1s.

Bathgate (Alexander) *Waitaruna: A Story of New Zealand Life.* Crown 8vo, cloth, 5s.

Batley (A. W.) *Etched Studies for Interior Decoration.* Imperial folio, 52s. 6d.

THE BAYARD SERIES.

Edited by the late J. HAIN FRISWELL.

Comprising Pleasure Books of Literature produced in the Choicest Style as Companionable Volumes at Home and Abroad.

"We can hardly imagine better books for boys to read or for men to ponder over."—*Times.*

Price 2s. 6d. *each Volume, complete in itself, flexible cloth extra, gilt edges, with silk Headbands and Registers.*

The Story of the Chevalier Bayard. By M. De Berville.
De Joinville's St. Louis, King of France.
The Essays of Abraham Cowley, including all his Prose Works.
Abdallah ; or, The Four Leaves. By Edouard Laboullaye.
Table-Talk and Opinions of Napoleon Buonaparte.
Vathek : An Oriental Romance. By William Beckford.
Words of Wellington : Maxims and Opinions of the Great Duke.
Dr. Johnson's Rasselas, Prince of Abyssinia. With Notes.
Hazlitt's Round Table. With Biographical Introduction.
The Religio Medici, Hydriotaphia, and the Letter to a Friend. By Sir Thomas Browne, Knt.
Ballad Poetry of the Affections. By Robert Buchanan.

Coleridge's Christabel, and other Imaginative Poems. With Preface by Algernon C. Swinburne.
Lord Chesterfield's Letters, Sentences, and Maxims. With Introduction by the Editor, and Essay on Chesterfield by M. de Ste.-Beuve, of the French Academy.
The King and the Commons. A Selection of Cavalier and Puritan Songs. Edited by Professor Morley.
Essays in Mosaic. By Thos. Ballantyne.
My Uncle Toby ; his Story and his Friends. Edited by P. Fitzgerald.
Reflections ; or, Moral Sentences and Maxims of the Duke de la Rochefoucauld.
Socrates : Memoirs for English Readers from Xenophon's Memorabilia. By Edw. Levien.
Prince Albert's Golden Precepts.

A Case containing 12 *Volumes, price* 31s. 6d.; *or the Case separately, price* 3s. 6d.

Bell (Major) : *Rambla—Spain. From Irun to Cerbere.* Crown 8vo, 8s. 6d.

Beumers' German Copybooks. In six gradations at 4d. each.

Biart (Lucien) Adventures of a Young Naturalist. Edited and adapted by PARKER GILLMORE. With 117 Illustrations on Wood. Post 8vo, cloth extra, gilt edges, New Edition, 7s. 6d.

Bickersteth's Hymnal Companion to Book of Common Prayer may be had in various styles and bindings from 1d. to 21s. *Price List and Prospectus will be forwarded on application.*

Bickersteth (Rev. E. H., M.A.) The Clergyman in his Home. Small post 8vo, 1s.

—— *Evangelical Churchmanship and Evangelical Eclecticism.* 8vo, 1s.

—— *From Year to Year: a Collection of Original Poetical Pieces.* Small post 8vo.

—— *The Master's Home-Call; or, Brief Memorials of Alice* Frances Bickersteth. 20th Thousand. 32mo, cloth gilt, 1s.

—— *The Master's Will.* A Funeral Sermon preached on the Death of Mrs. S. Gurney Buxton. Sewn, 6d. ; cloth gilt, 1s.

—— *The Shadow of the Rock.* A Selection of Religious Poetry. 18mo, cloth extra, 2s. 6d.

—— *The Shadowed Home and the Light Beyond.* 7th Edition, crown 8vo, cloth extra, 5s.

Bilbrough (E. J.) " Twixt France and Spain." [*In the press.*

Biographies of the Great Artists (Illustrated). Crown 8vo, emblematical binding, 3s. 6d. per volume, except where the price is given.

Claude Lorrain.*
Correggio, by M. E. Heaton, 2s. 6d.
Della Robbia and Cellini, 2s. 6d.
Albrecht Dürer, by R. F. Heath.
Figure Painters of Holland.
Fra Angelico, Masaccio, and Botticelli.
Fra Bartolommeo, Albertinelli, and Andrea del Sarto.
Gainsborough and Constable.
Ghiberti and Donatello, 2s. 6d.
Giotto, by Harry Quilter.
Hans Holbein, by Joseph Cundall.
Hogarth, by Austin Dobson.
Landseer, by F. G. Stevens.
Lawrence and Romney, by Lord Ronald Gower, 2s. 6d.
Leonardo da Vinci.
Little Masters of Germany, by W. B. Scott.
Mantegna and Francia.
Meissonier, by J. W. Mollett, 2s. 6d.
Michelangelo Buonarotti, by Clément.
Murillo, by Ellen E. Minor, 2s. 6d.
Overbeck, by J. B. Atkinson.
Raphael, by N. D'Anvers.
Rembrandt, by J. W. Mollett.
Reynolds, by F. S. Pulling.
Rubens, by C. W. Kett.
Tintoretto, by W. R. Osler.
Titian, by R. F. Heath.
Turner, by Cosmo Monkhouse.
Vandyck and Hals, by P. R. Head.
Velasquez, by E. Stowe.
Vernet and Delaroche, by J. R. Rees.
Watteau, by J. W. Mollett, 2s. 6d.
Wilkie, by J. W. Mollett.

* *Not yet published.*

Bird (F. J.) American Practical Dyer's Companion. 8vo, 42*s*.
Bird (H. E.) Chess Practice. 8vo, 2*s*. 6*d*.
Black (Wm.) Novels. See " Low's Standard Library."
Blackburn (Henry) Breton Folk: An Artistic Tour in Brittany.
 With 171 Illustrations by RANDOLPH CALDECOTT. Imperial 8vo, cloth extra, gilt edges, 21*s*.; plainer binding, 10*s*. 6*d*.
—— *Pyrenees (The).* With 100 Illustrations by GUSTAVE DORÉ, corrected to 1881. Crown 8vo, 7*s*. 6*d*.
Blackmore (R. D.) Lorna Doone. Édition de luxe. Crown 4to, very numerous Illustrations, cloth, gilt edges, 31*s*. 6*d*.; parchment, uncut, top gilt, 35*s*. Cheap Edition, small post 8vo, 6*s*.
—— *Novels.* See " Low's Standard Library."
Blaikie (William) How to get Strong and how to Stay so.
 A Manual of Rational, Physical, Gymnastic, and other Exercises. With Illustrations, small post 8vo, 5*s*.
Boats of the World, Depicted and Described by one of the Craft.
 With Coloured Plates, showing every kind of rig, 4to, 3*s*. 6*d*.
Bock (Carl). The Head Hunters of Borneo: Up the Mahakkam, and Down the Barita; also Journeyings in Sumatra. 1 vol., super-royal 8vo, 32 Coloured Plates, cloth extra, 36*s*.
—— *Temples and Elephants.* A Narrative of a Journey through Upper Siam and Lao. With numerous Coloured and other Illustrations, 8vo.
Bonwick (James) First Twenty Years of Australia. Crown 8vo, 5*s*.
—— *Port Philip Settlement.* 8vo, numerous Illustrations, 21*s*.
Borneo. See BOCK.
Bosanquet (Rev. C.) Blossoms from the King's Garden: Sermons for Children. 2nd Edition, small post 8vo, cloth extra, 6*s*.
Boussenard (L.) Crusoes of Guiana; or, the White Tiger.
 Illustrated by J. FERAT. 7*s*. 6*d*.
Boy's Froissart. King Arthur. Mabinogion. Percy. See LANIER.
Bradshaw (J.) New Zealand as it is. 8vo, 12*s*. 6*d*.
Brassey (Lady) Tahiti. With 31 Autotype Illustrations after Photos. by Colonel STUART-WORTLEY. Fcap. 4to, very tastefully bound, 21*s*.
Braune (Wilhelm) Gothic Grammar. Translated by G. H. BULG. 3*s*. 6*d*.

Brisse (Baron) Ménus (366, *one for each day of the year*). Each Ménu is given in French and English, with the recipe for making every dish mentioned. Translated from the French of BARON BRISSE, by Mrs. MATTHEW CLARKE. 2nd Edition. Crown 8vo, 5s.

British Fisheries Directory, 1883-84. Small 8vo, 2s. 6d.

Brittany. See BLACKBURN.

Broglie (Duc de) Frederick II. and Maria Theresa. 2 vols., 8vo, 30s.

Browne (G. Lathom) Narratives of Nineteenth Century State Trials. First Period: From the Union with Ireland to the Death of George IV., 1801—1830. 2nd Edition, 2 vols., crown 8vo, cloth, 26s.

Browne (Lennox) and Behnke (Emil) Voice, Song, and Speech. Medium 8vo, cloth.

Bryant (W. C.) and Gay (S. H.) History of the United States. 4 vols., royal 8vo, profusely Illustrated, 60s.

Bryce (Rev. Professor) Manitoba: its History, Growth, and Present Position. Crown 8vo, with Illustrations and Maps, 7s. 6d.

Bunyan's Pilgrim's Progress. With 138 original Woodcuts. Small post 8vo, cloth gilt, 3s. 6d.

Burnaby (Capt.) On Horseback through Asia Minor. 2 vols., 8vo, 38s. Cheaper Edition, crown 8vo, 10s. 6d.

Burnaby (Mrs. F.) High Alps in Winter; or, Mountaineering in Search of Health. By Mrs. FRED BURNABY. With Portrait of the Authoress, Map, and other Illustrations. Handsomely bound in cloth, 14s.

Butler (W. F.) The Great Lone Land; an Account of the Red River Expedition, 1869-70. With Illustrations and Map. Fifth and Cheaper Edition, crown 8vo, cloth extra, 7s. 6d.

—— *Invasion of England, told twenty years after, by an Old Soldier.* Crown 8vo, 2s. 6d.

—— *Red Cloud; or, the Solitary Sioux.* Imperial 16mo, numerous illustrations, gilt edges, 7s. 6d.

—— *The Wild North Land; the Story of a Winter Journey* with Dogs across Northern North America. Demy 8vo, cloth, with numerous Woodcuts and a Map, 4th Edition, 18s. Cr. 8vo, 7s. 6d.

Buxton (H. J. W.) Painting, English and American. With numerous Illustrations. Crown 8vo, 5s.

CADOGAN (Lady A.) Illustrated Games of Patience.
Twenty-four Diagrams in Colours, with Descriptive Text. Foolscap 4to, cloth extra, gilt edges, 3rd Edition, 12s. 6d.

California. See "Nordhoff."

Cambridge Staircase (A). By the Author of "A Day of my Life at Eton." Small crown 8vo, cloth, 2s. 6d.

Cambridge Trifles; or, Splutterings from an Undergraduate Pen. By the Author of "A Day of my Life at Eton," &c. 16mo, cloth extra, 2s. 6d.

Capello (H.) and Ivens (R.) From Benguella to the Territory of Yacca. Translated by ALFRED ELWES. With Maps and over 130 full-page and text Engravings. 2 vols., 8vo, 42s.

Carleton (W.). See "Rose Library."

Carlyle (T.) Reminiscences of my Irish Journey in 1849. Crown 8vo, 7s. 6d.

Carnegie (A.) American Four-in-Hand in Britain. Small 4to, Illustrated, 10s. 6d.

Chairman's Handbook (The). By R. F. D. PALGRAVE, Clerk of the Table of the House of Commons. 5th Edition, enlarged and re-written, 2s.

Challamel (M. A.) History of Fashion in France. With 21 Plates, coloured by hand, satin-wood binding, imperial 8vo, 28s.

Changed Cross (The), and other Religious Poems. 16mo, 2s. 6d.

Charities of London. See Low's.

Chattock (R. S.) Practical Notes on Etching. Second Edition, 8vo, 7s. 6d.

Chess. See BIRD (H. E.).

China. See COLQUHOUN.

Choice Editions of Choice Books. 2s. 6d. each. Illustrated by C. W. COPE, R.A., T. CRESWICK, R.A., E. DUNCAN, BIRKET FOSTER, J. C. HORSLEY, A.R.A., G. HICKS, R. REDGRAVE, R.A., C. STONEHOUSE, F. TAYLER, G. THOMAS, H. J. TOWNSHEND, E. H. WEHNERT, HARRISON WEIR, &c.

Bloomfield's Farmer's Boy.	Milton's L'Allegro.
Campbell's Pleasures of Hope.	Poetry of Nature. Harrison Weir.
Coleridge's Ancient Mariner.	Rogers' (Sam.) Pleasures of Memory.
Goldsmith's Deserted Village.	Shakespeare's Songs and Sonnets.
Goldsmith's Vicar of Wakefield.	Tennyson's May Queen.
Gray's Elegy in a Churchyard.	Elizabethan Poets.
Keat's Eve of St. Agnes.	Wordsworth's Pastoral Poems.

"Such works are a glorious beatification for a poet."—*Athenæum.*

Christ in Song. By Dr. PHILIP SCHAFF. A New Edition, revised, cloth, gilt edges, 6s.

Chromo-Lithography. See "Audsley."

Cid (Ballads of the). By the Rev. GERRARD LEWIS. Fcap. 8vo, parchment, 2s. 6d.

Clay (Charles M.) Modern Hagar. 2 vols., crown 8vo, 21s. See also "Rose Library."

Colquhoun (A. R.) Across Chrysê; From Canton to Mandalay. With Maps and very numerous Illustrations, 2 vols., 8vo, 42s.

Composers. See "Great Musicians."

Confessions of a Frivolous Girl (The): A Novel of Fashionable Life. Edited by ROBERT GRANT. Crown 8vo, 6s. Paper boards, 1s.

Cook (Dutton) Book of the Play. New and Revised Edition. 1 vol., cloth extra, 3s. 6d.

—— *On the Stage: Studies of Theatrical History and the Actor's Art.* 2 vols., 8vo, cloth, 24s.

Coote (W.) Wanderings South by East. Illustrated, 8vo, 21s. New and Cheaper Edition, 10s. 6d.

—— *Western Pacific.* Illustrated, crown 8vo, 2s. 6d.

Costume. See SMITH (J. MOYR).

Cruise of the Walnut Shell (The). An instructive and amusing Story, told in Rhyme, for Children. With 32 Coloured Plates. Square fancy boards, 5s.

Curtis (C. B.) Velazquez and Murillo. With Etchings &c., Royal 8vo, 31s. 6d.; large paper, 63s.

Cutcliffe (H. C.) Trout Fishing in Rapid Streams. Cr. 8vo, 3s. 6d.

*D*ANVERS (N.) *An Elementary History of Art.* Crown 8vo, 10s. 6d.

—— *Elementary History of Music.* Crown 8vo, 2s. 6d.

—— *Handbooks of Elementary Art—Architecture; Sculpture; Old Masters; Modern Painting.* Crown 8vo, 3s. 6d. each.

Day of My Life (A); or, Every-Day Experiences at Eton. By an ETON BOY, Author of "About Some Fellows." 16mo, cloth extra, 2s. 6d. 6th Thousand.

Day's Collacon: an Encyclopædia of Prose Quotations. Imperial 8vo, cloth, 31s. 6d.

Decoration. Vol. II., folio, 6s. Vols. III., IV., V., and VI., New Series, folio, 7s. 6d. each.

—— See also BATLEY.

De Leon (E.) Egypt under its Khedives. With Map and Illustrations. Crown 8vo, 4s.

Don Quixote, Wit and Wisdom of. By EMMA THOMPSON. Square fcap. 8vo, 3s. 6d.

Donnelly (Ignatius) Atlantis; or, the Antediluvian World. Crown 8vo, 12s. 6d.

—— *Ragnarok: The Age of Fire and Gravel.* Illustrated, Crown 8vo, 12s. 6d.

Dos Passos (J. R.) Law of Stockbrokers and Stock Exchanges. 8vo, 35s.

Dougall (James Dalziel, F.S.A., F.Z.A.) Shooting: its Appliances, Practice, and Purpose. New Edition, revised with additions. Crown 8vo, cloth extra, 7s. 6d.

"The book is admirable in every way. . . . . We wish it every success."—*Globe.*
"A very complete treatise. . . . . Likely to take high rank as an authority on shooting."—*Daily News.*

Drama. See ARCHER, COOK (DUTTON), WILLIAMS (M.).

Durnford (Col. A. W.) A Soldier's Life and Work in South Africa, 1872-9. 8vo, 14s.

Dyeing. See BIRD (F. J.).

EDUCATIONAL Works published in Great Britain. Classified Catalogue. Second Edition, revised and corrected, 8vo, cloth extra, 5s.

Egypt. See "De Leon," "Foreign Countries," "Senior."

Eidlitz (Leopold) Nature and Functions of Art (The); and especially of Architecture. Medium 8vo, cloth, 21s.

Electricity. See GORDON.

Emerson Birthday Book. Extracts from the Writings of R. W. Emerson. Square 16mo, cloth extra, numerous Illustrations, very choice binding, 3s. 6d.

Emerson (R. W.) Life. By G. W. COOKE. Crown 8vo, 8s. 6d.

English Catalogue of Books. Vol. III., 1872—1880. Royal 8vo, half-morocco, 42s.

English Philosophers. Edited by E. B. IVAN MÜLLER, M.A.

A series intended to give a concise view of the works and lives of English thinkers. Crown 8vo volumes of 180 or 200 pp., price 3s. 6d. each.

Francis Bacon, by Thomas Fowler.
Milton, by W. H. S. Monck.
*ley and James Mill, by G. S. *er.

*John Stuart Mill, by Miss Helen Taylor.
Shaftesbury and Hutcheson, by Professor Fowler.
Adam Smith, by J. A. Farrer.

* *Not yet published.*

Episodes in the Life of an Indian Chaplain. Crown 8vo, cloth extra, 12s. 6d.

Episodes of French History. Edited, with Notes, Maps, and Illustrations, by GUSTAVE MASSON, B.A. Small 8vo, 2s. 6d. each.
1. Charlemagne and the Carlovingians.
2. Louis XI. and the Crusades.
3. Part I. Francis I. and Charles V.
   ,, II. Francis I. and the Renaissance.
4. Henry IV. and the End of the Wars of Religion.

Esmarch (*Dr. Friedrich*) *Handbook on the Treatment of Wounded in War.* Numerous Coloured Plates and Illustrations, 8vo, strongly bound, 1l. 8s.

Etcher (*The*). Containing 36 Examples of the Original Etched-work of Celebrated Artists, amongst others: BIRKET FOSTER, J. E. HODGSON, R.A., COLIN HUNTER, J. P. HESELTINE, ROBERT W. MACBETH, R. S. CHATTOCK, &c. Vols. for 1881 and 1882, imperial 4to, cloth extra, gilt edges, 2l. 12s. 6d. each.

Etching. See BATLEY, CHATTOCK.

Etchings (*Modern*) *of Celebrated Paintings.* 4to, 31s. 6d.

FARM Ballads, Festivals, and Legends. See " Rose Library."

Fashion (*History of*). See "Challamel."

Fawcett (*Edgar*) *A Gentleman of Leisure.* 1s.

Fechner (*G. T.*) *On Life after Death.* 12mo, vellum, 2s. 6d.

Felkin (*R. W.*) *and Wilson* (*Rev. C. T.*) *Uganda and the Egyptian Soudan.* With Map, numerous Illustrations, and Notes. By R. W. FELKIN, F.R.G.S., &c., &c.; and the Rev. C. T. WILSON, M.A. Oxon., F.R.G.S. 2 vols., crown 8vo, cloth, 28s.

Fenn (*G. Manville*) *Off to the Wilds: A Story for Boys.* Profusely Illustrated. Crown 8vo, 7s. 6d.

Ferguson (*John*) *Ceylon in* 1883. With numerous Illustrations. Crown 8vo.

Ferns. See HEATH.

Fields (*J. T.*) *Yesterdays with Authors.* New Ed., 8vo., 16s.

Florence. See "Yriarte."

Flowers of Shakespeare. 32 beautifully Coloured Plates, with the passages which refer to the flowers. Small 4to, 5s.

Foreign Countries and British Colonies. A series of Descriptive Handbooks. Each volume will be the work of a writer who has special acquaintance with the subject. Crown 8vo, 3s. 6d. each.

Australia, by J. F. Vesey Fitzgerald.
Austria, by D. Kay, F.R.G.S.
*Canada, by W. Fraser Rae.
Denmark and Iceland, by E.C.Otté.
Egypt, by S. Lane Poole, B.A.
France, by Miss M. Roberts.
Germany, by S. Baring-Gould.
Greece, by L. Sergeant, B.A.
*Holland, by R. L. Poole.
Japan, by S. Mossman.
*New Zealand.
*Persia, by Major-Gen. Sir F. Goldsmid.
Peru, by Clements R. Markham, C.B.
Russia, by W. R. Morfill, M.A.
Spain, by Rev. Wentworth Webster.
Sweden and Norway, by F. H. Woods.
*Switzerland, by W. A. P. Coolidge, M.A.
*Turkey-in-Asia, by J. C. McCoan, M.P.
West Indies, by C. H. Eden, F.R.G.S.

* *Not ready yet.*

Fortunes made in Business. 2 vols., demy 8vo, cloth, 32s.

Franc (Maud Jeanne). The following form one Series, small post 8vo, in uniform cloth bindings, with gilt edges:—

Emily's Choice. 5s.
Hall's Vineyard. 4s.
John's Wife: A Story of Life in South Australia. 4s.
Marian; or, The Light of Some One's Home. 5s.
Silken Cords and Iron Fetters. 4s.
Vermont Vale. 5s.
Minnie's Mission. 4s.
Little Mercy. 4s.
Beatrice Melton's Discipline. 4s.
No Longer a Child. 4s.
Golden Gifts. 4s.
Two Sides to Every Question. 4s.

Francis (F.) War, Waves, and Wanderings, including a Cruise in the "Lancashire Witch." 2 vols., crown 8vo, cloth extra, 24s.

Frederick the Great. See "Broglie."

French. See "Julien."

Froissart. See "Lanier."

GENTLE Life (Queen Edition). 2 vols. in 1, small 4to, 6s.

THE GENTLE LIFE SERIES.

Price 6s. each; or in calf extra, price 10s. 6d.; Smaller Edition, cloth extra, 2s. 6d., except where price is named.

The Gentle Life. Essays in aid of the Formation of Character of Gentlemen and Gentlewomen.

About in the World. Essays by Author of "The Gentle Life."

Like unto Christ. A New Translation of Thomas à Kempis' "De Imitatione Christi."

Familiar Words. An Index Verborum, or Quotation Handbook. 6s.

Essays by Montaigne. Edited and Annotated by the Author of "The Gentle Life."

The Gentle Life. 2nd Series.

The Silent Hour: Essays, Original and Selected. By the Author of "The Gentle Life."

Half-Length Portraits. Short Studies of Notable Persons. By J. HAIN FRISWELL.

Essays on English Writers, for the Self-improvement of Students in English Literature.

Other People's Windows. By J. HAIN FRISWELL. 6s.

A Man's Thoughts. By J. HAIN FRISWELL.

The Countess of Pembroke's Arcadia. By Sir PHILIP SIDNEY. New Edition, 6s.

George Eliot: a Critical Study of her Life. By G. W. COOKE. Crown 8vo, 10s. 6d.

German. See BEUMER.

Germany. By S. BARING-GOULD. Crown 8vo, 3s. 6d.

Gibbs (J. R.) British Honduras, Historical and Descriptive. Crown 8vo, 7s. 6d.

Gilder (W. H.) Ice-Pack and Tundra. An Account of the Search for the "Jeannette." 8vo, 18s.

—— *Schwatka's Search.* Sledging in quest of the Franklin Records. Illustrated, 8vo, 12s. 6d.

Gilpin's Forest Scenery. Edited by F. G. HEATH. Large post 8vo, with numerous Illustrations. Uniform with "The Fern World," re-issued, 7s. 6d.

Glas (John) The Lord's Supper. Crown 8vo, 5s.

Gordon (J. E. H., B.A. Cantab.) Four Lectures on Electric Induction. Delivered at the Royal Institution, 1878-9. With numerous Illustrations. Cloth limp, square 16mo, 3s.

—— *Electric Lighting.* [*In preparation.*

—— *Physical Treatise on Electricity and Magnetism.* New Edition, revised and enlarged, with coloured, full-page, and other Illustrations. 2 vols., 8vo, 42s.

Gouffé. The Royal Cookery Book. By JULES GOUFFÉ; translated and adapted for English use by ALPHONSE GOUFFÉ, Head Pastrycook to Her Majesty the Queen. Illustrated with large plates printed in colours. 161 Woodcuts, 8vo, cloth extra, gilt edges, 42s.

—— Domestic Edition, half-bound, 10s. 6d.

Great Artists. See "Biographies."

Great Historic Galleries of England (*The*). Edited by LORD RONALD GOWER, F.S.A., Trustee of the National Portrait Gallery. Illustrated by 24 large and carefully executed *permanent* Photographs of some of the most celebrated Pictures by the Great Masters. Vol. I., imperial 4to, cloth extra, gilt edges, 36s. Vol. II., with 36 large permanent photographs, 2l. 12s. 6d.

Great Musicians. Edited by F. HUEFFER. A Series of Biographies, crown 8vo, 3s. each :—

Bach.	Handel.	Purcell.
*Beethoven.	*Haydn.	Rossini.
*Berlioz.	*Marcello.	Schubert.
English Church Composers. By BARETT.	Mendelssohn.	*Schumann.
	Mozart.	Richard Wagner.
*Gluck.	*Palestrina.	Weber.

* *In preparation.*

Grohmann (W. A. B.) Camps in the Rockies. 8vo, 12s. 6d.

Guizot's History of France. Translated by ROBERT BLACK. Super-royal 8vo, very numerous Full-page and other Illustrations. In 8 vols., cloth extra, gilt, each 24s. This work is re-issued in cheaper binding, 8 vols., at 10s. 6d. each.

"It supplies a want which has long been felt, and ought to be in the hands of all students of history."—*Times.*

—————— *Masson's School Edition.* The History of France from the Earliest Times to the Outbreak of the Revolution; abridged from the Translation by Robert Black, M.A., with Chronological Index, Historical and Genealogical Tables, &c. By Professor GUSTAVE MASSON, B.A., Assistant Master at Harrow School. With 24 full-page Portraits, and many other Illustrations. 1 vol., demy 8vo, 600 pp., cloth extra, 10s. 6d.

Guizot's History of England. In 3 vols. of about 500 pp. each, containing 60 to 70 Full-page and other Illustrations, cloth extra, gilt, 24s. each; re-issue in cheaper binding, 10s. 6d. each.

"For luxury of typography, plainness of print, and beauty of illustration, these volumes, of which but one has as yet appeared in English, will hold their own against any production of an age so luxurious as our own in everything, typography not excepted."—*Times.*

Guyon (Mde.) Life. By UPHAM. 6th Edition, crown 8vo, 6s.

HALL (W. W.) How to Live Long; or, 1408 *Health Maxims,* Physical, Mental, and Moral. By W. W. HALL, A.M., M.D. Small post 8vo, cloth, 2s. 2nd Edition.

Harper's Christmas No., 1882. Elephant folio, 2s. 6d.

Harper's Monthly Magazine. Published Monthly. 160 pages, fully Illustrated. 1s.
    Vol. I. December, 1880, to May, 1881.
    ,, II. June to November, 1881.
    ,, III. December, 1881, to May, 1882.
    ,, IV. June to November, 1882.
    ,, V. December, 1882, to May, 1883.
Super-royal 8vo, 8s. 6d. each.

"'Harper's Magazine' is so thickly sown with excellent illustrations that to count them would be a work of time; not that it is a picture magazine, for the engravings illustrate the text after the manner seen in some of our choicest *éditions de luxe.*"—*St. James's Gazette.*
"It is so pretty, so big, and so cheap. . . . An extraordinary shillingsworth—160 large octavo pages, with over a score of articles, and more than three times as many illustrations."—*Edinburgh Daily Review.*
"An amazing shillingsworth . . . combining choice literature of both nations."—*Nonconformist.*

Hatton (Joseph) Journalistic London: with Engravings and Portraits of Distinguished Writers of the Day. Fcap. 4to, 12s. 6d.

—— *Three Recruits, and the Girls they left behind them.* Small post 8vo, 6s.
"It hurries us along in unflagging excitement."—*Times.*

—— See also "Low's Standard Novels."

Heath (Francis George). Autumnal Leaves. New Edition, with Coloured Plates in Facsimile from Nature. Crown 8vo, 14s.

—— *Burnham Beeches.* Illustrated, small 8vo, 1s.

—— *Fern Paradise.* New Edition, with Plates and Photos., crown 8vo, 12s. 6d.

—— *Fern World.* With Nature-printed Coloured Plates. New Edition, crown 8vo, 12s. 6d.

—— *Gilpin's Forest Scenery.* Illustrated, 8vo, 12s. 6d.; New Edition, 7s. 6d.

—— *Our Woodland Trees.* With Coloured Plates and Engravings. Small 8vo, 12s. 6d.

—— *Peasant Life in the West of England.* Crown 8vo, 10s. 6d.

—— *Sylvan Spring.* With Coloured, &c., Illustrations. 12s. 6d.

—— *Trees and Ferns.* Illustrated, crown 8vo, 3s. 6d.

—— *Where to Find Ferns.* Crown 8vo, 2s.

Heber (Bishop) Hymns. Illustrated Edition. With upwards of 100 beautiful Engravings. Small 4to, handsomely bound, 7s. 6d. Morocco, 18s. 6d. and 21s. New and Cheaper Edition, cloth, 3s. 6d.

Heldmann (Bernard) Mutiny on Board the Ship "Leander."
Small post 8vo, gilt edges, numerous Illustrations, 7s. 6d.

Henty (G. A.) Winning his Spurs. Numerous Illustrations. Crown 8vo, 5s.

—— *Cornet of Horse : A Story for Boys.* Illustrated, crown 8vo, 5s.

—— *Jack Archer: Tale of the Crimea.* Illust., crown 8vo, 5s.

Herrick (Robert) Poetry. Preface by AUSTIN DOBSON. With numerous Illustrations by E. A. ABBEY. 4to, gilt edges, 42s.

History and Principles of Weaving by Hand and by Power. With several hundred Illustrations. By ALFRED BARLOW. Royal 8vo, cloth extra, 1l. 5s. Second Edition.

Hitchman (Francis) Public Life of the Right Hon. Benjamin Disraeli, Earl of Beaconsfield. New Edition, with Portrait. Crown 8vo, 3s. 6d.

Hole (Rev. Canon) Nice and Her Neighbours. Small 4to, with numerous choice Illustrations, 12s. 6d.

Holmes (O. W.) The Poetical Works of Oliver Wendell Holmes. In 2 vols., 18mo, exquisitely printed, and chastely bound in limp cloth, gilt tops, 10s. 6d.

Hoppus (J. D.) Riverside Papers. 2 vols., 12s.

Hovgaard (A.) See "Nordenskiöld's Voyage." 8vo, 21s.

Hugo (Victor) "Ninety-Three." Illustrated. Crown 8vo, 6s

—— *Toilers of the Sea.* Crown 8vo, fancy boards, 2s.

—— *and his Times.* Translated from the French of A. BARBOU by ELLEN E. FREWER. 120 Illustrations, many of them from designs by Victor Hugo himself. Super-royal 8vo, cloth extra, 24s.

—— *History of a Crime (The); Deposition of an Eye-witness.* The Story of the Coup d'État. Crown 8vo, 6s.

Hundred Greatest Men (The). 8 portfolios, 21s. each, or 4 vols., half-morocco, gilt edges, 10 guineas.

Hutchinson (Thos.) Diary and Letters. Demy 8vo, cloth, 16s.

Hutchisson (W. H.) Pen and Pencil Sketches: Eighteen Years in Bengal. 8vo, 18s.

Hygiene and Public Health (A Treatise on). Edited by A. H. BUCK, M.D. Illustrated by numerous Wood Engravings. In 2 royal 8vo vols., cloth, 42s.

Hymnal Companion of Common Prayer. See BICKERSTETH.

ILLUSTRATED Text-Books of Art-Education. Edited by EDWARD J. POYNTER, R.A. Each Volume contains numerous Illustrations, and is strongly bound for the use of Students, price 5s. The Volumes now ready are:—

PAINTING.

Classic and Italian. By PERCY R. HEAD.
German, Flemish, and Dutch.

French and Spanish.
English and American.

ARCHITECTURE.

Classic and Early Christian.
Gothic and Renaissance. By T. ROGER SMITH.

SCULPTURE.

Antique: Egyptian and Greek. | Renaissance and Modern.
Italian Sculptors of the 14th and 15th Centuries.

ORNAMENT.

Decoration in Colour. | Architectural Ornament.

Irving (Washington). Complete Library Edition of his Works in 27 Vols., Copyright, Unabridged, and with the Author's Latest Revisions, called the "Geoffrey Crayon" Edition, handsomely printed in large square 8vo, on superfine laid paper. Each volume, of about 500 pages, fully Illustrated. 12s. 6d. per vol. *See also* "Little Britain."

———————————— ("American Men of Letters.") 2s. 6d.

JAMES (C.) Curiosities of Law and Lawyers. 8vo, 7s. 6d.

Japan. See AUDSLEY.

Jarves (J. J.) Italian Rambles. Square 16mo, 5s.

Johnson (O.) W. Lloyd Garrison and his Times. Crown 8vo, 12s. 6d.

Jones (Major) The Emigrants' Friend. A Complete Guide to the United States. New Edition. 2s. 6d.

Jones (Mrs. Herbert) Sandringham: Past and Present. Illustrated, crown 8vo, 8s. 6d.

Julien (F.) English Student's French Examiner. 16mo. 2s.

—— *First Lessons in Conversational French Grammar.* Crown 8vo, 1s.

—— *Conversational French Reader.* 16mo, cloth, 2s. 6d.

—— *Petites Leçons de Conversation et de Grammaire.* New Edition, 3s. 6d.; without Phrases, 2s. 6d.

—— *Phrases of Daily Use.* Limp cloth, 6d.

Jung (Sir Salar) Life of. [*In the press*

KEMPIS (Thomas à) Daily Text-Book. Square 16mo, 2s. 6d.; interleaved as a Birthday Book, 3s. 6d.
Kingston (W. H. G.) Dick Cheveley. Illustrated, 16mo, gilt edges, 7s. 6d.; plainer binding, plain edges, 5s.
—— —— *Fresh and Salt Water Tutors: A Story.* 3s. 6d.
—— —— *Heir of Kilfinnan.* Uniform, 7s. 6d.; also 5s.
—— —— *Snow-Shoes and Canoes.* Uniform, 7s. 6d.; also 5s.
—— —— *Two Supercargoes.* Uniform, 7s. 6d.; also 5s.
—— —— *With Axe and Rifle.* Uniform, 7s. 6d.; also 5s.
Knight (E. F.) Albania and Montenegro. Illust. 8vo. 12s. 6d.
Knight (E. J.) The Cruise of the "Falcon." A Voyage round the World in a 30-Ton Yacht. Numerous Illust. 2 vols., crown 8vo.

LAMBERT (O.) Angling Literature in England; and Descriptions of Fishing by the Ancients. With a Notice of some Books on other Piscatorial Subjects. Fcap. 8vo, vellum, top gilt, 3s. 6d.
Lanier (Sidney) The Boy's Froissart, selected from the Chronicles of England, France, and Spain. Illustrated, extra binding, gilt edges, crown 8vo, 7s. 6d.
—— —— *Boy's King Arthur.* Uniform, 7s. 6d.
—— —— *Boy's Mabinogion; Original Welsh Legends of King* Arthur. Uniform, 7s. 6d.
—— —— *Boy's Percy: Ballads of Love and Adventure,* selected from the "Reliques." Uniform, 7s. 6d.
Lansdell (H.) Through Siberia. 2 vols., demy 8vo, 30s.; New Edition, very numerous illustrations, 8vo, 10s. 6d.
Larden (W.) School Course on Heat. Second Edition, Illustrated, crown 8vo, 5s.
Lathrop (G. P.) In the Distance. 2 vols., crown 8vo, 21s.
Legal Profession: Romantic Stories. 7s. 6d.
Lennard (T. B.) To Married Women and Women about to ': Married, &c. 6d.
Lenormant (F.) Beginnings of History. Crown 8vo, 12s. 6d.
Leonardo da Vinci's Literary Works. Edited by Dr. JEAN PAUL RICHTER. Containing his Writings on Painting, Sculpture, and Architecture, his Philosophical Maxims, Humorous Writings, and Miscellaneous Notes on Personal Events, on his Contemporaries, on Literature, &c.; for the first time published from Autograph Manuscripts. By J. P. RICHTER, Ph.Dr., Hon. Member of the Royal and Imperial Academy of Rome, &c. 2 vols., imperial 8vo, containing about 200 Drawings in Autotype Reproductions, and numerous other Illustrations. Twelve Guineas.

Leyland (R. W.) Holiday in South Africa. Crown 8vo, 12s. 6d.

Library of Religious Poetry. A Collection of the Best Poems of all Ages and Tongues. Edited by PHILIP SCHAFF, D.D., LL.D., and ARTHUR GILMAN, M.A. Royal 8vo, 1036 pp., cloth extra, gilt edges, 21s.; re-issue in cheaper binding, 10s. 6d.

Lindsay (W. S.) History of Merchant Shipping and Ancient Commerce. Over 150 Illustrations, Maps, and Charts. In 4 vols., demy 8vo, cloth extra. Vols. 1 and 2, 11s. each; vols. 3 and 4, 14s. each. 4 vols. complete, 50s.

Lillie (Lucy E.) Prudence: a Story of Æsthetic London. Small 8vo, 5s.

Little Britain; together with *The Spectre Bridegroom*, and *A Legend of Sleepy Hollow.* By WASHINGTON IRVING. An entirely New *Edition de luxe*, specially suitable for Presentation. Illustrated by 120 very fine Engravings on Wood, by Mr. J. D. COOPER. Designed by Mr. CHARLES O. MURRAY. Re-issue, square crown 8vo, cloth, 6s.

Logan (Sir William E.) Life. By BERNARD J. HARRINGTON. 8vo, 12s. 6d.

Long (Mrs. W. H. C.) Peace and War in the Transvaal. 12mo, 3s. 6d.

Low's Standard Library of Travel and Adventure. Crown 8vo, bound uniformly in cloth extra, price 7s. 6d., except where price is given.

1. The Great Lone Land. By Major W. F. BUTLER, C.B.
2. The Wild North Land. By Major W. F. BUTLER, C.B.'
3. How I found Livingstone. By H. M. STANLEY.
4. Through the Dark Continent. By H. M. STANLEY. 12s. 6d.
5. The Threshold of the Unknown Region. By C. R. MARKHAM. (4th Edition, with Additional Chapters, 10s. 6d.)
6. Cruise of the Challenger. By W. J. J. SPRY, R.N.
7. Burnaby's On Horseback through Asia Minor. 10s. 6d.
8. Schweinfurth's Heart of Africa. 2 vols., 15s.
9. Marshall's Through America.
10. Lansdell's Through Siberia. Illustrated and unabridged, 10s. 6d.

Low's Standard Novels. Small post 8vo, cloth extra, 6s. each, unless otherwise stated.

Work. A Story of Experience. By LOUISA M. ALCOTT.
A Daughter of Heth. By W. BLACK.
In Silk Attire. By W. BLACK.
Kilmeny. A Novel. By W. BLACK.

Low's Standard Novels—continued.

Lady Silverdale's Sweetheart. By W. BLACK.
Sunrise. By W. BLACK.
Three Feathers. By WILLIAM BLACK.
Alice Lorraine. By R. D. BLACKMORE.
Christowell, a Dartmoor Tale. By R. D. BLACKMORE.
Clara Vaughan. By R. D. BLACKMORE.
Cradock Nowell. By R. D. BLACKMORE.
Cripps the Carrier. By R. D. BLACKMORE.
Erema; or, My Father's Sin. By R. D. BLACKMORE.
Lorna Doone. By R. D. BLACKMORE.
Mary Anerley. By R. D. BLACKMORE.
An English Squire. By Miss COLERIDGE.
Mistress Judith. A Cambridgeshire Story. By C. C. FRASER-TYTLER.
A Story of the Dragonnades; or, Asylum Christi. By the Rev. E. GILLIAT, M.A.
A Laodicean. By THOMAS HARDY.
Far from the Madding Crowd. By THOMAS HARDY
The Hand of Ethelberta. By THOMAS HARDY.
The Trumpet Major. By THOMAS HARDY.
Two on a Tower. By THOMAS HARDY.
Three Recruits. By JOSEPH HATTON.
A Golden Sorrow. By Mrs. CASHEL HOEY. New Edition.
Out of Court. By Mrs. CASHEL HOEY.
History of a Crime: The Story of the Coup d'État. VICTOR HUGO.
Ninety-Three. By VICTOR HUGO. Illustrated.
Adela Cathcart. By GEORGE MAC DONALD.
Guild Court. By GEORGE MAC DONALD.
Mary Marston. By GEORGE MAC DONALD.
Stephen Archer. New Edition of "Gifts." By GEORGE MAC DONALD.
The Vicar's Daughter. By GEORGE MAC DONALD.
Weighed and Wanting. By GEORGE MAC DONALD.
Diane. By Mrs. MACQUOID.
Elinor Dryden. By Mrs. MACQUOID.
My Lady Greensleeves. By HELEN MATHERS.
John Holdsworth. By W. CLARK RUSSELL.
A Sailor's Sweetheart. By W. CLARK RUSSELL.

List of Publications.

Wreck of the Grosvenor. By W. CLARK RUSSELL.
The Lady Maud. By W. CLARK RUSSELL.
Little Loo. By W. CLARK RUSSELL.
My Wife and I. By Mrs. BEECHER STOWE.
Poganuc People, Their Loves and Lives. By Mrs. B. STOWE.
Ben Hur: a Tale of the Christ. By LEW. WALLACE.
Anne. By CONSTANCE FENIMORE WOOLSON.
For the Major. By CONSTANCE FENIMORE WOOLSON. 5s.

Low's Handbook to the Charities of London (Annual). Edited and revised to date by C. MACKESON, F.S.S., Editor of "A Guide to the Churches of London and its Suburbs," &c. Paper, 1s.; cloth, 1s. 6d.

McCORMICK (R., R.N.). Voyages of Discovery in the Arctic and Antarctic Seas in the "Erebus" and "Terror," in Search of Sir John Franklin, &c., with Autobiographical Notice by R. McCORMICK, R.N., who was Medical Officer to each Expedition. With Maps and very numerous Lithographic and other Illustrations. 2 vols., royal 8vo, 52s. 6d.

Macdonald (A.) "Our Sceptred Isle" and its World-wide Empire. Small post 8vo, cloth, 4s.

MacDonald (G.) Orts. Small post 8vo, 6s.

—— See also "Low's Standard Novels."

Macgregor (John) "Rob Roy" on the Baltic. 3rd Edition, small post 8vo, 2s. 6d.; cloth, gilt edges, 3s. 6d.

—— *A Thousand Miles in the "Rob Roy" Canoe.* 11th Edition, small post 8vo, 2s. 6d.; cloth, gilt edges, 3s. 6d.

—— *Description of the "Rob Roy" Canoe.* Plans, &c., 1s.

—— *Voyage Alone in the Yawl "Rob Roy."* New Edition, thoroughly revised, with additions, small post 8vo, 5s.; boards, 2s. 6d.

Macquoid (Mrs.). See LOW'S STANDARD NOVELS.

Magazine. See DECORATION, ETCHER, HARPER, UNION JACK.

Magyarland. A Narrative of Travels through the Snowy Car- pathians, and Great Alföld of the Magyar. By a Fellow of the Carpathian Society (Diploma of 1881), and Author of "The Indian Alps." 2 vols., 8vo, cloth extra, with about 120 Woodcuts from the Author's own sketches and drawings, 38s.

Manitoba. See RAE.

Maria Theresa. See BROGLIE.

Marked "In Haste." A Story of To-day. Crown 8vo, 8s. 6d.

Markham (Admiral) A Naval Career during the Old War.
8vo, cloth, 14s.

Markham (C. R.) The Threshold of the Unknown Region.
Crown 8vo, with Four Maps, 4th Edition. Cloth extra, 10s. 6d.

—— *War between Peru and Chili*, 1879-1881. Crown 8vo, with four Maps, &c. Third Edition. 10s. 6d. See also "Foreign Countries."

Marshall (W. G.) Through America. New Edition, crown 8vo, with about 100 Illustrations, 7s. 6d.

Martin (J. W.) Float Fishing and Spinning in the Nottingham Style. Crown 8vo, 2s. 6d.

Marvin (Charles) Russian Advance towards India. 8vo, 16s.

Maury (Commander) Physical Geography of the Sea, and its Meteorology. Being a Reconstruction and Enlargement of his former Work, with Charts and Diagrams. New Edition, crown 8vo, 6s.

Men of Mark: a Gallery of Contemporary Portraits of the most Eminent Men of the Day taken from Life, especially for this publication Complete in Seven Vols., handsomely bound, cloth, gilt edges, 25s. each.

Mendelssohn Family (The), 1729—1847. From Letters and Journals. Translated from the German of SEBASTIAN HENSEL. 3rd Edition, 2 vols., 8vo, 30s.

Mendelssohn. See also "Great Musicians."

Mitford (Mary Russell) Our Village. Illustrated with Frontispiece Steel Engraving, and 12 full-page and 157 smaller Cuts. Crown 4to, cloth, gilt edges, 21s.; cheaper binding, 10s. 6d.

Mollett (J. W.) Illustrated Dictionary of Words used in Art and Archæology. Explaining Terms frequently used in Works on Architecture, Arms, Bronzes, Christian Art, Colour, Costume, Decoration, Devices, Emblems, Heraldry, Lace, Personal Ornaments, Pottery, Painting, Sculpture, &c., with their Derivations. Illustrated with 600 Wood Engravings. Small 4to, strongly bound in cloth, 15s.

Morley (H.) English Literature in the Reign of Victoria. The 2000th volume of the Tauchnitz Collection of Authors. 18mo, 2s. 6d.

Muller (E.) Noble Words and Noble Deeds. Containing many Full-page Illustrations by PHILIPPOTEAUX. Square imperial 16mo, cloth extra, 7s. 6d.; plainer binding, plain edges, 5s.

Music. See "Great Musicians."

NEWBIGGIN'S Sketches and Tales. 18mo, 4s.

New Child's Play (A). Sixteen Drawings by E. V. B. Beautifully printed in colours, 4to, cloth extra, 12s. 6d.

New Zealand. See BRADSHAW.

Newfoundland. See RAE.

Norbury (Henry F.) Naval Brigade in South Africa. Crown 8vo, cloth extra, 10s. 6d.

Nordenskiöld's Voyage around Asia and Europe. A Popular Account of the North-East Passage of the "Vega." By Lieut. A. HOVGAARD, of the Royal Danish Navy, and member of the "Vega" Expedition. 8vo, with about 50 Illustrations and 3 Maps, 21s.

Nordhoff (C.) California, for Health, Pleasure, and Residence. New Edition, 8vo, with Maps and Illustrations, 12s. 6d.

Northern Fairy Tales. Translated by H. L. BRAEKSTAD. 5s.

Nothing to Wear; and Two Millions. By W. A. BUTLER New Edition. Small post 8vo, in stiff coloured wrapper, 1s.

Nursery Playmates (Prince of). 217 Coloured Pictures for Children by eminent Artists. Folio, in coloured boards, 6s.

O'BRIEN (P. B.) Fifty Years of Concessions to Ireland. 8vo.

—— *Irish Land Question, and English Question.* New Edition, fcap. 8vo, 2s.

Our Little Ones in Heaven. Edited by the Rev. H. ROBBINS. With Frontispiece after Sir JOSHUA REYNOLDS. Fcap., cloth extra, New Edition—the 3rd, with Illustrations, 5s.

Outlines of Ornament in all Styles. A Work of Reference for the Architect, Art Manufacturer, Decorative Artist, and Practical Painter. By W. and G. A. AUDSLEY, Fellows of the Royal Institute of British Architects. Only a limited number have been printed and the stones destroyed. Small folio, 60 plates, with introductory text, cloth gilt, 31s. 6d.

Owen (Douglas) Marine Insurance Notes and Clauses. 10s. 6d.

PALGRAVE (R. F. D.). See "Chairman's Handbook."

Palliser (Mrs.) A History of Lace, from the Earliest Period.
A New and Revised Edition, with additional cuts and text, upwards of 100 Illustrations and coloured Designs. 1 vol., 8vo, 1*l*. 1*s*.

—— *Historic Devices, Badges, and War Cries.* 8vo, 1*l*. 1*s*.

—— *The China Collector's Pocket Companion.* With upwards of 1000 Illustrations of Marks and Monograms. 2nd Edition, with Additions. Small post 8vo, limp cloth, 5*s*.

Perseus, the Gorgon Slayer. Numerous coloured Plates, square 8vo, 5*s*.

Pharmacopœia of the United States of America. 8vo, 21*s*.

Photography (History and Handbook of). See TISSANDIER.

Pinto (Major Serpa) How I Crossed Africa: from the Atlantic to the Indian Ocean, Through Unknown Countries ; Discovery of the Great Zambesi Affluents, &c.—Vol. I., The King's Rifle. Vol. II., The Coillard Family. With 24 full-page and 118 half-page and smaller Illustrations, 13 small Maps, and 1 large one. 2 vols., demy 8vo, cloth extra, 42*s*.

Pocock. See ARNOLD (G. M.).

Poe (E. A.) The Raven. Illustrated by GUSTAVE DORÉ. Imperial folio, cloth, 63*s*.

Poems of the Inner Life. Chiefly from Modern Authors. Small 8vo, 5*s*.

Polar Expeditions. See KOLDEWEY, MARKHAM, MACGAHAN, NARES, NORDENSKIÖLD, GILDER, MCCORMICK.

Politics and Life in Mars. 12mo, 2*s*. 6*d*.

Powell (W.) Wanderings in a Wild Country; or, Three Years among the Cannibals of New Britain. Demy 8vo, Map and numerous Illustrations, 18*s*.

Prisons, Her Majesty's, their Effects and Defects. New and cheaper Edition, 6*s*.

Poynter (Edward J., R.A.). See "Illustrated Text-books."

Publishers' Circular (The), and General Record of British and Foreign Literature. Published on the 1st and 15th of every Month, 3*d*.

List of Publications. 23

RAE (*W. Fraser*) *From Newfoundland to Manitoba ;* a Guide through Canada's Maritime, Mining, and Prairie Provinces. With Maps. Crown 8vo, 6s.

Rambaud (A.) History of Russia. 2 vols., 8vo, 36s.

Reber (F.) History of Ancient Art. 8vo, 18s.

Redford (G.) Ancient Sculpture. Crown 8vo, 5s.

Reid (T. W.) Land of the Bey. Post 8vo, 10s. 6d.

Rémusat (Madame de), Memoirs of, 1802—1808. By her Grandson, M. PAUL DE RÉMUSAT, Senator. Translated by Mrs. CASHEL HOEY and Mr. JOHN LILLIE. 4th Edition, cloth extra. 2 vols., 8vo, 32s.

——— *Selection from the Letters of Madame de Rémusat to her* Husband and Son, from 1804 to 1813. From the French, by Mrs. CASHEL HOEY and Mr. JOHN LILLIE. In 1 vol., demy 8vo (uniform with the "Memoirs of Madame de Rémusat," 2 vols.), cloth extra, 16s.

Richter (Dr. Jean Paul) Italian Art in the National Gallery. 4to. Illustrated. Cloth gilt, 2l. 2s.; half-morocco, uncut, 2l. 12s. 6d.

——— See also LEONARDO DA VINCI.

Robin Hood; Merry Adventures of. Written and illustrated by HOWARD PYLE. Imperial 8vo, cloth. [*In the press.*

Robinson (Phil) In my Indian Garden. With a Preface by EDWIN ARNOLD, M.A., C.S.I., &c. Crown 8vo, limp cloth, 4th Edition, 3s. 6d.

——— *Noah's Ark. A Contribution to the Study of Unnatural* History. Small post 8vo, 12s. 6d.

——— *Sinners and Saints : a Tour across the United States of* America, and Round them. Crown 8vo, 10s. 6d.

——— *Under the Punkah.* Crown 8vo, limp cloth, 5s.

Robinson (Sergeant) Wealth and its Sources. Stray Thoughts. 5s.

Roland ; the Story of. Crown 8vo, illustrated, 6s.

Romantic Stories of the Legal Profession. Crown 8vo, cloth, 7s. 6d.

Rose (J.) Complete Practical Machinist. New Edition, 12mo, 12s. 6d.

Rose Library (The). Popular Literature of all Countries. Each volume, 1*s*.; cloth, 2*s*. 6*d*. Many of the Volumes are Illustrated—

Little Women. By LOUISA M. ALCOTT. Dble. vol., 2*s*.
Little Women Wedded. Forming a Sequel to "Little Women."
Little Women and Little Women Wedded. 1 vol., cloth gilt, 3*s*. 6*d*.
Little Men. By L. M. ALCOTT. 2*s*.; cloth gilt, 3*s*. 6*d*.
An Old-Fashioned Girl. By LOUISA M. ALCOTT. 2*s*.; cloth, 3*s*. 6*d*.
Work. A Story of Experience. By L. M. ALCOTT. 2 vols., 1*s*. each.
Stowe (Mrs. H. B.) The Pearl of Orr's Island.
——— **The Minister's Wooing.**
——— **We and our Neighbours.** 2*s*.; cloth, 3*s*. 6*d*.
——— **My Wife and I.** 2*s*.; cloth gilt, 3*s*. 6*d*.
Hans Brinker; or, the Silver Skates. By Mrs. DODGE.
My Study Windows. By J. R. LOWELL.
The Guardian Angel. By OLIVER WENDELL HOLMES.
My Summer in a Garden. By C. D. WARNER.
Dred. Mrs. BEECHER STOWE. 2*s*.; cloth gilt, 3*s*. 6*d*.
Farm Ballads. By WILL CARLETON.
Farm Festivals. By WILL CARLETON.
Farm Legends. By WILL CARLETON.
The Clients of Dr. Bernagius. 2 parts, 1*s*. each.
The Undiscovered Country. By W. D. HOWELLS.
Baby Rue. By C. M. CLAY.
The Rose in Bloom. By L. M. ALCOTT. 2*s*.; cloth gilt, 3*s*. 6*d*.
Eight Cousins. By L. M. ALCOTT. 2*s*.; cloth gilt, 3*s*. 6*d*.
Under the Lilacs. By L. M. ALCOTT. 2*s*.; also 3*s*. 6*d*.
Silver Pitchers. By LOUISA M. ALCOTT.
Jimmy's Cruise in the "Pinafore," and other Tales. By LOUISA M. ALCOTT. 2*s*.; cloth gilt, 3*s*. 6*d*.
Jack and Jill. By LOUISA M. ALCOTT. 2*s*.
Hitherto. By the Author of the "Gayworthys." 2 vols., 1*s*. each; 1 vol., cloth gilt, 3*s*. 6*d*.
Friends: a Duet. By E. STUART PHELPS.
A Gentleman of Leisure. A Novel. By EDGAR FAWCETT.
The Story of Helen Troy.

Round the Yule Log: Norwegian Folk and Fairy Tales. Translated from the Norwegian of P. CHR. ASBJÖRNSEN. With 100 Illustrations after drawings by Norwegian Artists, and an Introduction by E. W. Gosse. Imperial 16mo, cloth extra, gilt edges, 7*s*. 6*d*.

Rousselet (Louis) Son of the Constable of France. Small post 8vo, numerous Illustrations, 5*s.*

—— *The Drummer Boy: a Story of the Days of Washington.* Small post 8vo, numerous Illustrations, 5*s.*

Russell (W. Clark) The Lady Maud. 3 vols., crown 8vo, 31*s.* 6*d.* New Edition, small post 8vo, 6*s.*

—— *Little Loo.* 6*s.*

—— *My Watch Below; or, Yarns Spun when off Duty.* 2nd Edition, crown 8vo, 2*s.* 6*d.*

—— *Sailor's Language.* Illustrated. Crown 8vo, 3*s.* 6*d.*

—— *Sea Queen.* 3 vols., crown 8vo, 31*s.* 6*d.*

—— *Wreck of the Grosvenor.* 4to, sewed, 6*d.*

—— See also LOW'S STANDARD NOVELS.

Russell (W. H., LL.D.) Hesperothen: Notes from the Western World. A Record of a Ramble through part of the United States, Canada, and the Far West, in the Spring and Summer of 1881. By W. H. RUSSELL, LL.D. 2 vols., crown 8vo, cloth, 24*s.*

—— *The Tour of the Prince of Wales in India.* By W. H. RUSSELL, LL.D. Fully Illustrated by SYDNEY P. HALL, M.A. Super-royal 8vo, cloth extra, gilt edges, 52*s.* 6*d.*; Large Paper Edition, 84*s.*

SAINTS and their Symbols: A Companion in the Churches and Picture Galleries of Europe. With Illustrations. Royal 16mo, cloth extra, 3*s.* 6*d.*

Scherr (Prof. J.) History of English Literature. Translated from the German. Crown 8vo, 8*s.* 6*d.*

Schuyler (Eugène). The Life of Peter the Great. By EUGÈNE SCHUYLER, Author of "Turkestan." 2 vols., 8vo.

Schweinfurth (Georg) Heart of Africa. Three Years' Travels and Adventures in the Unexplored Regions of Central Africa, from 1868 to 1871. With Illustrations and large Map. 2 vols., crown 8vo, 15*s.*

Scott (Leader) Renaissance of Art in Italy. 4to, 31*s.* 6*d.*

Sedgwick (Major W.) Light the Dominant Force of the Universe.
7s. 6d.

Senior (Nassau W.) Conversations and Journals in Egypt and
Malta. 2 vols., 8vo, 24s.

Shadbolt (S. H.) South African Campaign, 1879. Compiled by J. P. MACKINNON (formerly 72nd Highlanders) and S. H. SHADBOLT; and dedicated, by permission, to Field-Marshal H.R.H. the Duke of Cambridge. Containing a portrait and biography of every officer killed in the campaign. 4to, handsomely bound in cloth extra, 2l. 10s.

—— *The Afghan Campaigns of* 1878—1880. By SYDNEY SHADBOLT, Joint Author of "The South African Campaign of 1879." 2 vols., royal quarto, cloth extra, 3l.

Shakespeare. Edited by R. GRANT WHITE. 3 vols., crown 8vo, gilt top, 36s.; *édition de luxe,* 6 vols., 8vo, cloth extra, 63s.

—— See also "Flowers of Shakespeare."

Sidney (Sir P.) Arcadia. New Edition, 6s.

Siegfried: The Story of. Crown 8vo, illustrated, cloth, 6s.

Sikes (Wirt). Rambles and Studies in Old South Wales. With numerous Illustrations. Demy 8vo, 18s.

—— *British Goblins, Welsh Folk Lore.* New Edition, 8vo, 18s.

—— *Studies of Assassination.* 16mo, 3s. 6d.

Sir Roger de Coverley. Re-imprinted from the "Spectator." With 125 Woodcuts, and steel Frontispiece specially designed and engraved for the Work. Small fcap. 4to, 6s.

Smith (G.) Assyrian Explorations and Discoveries. By the late GEORGE SMITH. Illustrated by Photographs and Woodcuts. Demy 8vo, 6th Edition, 18s.

—— *The Chaldean Account of Genesis.* By the late G. SMITH, of the Department of Oriental Antiquities, British Museum. With many Illustrations. Demy 8vo, cloth extra, 6th Edition, 16s. An entirely New Edition, completely revised and re-written by the Rev. PROFESSOR SAYCE, Queen's College, Oxford. Demy 8vo, 18s.

Smith (J. Moyr) Ancient Greek Female Costume. 112 full-page Plates and other Illustrations. Crown 8vo, 7s. 6d.

—— *Hades of Ardenne: a Visit to the Caves of Han.* Crown 8vo, Illustrated, 5s.

Smith (T. Roger) Architecture, Gothic and Renaissance. Illustrated, crown 8vo, 5s.

———————————————— *Classic and Early Christian.* Illustrated. Crown 8vo, 5s.

South Kensington Museum. Vol. II., 21s.

Spanish and French Artists. By GERARD SMITH. (Poynter's Art Text-books.) 5s. [*In the press.*

Spry (W. J. J., R.N.) The Cruise of H.M.S. "Challenger." With Route Map and many Illustrations. 6th Edition, demy 8vo, cloth, 18s. Cheap Edition, crown 8vo, with some of the Illustrations, 7s. 6d.

Stack (E.) Six Months in Persia. 2 vols., crown 8vo, 24s.

Stanley (H. M.) How I Found Livingstone. Crown 8vo, cloth extra, 7s. 6d.; large Paper Edition, 10s. 6d.

———— *"My Kalulu," Prince, King, and Slave.* A Story from Central Africa. Crown 8vo, about 430 pp., with numerous graphic Illustrations after Original Designs by the Author. Cloth, 7s. 6d.

———— *Coomassie and Magdala.* A Story of Two British Campaigns in Africa. Demy 8vo, with Maps and Illustrations, 16s.

———— *Through the Dark Continent.* Cheaper Edition, crown 8vo, 12s. 6d.

Stenhouse (Mrs.) An Englishwoman in Utah. Crown 8vo, 2s. 6d.

Stoker (Bram) Under the Sunset. Crown 8vo, 6s.

Story without an End. From the German of Carové, by the late Mrs. SARAH T. AUSTIN. Crown 4to, with 15 Exquisite Drawings by E. V. B., printed in Colours in Fac-simile of the original Water Colours; and numerous other Illustrations. New Edition, 7s. 6d.

———— square 4to, with Illustrations by HARVEY. 2s. 6d.

Stowe (Mrs. Beecher) Dred. Cheap Edition, boards, 2s. Cloth, gilt edges, 3s. 6d.

———— *Footsteps of the Master.* With Illustrations and red borders. Small post 8vo, cloth extra, 6s.

———— *Geography.* With 60 Illustrations. Square cloth, 4s. 6d.

———— *Little Foxes.* Cheap Edition, 1s.; Library Edition, 4s. 6d.

———— *Betty's Bright Idea.* 1s.

Stowe (*Mrs. Beecher*) *My Wife and I; or, Harry Henderson's History.* Small post 8vo, cloth extra, 6s.*

—————— *Minister's Wooing.* 5s.; Copyright Series, 1s. 6d.; cl., 2s.*

—————— *Old Town Folk.* 6s.; Cheap Edition, 2s. 6d.

—————— *Old Town Fireside Stories.* Cloth extra, 3s. 6d.

—————— *Our Folks at Poganuc.* 6s.

—————— *We and our Neighbours.* 1 vol., small post 8vo, 6s. Sequel to "My Wife and I."*

—————— *Pink and White Tyranny.* Small post 8vo, 3s. 6d. Cheap Edition, 1s. 6d. and 2s.

—————— *Poganuc People: their Loves and Lives.* Crown 8vo, cloth, 6s.

—————— *Queer Little People.* 1s.; cloth, 2s.

—————— *Chimney Corner.* 1s.; cloth, 1s. 6d.

—————— *The Pearl of Orr's Island.* Crown 8vo, 5s.*

—————— *Woman in Sacred History.* Illustrated with 15 Chromo-lithographs and about 200 pages of Letterpress. Demy 4to, cloth extra, gilt edges, 25s.

Sullivan (*A. M., late M.P.*) *Nutshell History of Ireland.* From the Earliest Ages to the Present Time. Paper boards, 6d.

TACCHI (*A.*) *Madagascar and the Malagasy Embassy.* Demy 8vo, cloth.

Taine (*H. A.*) "*Les Origines de la France Contemporaine*" Translated by JOHN DURAND.
    Vol. 1. **The Ancient Regime.** Demy 8vo, cloth, 16s.
    Vol. 2. **The French Revolution.** Vol. 1. do.
    Vol. 3. **Do.** do. Vol. 2. do.

Talbot (*Hon. E.*) *A Letter on Emigration.* 1s.

Tauchnitz's *English Editions of German Authors.* Each volume, cloth flexible, 2s.; or sewed, 1s. 6d. (Catalogues post free on application.)

Tauchnitz (*B.*) *German and English Dictionary.* Paper, 1s. 6d.; cloth, 2s.; roan, 2s. 6d.

* *See also* Rose Library.

Tauchnitz (B.) French and English Dictionary. Paper, 1s. 6d.; cloth, 2s.; roan, 2s. 6d.

—— *Italian and English Dictionary.* Paper, 1s. 6d.; cloth, 2s.; roan, 2s. 6d.

—— *Spanish and English.* Paper, 1s. 6d.; cloth, 2s.; roan, 2s. 6d.

Taylor (W. M.) Paul the Missionary. Crown 8vo, 7s. 6d.

Thausing (Prof.) Preparation of Malt and the Fabrication of Beer. 8vo, 45s.

Theakston (Michael) British Angling Flies. Illustrated. Cr 8vo, 5s.

Thoreau. By SANBORN. (American Men of Letters.) Crown 8vo, 2s. 6d.

Thousand Years Hence (A). By NUNSOWE GREENE. Crown 8vo, 6s.

Tolhausen (Alexandre) Grand Supplément du Dictionnaire Technologique. 3s. 6d.

Tolmer (Alexander) Reminiscences of an Adventurous and Chequered Career. 2 vols., 21s.

Trials. See BROWNE.

Tristram (Rev. Canon) Pathways of Palestine: A Descriptive Tour through the Holy Land. First Series. Illustrated by 44 Permanent Photographs. 2 vols., folio, cloth extra, gilt edges, 31s. 6d. each.

Tuckerman (Bayard) History of English Prose and Fiction. 8s. 6d.

Tunis. See REID.

Turner (Edward) Studies in Russian Literature. Crown 8vo, 8s. 6d.

UNION Jack (The). Every Boy's Paper. Edited by G. A. HENTY. Profusely Illustrated with Coloured and other Plates. Vol. I., 6s. Vols. II., III., IV., 7s. 6d. each.

Up Stream: A Journey from the Present to the Past. Pictures and Words by R. ANDRÉ. Coloured Plates, 4to, 5s.

BOOKS BY JULES VERNE.

***CELEBRATED TRAVELS* and *TRAVELLERS*.** 3 Vols., Demy 8vo, 600 pp., upwards of 100 full-page Illustrations, 12s. 6d.; gilt edges, 14s. each :—

I. The Exploration of the World.
II. The Great Navigators of the Eighteenth Century.
III. The Great Explorers of the Nineteenth Century.

☞ The letters appended to each book refer to the various Editions and Prices given at the foot of the page.

  a e TWENTY THOUSAND LEAGUES UNDER THE SEA.
  a e HECTOR SERVADAC.
  a e THE FUR COUNTRY.
  a f FROM THE EARTH TO THE MOON, AND A TRIP ROUND IT.
  a e MICHAEL STROGOFF, THE COURIER OF THE CZAR.
  a e DICK SANDS, THE BOY CAPTAIN.
  b c d FIVE WEEKS IN A BALLOON.
  b c d ADVENTURES OF THREE ENGLISHMEN AND THREE RUSSIANS.
  b c d AROUND THE WORLD IN EIGHTY DAYS.
  b c { *d* A FLOATING CITY.
       { *d* THE BLOCKADE RUNNERS.
  b c { *d* { DR. OX'S EXPERIMENT.
         { MASTER ZACHARIUS.
       { *d* { A DRAMA IN THE AIR.
          { A WINTER AMID THE ICE.
  b c { *d* THE SURVIVORS OF THE "CHANCELLOR."
       { *d* MARTIN PAZ.
  b c d THE CHILD OF THE CAVERN.
         THE MYSTERIOUS ISLAND, 3 Vols. :—
  b c d   I. DROPPED FROM THE CLOUDS.
  b c d   II. ABANDONED.
  b c d   III. SECRET OF THE ISLAND.
  b c { *d* THE BEGUM'S FORTUNE.
       { THE MUTINEERS OF THE "BOUNTY."
  b c d THE TRIBULATIONS OF A CHINAMAN.
         THE STEAM HOUSE, 2 Vols. :—
  b c   I. DEMON OF CAWNPORE.
  b c   II. TIGERS AND TRAITORS.
         THE GIANT RAFT, 2 Vols. :—
  b   I. EIGHT HUNDRED LEAGUES ON THE AMAZON.
  b   II. THE CRYPTOGRAM.
  b   GODFREY MORGAN.
         THE GREEN RAY. Cloth, gilt edges, 6s.; plain edges, 5s.

  a Small 8vo, very numerous Illustrations, handsomely bound in cloth, with gilt edges, 10s. 6d.; ditto, plainer binding, 5s.
  b Large imperial 16mo, very numerous Illustrations, handsomely bound in cloth, with gilt edges, 7s. 6d.
  c Ditto, plainer binding, 3s. 6d.
  d Cheaper Edition, 1 Vol., paper boards, with some of the Illustrations, 1s.; bound in cloth, gilt edges, 2s.
  e Cheaper Edition as (*d*), in 2 Vols., 1s. each; bound in cloth, gilt edges, 1 Vol., 3s. 6d.
  f Same as (*e*), except in cloth, 2 Vols., gilt edges, 2s. each.

VELAZQUEZ and Murillo. By C. B. CURTIS. With Original Etchings. Royal 8vo, 31*s.* 6*d.*; large paper, 63*s.*

Victoria (Queen) Life of. By GRACE GREENWOOD. With numerous Illustrations. Small post 8vo, 6*s.*

Vincent (F.) Norsk, Lapp, and Finn. By FRANK VINCENT, Jun., Author of "The Land of the White Elephant," "Through and Through the Tropics," &c. 8vo, cloth, with Frontispiece and Map, 12*s.*

Viollet-le-Duc (E.) Lectures on Architecture. Translated by BENJAMIN BUCKNALL, Architect. With 33 Steel Plates and 200 Wood Engravings. Super-royal 8vo, leather back, gilt top, with complete Index, 2 vols., 3*l.* 3*s.*

Vivian (A. P.) Wanderings in the Western Land. 3rd Edition, 10*s.* 6*d.*

Voyages. See MCCORMICK.

WALLACE (L.) Ben Hur: A Tale of the Christ. Crown 8vo, 6*s.*

Waller (Rev. C. H.) The Names on the Gates of Pearl, and other Studies. By the Rev. C. H. WALLER, M.A. New Edition. Crown 8vo, cloth extra, 3*s.* 6*d.*

—— *A Grammar and Analytical Vocabulary of the Words in* the Greek Testament. Compiled from Brüder's Concordance. For the use of Divinity Students and Greek Testament Classes. By the Rev. C. H. WALLER, M.A. Part I. The Grammar. Small post 8vo, cloth, 2*s.* 6*d.* Part II. The Vocabulary, 2*s.* 6*d.*

—— *Adoption and the Covenant.* Some Thoughts on Confirmation. Super-royal 16mo, cloth limp, 2*s.* 6*d.*

—— *Silver Sockets; and other Shadows of Redemption.* Eighteen Sermons preached in Christ Church, Hampstead. Small post 8vo, cloth, 6*s.*

Warner (C. D.) Back-log Studies. Boards, 1*s.* 6*d.*; cloth, 2*s.*

Washington Irving's Little Britain. Square crown 8vo, 6*s.*

Webster. (American Men of Letters.) 18mo, 2*s.* 6*d.*

Weismann (A.) Studies in the Theory of Descent. One of the most complete of recent contributions to the Theory of Evolution. With a Preface by the late CHARLES DARWIN, F.R.S., and numerous Coloured Plates. 2 vols., 8vo, 40*s.*

Wheatley (H. B.) and Delamotte (P. H.) Art Work in Porcelain. Large 8vo, 2*s.* 6*d.*

—— *Art Work in Gold and Silver. Modern.* Large 8vo, 2*s.* 6*d.*

White (Rhoda E.) From Infancy to Womanhood. A Book of Instruction for Young Mothers. Crown 8vo, cloth, 10*s.* 6*d.*

White (R. G.) England Without and Within. New Edition, crown 8vo, 10s. 6d.

Whittier (J. G.) The King's Missive, and later Poems. 18mo, choice parchment cover, 3s. 6d.

―――― *The Whittier Birthday Book.* Extracts from the Author's writings, with Portrait and numerous Illustrations. Uniform with the "Emerson Birthday Book." Square 16mo, very choice binding, 3s. 6d.

―――― *Life of.* By R. A. UNDERWOOD. Cr. 8vo, cloth, 10s. 6d.

Wild Flowers of Switzerland. With Coloured Plates, life-size, from living Plants, and Botanical Descriptions of each Example. Imperial 4to, 52s. 6d.

Williams (C. F.) The Tariff Laws of the United States. 8vo, cloth, 10s. 6d.

Williams (H. W.) Diseases of the Eye. 8vo, 21s.

Williams (M.) Some London Theatres: Past and Preesnt. Crown 8vo, 7s. 6d.

Wills, A Few Hints on Proving, without Professional Assistance. By a PROBATE COURT OFFICIAL. 5th Edition, revised, with Forms of Wills, Residuary Accounts, &c. Fcap. 8vo, cloth limp, 1s.

Winckelmann (John) History of Ancient Art. Translated by JOHN LODGE, M.D. With very numerous Plates and Illustrations. 2 vols., 8vo, 36s.

Winks (W. E.) Lives of Illustrious Shoemakers. With eight Portraits. Crown 8vo, 7s. 6d.

Woodbury (Geo. E.) History of Wood Engraving. Illustrated, 8vo, 18s.

Woolsey (C. D., LL.D.) Introduction to the Study of International Law; designed as an Aid in Teaching and in Historical Studies. 5th Edition, demy 8vo, 18s.

Woolson (Constance F.) See "Low's Standard Novels."

Wright (the late Rev. Henry) The Friendship of God. With Biographical Preface by the Rev. E. H. BICKERSTETH, Portrait, &c. Crown 8vo, 6s.

*Y*RIARTE *(Charles) Florence: its History.* Translated by C. B. PITMAN. Illustrated with 500 Engravings. Large imperial 4to, extra binding, gilt edges, 63s.

History; the Medici; the Humanists; letters; arts; the Renaissance; illustrious Florentines; Etruscan art; monuments; sculpture; painting.

London:
SAMPSON LOW, MARSTON, SEARLE, & RIVINGTON,
CROWN BUILDINGS, 188, FLEET STREET, E.C.